"Mountains are global commons and unique ecosystems that sustain both upland and lowland communities through their vital contributions to water, biodiversity, climate regulation, and livelihoods. Yet, despite their immense ecological and socio-economic significance to the wider societies, mountain regions remain among the most marginalised and neglected landscapes and communities in development policy and practice. Today, climate change has emerged as a major stressor, with rapid elevation-dependent warming leading to accelerating glacier retreat and increasing frequency of glacial lakes outburst floods (GOLFs), ecological degradation, and disaster risks that threaten the very foundations of mountain societies and ecosystems. *Indian Himalayan Economies: Challenges, Prospects, and Sustainable Development* is a timely and significant contribution to the growing discourse on sustainable mountain development. Combining interdisciplinary scholarship with strong policy relevance, the book offers an integrated and insightful perspective on economic transformation, environmental sustainability, resilience, and inclusive development in fragile mountain ecosystems."

—**Pema Gyamtsho,** *Director General, ICIMOD, Nepal*

"Himalayan economies face a unique set of challenges shaped by fragile ecosystems, geographic isolation, climate vulnerability, and evolving socio-economic dynamics. This book provides a comprehensive and insightful exploration of sustainable mountain economies by integrating the economic, social, and environmental dimensions—the three mutually reinforcing pillars of sustainable development within the broader context of mountain systems. By highlighting emerging challenges, opportunities, and pathways for resilience, the book offers valuable perspectives for researchers, policymakers, development practitioners, and students engaged in mountain development and sustainability."

—**Sangam Shrestha,** *Professor, Water Engineering and Management (WEM) Co-Director, Global Water & Sanitation Center (GWSC), Asian Institute of Technology (AIT), Thailand*

"*Indian Himalayan Economies: Challenges, Prospects, and Sustainable Development* is a valuable contribution to the ongoing debate on sustainable mountain development. Climate change and socio-economic pressures are increasingly undermining fragile mountain economies, making this volume especially timely. The authors advance a strategic vision for the Indian Himalaya that integrates economic progress with ecological sustainability, while engaging with the broader debate on how marginalised mountain people and environments can be mainstreamed into national development priorities. Though focused on India, the insights carry relevance for other parts of the Hindu Kush Himalayas, making this book an important resource for scholars, policymakers, and practitioners concerned with the future of mountain regions."

—**Mahesh Banskota,** *Former Deputy Director General of ICIMOD, former Country Representative of the International Union for Conservation of Nature (IUCN), Nepal, and Visiting Professor, School of Arts, Kathmandu University, Nepal*

"*Indian Himalayan Economies: Challenges, Prospects and Sustainable Development* by Balwant S. Mehta and Ishwar Chandra Awasthi offers a timely and comprehensive exploration of the unique development challenges facing the Himalayan states. Characterised by fragile ecosystems, difficult terrain, rich natural resources, and deep socio-economic diversity, the Himalayan region requires a development paradigm distinct from that of the rest of India. The book critically examines how past development strategies, often insensitive to mountain realities, have contributed to environmental degradation, deforestation, unplanned infrastructure growth, and increasing vulnerability to natural disasters. Combining rigorous analysis with strong policy relevance, the authors highlight pathways for sustainable and inclusive development rooted in ecological balance, local livelihoods, and community resilience. Covering sectors such as agriculture, horticulture, tourism, skills, and small-scale industries, this volume is an invaluable resource for scholars, policymakers, students, and practitioners seeking to build a greener, more equitable, and resilient future for the Indian Himalayan region."

—**Atul Sarma,** *Former Vice-Chancellor of Rajiv Gandhi University, Itanagar and former Member of the Thirteenth Finance Commission, Government of India and consultant to several international agencies, including ADB, FAO, ESCAP, IDRC, and UNIDO*

Indian Himalayan Economies

This book explores the interconnected challenges of economic development, social progress, and environmental protection in India's mountainous regions. While these regions have recorded steady growth, rising per capita incomes, and improvements in education, their economies continue to face deep structural constraints, including persistent inequalities, limited employment generation, distress-driven migration, gaps in access to healthcare, and growing ecological stress. Using a mountain development framework that integrates socio-economic advancement with environmental sustainability, the book critically explores the tensions between growth and long-term sustainable development. A distinctive strength of the volume is its comprehensive coverage of all Indian Himalayan states, offering an integrated perspective not previously attempted in a single study. It will serve as a valuable resource for students, researchers, and practitioners engaged in sustainable development, economics, disaster management, education, minority studies, and South Asian studies. This is a must-read for anyone seeking to understand mountain economies, and its insights are equally relevant for similar mountainous regions across the world.

Balwant Singh Mehta is Professor at the Institute for Human Development, New Delhi. His research interests include employment, inequality, poverty, child welfare, education, and health. He has authored 10 books and over 100 journal articles. His recent books include *Poverty in India Using a Machine Learning Approach* (2024) and *Future of Work: Opportunities and Challenges* (2025).

Ishwar Chandra Awasthi is Professor at the Institute for Human Development, New Delhi. His research focuses on labour, employment, livelihoods, and development evaluation. He has published over six dozen papers. Key books include *Livelihood Diversities in Mountain Economy* (2012) and *Women and Labour Market Dynamics* (2019).

Indian Himalayan Economies

Challenges, Prospects, and Sustainable Development

Balwant Singh Mehta and Ishwar Chandra Awasthi

Routledge
Taylor & Francis Group
LONDON AND NEW YORK

First published 2027
by Routledge
4 Park Square, Milton Park, Abingdon, Oxon OX14 4RN

and by Routledge
605 Third Avenue, New York, NY 10158

Routledge is an imprint of the Taylor & Francis Group, an informa business

British Library Cataloguing-in-Publication Data
A catalogue record for this book is available from the British Library

ISBN: 978-1-032-97588-7 (hbk)
ISBN: 978-1-032-97783-6 (pbk)
ISBN: 978-1-003-59541-0 (ebk)

DOI: 10.4324/ 9781003595410

Typeset in Sabon
by Apex CoVantage, LLC

"Dedicated to the cherished memory of Late Professor T. S. Papola, a distinguished development economist whose pioneering scholarship on the Indian Himalayan economies continues to guide and inspire our work, and whose vision profoundly motivated the creation of this book".

Contents

Illustrations

Figures

Maps

Tables

प्रो. रमेश चन्द
सदस्य
Prof. Ramesh Chand
MEMBER

सत्यमेव जयते

भारत सरकार
नीति आयोग, संसद मार्ग
नई दिल्ली-110 001
Government of India
NATIONAL INSTITUTION FOR TRANSFORMING INDIA
NITI Aayog, Parliament Street
New Delhi-110 001
Tele. : 23096756, 23096774 Fax : 23730678
E-mail : rc.niti@gov.in

FOREWORD

Himalayan economies face severe, mountain-specific constraints – especially across the Hindu Kush Himalayan (HKH) region – where rapid climate change, rising temperatures, environmental degradation, deforestation, and unplanned infrastructure development have increased vulnerability and the frequency of natural hazards, with cascading impacts on lives and livelihoods.

The book Indian Himalayan Economies: Challenges, Prospects, and Sustainable Development re-examines the principal challenges confronting the Indian Himalaya. Organized into eight focused chapters, the book combines empirical evidence with thematic and comparative perspectives to illuminate state-level concerns and derive practical policy insights. It persuasively argues that conventional development paradigms – shaped largely by plains and urban experience – are often inadequate or counterproductive in mountain contexts, because they neglect unique topographical, ecological, and socio-economic features. The authors advocate a mountain-specific, sustainable development framework that integrates economic, social, and environmental dimensions as mutually reinforcing pillars of resilience.

The book's documentation of successful entrepreneurial initiatives across Indian Himalayan states is particularly valuable, offering replicable models and lessons for other mountain regions. It also proposes policy suggestions with potential direct relevance to practitioners and policymakers. At the same time, the volume could engage more deeply with certain economic challenges – most notably the impacts of climate change on agriculture and river systems, livelihood insecurity, the need for climate-resilient and diversified planning, and a more comprehensive assessment of water, biodiversity, and ecosystem services.

Overall, the book is a timely and useful contribution to debates on Himalayan development. I congratulate the authors on this important effort; the work will be of interest to scholars, policymakers, and practitioners concerned with mountain economies.

(Ramesh Chand)

Date: 9th March, 2026

स्वच्छ भारत
एक कदम स्वच्छता की ओर

Preface

This book is born out of the Authors long-standing engagement with the diverse landscapes and communities of the Indian Himalayan region. Working across different Himalayan states has offered deep insights into the many multifaceted challenges these regions face. This book is a humble attempt to understand these issues more clearly and explore practical policy solutions that can truly make a difference.

Mountains across the world – whether the Himalayas, the Alps, or the Andes – share similar physical traits: steep slopes, fragile ecosystems, and difficult terrain. While they hold immense natural wealth – rivers, forests, minerals, and tourism potential – they often remain politically and economically sidelined. Many of these regions remain isolated and underdeveloped, struggling with poor connectivity, environmental fragility, and limited economic opportunities. The Indian Himalayan states – Jammu and Kashmir, Ladakh, Uttarakhand, Himachal Pradesh, and the North-eastern states, including Arunachal Pradesh, Manipur, Meghalaya, Mizoram, Nagaland, Sikkim, Tripura, North Cachar Hills, Karbi Anglong, and Darjeeling – face similar problems. Agriculture remains the backbone of their economies, often practised with limited resources and traditional tools. But with growing populations and mounting pressure on land, the region is being pushed to shift towards new sources of livelihoods. Yet poor infrastructure, difficult geography, and the lack of supportive institutions make this transition extremely hard.

Development has brought both hope and new risks. Improved roads may offer access but also expose these regions to environmental degradation and resource exploitation. Migration – especially of the young and educated – is on the rise, leaving behind ageing populations, increasing women's workloads, and weakening the village economy. At the same time, trade relations often favour the plains, leading to the depletion of mountain resources without adequate returns. While some states, like Himachal Pradesh, have found success in horticulture and others, like Uttarakhand, in tourism, most Himalayan regions continue to depend heavily on central grants and the government sector. Local industries remain underdeveloped, and natural resource potential is yet to be fully tapped. Differences in geography, resources, and culture call for state-specific development strategies rather than one-size-fits-all solutions.

A recurring issue across all states is out-migration. Driven by limited job opportunities, poor healthcare, and lack of higher education facilities, people – often entire families – are moving to urban areas. This kind of migration, often forced rather than voluntary, reflects deep regional imbalances. Migrants, once they leave, often struggle to access basic entitlements due to the lack of a national database. A comprehensive, updated database of migrant workers is urgently needed to support effective policies. Reducing distress migration means strengthening local economies – especially agriculture and allied sectors – while creating jobs through tourism, horticulture, and small industries. Education and skills development aligned with market needs can help retain youth in the hills. Promoting traditional knowledge and ecological sustainability should go hand in hand with economic development. The goal is not just to grow, but to grow inclusively. Development must ensure decent work, gender equality, and access to basic services like healthcare and education. This aligns with the global vision of the Sustainable Development Goals (SDGs), especially SDG 8, which emphasises inclusive and sustainable economic growth.

This book focuses on key aspects of Himalayan economies – employment, livelihoods, education, health, and poverty. Using indicators like Gross State Value Added (GSVA), employment rates, and sectoral shifts, it examines how jobs are created, who benefits, and what more needs to be done. It draws from major data sources, including PLFS, ASI, UDISE+, and government policy documents, to analyse how policies have impacted these sectors. Education plays a vital role in shaping future opportunities. While access has improved in many Himalayan states, serious challenges remain – teacher shortages, inadequate infrastructure, poor digital access, and high dropout rates, especially in remote areas. The analysis looks at both school and higher education, vocational training, and the role of policy reforms, such as NEP 2020, in bridging educational gaps.

Healthcare is another critical area. The tough terrain, remote villages, and lack of facilities often keep quality health services out of reach. This book examines public health indicators, maternal and child health, and government schemes such as Ayushman Bharat and NRHM. It evaluates how well these programmes serve the mountain communities and where the gaps lie. Poverty and inequality continue to challenge the development narrative. Even though there are signs of progress, disparities between the plains and hills persist. This book explores poverty using multiple indicators – from income and consumption metrics to multidimensional poverty indices. It also examines inequality using measures like the Gini coefficient and Engel curve. Disasters – from landslides to floods and earthquakes – are a constant threat in the Himalayas, yet disaster management often remains reactive rather than proactive. A mountain-specific approach to disaster planning is critical. Effective early warning systems, local capacity building, and better alignment with development planning are needed to reduce the long-term impact of these events. Despite the formation of disaster management authorities, implementation remains weak in many states. Recovery from disasters requires short-, medium-, and long-term strategies that are integrated into broader development plans. Building resilience – through better infrastructure, community-based efforts, and ecological restoration – is essential for long-term sustainability.

This book is an attempt to bring together these many threads – livelihoods, migration, education, health, poverty, and disaster risk – into a coherent understanding of mountain development. With climate change accelerating and its impacts already visible in the Himalayas, it is time to rethink how we approach development in these regions. We hope this book helps build a deeper understanding of the unique challenges and opportunities of the Indian Himalayan region. It is intended as a useful resource not only for scholars and students but also for policymakers, practitioners, and anyone committed to building a greener, fairer, and more resilient future for our mountain communities. The authors sincerely thank the anonymous reviewers for their insightful comments and valuable suggestions, which have greatly strengthened the arguments and analysis.

We are indeed grateful to Professor Ramesh Chand, Member, NITI Aayog, for kindly writing the foreword to this book. We consider it a privilege and an honour that he agreed to share his valuable insights and perspectives through the foreword, which greatly enhances the significance and value of this volume.

Authors

Abbreviations

AFSPA	Armed Forces (Special Powers) Act
AISHE	All India Survey on Higher Education
ASER	Annual Status of Education Report
CBD	Convention on Biological Diversity
DDU-GKY	Deen Dayal Upadhyaya Grameen Kaushalya Yojana
EUS	Employment and Unemployment Survey
FAO	Food and Agriculture Organization of the United Nations
GER	Gross Enrolment Ratio
GKRA	Garib Kalyan Rojgar Abhiyaan
GNOMO	Global Network of Mountain Observatories
GSDP	Gross State Domestic Product
GVA	Gross Value Added
HDI	Human Development Index
HKH	Hindu Kush Himalayas
ICDS	Integrated Child Development Services
ICIMOD	International Centre for Integrated Mountain Development
IER	Incremental Efficiency Ratio
IHR	Indian Himalayan region
IIPS	International Institute for Population Sciences
ICT	Information and Communication Technology
IMRs	Infant Mortality Rates
LFPR	Labour Force Participation Rate
MMR	Maternal Mortality Ratio
MGNREGA	Mahatma Gandhi National Rural Employment Guarantee Act
MHRD	Ministry of Human Resource Development (now Ministry of Education)
MPI	Multidimensional Poverty Index
MPCE	Monthly Per Capita Expenditure
NAPS	National Apprenticeship Promotion Scheme
NCRMP	National Cyclone Risk Mitigation Project
NERCORMP	North-eastern Region Community Resource Management Project

NEP	National Education Policy
NER	North-eastern Region
NESIDS	North-east Special Infrastructure Development Scheme
NFHS	National Family Health Survey
NGOs	Non-Governmental Organisations
NHM	National Health Mission
NITI	National Institution for Transforming India (NITI Aayog)
NSS	National Sample Survey
NSDC	National Skill Development Corporation
NSO	National Statistical Office
NSSO	National Sample Survey Organisation
NULM	National Urban Livelihoods Mission
NUHM	National Urban Health Mission
NUEPA	National University of Educational Planning and Administration
OOP	Out-of Pocket (Expenditure on Health)
OECD	Organisation for Economic Co-operation and Development
OPHI	Oxford Poverty and Human Development Initiative
PDS	Public Distribution System
PLFS	Periodic Labour Force Survey
PMJAY	Pradhan Mantri Jan Arogya Yojana (Ayushman Bharat)
PMKVY	Pradhan Mantri Kaushal Vikas Yojana
RMSA	Rashtriya Madhyamik Shiksha Abhiyan
RTE	Right to Education Act
SDG	Sustainable Development Goal
SDMAs	State Disaster Management Authorities
SSA	Sarva Shiksha Abhiyan
TFR	Total Fertility Rate
UDISE+	Unified District Information System for Education Plus
UNDP	United Nations Development Programme
UNCED	United Nations Conference on Environment and Development
UNESCO	United Nations Educational, Scientific and Cultural Organization
UNDMT	United Nations Disaster Management Team
UNFCCC	United Nations Framework Convention on Climate Change
WPR	Worker-Population Ratio

1 Development Challenges and Issues in Mountain Economies

1.1 Overview

Mountain regions are among the most distinct and complex landscapes on Earth. They are shaped by steep slopes, unique ecological systems, and a high degree of physical instability. These natural features make them incredibly sensitive to environmental changes and disturbances, often with severe consequences for the people who inhabit them. Globally, mountains cover about 24 per cent of the Earth's land surface (Kapos et al., 2000) and are home to approximately 1.1 billion people, accounting for around 15 per cent of the world's population (Romeo et al., 2022). These regions are not just vital for the people who live there; they play an essential role in sustaining life far beyond their boundaries. Mountains are often referred to as the "water towers of the world" because they provide freshwater to more than half of the world's population. This water is crucial for drinking, sanitation, and especially for agriculture in downstream lowland areas. By feeding rivers and replenishing aquifers, mountain-sourced water supports irrigation and food production at a global scale. Without it, food security would be severely threatened in many parts of the world.

Despite their global importance, mountain regions remain some of the most neglected areas in terms of development and policy focus. Around 90 per cent of mountain populations live in developing countries, and a significant portion of them face harsh living conditions. Half of these people experience food insecurity and a large number live in poverty (FAO, 2019). Many mountain communities are politically and economically marginalised, often lacking the infrastructure, services, and investment needed to thrive. The combination of ecological fragility and socio-economic vulnerability makes mountain development both a challenge and a necessity. Yet mountains hold immense potential. They are rich in natural resources such as freshwater, forests, minerals, and biodiversity. They also have significant potential for hydropower and tourism, especially eco-tourism, which can provide sustainable income if managed properly. As human populations grow and demand for natural resources increases, the ecosystem services offered by mountain regions – particularly water – are becoming even more vital. However, this

DOI: 10.4324/ 9781003595410-1

rising demand also puts pressure on these fragile ecosystems, highlighting the need for sustainable management practices.

Historically, mountain issues received little attention in global development discussions. This changed in 1992 during the United Nations Conference on Environment and Development (UNCED) held in Rio de Janeiro, Brazil. For the first time, mountains were formally recognised on the global agenda. Chapter 13 of Agenda 21, titled "Managing Fragile Ecosystems: Sustainable Mountain Development," marked a turning point. It called on world leaders to acknowledge the vulnerabilities of mountain ecosystems and commit to their sustainable development. This was a foundational moment that brought mountain concerns into mainstream environmental and developmental dialogues.

The international community continued to build on this momentum. In 2002, the United Nations declared the International Year of Mountains, which led to the creation of the International Partnership for Sustainable Development in Mountain Regions. This partnership aimed to foster co-operation across countries and organisations in protecting mountain ecosystems and improving the livelihoods of mountain communities. Regional efforts such as the Alpine Convention (1991) and the Carpathian Convention (2003) also contributed to a growing movement for mountain sustainability. Further steps were taken in 2004, when the Convention on Biological Diversity (CBD) launched a special programme to address mountain biodiversity. The Rio+20 Summit in 2012 again brought mountain concerns to the forefront, and the 2030 Agenda for Sustainable Development included specific targets related to mountains, reaffirming their global significance. In 2017, the Mountain Partnership launched a new Framework for Action to align mountain development with global goals such as the Paris Agreement. More recently, the UN declared 2022 as the International Year of Sustainable Mountain Development, further emphasising the urgent need to address poverty, food insecurity, and environmental degradation in mountain regions (Romeo et al., 2022).

These international developments have inspired a growing network of organisations dedicated to mountain issues. Today, there are hundreds of stakeholders involved in promoting sustainable mountain development. These include international agencies like the FAO and UNEP, regional initiatives such as the Asia Pacific Mountain Network and the African Highlands Initiative, and research centres such as the International Centre for Integrated Mountain Development (ICIMOD) and *Mountain Research and Development*. The Mountain Partnership alone has 593 members, including 68 governments, 23 intergovernmental organisations, and over 500 non-governmental organisations and academic institutions (FAO, 2024). This diverse coalition reflects the increasing recognition of the strategic importance of mountain ecosystems.

The concept of mountain regions has also evolved over time. Early understandings focused on their physical and ecological characteristics. More recent approaches have incorporated the cultural, economic, and institutional dimensions of mountain life. Scholars have described mountains as commons – areas governed by shared rules of access and use, often based on traditional knowledge and practices. Issues of property rights, environmental justice, and collective management are central themes in the literature on mountain development (Debarbieux & Price, 2010). One influential framework for understanding mountain regions identifies a set of common features, or "specificities," that distinguish them from other areas. These include inaccessibility, fragility, marginality, and diversity (Price, 1981; Ives & Messerli, 1989b; Allan et al., 1988). These are referred to as first-order specificities. In response to these challenges, mountain communities have developed adaptive strategies over time, based on deep local knowledge and trial-and-error learning. These are known as second-order specificities and include natural suitability and adaptive human mechanisms (Jodha, 1992a).

Inaccessibility in mountain areas results from steep slopes, high altitudes, rough terrain, and frequent natural hazards such as landslides and avalanches. These conditions limit mobility and increase the cost of building and maintaining infrastructure. Fragility reflects the delicate balance of mountain ecosystems, which are easily disturbed by overuse, deforestation, and climate change. Marginality stems from isolation – both geographic and economic – that prevents mountain communities from fully participating in national or global markets. Meanwhile, diversity is a defining strength of mountain areas. It includes not only ecological variety but also social, cultural, and economic differences that vary from one mountain region to another. This diversity can be an advantage. Many mountain regions produce unique or high-value products such as medicinal herbs, specialty fruits and vegetables, or artisanal crafts. These products offer potential for niche markets and sustainable livelihoods – provided that access to markets and infrastructure is improved. The rich cultural and religious heritage found in mountains also adds to their value. Many of the world's most linguistically and religiously diverse areas are found in mountainous regions, offering opportunities for cultural tourism and intercultural learning (Debarbieux & Price, 2010).

Adaptation in mountain regions refers to how human societies adjust to environmental challenges to sustain their way of life. This often involves indigenous knowledge systems that have developed over generations. Such systems include agricultural practices suited to high altitudes, traditional water harvesting methods, and community-based forest management. These practices are crucial for resilience and sustainability in fragile mountain ecosystems (Ives, 2022).

In sum, mountain regions matter – not only to the people who live there, but to the world as a whole. They are central to the global water cycle, biodiversity conservation, and climate stability. Yet they are also places of poverty, vulnerability, and neglect. Understanding the unique characteristics and challenges of mountains is essential for crafting effective policies and development strategies. As the world confronts the twin crises of climate change and biodiversity loss, mountain regions can no longer be an afterthought. They must be recognised as vital components of our shared environmental and socio-economic future. In this context, this chapter outlines the theoretical perspective on the mountain economy used in this book to understand development and structural change, issues, and opportunities, and lays the foundation for a deeper exploration of mountain development challenges and the need for inclusive, sustainable, and resilient solutions tailored to these extraordinary landscapes.

After the introductory section and theoretical perspectives, the second part of this chapter focuses on key development aspects of mountain economies, examining how geographic, ecological, and socio-economic factors shape growth patterns, livelihoods, and resource use. The third section explores the commonalities and interdependencies shared by mountain areas across the globe, highlighting their ecological significance, socio-economic linkages with downstream regions, and the need for integrated and cooperative approaches to sustainable development. The fourth section outlines the chapterisation and overall structure of the book, providing a roadmap of the key themes and issues addressed in each chapter. Finally, the fifth section offers a summary and conclusion, synthesising the main ideas discussed and setting the stage for the chapters that follow.

1.2 Theoretical Perspectives on Mountain Economies

Theoretical foundations and conceptual aspects for understanding mountain economies draw upon diverse disciplines, including development economics, geography, environmental studies, and political economy. Globally, scholarship recognises that mountain regions are marked by physical isolation, ecological fragility, and cultural distinctiveness – factors that shape their economic structures and development trajectories (Jodha, 1992a). Several international development theories and concepts provide useful lenses for examining the structural challenges and opportunities of mountain economies.

Modernisation theory – linear transition and its limits. Modernisation theory frames development as a linear shift from traditional to modern economies; while it offers a baseline for analysing changes in occupational structures and market integration, it inadequately addresses the geographic constraints and ecological limits inherent to mountain regions.

Dependency theory – periphery–core dynamics. Dependency theory offers a contrasting perspective, underscoring how mountain states in India often serve as peripheral resource suppliers – such as hydropower, timber, and tourism – to lowland and urban cores, thereby perpetuating structural inequalities (Frank, 1967).

Sustainable development theory – balancing ecology, livelihoods, and culture. Sustainable development theory, articulated in the Brundtland Report (1987) and reinforced through the Mountain Agenda at the Rio Earth Summit (1992), is particularly pertinent. It emphasises the need to balance ecological integrity, livelihood security, and cultural preservation. Within the Indian context, the Sustainable Livelihoods Approach (Chambers & Conway, 1992) has been widely adopted in mountain development initiatives, focusing on enhancing resilience through diversification of livelihood assets.

Political economy of resource governance – asymmetries and institutions. From a political economy standpoint, mountain states contend with asymmetric power relations in resource governance, fiscal transfers, and policy formulation. The Resource Curse Hypothesis – traditionally applied to mineral-rich economies – finds a partial parallel in the hydropower-rich Himalayan states, where large-scale projects generate revenue but also trigger ecological degradation and social displacement (Rasul & Molden, 2014).

Spatial economics – topography, access, and growth poles. Spatial economics provides additional analytical tools for understanding mountain economies. Central Place Theory (Christaller, 1933) explains settlement hierarchies; however, in mountainous regions, market accessibility is shaped less by linear distance and more by topography, road infrastructure, and seasonal constraints. Growth Pole Theory (Perroux, 1950) posits that strategic investment in urban or semi-urban hubs can stimulate regional development through spillover effects. In the Indian Himalayan context, centres such as Shimla, Gangtok, and Itanagar function as growth poles, concentrating services, education, and administrative activities. However, mountain specificities make it difficult to spread the benefits widely.

Cumulative causation – migration and divergence. The cumulative causation theory, enunciated by Myrdal (1957), argues that the continued out-migration of skilled labour and youth to lowland areas reinforces regional disparities and inequalities, creating a self-perpetuating cycle of underdevelopment. Coping with such unbalanced growth and inequality requires policies that promote decentralised development and foster value-added local industries, thereby strengthening the resilience of mountain economies.

Ecological economics – environmental limits and natural capital. In view of the environmental sensitivity of mountain regions, ecological economics provides a theoretical framework by embedding environmental limits within development planning (Costanza et al., 1997). This framework recognises natural capital – forests, glaciers, water, non-renewable resources like fossil fuels and minerals, and biodiversity resources – which is critical to long-term sustainable development.

Resilience theory – adaptive capacity to shocks. Resilience theory, associated with Holling (1973), emphasises the importance of adaptive capacity in socio-ecological systems, a concept highly relevant to mountain economies facing numerous challenges from climate change and other disasters. The increased vulnerability of Indian Himalayan states to climate-induced disasters results in colossal losses to infrastructure, lives, and livelihoods, making it imperative to adopt development frameworks suited to these regions. For instance, the devastating 2013 Uttarakhand floods have exposed the dangers of unregulated construction in ecologically fragile regions.

Globalisation and value chains – opportunities and exposure. Globalisation theories argue that liberalisation and market integration can generate both opportunities and heightened vulnerabilities. In mountain economies, access to markets has expanded – for example, high-value horticulture in Himachal Pradesh, adventure tourism in Ladakh, and other niche mountain products – but this has also increased exposure to external demand fluctuations. The Global Commodity Chain framework provides a useful tool for integrating mountain products into global markets; however, such integration perpetuates persistent power asymmetries, with local producers in mountain regions most often remaining price-takers rather than price-setters (Gereffi et al., 2005).

Cultural economy – heritage and local knowledge. In India's mountain states, indigenous agricultural systems, traditional crafts, community-based tourism, resource management, biodiversity conservation, and climate change adaptation collectively contribute to sustainable development. The Cultural Economy approach underscores the role of heritage, identity, and local knowledge in shaping economic strategies, advocating for the use of local resources, capacities, and institutions (Ray, 1998). The notable example is Sikkim's shift to organic farming that embraces the local agroecological practices.

Location models and endogenous development – mountain-specific fit. Classical location models, such as von Thünen's concentric zones, fail to capture the spatial and topographical specificities of mountain regions. In contrast, the Sustainable Livelihoods Approach (SLA) and Endogenous Development Models provide better perspectives by integrating environmental factors, social capital, and institutional capacity. This holds true for the Indian Himalayan economies, particularly the North-Eastern states, which reflect a complex interplay of resource constraints, environmental vulnerability, and socio-political marginalisation.

Institutional economics – commons and community governance. Institutional economics emphasises the crucial role of institutions in managing common property resources. For example, Van Panchayats in Uttarakhand illustrate community-led governance that balances ecological sustainability with livelihood needs. Strengthening participatory governance through community and local institutions can foster development suited to the specific needs of mountain ecosystems.

Himalayan environmental degradation thesis – evidence over assumption. A strand of scholarship in the 1970s–1980s predicted widespread deforestation, disasters, and ecological imbalance in the Himalaya, exacerbated by population pressures; even the World Bank warned of limited forest access. These pessimistic views were strongly criticised, with scholars arguing for evidence-based assessments over myths and unsubstantiated assumptions (Ives & Messerli, 1989b; Ives, 2022).

Integrative framework – multi-theory synthesis. No single theoretical perspective adequately captures the complexity of mountain economies, which often face challenges arising from their specific characteristics. In view of this, a multi-theoretical synthesis is required – combining the Sustainable Livelihoods Approach, Ecological Economics, and Endogenous Development Theory – to offer a more comprehensive framework for achieving long-term, inclusive, and sustainable development in the context of mountain regions.

Throughout the book, these theories and concepts are applied, wherever appropriate, to explain the development trajectory of mountain economies.

1.3 Development Dynamics of Mountain Economies

Mountain regions across the globe – whether in Europe, South America, or Asia – share a number of strikingly similar ecological, social, and economic characteristics. These areas, despite their diversity in culture and geography, face comparable challenges arising from their steep terrain, fragile ecosystems, isolation, and vulnerability to both natural and human-induced pressures. From the towering Alps of Europe and the expansive Andes of South America to the vast Hindu Kush Himalayan (HKH) region of South and Central Asia, mountain economies are shaped by a complex interplay of environmental constraints and socio-economic marginality. These shared traits have significant implications for development, livelihoods, and the sustainability of mountain ecosystems. Annexure Chapter 1 highlights the bio-climatic similarities of these regions, which help explain the common developmental concerns they encounter.

A key challenge for many mountain regions, particularly in developing and underdeveloped countries, is the growing degradation of natural resources. This degradation stems largely from overuse and the intensifying pressure of expanding populations, leading to adverse environmental changes. As a result, biomass productivity has declined, ecosystem services have diminished, and mountain communities have increasingly found themselves on the margins of development. This marginalisation is further compounded by weak economic integration, poor infrastructure, and limited access to public services. According to Huddleston et al. (2003), about half of the rural population living in mountain areas of developing or transition economies faces food insecurity. This alarming situation is particularly evident in countries with large mountainous zones and fragile economic systems, where people suffer from chronic undernourishment, inadequate access to clean water, and limited opportunities for women in formal wage employment, especially outside the agricultural sector (Wymann von Dach et al., 2006).

The vulnerability of mountain populations has been further exposed in recent years by global crises such as the COVID-19 pandemic. The pandemic intensified the already difficult conditions in these regions, where livelihoods were disrupted by lockdowns, health systems were overstretched, and access to markets and essential services became even more difficult. This health crisis came on top of long-standing issues such as climate change, natural disasters, and political instability. Despite these challenges, it is important to note that the economic conditions of mountain regions are not uniform. For instance, while some communities may be trapped in subsistence economies, others have benefitted from access to tourism, niche markets, or remittances. This variation underscores the need for context-specific strategies for mountain development.

One of the most pressing issues faced by mountain economies is their high exposure to natural hazards such as landslides, earthquakes, avalanches, and epidemics. These risks are often intensified by human activities, such as deforestation, poorly planned infrastructure, and unsustainable agricultural practices. In several mountain regions, particularly those plagued by political instability, conflict adds another layer of vulnerability. Studies by Libiszewski and Bachler (1997) have shown that mountain areas often become the battleground for ethnic tensions, resource conflicts, and wars, further undermining development prospects. This is particularly true in parts of the HKH region, where minority groups have historically faced both social exclusion and exploitation of natural resources. Conflict not only disrupts lives and livelihoods but also deters much-needed investment and weakens governance systems in these regions.

While developing mountain regions struggle with a multitude of challenges, the historical development of mountain economies in Europe offers important lessons. During the 18th century, mountain areas like the Alps faced conditions not unlike those currently observed in the Andes or the HKH. During the Little Ice Age (AD 1500–1850), many Alpine communities experienced severe poverty, widespread malnutrition, and significant out-migration. However, the transformation of these regions began with the Industrial Revolution, which linked the Alpine economies with booming industrial centres in the lowlands. Improved transportation networks – such as railways and navigable routes – enabled trade and movement of people, while technological innovation and state support played a crucial role in stimulating economic activities. Out-migration also helped reduce population pressures, while remittances contributed to household incomes and investment in local economies.

The success of European mountain development can be attributed in large part to deliberate efforts to integrate mountain areas with broader national economies. The introduction of the potato as a staple crop, the expansion of railway networks, the growth of tourism, and the popularity of winter sports all contributed to the revitalisation of the Alpine economy. Over time, Alpine countries invested in hydropower-based industries, provided subsidies for mountain farmers, and ensured that mountain development was included in national policy agendas. Today, more than half the population in the Alps lives in urban areas, and tourism remains a thriving sector, drawing millions of visitors each year. Governments in countries like Switzerland, Austria, Germany, France, and Norway have institutionalised support for mountain development through a combination of subsidies, protective legislation, and strong political commitment.

Yet despite the overall success, European mountain economies are not without their disparities. Scholars such as Bätzing et al. (1996) caution against generalising the Alpine success story, noting that development remains concentrated in a few accessible and attractive areas, while large parts of the Alpine zone continue to suffer from economic decline and population loss. In the French and Italian Alps, for example, many communities are still dependent on traditional agriculture and lack viable alternatives such as industry or tourism. These areas remain reliant on subsidies and have limited access to diversified economic opportunities. This underlines the importance of continued policy support and the need to design development strategies that are inclusive and equitable, ensuring that no part of the mountain region is left behind.

In contrast, many of the world's least developed mountain areas are still characterised by subsistence economies dominated by agriculture, livestock rearing, forestry, and small-scale horticulture. These activities are usually labour-intensive, rely on family labour, and make limited use of modern technologies or external inputs. Traditional enterprises are often rooted in local cultures and make use of indigenous knowledge systems, but they face major constraints such as limited market access, poor infrastructure, and low levels of investment. As a result, these economies tend to be closed and self-reliant, with minimal surplus for trade or reinvestment. Although such systems can be ecologically sustainable and culturally appropriate, they often generate low levels of income and limited prospects for economic growth.

The increasing population pressure in many mountain regions has worsened the problem of land scarcity. As demand for food rises, agricultural activities have expanded into previously uncultivated or marginal lands, including forested areas and steep slopes. This expansion has serious ecological consequences, including deforestation, soil erosion, and loss of biodiversity. In many cases, these environmental impacts reduce the long-term productivity of land and forests, making the existing livelihoods even more vulnerable. Unsustainable land use practices also increase the risks of natural disasters and contribute to climate change, creating a vicious cycle of poverty and environmental degradation.

Nevertheless, there have been some positive developments in recent decades. Many governments have recognised the strategic importance of mountain regions and have taken deliberate steps to promote their integration into national development agendas. Infrastructure development – such as the construction of roads, bridges, and telecommunications networks – has improved accessibility and connected remote mountain communities with markets, services, and opportunities. Public investments in education, healthcare, and rural development have begun to reduce the isolation of mountain populations and have expanded their capabilities. Sector-specific programmes targeting agriculture, horticulture, livestock, tourism, and renewable energy have opened new pathways for economic growth. These interventions have not only improved incomes but also fostered greater awareness about environmental sustainability and resource conservation.

Overall, the development dynamics of mountain economies are shaped by a unique blend of environmental limitations, socio-economic challenges, and historical trajectories. While mountain regions in developed countries have managed to transform their economies through connectivity, institutional support, and diversification, many developing mountain areas continue to face poverty, exclusion, and environmental degradation. However, with the right policy frameworks, investment in infrastructure, and support for traditional and innovative livelihood strategies, mountain economies can unlock their potential and achieve inclusive and sustainable development. A comprehensive approach that builds on local strengths while addressing structural disadvantages is essential for ensuring that mountain communities are not left behind in the global pursuit of prosperity and sustainability.

1.4 Commonalities and Interdependencies

Despite numerous initiatives in mountain regions – implemented through various programmes and projects by national governments and donor agencies – and growing international concern for environmental sustainability, these areas have largely continued to lag in development, with the exception of those in developed countries. A key reason for this shortfall is that development efforts have often been driven by external flatlander or mainstream institutions, frequently overlooking or neglecting mountain-specific perspectives. Therefore, it is crucial to incorporate essential prerequisites to achieve the long-term goal of sustainable development (Ives et al., 1997). The obstacles to sustainable development in poorer countries are significantly more severe than those encountered by mountain regions in industrialised nations. The key challenges and concerns in these countries include:

1.4.1 Mountain Specificities

Mountain-specific characteristics are often overlooked during the design and implementation of development programmes, with many sectoral projects created for non-mountain contexts. Such macro-level decisions frequently fail to align with local realities, and inter-sectoral linkages are commonly ignored, resulting in projects that have minimal effectiveness and relevance in mountainous areas. This oversight stems from a lack of consideration for "mountain perspectives," defined by Jodha et al. (1992) as "the explicit or implicit consideration of specific mountain conditions and characteristics and their operational implications in planning and executing interventions in mountain regions."

The ultimate objective is to achieve what has been aptly described at the World Summit on Sustainable Development:

> [S]ustainable management of mountain resources means enabling mountain populations to earn a livelihood, providing protection against

> natural hazards, enhancing conservation of natural resources, safeguarding social and cultural traditions, and supporting development that takes account of the special features of mountain regions, and ensures that the interests of both mountain and lowland populations become equal parts of a fundamental social contract.
>
> (WSSD, 2002)

A global survey highlights that strong local governance improves residents' well-being, but effective governance mechanisms are lacking. Enhancing governance and sustainability requires context-specific approaches and inclusive collaborations among diverse stakeholders within and beyond mountain communities (Tucker et al., 2021).

In recent years, the Mountain Research Initiative and its partners have led efforts to create a global network of observatories focused on the sustainability of mountain social and ecological systems (Greenwood, 2013). This effort led to the formation of the Global Network of Mountain Observatories (GNOMO) (http://gnomo.ucnrs.org), an interdisciplinary platform designed to improve communication, promote collaboration, and standardise methods for assessing similarities and differences across mountain regions worldwide (Flint, 2016).

There is evidence of large-scale infrastructure projects, such as dams, hydropower plants, and mineral exploration, being developed in these regions without accounting for their fragility and the environmental risks involved. Furthermore, due to weak ancillary linkages, the benefits from such projects – such as water, irrigation, and power – primarily flow to lowland areas, leaving highland agriculture and other local sectors largely unimproved.

Across countries, some of the successful cases show that incorporating mountain-specific needs into development policies has led to rapid shifts from traditional crops to diverse, market-oriented products in the HKH region (see Annexure Chapter 1).

1.4.2 *Subsistence Agriculture and Food Deficits*

Mountain agriculture includes a range of land-based activities – such as crop cultivation, horticulture, animal husbandry, and forestry – practised in an integrated manner. Traditionally, it has been characterised by low yields and a subsistence-oriented approach, relying on local resources and traditional methods, with limited production for market sale. This system linked closely with other land-based activities, using adaptation mechanisms with few external connections. Over time, changes in land use, cropping patterns, inputs, and livestock composition have occurred due to population growth, improved accessibility, government interventions, and market expansion. While cereal crop areas have generally stagnated, productivity has risen in some regions through crop diversification and fertilisers, though high-value cash crops have declined as small-scale livestock dairies have grown (Tulachan,

2000). Increased population pressure has also pushed land use into marginal and forest areas, straining resources and impacting ecology. Despite intensified production, foodgrain output still falls short of demand, leading many to adopt multiple livelihood strategies. Mountain agriculture faces mounting challenges due to land fragmentation, displacement of marginalised farmers, landlessness, natural disasters, and the increasing pressure of a young population, making it increasingly unsustainable.

1.4.3 Persistent Human Poverty

Human poverty in mountain regions is driven by complex forces within the unique mountain environment, creating compounding effects that perpetuate poverty for large populations. In China, for instance, most of the 80 million poor people in 1993 were from mountain-dwelling minorities. Other extremely poor mountainous countries include Nepal, Bhutan, and Afghanistan. Regions like Uttarakhand (India), Northern Pakistan, and Xizang in China also had high poverty levels, often obscured by aggregated census data (Ives, 1997). Over 60 per cent of the rural Andean population lives in extreme poverty (Denniston, 1995). Apart from China, the countries in the HKH region fall below the global average on the Human Development Index (Wester et al., 2019). Mountainous and landlocked countries, such as Nepal, Ethiopia, and Bolivia, often rank among the world's poorest, and even mountain regions in developed countries like Austria and Switzerland tend to be less affluent than their lowland areas (Ives, 1997).

Poverty in mountain regions is closely tied to subsistence agriculture on fragmented, rain-fed plots with low productivity and limited scope for technological advancement, leading to food deficits and reliance on imported grains. This dependence on low-yield agriculture drives households to diversify livelihoods through off-farm and non-farm activities. Pluriactivity is common as a coping strategy, with significant out-migration from these areas, which affects the origin communities by depleting the workforce for agriculture, often placing the burden on women and increasing their labour.

Isolation also limits access to essential public services and raises the cost of living due to higher local prices. Conventional poverty surveys based on consumption levels often underestimate mountain poverty (as seen in India, Nepal, and Pakistan), as they overlook mountain-specific needs such as higher calorie intake, warm clothing, and sturdy shelters. Factoring in these necessities would reveal significantly higher poverty levels in mountain areas than standard surveys suggest (Papola, 2002).

1.4.4 Exploitative Terms of Trade and Exploitative Linkage Relations

Mountain economies have unique advantages over lowland economies due to their natural resources, such as water, forests, minerals, tourism potential, and niche products like herbs and specialty crops. These resources create potential trade and economic linkages with lowland areas. However, mountain regions face significant challenges in leveraging these resources due to issues like inaccessibility, fragility, and marginality, limiting their engagement in external trade and maintaining their economic marginality (Jodha, 1992a).

These dynamics form a hinterland–metropolis relationship, where mountains supply raw materials to lowland economies, which benefit with minimal value addition for the highlands. For instance, timber, water, and minerals are extracted from the mountains primarily for lowland use, while the flow of goods back to the highlands – mostly consumer items like foodgrains – is limited. This one-sided trade, favouring lowland regions, leaves mountain areas at an economic disadvantage.

Infrastructure investments in mountain regions, aimed at fostering development, have mixed effects. Roads and communication networks improve accessibility and connect mountain communities with lowland markets, enhancing aspirations and opportunities. Yet infrastructure alone does not stimulate local economic growth and often results in negative "backwash" effects rather than fostering indigenous development. Large-scale projects, like dam construction, hydropower, and mining, frequently neglect the ecological and social needs of mountain communities, enabling more intensive resource extraction while yielding few local economic benefits. These projects disrupt local habitats and displace communities, with the benefits primarily flowing to lowland regions.

Out-migration from mountains is another consequence of the limited economic base and lack of opportunities. Although remittances provide some income, the loss of human resources burdens local communities, especially women, who bear increased agricultural and household responsibilities.

An integrated approach to highland–lowland development is essential to address these imbalances, as the development of each region is interdependent. Compensatory mechanisms are needed to ensure fairer benefits for mountain regions from their resource contributions to lowland economies (Jodha, 1992a). In a liberalised economy, mountain regions in areas like the Andes and Himalayas face further disadvantages due to limited cost advantages and subsistence-level agriculture, exacerbating inequalities. This effect may be less pronounced in the Western Alps, where lower population growth and a well-established tourism industry provide more stable economic alternatives (Rieder & Wyder, 1997).

1.4.5 Gender Inequity and Drudgery

Women are the primary contributors to mountain agriculture and central to household responsibilities, handling nearly all agricultural tasks except ploughing. They collect fodder, fetch water from distant sources, and manage various household duties like cooking, washing, and childcare. Some of the most strenuous tasks include gathering fuelwood, fodder, and water, which, due to environmental degradation, now require longer, more gruelling journeys. Overburdened with these activities, women have little to no access or control over key resources like land, and most household decisions – such as asset management, children's education, or migration – are made by men. Male out-migration further intensifies women's workload, leaving them to take on traditionally male tasks. Women have limited access to the labour market, and cultural norms restrict their employment options. Moreover, social discrimination impacts women's access to food, health, education, and increases their workloads, perpetuating poverty and inequality. This entrenched gender discrimination is widespread across much of the HKH region.

The gendered vulnerabilities to climate change, driven by the increasing intensity and frequency of natural hazards, have significant impacts on women and girls. These challenges greatly exacerbate their drudgery and overall vulnerability (Goodrich et al., 2019).

1.4.6 Environmental Degradation

Environmental degradation is the result of multiple factors that negatively affect environmental capital, including species, habitats, ecosystems, and natural resource stocks. While degradation is a natural process, human activities – whether for subsistence, development, or commercial purposes – exacerbate it. Historically, population growth led to the expansion of agricultural land into marginal and forested areas to meet food needs, often resulting in deforestation. Increased demand for fuel, fodder, and other natural resources further strained forest ecosystems. Timber, a key commercial resource, has been heavily exploited by traders, contractors, and even government agencies, further depleting forest resources. Reckless deforestation in upstream areas has also caused downstream damage, such as floods. Disasters like landslides, earthquakes, and forest fires are increasingly common in mountain regions. Large-scale, unplanned construction projects have had serious environmental consequences due to a lack of knowledge about mountain-specific construction practices. Government policies, development projects, and commercial interests that overlook environmental considerations have also contributed to the degradation. These factors have significant impacts on both the environment's sustainability and the livelihoods of mountain populations. The relationship between economic growth and the natural environment is central to sustainable development. While economic growth can improve human well-being and provide resources to address environmental issues, it can also lead to the overuse and degradation of natural resources if incentives for their sustainable use are not in place and external costs are not considered. Historically, economic growth has often meant converting natural resources into other forms of capital. Today, maintaining healthy ecosystems that support both economic and social development is essential for long-term sustainability, especially when no substitutes are available (OECD, 2001).

Mountain economies are particularly vulnerable to natural disasters due to their fragile ecosystems and unsustainable resource management. Over-exploitation and environmental degradation exacerbate issues like floods, landslides, and earthquakes, leading to significant losses in life, property, and resources (Awasthi et al., 2014). Regions such as the European Alps, Andes, and Hindu Kush Himalayas (HKH) share common challenges, including resource depletion, declining biomass, and heightened disaster risks like avalanches and diseases (Li Tianchi et al., 2001).

Climate change further intensifies these vulnerabilities. In Europe and Central Asia, rising temperatures and glacier melt threaten water supplies, while droughts and floods, often worsened by deforestation and overgrazing, damage infrastructure and livelihoods (World Bank Blogs, 2021). Similarly, the Andes face frequent earthquakes, landslides, and floods, with interlinked events like rainfall-induced landslides causing severe impacts (CLIENT II, 2018).

The HKH region is one of the most disaster-prone areas, experiencing recurring floods, landslides, and earthquakes. Between 2000 and 2013, major floods claimed over 10,000 lives and displaced 50 million people (GRID-Arendal, 2018). Recent record rainfall in China caused catastrophic flooding, collapsing 59,000 homes and damaging 150,000 others, highlighting the escalating risks associated with climate change. Sustainable development's foundation lies in integrating economic, social, and environmental dimensions – a triad of mutually reinforcing pillars essential for mountain economies.

1.4.7 Lack of Integration into Regional and Global Economies

Mountain economies possess unique characteristics and specificities that often leave them marginalised and isolated from the rest of the world. While they have gradually become more connected through advances in transport and communication, they remain only partially integrated into national and global economies. Some mountain regions of Europe have been integrated primarily because of strong linkages to mainstream economies. Globalisation has increased vulnerability in other mountain regions due to limited access to larger markets. Although mountain economies are rich in water, forest, and mineral resources, the benefits derived from these assets are highly inequitable, with most gains flowing to lowland populations rather than highland communities. Economic integration in these regions through trade, investment, and migration has often been limited. Due to weak linkages, most of the benefits are accrued by lowland populations, leaving highland communities largely deprived of these advantages.

Mountain environments, characterised by limited accessibility, fragility, marginality, and diversity, encourage diversified resource use and a balance between production and conservation. However, globalisation, driven by market forces prioritising profitability and external demand, promotes narrow specialisation, intensive resource use, and environmental degradation. In the Hindu Kush–Himalayan region, this is evident in cash crop monocultures, heavy chemical input reliance, reduced diversification, and overextraction of resources, leading to negative local impacts (Jodha, 2000). The niche products of these areas, such as fruits, off-season vegetables, seeds, medicinal plants, and herbs, are often undervalued due to insufficient market information, inadequate incentives, limited access to relevant technologies, poor infrastructure, and a lack of support systems, despite their high demand and profitability.

1.4.8 Ethnic Pluralism and Development Dynamics

A prominent feature of mountain economies – worldwide and in India – is their rich ethnic diversity. This diversity is deeply rooted in geography: rugged terrain and limited connectivity historically nurtured the emergence of numerous small communities, each with distinct languages, customs, and social norms. In the Indian Himalaya and North-East, ethnic identity significantly shapes livelihoods, governance systems, and interactions with the state. For example, in Nagaland and Mizoram, customary land ownership underpins community life and economic activity, while in Ladakh and Himachal Pradesh, Buddhist and tribal traditions influence farming practices and resource use (Dutta, 2016).

Ethnicity often strengthens resilience by fostering social cohesion and mutual support within communities. Yet it can also pose challenges to wider integration. Development policies that overlook cultural norms or apply uniform solutions risk creating mistrust or resistance. Land market reforms, for instance, may clash with communal ownership traditions, causing tension between state objectives and community rights. By contrast, culturally sensitive approaches – such as Sikkim's organic farming policy, which builds on indigenous practices – show how aligning development strategies with community values can foster sustainable and broadly accepted outcomes.

1.4.9 Borders, Boundaries, and Development Trajectories

Border location is another defining characteristic of many mountain economies. In India, several Himalayan and North-Eastern states share long – and in some cases disputed – boundaries with multiple countries:

- Jammu and Kashmir and Ladakh with Pakistan and China
- Arunachal Pradesh with China
- Sikkim and Uttarakhand with China and Nepal
- Himachal Pradesh with Tibet (China)
- North-Eastern states with Myanmar, Bhutan, and Bangladesh

Such locations bring a mix of opportunities and challenges. On the positive side, cross-border trade can stimulate local economies, as seen in traditional trade corridors like the Nathu La Pass in Sikkim or Moreh in Manipur. Cultural exchanges across borders often enrich local traditions, crafts, and markets. Yet in sensitive geopolitical contexts, borders can also impose severe restrictions – limiting mobility, creating militarised zones, and sometimes displacing communities (Singh, 2018).

In many cases, infrastructure development in these regions is shaped more by security considerations than by local economic priorities, leading to mismatches between what is built and what communities actually need. For example, road construction in Arunachal Pradesh may focus on troop mobility rather than improving market access, while movement restrictions in Ladakh's border villages limit tourism and trade opportunities. In disputed territories such as Aksai Chin or along the McMahon Line, recurrent tensions and occasional skirmishes can halt development initiatives altogether (Chakrabarti & Patra, 2019; Hussain, 2013).

1.4.10 *Security Concerns*

Security concerns in mountain economies extend beyond conventional military threats to include insurgency, cross-border smuggling, human trafficking, and environmental risks with security dimensions. In parts of India's North-East, insurgent movements have historically contested state authority, undermined governance, and deterred private investment. Prolonged conflicts in states like Nagaland and Manipur have disrupted transport networks, escalated the costs of development projects, and led to militarisation, with significant impacts on civilian life.

Security imperatives can sometimes skew development priorities. In border districts, for example, resources may be channelled into constructing military roads rather than investing in rural schools or healthcare facilities. Although such roads may eventually serve civilian needs, their initial design often disregards local economic patterns. Likewise, stringent security protocols can restrict tourism in areas that otherwise hold strong visitor appeal.

Pathways to inclusive and resilient mountain development in both global and Indian contexts suggest that success depends on integrating social cohesion, cultural respect, and security needs into economic planning. Experiences such as peace parks in the Andes or community-based tourism in the Alps demonstrate that security and development can go hand in hand. For India, locally adapted approaches – such as joint development zones in stable border areas, inter-community cultural events, and education that bridges ethnic divides – can foster trust and cooperation. Ultimately, mountain development is as much a social and political process as it is an economic one, and neglecting these dimensions risks undermining both projects and community–state relations.

1.5 Chapterisation

This book is structured into seven comprehensive chapters, each addressing a key facet of mountain development, with a particular focus on the Indian Himalayan region.

Chapter 1 draws upon a range of theoretical perspectives across diverse disciplines to develop a comprehensive understanding of the structural challenges and opportunities that shape mountain economies. By integrating insights from development economics, geography, environmental studies, political economy, and cultural economy, it presents a multidimensional framework for analysing the distinctive features, constraints, and development potential of these regions. It also sets the stage by exploring the development challenges common to mountain regions across the world. Despite being endowed with rich natural resources – such as freshwater, hydropower, forests, minerals, and tourism potential – these regions often remain economically and politically marginalised. Their typical characteristics, including geographical inaccessibility, ecological fragility, and social heterogeneity, render them especially vulnerable to environmental disruptions and natural hazards. Mountain ranges such as the Alps, Andes, and Hindu Kush Himalayas (HKH) face similar structural issues like resource depletion, poverty, and exclusion from mainstream development, though their development outcomes vary. While European mountain economies have witnessed considerable progress, the Andes and HKH continue to struggle with underdevelopment. Accelerating climate change, particularly the rapid deglaciation of the Himalayas, is altering regional hydrology and threatening long-term water security and livelihoods. In underdeveloped mountain economies, reliance on subsistence agriculture, horticulture, animal husbandry, and forestry – activities constrained by labour intensity, limited infrastructure, and small landholdings – compounds the challenges. These difficulties are further intensified by environmental degradation, persistent out-migration, and unsuitable, top-down development approaches. To address these issues, a mountain-specific development paradigm is essential – one that integrates economic growth with equity, ecological sustainability, and gender justice, echoing the aspirations of the World Summit on Sustainable Development.

Chapter 2 focuses on the development challenges specific to the Indian Himalayan region, which spans thirteen states and regions including Jammu and Kashmir, Ladakh, Himachal Pradesh, Uttarakhand, the North-eastern states, and parts of Assam and West Bengal.[1] These regions face multiple structural problems such as fragile agriculture, poverty, ecological vulnerability, and limited access to sustainable livelihoods – further complicated by gendered divisions of labour and constrained development opportunities. Population pressures and limited land availability have prompted a shift toward non-traditional occupations, yet development outcomes remain mixed. Improved connectivity has enhanced access but simultaneously intensified ecological stress and resource exploitation. Trade imbalances, environmental degradation, and migration patterns have further strained local systems. Agricultural productivity is constrained by poor infrastructure, fragmented markets, and delicate ecosystems, while industrialisation remains stunted due to the lack of institutional support for small-scale enterprises. Despite significant reserves of human and natural capital, the region continues to depend heavily on financial support from the central government. The diversity of socio-cultural and ecological contexts demands differentiated development strategies – Himachal Pradesh, for instance, has leveraged horticulture successfully, whereas Jammu and Kashmir remains dependent on tourism, and the North-east continues to lag industrially. Across the region, natural disasters remain a constant and growing risk, reinforcing the urgency for tailored and context-specific development approaches.

Chapter 3 delves into labour market trends and migration patterns in the Indian Himalayan states, shedding light on employment structures, regional disparities, and gendered outcomes. Labour force participation is on the rise, but this has not always translated into employment gains, especially for educated women. While some states like Sikkim have succeeded in generating employment, others such as Mizoram continue to struggle with underemployment. Despite the growth of self-employment and regular salaried jobs, informality remains prevalent – even within the organised sector – reflecting the weak enforcement of labour standards and protections. Migration trends, largely driven by aspirations for better education, employment, and living conditions, exhibit clear male–female distinctions and highlight serious gaps in official data and policy attention. Addressing these complex labour dynamics requires state-specific, multidimensional strategies that promote local industries, improve vocational training systems, enhance physical and digital infrastructure, and actively foster gender-inclusive development.

Chapter 4 turns to human capital, examining the state of education and healthcare in the Himalayan region. Despite progress, persistent gaps in access, infrastructure, affordability, and service quality continue to undermine the region's human development potential. Strengthening the education system by investing in school infrastructure, teacher recruitment, digital learning tools, and locally relevant vocational training is urgently needed. On the health front, geographic remoteness, human resource shortages, and chronic underfunding hamper service delivery. Strengthening primary healthcare, integrating traditional knowledge with modern medical systems, and promoting telemedicine are critical to overcoming these challenges. High levels of out-of-pocket spending, significant maternal and child health disparities, and poor nutrition further constrain human development outcomes. To make a tangible difference, national programmes such as Ayushman Bharat and Anemia Mukt Bharat must be implemented in region-specific ways that respond to local realities. An integrated and well-coordinated approach that combines education, technology, and equity-focused service delivery can help build a more resilient and empowered population in these mountain states.

Chapter 5 explores poverty and inequality across Himalayan economies, focusing on income levels and multidimensional deprivation. While many states have recorded improvements in poverty reduction and service delivery – largely due to targeted interventions and social welfare schemes – substantial disparities persist across states. Sikkim and Himachal Pradesh have made significant headway, but Meghalaya, Nagaland, and others continue to register high poverty levels. Although rural inequality has declined in several areas, urban inequality remains a pressing issue, particularly in Sikkim, where income gaps are widening in urban centres. Addressing these disparities calls for inclusive growth strategies that strengthen last-mile service delivery, improve access to opportunities in remote regions, and foster greater social inclusion. The integration of climate resilience into poverty alleviation programmes and the enhancement of institutional capacity, especially in lagging states, will be vital to ensuring long-term, sustainable development outcomes.

Chapter 6 shifts focus to sustainability and disaster management in the Himalayan economies, where climate change and ecological fragility have intensified the frequency and severity of natural disasters such as landslides, earthquakes, floods, and wildfires. Despite the creation of State Disaster Management Authorities (SDMAs), the region's response remains largely reactive and fragmented. To build resilience, a proactive and integrated approach to disaster risk reduction is essential. This includes investment in early warning systems, community-based preparedness, and the mainstreaming of disaster management into broader development planning. Global experiences – such as Bangladesh's flood management systems or the lessons from Hurricane Katrina – highlight that institutional readiness and strategic planning often matter more than resource availability. Effective disaster recovery requires a layered strategy encompassing short-, medium-, and long-term measures, all aligned with sustainability, resilience building, and livelihood restoration. Ultimately, the development of a region-specific, holistic disaster management framework is not just desirable but indispensable.

Chapter 7 presents several success stories from across the Himalayan states that highlight innovative approaches delivering tangible socio-economic and environmental benefits. These examples reflect the creativity and resilience of mountain communities while offering tested models that can be adapted and replicated in other parts of the region to address similar challenges.

Chapter 8 brings together insights from the preceding discussions and presents a strategic vision for inclusive and sustainable development in the Indian Himalayan region. It consolidates the thematic lessons from each chapter – ranging from livelihoods and human capital to migration, poverty, and disaster preparedness – into a coherent policy framework. The path forward must be shaped by locally grounded, spatially differentiated, and ecologically sensitive strategies. Building a resilient mountain future will require sustained investments in human development, promotion of gender equity, creation of sustainable livelihood options, and robust climate adaptation mechanisms. Strengthening institutions and governance structures is equally crucial. Above all, this vision seeks to balance the imperatives of economic growth with ecological conservation and community well-being, laying the foundation for a truly sustainable mountain development paradigm.

1.6 Chapter Summary and Conclusion

The chapter utilises a range of theoretical perspectives from multiple disciplines to build a comprehensive understanding of the structural challenges and opportunities that shape mountain economies.

Mountain regions share several common features, including distinct biophysical characteristics, heightened environmental concerns, subsistence-based agriculture, underdevelopment, and the marginalisation of local populations, ethnic pluralism, borders, boundaries, and security concerns. However, these areas also possess unique advantages, such as rich forest resources, abundant water sources, tourism potential, and other niche products, which offer them a comparative edge over non-mountain regions. While some areas have successfully leveraged these assets through effective development strategies, many others have struggled due to inadequate infrastructure and limited developmental initiatives. As a result, the development paths of mountain regions differ significantly, shaped by variations in growth drivers.

During the eighteenth century, the mountain region of Europe had similar conditions as many mountain regions of poor HKH or Andean regions have today. The mountain region of Europe developed during the late eighteenth and early nineteenth centuries, credited to strong external linkages from the regions experiencing the Industrial Revolution and fast agricultural growth. The Industrial Revolution had changed the production relationship, which had benefited mountain region significantly. The development of transportation such as railways and navigation had facilitated trade and out-migration from the mountain regions, which helped reduce demographic pressures to a certain extent. External linkages to the areas experiencing fast growth in employment and incomes had favoured the growth of mountain areas in terms of infrastructural development, employment opportunities, education, and skill and tourism development, while linkages in the Andean and HKH regions have been mostly to the regions or areas that are marginally better off than mountain areas (Banskota, 2000).

The population growth in these regions is significantly higher, and this has had an adverse effect on the environment and ecology. Infrastructure development is still at a nascent stage in these regions with limited internal linkages. The tourism industry has been promoted in many parts of the HKH region, but environmental considerations are neglected and internal linkages are often found weak. Many mountain economies in the Alps are helped by national economies in the form of subsidies and greater flow of funds to ameliorate inequalities. Development strategies in countries such as Austria, France, Slovenia, and Switzerland are more *proactive*, focusing on building a modern mountain economy centred on the tourism industry, high-quality agricultural products, agro-tourism, improved transport infrastructure, and in some cases, high-tech industries and specialised service sector activities, like healthcare and spas (Mountain Areas in Europe, 2004).

The goal, as outlined at the World Summit on Sustainable Development (WSSD, 2002), is to sustainably manage mountain resources by enabling livelihoods, protecting against natural hazards, conserving resources, preserving cultural traditions, and fostering development tailored to mountain-specific needs while balancing the interests of both mountain and lowland populations. In line with this vision, the Mountain Research Initiative has established the Global Network of Mountain Observatories (GNOMO), an interdisciplinary effort to study mountain sustainability, promote collaboration, and align methodologies across global mountain landscapes (Greenwood, 2013; Flint, 2016).

Therefore, it is essential to develop a mountain-specific framework that promotes growth with equity while addressing key issues such as mountain agriculture, persistent poverty, sustainable livelihoods, environmental conservation, and gender concerns. This framework should adopt an integrated development approach that effectively incorporates the unique characteristics of mountain regions to achieve the desired outcomes.

Note

1 Assam has only two hill districts (Karbi Anglong and Dima Hasao), and West Bengal has one (Darjeeling). Hence, most of the analysis is restricted to the ten hill states.

2 Development Issues in Indian Himalayan Economies

2.1 Introduction

The economies of the hill and mountain regions, including those in the Indian Himalayan belt, have historically remained on the margins of mainstream development. These areas were traditionally dependent on subsistence agriculture, supported by limited access to transport, communication, and basic infrastructure. This subsistence-based economy was deeply linked to a social system that emphasised mutual obligations and collective livelihood security. In such settings, traditional village industries also emerged over time, making use of local raw materials and community skills. These industries, however, were largely informal and produced goods for local consumption, with very little surplus available for trade or reinvestment. As a result, they operated on narrow economic margins and were largely restricted to primary processing and low-value activities (Awasthi, 2012).

The structure of the local economy fostered a form of trade that was more communal than market-driven. Instead of being connected to wider commercial markets, trade was often based on barter or direct exchange within villages to meet immediate needs. When trade did occur beyond local boundaries, it was usually to obtain essential non-food items that could not be produced locally. This limited engagement with external markets was also supplemented by remittances sent by family members who had migrated elsewhere for work. Migration, in fact, became a necessary part of household survival, as income from local sources remained insufficient to meet growing needs.

Given the difficult terrain, poor connectivity, ecological sensitivity, and limited economic options, hill areas posed unique challenges for development planning. Recognising these concerns, tailored planning efforts began to take shape in the 1970s. The Fifth Five Year Plan of India marked a turning point when specific attention was directed to the development of hill and tribal regions through dedicated initiatives. Several schemes such as the Special Hill Area Development Programme, the Hill Sub-plan, the Tribal Sub-plan, and the Western Ghats and North-eastern development programmes were introduced. These efforts were supported by generous grants and special

DOI: 10.4324/ 9781003595410-2

assistance from the central government, which provided financial resources to state governments through schemes like the special central assistance programme. In many cases, the funding was provided on a 90:10 ratio between the Centre and the State, allowing states to undertake priority development activities.

In some cases, states also received special financial packages to address their distinct developmental concerns. With time, these initiatives focused increasingly on infrastructure – particularly in constructing roads, expanding communication networks, electrification, education and healthcare services, commercial facilities, and agricultural modernisation. A wide range of sectoral development schemes targeting agriculture, horticulture, irrigation, animal husbandry, forestry, industry, and social welfare were introduced to accelerate progress in these remote and often neglected regions (Awasthi, 2012).

These efforts led to improvements in physical connectivity and opened up the region to new economic opportunities. The introduction of new technologies and the growing influence of development programmes helped raise awareness among people about modern livelihoods and alternative income-generating options. In many areas, the government's initiatives were supplemented by the efforts of non-governmental organisations (NGOs), which focused on improving farming practices, supporting women's livelihoods, and enhancing access to essential services. However, the outcomes of these development initiatives have not always been positive or uniform. The benefits have often been captured by those with relatively greater access to resources – such as landowners, educated individuals, skilled workers, or those living close to roads and market centres. This has created a dual economy in many mountain regions, where a small section benefits from development while a majority remain marginalised and excluded.

Natural resources such as timber, medicinal herbs, and minor forest products have come under growing pressure from commercial exploitation. Unscrupulous contractors and traders from outside the region often extract these resources in large volumes to meet the increasing demands of the plains. This one-way flow of resources has led to significant ecological damage in the hills, while the economic benefits have largely accrued to industries and consumers in urban areas. The hill regions, instead of gaining from their rich natural endowments, face resource depletion, environmental degradation, and worsening terms of trade. Overexploitation of forests and water sources has only added to the fragility of these ecosystems.

One of the more visible consequences of this pattern of development has been the increasing rate of out-migration. Faced with limited local opportunities, especially for youth and educated individuals, many families have moved or sent members to towns and cities in search of better livelihoods. This has resulted in significant demographic changes in mountain villages, including imbalanced sex ratios, increasing burden on women who remain behind, and rising dependence on remittances. Migration has also affected local agriculture and alternative livelihoods, leading to falling productivity and weakened community institutions. Improved road connectivity and access to outside regions have further accelerated this trend. While exposure to the outside world has raised aspirations, the limited scope for viable economic activities within the region has made it difficult to retain the working-age population, especially the youth.

Meanwhile, technological advances in agriculture that have benefited other parts of the country have had limited impact in the hills. The difficult terrain, small landholdings, scattered settlements, and lack of irrigation have made it hard to replicate the Green Revolution model here. While there has been a slow shift from traditional cereal farming to horticulture, especially fruit and vegetable cultivation, this transition has mostly occurred in areas with good road connectivity and better market access. Many remote regions still struggle with food insecurity and remain dependent on food imports from the plains. The hill environment does not support the typical conditions required for intensive agriculture – such as large-scale input use, economies of scale, or reliable infrastructure. Limited accessibility further drives up input costs and restricts the movement of produce, reducing the competitiveness of both staple and niche crops (Jodha, 2000).

The manufacturing sector in these regions remains almost negligible, except in the relatively more accessible tarai (plain) areas that offer better conditions for industrial activity. The fragile ecology, lack of railway networks, power shortages, small markets, and poor transportation infrastructure make the establishment of large-scale industry impractical in most hill districts. Though village and household-based industries – like those related to livestock products, food processing, and handicrafts – have received some support, they remain scattered, small in scale, and face stiff competition from better quality and cheaper products from the plains. Without institutional support and access to wider markets, many of these industries have either stagnated or declined over time (Papola, 1982).

This weak base in both agriculture and industry has important consequences for trade. The overall volume of trade remains low, even in areas where the region has potential comparative advantages – such as tourism, herbs, or unique forest products. Interestingly, the low level of trade has also shielded the region somewhat from overexploitation, but it has also prevented the benefits of economic integration from reaching these communities. The absence of a strong economic foundation leaves the mountain economies vulnerable to external shocks and dependent on government support.

The broader picture that emerges is one of isolation, ecological fragility, and socio-economic marginality, all reinforcing each other in a cycle of underdevelopment. Yet one of the most distinctive features of mountain regions is their immense diversity – cultural, ecological, linguistic, and occupational. This diversity is both a challenge and a strength. On one hand, it makes standardised solutions ineffective; on the other, it offers possibilities for crafting local, context-specific interventions that build on traditional knowledge and local strengths. When well understood and supported through appropriate policies, this diversity can play a crucial role in conserving biodiversity, protecting traditional ecosystems, and generating sustainable livelihoods based on local resources like herbs, medicinal plants, or ecotourism.

Despite their shared geographic and ecological traits, each hill state and sub-region exhibits its own development challenges and opportunities. The economies remain largely agrarian and dependent on natural resources, with weak industrial and service sectors. Much of the development has been exogenously driven, with a reliance on central government schemes and little internal resource mobilisation. Even though some states possess niche advantages and a wealth of natural resources, they have not been able to fully capitalise on these opportunities. The growth momentum in most cases has not emerged from within but has been shaped by external interventions and support.

This introductory section has outlined the historical evolution and structural challenges of hill economies, especially in the Himalayan region. While significant efforts have been made over the decades to support their development, the impact has often been uneven and limited in reach. The subsequent sections of this chapter will explore in greater detail the issues of diversity and development, examining sector-specific challenges in education, health, and poverty. These discussions will be closely linked to human development indicators and progress towards sustainable development goals and will serve as a foundation for the thematic focus of the chapters that follow.

2.2 Diversity and Development

2.2.1 Diversity and Development in the Indian Himalayan Region

The Indian Himalayan region (IHR) is a vast and diverse landscape encompassing 13 states and regions – Jammu and Kashmir (J&K), Ladakh, Himachal Pradesh, Uttarakhand, Arunachal Pradesh, Sikkim, Manipur, Meghalaya, Mizoram, Nagaland, Tripura, and the hill districts of Assam (Karbi Anglong and Dima Hasao) and West Bengal (Darjeeling) (Map 2.1). This region is not only ecologically fragile but also socio-culturally rich, home to numerous ethnic groups, languages, and traditions. Understanding its development dynamics requires a nuanced approach that respects its diversity and acknowledges its unique challenges and opportunities.

2.2.2 Demographic Characteristics

The population dynamics of the Himalayan region reflect a complex interplay of geographic, social, and economic factors. Many hill states have experienced population growth rates higher than the national average, particularly during the 2001–2011 decade (see Table 2.1). States such as Meghalaya, Arunachal Pradesh, and Manipur recorded some of the highest decadal

Map 2.1 Indian Himalayan region.

growth rates, driven by both natural increase and migration. However, notable exceptions exist. Nagaland, for instance, witnessed a sharp decline in population growth, likely due to out-migration and corrections in census methodology. The sex ratio in most Himalayan states is generally higher than the national average, especially in Meghalaya, Mizoram, and Manipur. This is an encouraging sign, reflecting relatively better gender parity in certain aspects of social life. However, this needs to be understood in the broader context of social indicators such as education, health, and employment.

In terms of population density, all Himalayan states have lower averages than the national figure. The sparsely populated Arunachal Pradesh has just 17 persons per square kilometre, while Tripura is relatively dense with 350 persons per square kilometre. These differences are influenced by factors like

Table 2.1 Demographic Profiles of the Himalayan States

State/s UTs	*Population (in 000)*		*Decadal Growth*	*Percentage of Urban Population*		*Sex Ratio*
	2001	*2011*	*2001–11*	*2001*	*2011*	*2011*
Arunachal Pradesh	1,098	1,384	26.0	20.41	23.0	938
Himachal Pradesh	6,078	6,865	12.9	9.79	10.0	972
Jammu and Kashmir	10,144	12,541	23.6	24.88	27.4	889
Manipur	2,294	2,856	24.5	23.88	29.2	985
Meghalaya	2,319	2,967	27.9	19.63	20.1	989
Mizoram	889	1,097	23.4	49.50	52.1	976
Nagaland	1,990	1,979	-0.6	17.74	28.9	931
Sikkim	541	611	12.9	11.10	25.2	890
Tripura	3,199	3,674	14.8	17.02	26.2	960
Uttarakhand	8,489	10,086	18.8	25.59	30.2	963
India	1,028,737	1,210,855	17.7	27.78	31.1	943

Source: Registrar General of India, Census of India.

terrain, forest cover, and availability of arable land. Urbanisation patterns show wide variation. While Himachal Pradesh remains predominantly rural with only about 10 per cent urban population, Mizoram is more urbanised, with over 50 per cent of its population living in urban areas as of 2011. Interestingly, urban growth in some states – such as Sikkim, Tripura, and Nagaland – can be attributed more to reclassification of rural areas into urban categories than to actual urban expansion or economic transformation. This trend calls for careful planning of urban infrastructure and services in newly classified urban areas.

2.2.3 *Education and Literacy*

Education is a crucial pillar of development, and most Himalayan states have shown commendable progress in improving literacy rates. Except for Arunachal Pradesh and Jammu and Kashmir, all other hill states have literacy rates that surpass the national average. Mizoram stands out with over 91 per cent literacy, second only to Kerala (see Table 2.2). States like Tripura, Himachal Pradesh, Uttarakhand, and Sikkim also boast high male literacy levels, above 85 per cent. However, gender disparity in literacy remains a concern in some states (Map 2.2). The gap between male and female literacy is especially wide in Jammu and Kashmir (over 26 percentage points), followed by Arunachal Pradesh. In contrast, states like Mizoram, Meghalaya, and Sikkim have managed to reduce the gender gap, indicating progress towards inclusive education (Map 2.2).

Beyond literacy, the gross enrolment ratio (GER) offers a broader picture of educational access across different stages. While India's National Education

Table 2.2 Literacy Rates (in %)

States/UTs	*Literacy Rates, 2011*			
	Person	*Male*	*Female*	*Gender Gap %*
Arunachal Pradesh	65.38	72.55	57.70	20.47
Himachal Pradesh	82.80	89.53	75.93	15.19
Jammu and Kashmir	67.16	76.75	56.43	26.50
Manipur	76.94	83.58	70.26	15.94
Meghalaya	74.43	75.95	72.89	4.29
Mizoram	91.33	93.35	89.27	4.37
Nagaland	79.60	82.75	76.11	8.02
Sikkim	82.20	87.30	76.43	12.45
Tripura	87.22	91.53	78.98	13.71
Uttarakhand	78.82	87.40	70.01	19.90
All India	74.04	82.14	65.46	**20.31**

Source: Registrar General of India, Census of India.

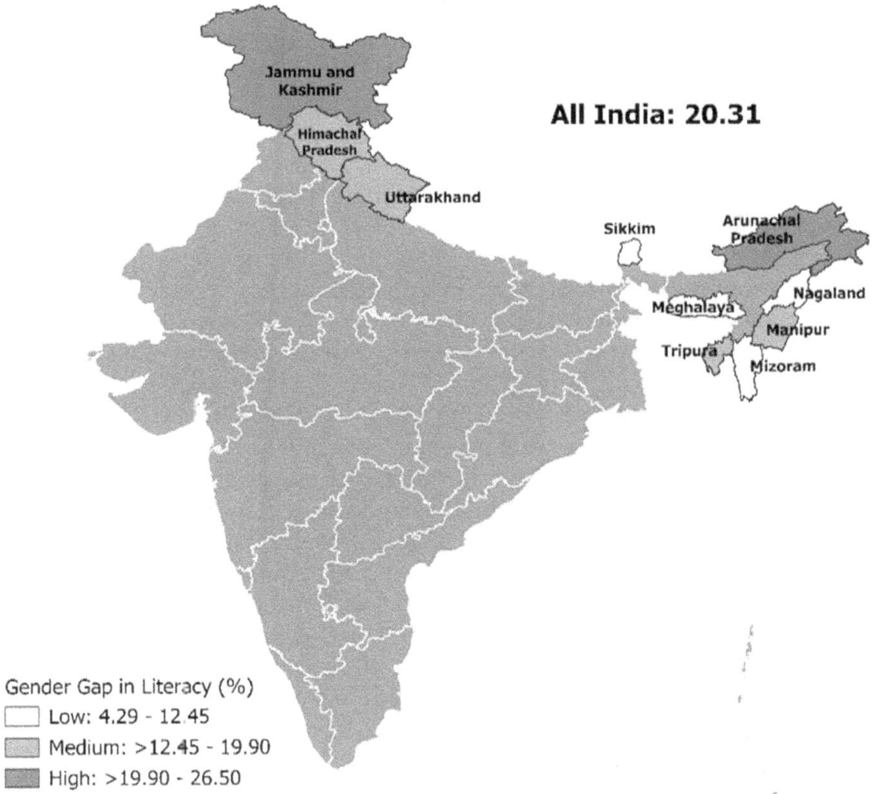

Map 2.2 Gender gap in literacy.

Source: Registrar General of India, Census of India.

Policy (NEP) 2020 sets ambitious targets – achieving 100 per cent GER in school education by 2030 and 50 per cent in higher education by 2035 – many Himalayan states lag behind, especially at secondary and higher education levels. GER at the secondary level is notably low in Arunachal Pradesh, Jammu and Kashmir, Manipur, Meghalaya, and Nagaland, with Nagaland and J&K among the lowest performers. A similar pattern continues at the higher secondary level and in tertiary education (see Annexure Chapter 2 and 3).

Despite the expansion of colleges and universities, GER in higher education remains well below the national average of 28 per cent in many states. Factors such as remoteness, inadequate infrastructure, and socio-economic constraints contribute to this shortfall. Addressing these issues will require targeted investments and flexible education delivery models, including digital and distance learning options.

2.2.4 *Health and Nutrition*

While some progress has been made in improving health outcomes, several challenges persist, especially in child nutrition and anaemia. According to data from the National Family Health Survey (NFHS), there has been a nationwide decline in stunting, wasting, and underweight prevalence among children under five. However, this overall improvement masks regional disparities.

In many Himalayan states, child nutrition indicators have either stagnated or worsened. States such as Himachal Pradesh, Meghalaya, Mizoram, Nagaland, and Tripura have witnessed an increase in stunting between 2015–16 (NFHS-4) and 2019–21 (NFHS-5). Meghalaya continues to have one of the highest proportions of stunted children, exceeding the national average. Similarly, wasting and underweight indicators have deteriorated in several states, reflecting persistent food insecurity, poor health services, and socio-economic vulnerabilities (see Annexure Chapter 2 and 3). The situation is compounded by rising anaemia among children aged 6–59 months. Nationally, the prevalence of anaemia increased from 59 per cent to 67 per cent between NFHS-4 and NFHS-5. Most Himalayan states, with the exception of Meghalaya and Uttarakhand, have reported increases in anaemia rates. This indicates deeper systemic issues related to nutrition, maternal health, and access to iron-rich food or supplements. On a positive note, infant and under-five mortality rates have declined across most Himalayan states, showing improvements in maternal and child healthcare. However, the benefits are uneven. Manipur, Meghalaya, and Tripura have experienced a reversal of trends with increased mortality rates, warranting urgent attention from public health authorities.

2.2.5 *Poverty and Inequality*

Poverty in the Himalayan region is a multidimensional phenomenon. While a detailed analysis is presented in Chapter 6, some key observations are worth noting here. Historically, poverty estimates in these states have been affected by the issue of "statistical invisibility." Many of the smaller hill states have low population sizes, making it difficult to derive state-specific poverty ratios from national surveys such as those conducted by the NSSO. Furthermore, poverty estimates for the North-east are often benchmarked to Assam, ignoring the wide differences between hill and plain regions.

Between 2004–05 and 2011–12, poverty ratios in most hill states showed a significant decline. Yet the incidence remained high in some areas, particularly in Arunachal Pradesh and Manipur, where poverty rates were estimated between 35 to 37 per cent – well above the national average. In absolute terms, Jammu and Kashmir, Manipur, and Uttarakhand have large numbers of people living below the poverty line. More recently, multidimensional poverty – measured using indicators such as health, education, and living standards – provides a more accurate picture. Based on NFHS-4 and NFHS-5 data, the Multidimensional Poverty Index (MPI) reveals notable improvements between 2015–16 and 2019–21. Most hill states have seen a decline in the MPI headcount ratio, with Arunachal Pradesh, Nagaland, Manipur, and Uttarakhand showing the sharpest reductions. Conversely, progress has been slower in Sikkim, Himachal Pradesh, and Tripura (see Annexure Chapter 2 and 3).

Nevertheless, some states such as Meghalaya and Nagaland continued to have higher multidimensional poverty in both survey periods, highlighting the need for targeted development efforts. Challenges such as poor infrastructure, limited livelihood opportunities, inadequate public services, and difficult terrain hinder the progress of poverty reduction programmes in many parts of the region.

This shows that India's Himalayan states present a unique demographic and developmental profile. While there have been impressive gains in education, literacy, and health indicators in several states, persistent gaps in nutrition, access to higher education, and poverty reduction remain. These disparities underline the need for region-specific strategies that account for the geographical, cultural, and economic diversity of the mountain states. Ensuring inclusive and sustainable development in the Himalayas requires not only better data and tailored policies but also meaningful participation from local communities in shaping their development pathways.

2.2.6 *Human Development Indicators in the Himalayan States*

The Human Development Index (HDI) is a powerful tool for measuring the overall progress of societies in terms of human well-being. Developed by the United Nations Development Programme (UNDP), HDI combines three crucial dimensions of human development: health, education, and standard of living. These dimensions are considered foundational to ensuring that individuals lead long, knowledgeable, and productive lives. Health is assessed through life expectancy at birth, reflecting how long people are expected to live under current mortality conditions. Education is captured using a

Table 2.3 Human Development Index and Gender Equality Score

States/UTs	*2022*	*2018*
	HDI Value	*Gender Equality Index Score SDG-5*
Arunachal Pradesh	0.668	32
Himachal Pradesh	0.715	42
Jammu and Kashmir	0.720	39
Manipur	0.668	25
Meghalaya	0.646	36
Mizoram	0.705	43
Nagaland	0.666	42
Sikkim	0.710	50
Tripura	0.617	38
Uttarakhand	0.667	41
All India	0.644	36

Sources: UNDP for HDI values; SDG India Index; NITI Aayog (2018).

combination of two indicators – average years of schooling for adults aged 25 and above, and expected years of schooling for children entering school. The third dimension, standard of living, is measured through gross national income (GNI) per capita, adjusted for purchasing power parity.

In the context of the Himalayan states of India, there has been a steady improvement in HDI over the years. States like Jammu and Kashmir, Himachal Pradesh, Sikkim, and Mizoram fall under the high human development category, while others remain in the medium human development range. However, disparities persist across these states, with Tripura recording the lowest HDI among them. These variations highlight the uneven distribution of resources, infrastructure, and services across the region. Yet it is encouraging to note that HDI values have improved across all the hill states, reflecting progress in health, education, and income indicators (see Table 2.3).

When examining human development from a gender equality perspective, significant concerns emerge. The pursuit of gender equality, as enshrined in Sustainable Development Goal (SDG) 5, requires the elimination of all forms of discrimination, violence, and harmful practices against women and girls. Gender equality also involves ensuring women's full participation in social, economic, and political life. Among the Himalayan states, gender equality scores range from 25 to 50, with Sikkim performing the best and Manipur the worst. Except for Sikkim, most of the hill states have lower gender equality scores, indicating persistent gender gaps in education, employment, and decision-making roles. Arunachal Pradesh and Manipur, in particular, score below the national average, highlighting the need for more focused gender-sensitive policies and interventions.

Table 2.4 State-wise Sustainable Development Goals (SDGs) Score

States/UTs	*2018*	*2019*	*2020*
Arunachal Pradesh	51	53	60
Himachal Pradesh	69	69	74
Jammu and Kashmir	53	59	66
Manipur	59	60	64
Meghalaya	52	54	60
Mizoram	59	56	68
Nagaland	51	57	61
Sikkim	58	65	71
Tripura	55	58	65
Uttarakhand	60	64	72
All India	57	60	66

Source: NITI Aayog, Government of India.

2.2.7 *Progress Towards the Sustainable Development Goals (SDGs)*

India, like many other nations, is committed to achieving the United Nations Sustainable Development Goals (SDGs) by 2030. These 17 goals encompass a wide range of economic, social, and environmental objectives, including poverty reduction, education, health, gender equality, climate action, and sustainable economic growth. India's composite SDG Index score, developed by NITI Aayog, has shown gradual improvement over the years – from 57 in 2018 to 60 in 2019, and further to 66 in 2020. These increasing scores are indicative of nationwide progress in achieving sustainable development outcomes.

The Himalayan states have also made notable strides. Himachal Pradesh, Mizoram, Sikkim, and Uttarakhand have performed better than the national average, reflecting stronger efforts in education, health, and environmental management. Additionally, states like Mizoram, Uttarakhand, Arunachal Pradesh, Jammu and Kashmir, and Tripura have registered significant improvements in their SDG scores between 2019 and 2020. This trend suggests effective implementation of development programmes and policies. However, some states such as Arunachal Pradesh, Manipur, Meghalaya, and Nagaland have continued to lag behind the all-India average in their 2020 scores. These disparities signal the need for region-specific strategies, enhanced institutional capacity, and sustained investments to ensure inclusive and balanced development across all mountain states (see Table 2.4).

2.2.8 *Economic Growth, Per Capita Income, and Sectoral Dynamics*

An important dimension of development is economic growth, often measured by gross state domestic product (GSDP) or net state domestic product (NSDP). The analysis of GSDP trends from 2011–12 to 2021–22 reveals a

Table 2.5 Gross State Domestic Product (GSDP) Constant Price, 2011–12 (Rs. Billions)

States/UTs	*GSDP*			*ACGR%*		
	2011–12	*2016–17*	*2021–22*	*2011–12 to 2016–17*	*2016–17 to 2021–22*	*2011–12 to 2021–22*
Arunachal Pradesh	110.6	148.9	198.0	6.1	5.9	6.0
Himachal Pradesh	727.2	1,030.5	1,264.3	7.2	4.2	5.7
Jammu and Kashmir	782.6	1,002.0	1,264.3	5.1	4.8	4.9
Manipur	129.1	170.8	205.1	5.8	3.7	4.7
Meghalaya	199.2	217.3	242.7	1.8	2.2	2.0
Mizoram	72.6	136.0	176.6	13.4	5.4	9.3
Nagaland	121.8	156.5	183.6	5.1	3.2	4.2
Sikkim	111.7	154.0	207.3	6.6	6.1	6.4
Tripura	192.1	305.4	394.9	9.7	5.3	7.5
Uttarakhand	1,153.3	1,677.0	1,934.1	7.8	2.9	5.3
All India	**8,631.5**	**12,223.3**	**15,155.5**	7.2	4.4	5.8

Source: Directorate of Economics and Statistics of respective state governments.

mixed performance among the hill states. Between 2011–12 and 2016–17, states like Mizoram, Tripura, and Uttarakhand performed relatively well, recording growth rates above the national average. Mizoram, in particular, stood out with an impressive average annual growth rate of over 13 per cent, while Jammu and Kashmir reported the lowest growth at about 5 per cent per annum. However, the subsequent period from 2016–17 to 2021–22 witnessed a general slowdown in growth across most states. This slowdown can be attributed to several factors. Most notably, the COVID-19 pandemic had a disproportionate impact on hill economies, especially those reliant on tourism, small businesses, and local services. Additionally, structural constraints such as limited infrastructure, high transportation costs, and vulnerability to climate-related shocks have continued to affect economic activity. Sectors such as hospitality, retail, and transport suffered heavy losses, resulting in declining incomes and slower recovery in these regions (see Table 2.5).

There is considerable inter-state variation in per-capita income across the Himalayan region. Sikkim and Uttarakhand outperform their peers, buoyed by robust tourism, hydropower generation and royalties, and – especially in Uttarakhand – industrial clusters in pharmaceuticals, automobiles, and FMCG; Sikkim's small population further lifts per-capita figures. In contrast, Tripura and Manipur rank lower, reflecting low-productivity agriculture

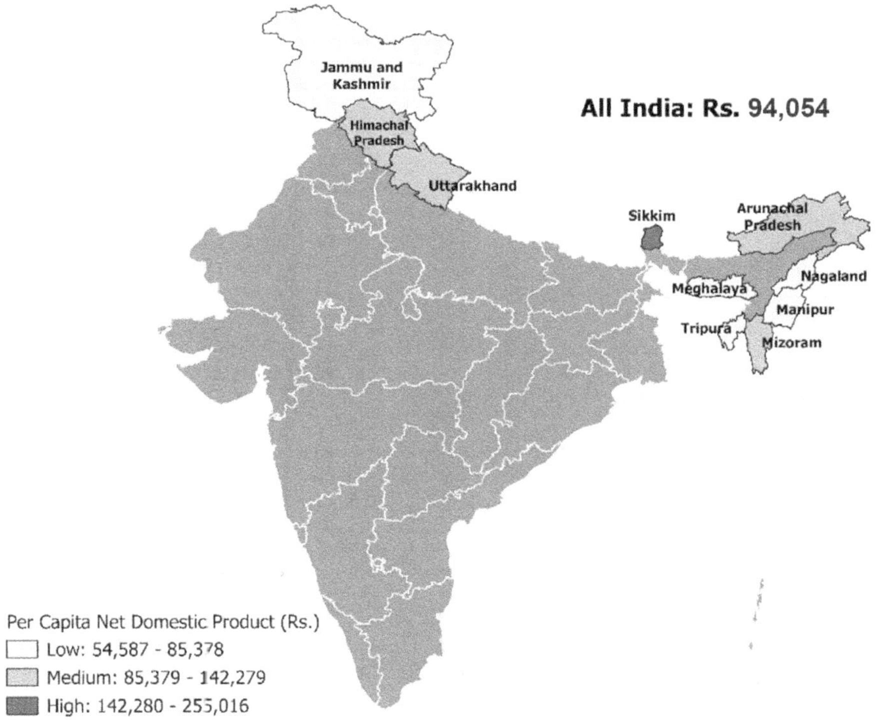

Map 2.3 Per capita net domestic product (Rs.).

Source: Directorate of Economics and Statistics of respective state governments.

(including hill farming) and a limited base of formal industry and tradable services (Map 2.3).

Between 2011–12 and 2016–17, Mizoram recorded the highest growth rate in per capita income at 11.4 per cent per annum, followed by Tripura at 8.2 per cent. On the other hand, states such as Meghalaya and Nagaland registered extremely low growth, with Meghalaya recording an alarming low of just 0.32 per cent per annum. During the next five-year period, per capita income growth declined for all states, with Uttarakhand registering the lowest growth rate at 0.22 per cent (see Table 2.6).

From a sectoral contribution perspective, significant shifts are visible. In most Himalayan states, the share of the primary sector (agriculture, forestry, etc.) in GSDP has declined between 2011–12 and 2022–23, indicating a slow move towards economic diversification. However, Tripura saw an increase in primary sector share, suggesting a different developmental

Table 2.6 Per Capita Net Domestic Product at Constant Price, 2011–12 (Rs.)

States/UTs	*GSDP per Capita (Rs.)*			*ACGR%*		
	2011–12	*2016–17*	*2021–22*	*2011–12 to 2016–17*	*2016–17 to 2021–22*	*2011–12 to 2021–22*
Arunachal Pradesh	73,540	91,311	1,04,617	4.42	2.76	3.59
Himachal Pradesh	87,721	1,22,208	1,42,279	6.86	3.09	4.96
Jammu and Kashmir	51,775	62,398	66,029	3.75	1.12	2.46
Manipur	39,762	47,151	54,587	3.47	2.97	3.22
Meghalaya	59,794	60,752	65,313	0.32	1.46	0.89
Mizoram	57,654	99,089	1,23,907	11.44	4.57	7.95
Nagaland	53,010	64,259	69,531	3.92	1.59	2.75
Sikkim	1,58,667	2,07,355	2,55,016	5.46	4.22	4.86
Tripura	47,155	69,860	85,378	8.18	4.09	6.12
Uttarakhand	1,00,314	1,38,784	1,40,322	6.71	0.22	3.41
All India	**63,462**	83,003	94,054	**5.52**	**2.53**	4.01

Source: Directorate of Economics and Statistics of respective state governments.

pathway. The secondary sector (manufacturing and construction) showed mixed trends – while its contribution increased in some states, it declined in others like Manipur, Meghalaya, Nagaland, Tripura, and Uttarakhand. The tertiary sector (services) generally gained a larger share in most states, except in Tripura, where its share actually declined (see Table 2.7 and Annexure Chapter 2 and 3).

This sectoral shift is echoed in employment trends. Although there has been a gradual decline in employment in agriculture, the transition to secondary and tertiary sectors remains slow and uneven. In some cases, such as Himachal Pradesh and Jammu and Kashmir, agricultural employment has actually increased, likely due to the growth of horticulture. States like Tripura witnessed a sharp decline in secondary sector employment – almost 50 percent – with a corresponding rise in services employment. Despite modest changes in economic structure, employment remains heavily concentrated in the primary sector, suggesting that structural transformation – a hallmark of sustained development – is yet to take firm root in the Himalayan region (see table Annexure Chapter 2).

2.2.9 *Labour Market Participation Trends*

While a detailed labour market analysis is covered in the subsequent chapter, a brief macro-overview is necessary to contextualise the broader development patterns in the hill states. Between 2011–12 and 2023–24, the labour force participation rate (LFPR) increased from 56 per cent to 60 per cent at

Table 2.7 Sectoral Share of Gross Domestic Product (in %)

States/UTs	*GSDP Share% Constant Prices (2011–12 = 100)*					
	2011–12			*2022–23*		
	Primary	*Secondary*	*Tertiary*	*Primary*	*Secondary*	*Tertiary*
Arunachal Pradesh	44.1	17.2	38.7	26.2	24.2	49.6
Himachal Pradesh	17.2	43.8	39.0	13.8	46.1	40.1
Jammu and Kashmir	17.9	27.6	54.4	15.7	26.2	58.1
Manipur	19.8	15.4	64.8	18.1	11.0	70.8
Meghalaya	22.3	33.0	44.7	18.1	18.8	63.1
Mizoram	20.8	19.8	59.4	16.1	29.3	54.6
Nagaland	31.4	12.4	56.2	25.2	10.5	64.3
Sikkim	8.3	62.8	28.8	6.5	63.7	29.8
Tripura	33.5	14.1	52.4	39.5	13.4	47.1
Uttarakhand	14.0	52.1	33.9	8.9	49.2	41.8
All India	21.7	29.3	49.0	17.5	28.1	54.4

Source: Directorate of Economics and Statistics of respective state governments.

the national level. This modest rise is largely attributed to a 10.5 percentage point increase in female LFPR, while male LFPR remained largely stagnant. This divergence reflects changing gender norms, reduced fertility rates, greater educational attainment among women, and increased demand for female labour in services and informal sectors.

Despite improvements, the Indian labour market remains male-dominated, and a considerable number of working-age men remain out of the labour force due to unemployment, underemployment, or ongoing education. In this context, a low LFPR signals underutilised human capital and calls for active labour market policies. In the Himalayan states, most exhibit higher LFPR than the national average – except Jammu and Kashmir and Uttarakhand. The female LFPR in rural areas is particularly encouraging, with Arunachal Pradesh, Himachal Pradesh, Meghalaya, and Sikkim reporting female LFPR of 70 per cent or more. This reflects the role of women in agriculture and household enterprises in mountain economies (see Annexure Chapter 2 and 3).

The worker–population ratio (WPR) has also shown improvement – especially for women – rising by 10.5 percentage points, while male WPR declined marginally. However, the male WPR dropped in both rural and urban areas, possibly due to discouraged youth unable to secure jobs aligned with their education or expectations (see Annexure Chapter 2). The unemployment rate, which was around 6 per cent in 2017–18, has declined steadily to 3.2 per cent in 2023–24. While this is a positive trend, the urban unemployment rate remains higher, especially among women. For example, in 2017–18, female unemployment in urban areas stood at 10.8 per cent, which declined to 7.1 per cent in 2023–24. Still, the unemployment situation in 2011–12 was better across most states, except Tripura and Nagaland, which saw a marked improvement in recent years (see Annexure Chapter 2 and 3). In general, female unemployment rates are higher in urban areas, while rural female unemployment in most hill states remains higher than male unemployment. These patterns underscore the need for inclusive job creation strategies, particularly targeting women, youth, and urban job seekers.

2.3 Diversity in Development Patterns in India's Himalayan States

The Himalayan states of India share many geographical and ecological features. Their mountainous terrain, cold climate, rich biodiversity, and dependence on natural resources create a common context. However, their paths of development have been far from uniform. States like the North-eastern states, Himachal Pradesh, Uttarakhand, and Jammu and Kashmir – while similar in physical setting – have followed distinct development journeys shaped by their histories, governance structures, policy choices, and institutional capacities. This chapter explores the different patterns of progress across these states, highlighting their achievements, challenges, and the need for context-sensitive development strategies.

2.3.1 Himachal Pradesh: A Model of Inclusive and Balanced Development

Himachal Pradesh has often been considered a success story among the hill states. The state's development has been inclusive and broad-based, reflecting a steady commitment to improving human well-being alongside economic growth. Education has been one of the strongest pillars of its development journey. The state has made significant efforts to ensure that all children, regardless of their gender or location, have access to schooling. Over time, this has led to high literacy levels, especially among girls. Schools are accessible even in remote villages, and public investment in school infrastructure has been complemented by community participation.

Health indicators have also shown consistent improvement. Maternal and child health outcomes are among the best in the Himalayan region. These human development achievements are closely linked with the state's relatively low levels of poverty. Multidimensional poverty – when people lack access to health, education, and decent living conditions – is limited, placing Himachal Pradesh in the high human development category.

Another striking feature of Himachal Pradesh is the active participation of women in the workforce. In both rural and urban areas, women contribute meaningfully to economic and community life. This high female labour force participation is the result of a strong tradition of women's involvement in agriculture and rural enterprises, as well as supportive policies that promote gender equality.

The economic structure of the state has also evolved in a balanced manner. Himachal Pradesh moved away from dependence on traditional agriculture by promoting horticulture. Cultivation of apple and other high-value crops has brought income stability to rural households, particularly to small and marginal farmers. Alongside agriculture, the state invested in rural roads, electricity, and irrigation, which made diversification possible. The promotion of livestock and dairy farming has also helped reduce rural poverty and improve food security.

Industrialisation in Himachal Pradesh has grown steadily. Using its locational advantage, the state attracted industries with support from central government policies. Today, the industrial base includes traditional crafts as well as modern sectors like electronics, pharmaceuticals, and processed foods. The business environment is relatively favourable, with simplified regulations and strong institutional support for start-ups and sustainable enterprises.

Tourism is another important driver of economic activity. The state has consciously developed a range of tourism experiences, from adventure and eco-tourism to spiritual and cultural travel. These efforts have not only created jobs and boosted local businesses but have also aimed to protect the environment. Sustainable tourism policies reflect a long-term vision to preserve the ecological richness of the Himalayas.

One of the most important economic assets of Himachal Pradesh is its hydropower potential. The state's rivers, fed by glaciers, have allowed the development of hydropower plants that contribute significantly to energy production in the region. Although a large share of these projects is managed by central agencies, the sector continues to provide income and employment to local communities.

2.3.2 Jammu and Kashmir: Complex Realities and Promising Sectors

Jammu and Kashmir presents a more complex picture. Despite having similar natural advantages, the state has experienced a slower pace of development. Historical conflicts, political instability, and administrative disruptions have influenced its growth trajectory. As a result, many development indicators lag behind those of its neighbour, Himachal Pradesh.

One of the key challenges lies in the demographic structure. The state has witnessed high population growth, and its sex ratio is among the lowest in the hill region. Gender disparities are also evident in literacy levels, with a considerable gap between male and female literacy. This points to the need for more inclusive and gender-sensitive educational planning.

While there have been some improvements in school enrolment, secondary and higher education participation remains weak. The state also continues to face issues related to multidimensional poverty. Although poverty has declined over time, large segments of the population remain deprived of basic services and opportunities. Gender empowerment remains a particular area of concern, with low female participation in education and employment.

Despite these social challenges, the state's economy has demonstrated resilience. In recent years, the services sector has shown strong performance. This growth, however, has not translated into broad-based income gains. Per capita income has improved only modestly, and income inequality remains a concern.

The labour market in Jammu and Kashmir is marked by low participation, especially among women. Unemployment is high, pointing to structural mismatches between education, skills, and available jobs. However, recent improvements in female labour participation suggest that with the right interventions, there is scope to change this trajectory.

Agriculture continues to play an important role in the state economy, with horticulture – particularly fruit cultivation – emerging as a promising sector. Apples, cherries, and other temperate fruits are major sources of income for rural households. Tourism, too, remains a vital contributor. The region's stunning landscapes, spiritual sites, and cultural heritage attract large numbers of visitors each year. The state government has launched policies to strengthen tourism infrastructure, with the aim of creating jobs and enhancing service quality.

Hydropower remains an underutilised asset. Although the state has significant potential, only a small portion has been harnessed. With better coordination between state and national agencies, and a focus on environmental sustainability, the sector could emerge as a major source of income and energy security.

2.3.3 Uttarakhand: Balancing Growth With Fragility

Uttarakhand offers a distinctive window into the development dynamics of India's hill states – a region marked by its ecological fragility and socio-economic aspirations. Since its formation in 2000, the state has undergone significant transformation. Urbanisation has expanded rapidly, education levels have risen steadily, and literacy – particularly among women – has improved impressively. School enrolment rates remain strong across all age groups, laying a solid foundation for long-term human development. Health outcomes have also advanced, with progress in maternal care, nutrition, and healthcare outreach. These indicators have contributed to relatively low poverty rates and moderate levels of multidimensional deprivation, suggesting a trajectory of inclusive development. Yet Uttarakhand's overall performance on the Human Development Index (HDI) remains middling, reflecting uneven progress across regions and communities.

The initial years of the state's economic journey were marked by robust industrial growth, particularly in areas such as Haridwar, Dehradun, and Rudrapur, where tax incentives and infrastructure development drew investment. However, this early momentum began to slow in the following decade. Between 2016 and 2021, economic growth rates dipped, before regaining some stability in recent years. The trajectory of per capita income mirrored this pattern – rising quickly in the early years before plateauing and then gradually recovering. While the industrial base has matured in certain pockets, the broader economy remains vulnerable to structural imbalances and environmental risks.

A critical challenge facing Uttarakhand is balancing its economic ambitions with ecological sustainability. The state is highly susceptible to natural disasters, including floods, landslides, and earthquakes – events that have become more frequent and intense due to climate change and unchecked construction. This fragility has prompted the state to emphasise disaster preparedness and climate resilience in its development planning. Simultaneously, there has been a push to diversify the economy through agro-based industries, hydropower, and tourism – sectors that can potentially generate employment while leveraging local resources.

Tourism has emerged as a cornerstone of Uttarakhand's economy. With its pilgrimage circuits, eco-tourism hubs, and adventure sports destinations, the state attracts millions of visitors annually. From Kedarnath and Badrinath to Rishikesh and Nainital, tourism sustains a wide range of livelihoods across urban and rural areas. Women, in particular, have benefited from jobs in hospitality, retail, and informal services, making tourism a key enabler of gender-inclusive development. The recently announced Tourism Policy aims to build on this momentum by offering targeted incentives for investments in hospitality, transport, and allied services. However, the expansion of tourism also raises critical concerns around environmental degradation, waste management, and overdevelopment in ecologically sensitive areas.

Hydropower represents another sector with transformative potential. The state's rivers and terrain provide a significant theoretical capacity for hydroelectric energy generation, but only a fraction of this has been realised so far. Responsible development in this sector – guided by robust environmental assessment, community engagement, and benefit-sharing – could strengthen the energy base, create employment, and contribute to sustainable growth. Yet concerns remain over displacement, ecological disruption, and the long-term viability of large-scale hydro projects in a climate-vulnerable region.

On the labour front, Uttarakhand has seen a gradual yet encouraging increase in labour force participation over the last decade. The labour force participation rate (LFPR) has risen consistently, with improvements noted across both genders. Female participation, in particular, increased notably between 2011–12 and 2021–22, suggesting a growing willingness and ability among women to seek work. The work participation rate (WPR) has also seen parallel gains, especially among women, reflecting actual absorption into work. Much of this employment remains informal or self-employed, often in agriculture or household enterprises. However, these trends do reflect a shift in social norms and the potential impact of education and livelihood initiatives.

Despite this progress, unemployment continues to be a significant concern. The state records a relatively higher unemployment rate compared to the national average. Urban youth unemployment – especially among educated males – has remained persistently high. Female unemployment in urban areas, while historically acute, has shown recent signs of decline. These patterns point to a mismatch between education and employability, a lack of formal job creation, and limited industrial diversification in sectors capable of absorbing the skilled and semi-skilled workforce. Addressing these issues requires rethinking vocational training, promoting micro-enterprises, and investing in new-age sectors such as renewable energy, IT services, and creative industries.

Regional disparities remain a defining feature of Uttarakhand's development story. A marked divide exists between the hill and plain regions. The plains – including Haridwar, Dehradun, and Udham Singh Nagar – have seen concentrated industrial growth, stronger connectivity, and better access to public services. These areas have attracted the bulk of investment and migration, acting as urban growth hubs. In contrast, the hill districts continue to struggle with poor infrastructure, low agricultural productivity, and limited employment opportunities. Rain-fed subsistence agriculture dominates, with little value addition or diversification. Out-migration from the hills, particularly of youth, remains a defining feature, driven by aspirations for better education, jobs, and living standards.

This internal migration has created a demographic imbalance, with many villages now home primarily to the elderly, women, and children. The resulting social and economic dislocation poses new challenges for governance, service delivery, and rural revitalisation. Meanwhile, within the hill districts themselves, there is considerable variation in resource availability, topography, and access to services. Tailored and decentralised development strategies are therefore essential – not only to reduce the hill-plains divide but also to empower communities to participate in and shape their own development.

Uttarakhand stands today at a critical juncture. It has made notable strides in health, education, and infrastructure, and it possesses the natural and human capital needed to sustain growth. But achieving this will depend on its ability to reconcile economic ambition with environmental stewardship, promote inclusive labour market policies, and address regional imbalances with nuance and care. The challenge is not just one of growth, but of sustainability, equity, and resilience in the face of a rapidly changing climate and socio-economic landscape.

2.3.4 The North-eastern States: A Region of Promise and Paradox

The North-eastern region of India, comprising the eight states of Arunachal Pradesh, Assam, Manipur, Meghalaya, Mizoram, Nagaland, Tripura, and Sikkim, remains one of the most culturally vibrant and geographically unique areas of the country. Nestled in the eastern Himalayan foothills and bordered by international frontiers, the region is endowed with rich biodiversity, fertile land, abundant water resources, and a multiplicity of ethnic groups and languages. Despite these natural and cultural endowments, the region continues to grapple with persistent developmental challenges rooted in historical neglect, geographical isolation, structural economic weaknesses, and complex socio-political dynamics.

Economically, the region has remained underdeveloped, with a heavy reliance on agriculture – especially subsistence and shifting cultivation – that offers low productivity and limited market integration. Though the region is rich in natural resources such as oil, gas, forests, and minerals, their exploitation remains constrained by inadequate infrastructure, ecological concerns, and weak private sector participation. Industrialisation is sparse, with only a few exceptions like Assam's tea industry or Tripura's natural gas-based units. The manufacturing sector remains underdeveloped across most states, and in some cases, early signs of de-industrialisation are evident. While the contribution of agriculture to the gross state domestic product (GSDP) has been declining, it is the services sector – driven primarily by government spending rather than dynamic market forces – that has emerged as the mainstay. This growth pattern, reliant on public employment and state subsidies, raises questions about the sustainability of economic expansion in the region.

The region's share in India's overall GDP remains disproportionately small – contributing merely 2.8 per cent in 2018–19 – with Assam alone accounting for two-thirds of that. Several factors contribute to this marginalisation, including poor physical and digital connectivity, high transportation costs, low investment levels, and recurring ethnic unrest. The narrow Siliguri Corridor, also known as the "Chicken's Neck," remains the region's lifeline to the rest of India but poses significant logistical and strategic vulnerabilities. Transport infrastructure, electricity consumption, and internet penetration in most North-eastern states fall well below the national average, impeding both economic growth and social development.

Demographically, the region presents a paradox of opportunity and pressure. Several North-eastern states – such as Arunachal Pradesh, Manipur, Meghalaya, and Mizoram – have recorded population growth rates higher than the national average, signalling a growing youth population that could be a demographic dividend. However, urbanisation remains limited in most parts of the region, with the exception of Mizoram, where over half the population resides in urban areas. The relatively high sex ratio across the region and steady improvements in literacy – particularly in states like Mizoram, which ranks second nationally – indicate progress in human development. Yet disparities remain stark: Arunachal Pradesh continues to struggle with low literacy and a persistent gender gap in education, while tribal and remote areas across the region face challenges in teacher availability and curriculum relevance, often exacerbated by language and cultural mismatches.

In the domain of health, accessibility remains a major concern, especially in rural and remote locations where infrastructure is poor and often disrupted by natural disasters such as floods and landslides. While innovative initiatives like boat clinics in Assam offer localized solutions, they remain limited in coverage. Similarly, although there have been improvements in educational enrolment and gender parity, the quality of public education and learning outcomes continue to suffer due to systemic gaps in delivery and monitoring.

Poverty and inequality continue to plague the region. As per recent estimates, the percentage of population below the poverty line remains high in states such as Manipur (37 per cent) and Arunachal Pradesh (35 per cent). Although multidimensional poverty has shown signs of decline, the pace has been uneven – Nagaland and Meghalaya, for instance, still register headcount ratios above the national average. Human Development Index (HDI) rankings place most North-eastern states in the medium category, with only Mizoram and Sikkim achieving high scores. Gender inequality, too, reveals a complex picture: while states like Mizoram and Sikkim have made commendable progress, others like Manipur and Arunachal Pradesh continue to show poor outcomes in terms of female labour participation, literacy, and representation.

Labour market dynamics in the North-east are shaped by high rates of unemployment and underemployment, particularly among educated youth. In states such as Nagaland and Tripura, the unemployment rate touched 18 and 13 per cent, respectively, in 2011–12, and more recent data suggest that joblessness remains a persistent issue in states like Arunachal Pradesh, Manipur, and Meghalaya. Although the labour force participation rate (LFPR) and worker–population ratio (WPR) have improved in some states, the gains are uneven – Mizoram, for example, has experienced stagnation or even decline in female and rural participation. A major concern is the lack of employment opportunities outside agriculture, which continues to absorb a significant share of the workforce despite its declining economic relevance. The paucity of industrial employment, coupled with limited avenues for entrepreneurship, has led to increased out-migration, particularly among youth, towards urban centres in mainland India.

From a macroeconomic standpoint, the region's performance has been uneven. Between 2011–12 and 2016–17, Mizoram posted the highest GSDP growth at 13.4 per cent, while Meghalaya lagged at just 1.8 per cent. The following period saw a deceleration in overall growth, with Mizoram still leading (4.6 per cent), but the pace remained well below potential. Per capita Net Domestic Product (NDP) patterns also reflected these disparities, with Meghalaya consistently at the lower end, indicating a widening income gap across and within the states.

Yet within these constraints lie opportunities for transformation. The shift from traditional agriculture to horticulture, floriculture, and the cultivation of high-value fruits and spices is gaining momentum, supported by targeted government schemes. Allied activities such as fisheries, piggery, and poultry are also being encouraged to diversify rural livelihoods. The region's immense hydropower potential and its unexplored tourism prospects – especially eco and cultural tourism – represent untapped drivers of economic growth. As India deepens its diplomatic and trade engagement with South-east Asia under the Act East Policy, the North-east could serve as a natural bridge, provided connectivity and local capacities are enhanced.

Recognising the region's challenges and potential, the Government of India has rolled out several institutional and policy interventions. The establishment of the Ministry of Development of the North Eastern Region (MDoNER) in 2001 marked a pivotal step towards coordinated development planning. Special financial arrangements – such as the 90:10 funding pattern for centrally sponsored schemes – have underscored the Centre's commitment. Flagship programmes like the North Eastern Region Community Resource Management Project (NERCORMP), the North East Special Infrastructure Development Scheme (NESIDS), and the formation of the NITI Forum for the North-east have aimed to address sector-specific gaps and foster participatory development.

Nonetheless, structural constraints remain formidable. Political marginalisation, intermittent insurgency, and a security-centric governance framework – exemplified by the continued imposition of the Armed Forces Special Powers Act (AFSPA) in several areas – have often sidelined developmental priorities. Inter-ethnic tensions around land rights, identity, and resource sharing persist, hampering regional cooperation and social cohesion. The demand for Inner Line Permits (ILPs) and growing resistance to "outsiders" reflect deeper anxieties around cultural erosion and economic displacement, calling for more inclusive and context-sensitive governance mechanisms.

Globalisation and liberalisation have had a profound impact on the hill states. The experience of North-east India shows that these processes have often widened inequalities, with benefits largely concentrated in select sectors and regions. While the region possesses significant development potential, weak local institutions and inadequate infrastructure continue to hamper progress. Employment generation remains limited, industrialisation sluggish, and agriculture still heavily dependent without sufficient modernisation. These states also rely substantially on central transfers. Given that the region is sensitive, ethnically diverse, and ecologically fragile, it requires context-specific and carefully designed development policies (Mishra & Upadhyay, 2017).

The trajectory of development in the region is inextricably bound to issues of ethnicity, land tenure, and citizenship, as exemplified in Arunachal Pradesh (Mishra & Upadhyay, 2017).

Progress on Sustainable Development Goals (SDGs) has been mixed. While the region as a whole has seen improvements since 2018, states like Arunachal Pradesh and Nagaland continue to rank among the lowest nationally. Moreover, the lack of effective integration into the broader framework of India's Act East Policy has meant that the region's strategic location has not been adequately leveraged for cross-border trade, connectivity, or economic diplomacy with South-east Asia.

The development trajectory of the North-eastern region embodies both promise and paradox. Its vast resources, strategic positioning, and youthful population offer significant developmental potential, but realising this promise demands more than financial investments or short-term schemes. What is required is a long-term vision anchored in inclusivity, sustainability, and regional cooperation. Prioritising integrated connectivity – through rail, road, air, and digital infrastructure – restoring traditional trade routes, fostering peace and social reconciliation, promoting skill development, and supporting local entrepreneurship must form the pillars of a renewed development agenda. With the right mix of policy innovation, institutional accountability, and participatory governance, the North-eastern states can emerge not just as a gateway to India's eastern frontier but as a model for resilient and inclusive development.

2.4 Chapter Summary and Conclusion

Despite sharing similar biophysical and ecological characteristics, India's hill states – Himachal Pradesh, Uttarakhand, Jammu and Kashmir, and the North-eastern region – exhibit markedly varied development patterns. These differences are shaped not just by geography, but by a complex interplay of policy choices, governance quality, institutional strength, and historical legacies. A common thread across the hill states is the continued reliance on the primary sector, with limited diversification into manufacturing or high-productivity services. Employment in agriculture remains high, while industrial activity is sparse and services are often dominated by low-value or government-aided sectors. Social, economic, and health indicators have shown progress, but often at a slower pace than the national average. Structural bottlenecks – such as infrastructure deficits, ecological vulnerability, and limited livelihood opportunities – continue to constrain inclusive and sustainable growth.

Himachal Pradesh stands out for its successful transition from a cereal-based agricultural economy to a high-value horticultural hub. It has achieved relatively high literacy, robust healthcare systems, and well-developed infrastructure, positioning it as a model for inclusive development. This progress has been underpinned by consistent investment in human development, the active participation of women, and the role of local governance institutions. The state also holds significant potential in hydropower, tourism, and agro-business, reinforced by policies that encourage private investment. In contrast, Jammu and Kashmir, while recording the lowest poverty ratio among hill states, faces critical challenges in industrial development and gender disparities in education and health. Rich in tourism, saffron cultivation, handicrafts, and hydro-resources, the region's development has been impeded by longstanding conflict, strained Indo-Pak relations, and internal instability. However, positive trends in the services sector – particularly tourism – highlight its untapped economic potential.

Uttarakhand, despite high literacy levels and a relatively narrow gender gap, has paradoxically recorded the highest poverty rate among hill states. The early momentum following its formation in 2000 has given way to development imbalances between the plains and hill districts. While endowed with rich natural resources and potential in hydroelectricity, tourism, and horticulture, economic infrastructure and institutional support remain underdeveloped. Recent trends, however, show sectoral growth, particularly in tourism and services. The state's focus on balancing ecological sustainability with development offers important lessons for other mountainous regions.

The North-eastern region – with its rich ethnic and ecological diversity – remains economically and industrially underdeveloped. Agriculture remains the primary source of livelihood, but productivity is low, and foodgrain dependency persists. High population growth, youth unemployment, and low per capita income further complicate the development landscape. Labour force participation has improved in parts of the region, especially among women, yet underemployment remains a persistent concern.

Despite various central initiatives – including the mandatory earmarking of 10 per cent of ministry budgets for the North-east and schemes like the North East Special Infrastructure Development Scheme (NESIDS) and the North Eastern Region Community Resource Management Project (NERCORMP) – long-term development outcomes have often been limited. The region continues to rely heavily on central transfers, with low internal revenue generation and private sector investment.

India's foreign policy has also historically underleveraged the North East's geographic proximity to South-east Asia. The closure of traditional trade routes and limited regional cooperation with neighbouring countries like Myanmar and Bangladesh have prevented the region from emerging as a dynamic trade and connectivity hub. Addressing this requires a paradigm shift that includes restoring trade routes, deepening diplomatic engagement, and investing in connectivity – both physical and emotional – with the rest of India and neighbouring countries. The experience of these hill states underscores that one-size-fits-all development strategies are insufficient. Common challenges – such as ecological fragility, natural disasters, and infrastructure deficits – demand regional cooperation and cross-learning. Yet development strategies must also be tailored to local realities. For these states to thrive, planning must be inclusive, gender-responsive, ecologically sensitive, and grounded in the aspirations of local communities.

Ultimately, unlocking the full potential of India's hill states requires coordinated action between central and state governments, strategic investment in education and infrastructure, promotion of entrepreneurship, and capacity building. Viewing development through a mountain-specific lens – as argued by Papola (2014), Chopra (2013), and Jodha et al. (1992) – demands attention to the region's distinct conditions and their practical implications. With thoughtful planning and inclusive governance, these regions can transform their structural constraints into opportunities for resilient, equitable, and sustainable growth.

3 Labour Market Dynamics and Migration in Indian Mountain Regions

3.1 Introduction

The primary objective of economic development is to improve people's quality of life by ensuring access to fundamental necessities alongside adequate livelihood opportunities. However, access alone is insufficient; the nature and returns of these opportunities are crucial in driving social and economic development. Therefore, the creation of adequate and sustainable livelihood opportunities is a key policy intervention aimed at addressing the needs of an expanding workforce. Sustainable Development Goal (SDG) 8 underscores the importance of sustained, inclusive, and sustainable economic growth, full and productive employment, and decent work for all, with an emphasis on gender equality (United Nations, 2015). The Himalayan region, comprising states such as Jammu and Kashmir, Himachal Pradesh, Uttarakhand, Assam, Arunachal Pradesh, Meghalaya, Manipur, Mizoram, Nagaland, Tripura, and Sikkim, is predominantly mountainous, with a significant proportion of its population residing in rural and hilly areas. Subsistence agriculture and tourism form the backbone of livelihoods in these regions. However, unique geographical challenges such as inaccessibility to infrastructure, markets, technology, and information, along with environmental fragility and marginality, have contributed to their underdevelopment. The limited, fragmented, and rain-fed agricultural land results in low productivity and income, further exacerbating economic disparities between the hilly and plain areas.

Another crucial demographic factor influencing the labour market is migration, which has become an integral part of the development process, especially in Himalayan regions. Migration occurs for various reasons, including better employment opportunities, higher income, and improved access to education and healthcare. Historically, migration has been driven by regional development disparities, with people from less developed areas moving to more developed regions in search of better prospects (Harris & Todaro, 1970). Rural-to-urban migration underscores these inequalities, and while migration can be an economic strategy, it is also a complex process involving various forms such as temporary, circular, long-term, and permanent migration. Initially, out-migration primarily involved able-bodied males, reflecting

DOI: 10.4324/9781003595410-3

strong ties to their places of origin. However, a lack of employment opportunities and inadequate social infrastructure, particularly in hilly districts in Himalayan regions, has led to distress-driven migration, creating significant challenges.

Migration from Himalayan states is not solely employment-driven; it also includes movements for education and healthcare, often involving entire families. This evolving migration pattern has significant implications for both places of origin and destinations. Migrant workers frequently face difficulties in accessing entitlements, making them one of the most marginalised groups in society (Deshingkar & Akter, 2009). In particular, out-migration is an inevitable aspect of economic development, driven by aspirations for better education, healthcare, and employment. However, there is a lack of studies covering these two important aspects across the Himalayan states in India.

Given this context, this chapter explores employment and livelihoods in the Himalayan states, with the aim not only of generating adequate livelihoods but also of ensuring decent and productive work for all residents. It also examines migration patterns and their underlying reasons. The chapter is structured into two main parts. The first part examines labour market dynamics, including patterns and trends in employment and livelihoods, labour force participation, employment rates, unemployment rates, and structural composition. It also explores the relationship between economic growth and employment, with a focus on Gross State Value Added (GSVA) across broad sectors such as agriculture, industry, and services. Employment quality is assessed by examining organised versus unorganised sectors, formal versus informal employment, and occupational distribution. The analysis also considers variations across gender and rural–urban divides. This chapter presents an analysis based on data from national censuses, labour force surveys, migration surveys, and published reports. Data sources include the Employment and Unemployment Surveys (EUS), Periodic Labour Force Surveys (PLFS), and GSVA data from the National Statistical Organisation (NSO) and state economic and statistical departments.

The second part examines migration patterns, particularly out-migration, attributed to push and pull factors such as employment prospects and socio-economic conditions. Migration trends and reasons are analysed using Census data (2001, 2011) and NSSO surveys (2007–08, 2020–21). Since Census of India migration data is available only up to 2011, PLFS data for 2020–21 is also utilised. Case studies from selected Himalayan states provide insights into recent migration patterns. Primary survey-based studies at the national and state levels are also incorporated to provide a comprehensive understanding of migration trends and labour market dynamics in the Himalayan states. The chapter also evaluates government livelihood programmes, addressing issues such as youth unemployment, livelihood risks, and emerging employment opportunities. The final section summarises the findings and provides policy recommendations.

3.2 Labour Market Dynamics

3.2.1 Labour Force Participation Rate

The labour force participation rate (LFPR) in the Himalayan states exhibits significant variation compared to the national average and across states. In 2024, LFPR in most Himalayan states remains higher than the national average, reflecting strong engagement of the workforce in economic activities (see Figure 3.1 and Annexure Chapter 3). Compared to the all-India LFPR, which has improved since 2012 but remains lower than its 2000 level, states such as Arunachal Pradesh, Meghalaya, Sikkim, and Nagaland have shown a significant resurgence in participation rates. This upward trend suggests an increase in employment opportunities and economic activities in these regions. Himachal Pradesh continues to maintain one of the highest participation rates, reinforcing its long-standing trend of strong workforce engagement. However, not all states have followed this positive trajectory – Mizoram has seen a decline in LFPR, indicating possible employment-related challenges that could stem from structural economic shifts or reduced opportunities in traditional sectors.

Looking at broader trends from 2000 to 2024, the LFPR in most Himalayan states was initially higher than the national average, largely due to the

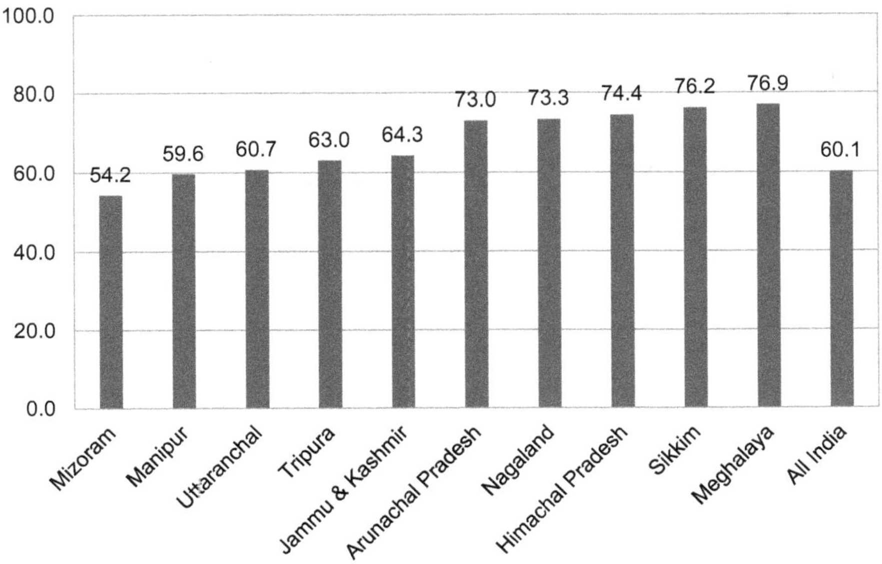

Figure 3.1 Labour force participation rate, 2024 (in %).

Source: EUS and PLFS, NSSO.

strong involvement of rural populations in agriculture and allied activities. Over time, a decline was observed by 2012, mirroring national patterns of economic transformation, urbanisation, and shifts away from agriculture. The literature on labour market trends suggests that this period saw increased mechanisation in agriculture, migration to non-farm employment, and structural adjustments in the economy, which contributed to the decline in workforce participation. The resurgence observed in 2024 aligns with the broader recovery seen at the national level but remains more pronounced in certain Himalayan states. Factors such as renewed employment in emerging sectors, policy initiatives promoting local economies, and an increasing focus on tourism, infrastructure, and service-based industries could explain this positive shift. However, the contrasting trend in Mizoram underscores the uneven nature of economic growth and employment opportunities within the region, reflecting the challenges of sectoral transitions and regional economic disparities. Thus, while overall LFPR in the Himalayan states remains higher than the national average, the variations across states highlight the complex interplay of economic policies, labour market dynamics, and sectoral transformations.

3.2.1.1 Male–Female Differences

The labour force participation rates (LFPR) by gender in the Himalayan states continue to show notable gender disparities in 2024, though some states have made significant progress in reducing the gap compared to the national average (see Figure 3.2 and Annexure Chapter 3). Male participation remains

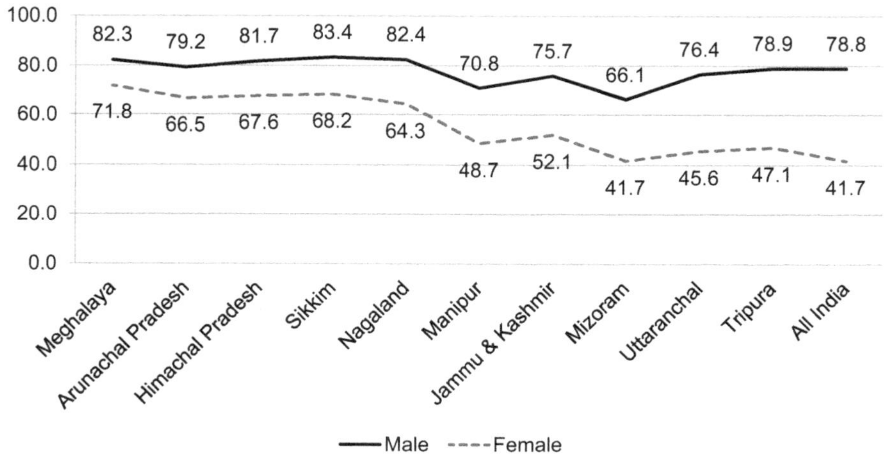

Figure 3.2 Labour force participation rate by gender, 2024 (in %).
Source: PLFS, NSSO.

consistently high across all states, with most exceeding the national male LFPR. However, female participation varies widely. In states like Meghalaya, Arunachal Pradesh, and Sikkim, female LFPR has increased substantially, reaching levels comparable to male participation. On the other hand, in states such as Mizoram, Tripura, and Uttarakhand, female participation remains relatively low, highlighting persistent barriers to workforce entry. At the national level, female LFPR has increased modestly but remains significantly lower than male LFPR, indicating that while some Himalayan states are witnessing a strong resurgence in female employment, gender disparities continue to shape labour market dynamics.

Examining trends from 2000 to 2024, the gender gap in workforce participation has been a defining characteristic of labour market shifts (see Annexure Chapter 3). In 2000, male LFPR across the Himalayan states was consistently high, while female participation varied, with some states showing relatively strong engagement and others displaying extremely low participation. By 2012, a notable decline in female LFPR was observed in most states, reflecting broader national trends linked to structural transformations in the economy. The literature highlights several factors contributing to this decline, including increased enrolment in education, lack of suitable employment opportunities, and socio-cultural norms restricting women's workforce engagement. However, by 2024, a resurgence in female LFPR is evident in many Himalayan states, suggesting a recovery driven by expanding employment in non-agricultural sectors, government initiatives promoting women's employment, and a gradual shift in societal attitudes towards female labour force participation.

A key question is whether female participation has led the fluctuations in overall LFPR. The data suggests that much of the decline in workforce participation between 2000 and 2012 was driven by the reduction in female LFPR, as male participation remained relatively stable. Similarly, the resurgence in 2024 appears to be fuelled by the significant increase in female LFPR in several states, particularly Arunachal Pradesh, Meghalaya, and Sikkim. This pattern indicates that fluctuations in overall LFPR are closely linked to changes in women's participation, reinforcing the argument in labour market literature that female workforce engagement is highly sensitive to economic, social, and policy-driven changes. Despite this recovery, the persistence of gender disparities in certain states underscores the need for targeted policy interventions to ensure sustained improvements in women's workforce participation across the region.

3.2.1.2 Rural–Urban Differences

Further, the LFPR in the Himalayan states continues to reflect a distinct rural–urban divide in 2024, with rural workforce participation remaining significantly higher than urban participation, a pattern consistent with the national trend. Rural LFPR in states such as Sikkim, Meghalaya, and Nagaland has rebounded strongly, indicating a revival of employment opportunities in agriculture, allied activities, and informal sectors (see Figure 3.3 and Annexure Chapter 3).

This resurgence contrasts with the national rural LFPR, which has also improved since 2012 but remains lower than in 2000. In urban areas, while workforce participation has generally increased in states like Nagaland and Himachal Pradesh, pointing to better employment prospects in cities, some states, such as Mizoram, have experienced a decline, suggesting challenges in urban labour absorption. At the national level, urban LFPR has remained relatively stable over the years, showing only marginal improvement, underscoring that urbanisation has not universally translated into higher workforce participation. Examining the trends from 2000 to 2024, rural LFPR in the Himalayan region has consistently been higher than urban LFPR, primarily due to the prevalence of subsistence agriculture and informal employment opportunities (see Annexure Chapter 3). However, between 2000 and 2012, rural LFPR saw a decline across most states, in line with national trends. The literature attributes this decline to factors such as the gradual transition away from agriculture, increasing rural-to-urban migration, and declining farm incomes. The subsequent recovery in 2024, particularly in rural Sikkim, Meghalaya, and Nagaland, suggests renewed labour engagement, possibly due to employment in diversified rural activities, including tourism, horticulture, and government-led livelihood programmes.

The fluctuation in overall LFPR appears to be primarily driven by changes in rural workforce participation. Between 2000 and 2012, the significant

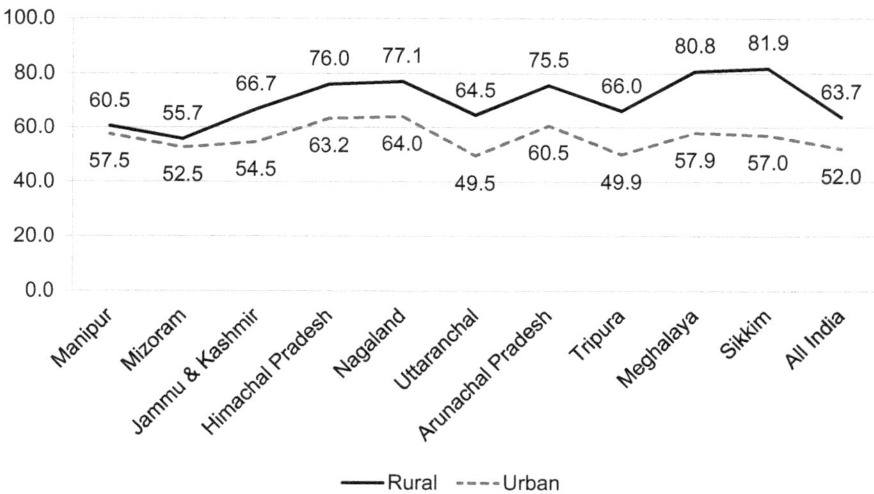

Figure 3.3 Labour force participation rate by sector, 2024 (in %).

Source: PLFS, NSSO.

drop in rural LFPR contributed to the overall decline in workforce participation, as urban LFPR remained relatively stable during this period. Similarly, the resurgence observed in 2024 aligns closely with the recovery in rural LFPR, indicating that rural labour market trends continue to play a dominant role in shaping overall workforce participation patterns. This suggests that policy measures aimed at enhancing rural employment opportunities, such as investment in agro-based industries, infrastructure development, and skill training programmes, are crucial for sustaining labour force engagement in the Himalayan region. However, the persistent rural–urban gap also highlights the need for targeted urban employment policies, particularly in states like Mizoram, where declining urban LFPR suggests underlying structural challenges in the urban labour market.

3.2.2 Worker–Population Ratio

In 2024, the worker–population ratio (WPR) in the Himalayan states exhibits notable gender disparities, mirroring the trends in Labour Force Participation Rate (LFPR) (see Figure 3.4 and Annexure Chapter 3). Compared to the all-India figures, most Himalayan states maintain higher workforce absorption, with both male and female WPRs exceeding national averages in several cases. The Himalayan states such as Arunachal Pradesh, Meghalaya, and Sikkim have witnessed a strong resurgence in female WPR, reflecting improved employment opportunities.

However, gender disparities persist, particularly in states like Mizoram and Tripura, where female WPR remains considerably lower than male WPR

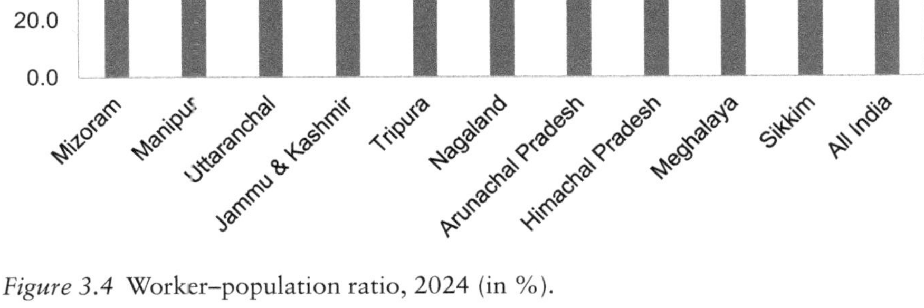

Figure 3.4 Worker–population ratio, 2024 (in %).

Source: PLFS, NSSO.

(Map 3.1). At the national level, while WPR has shown some recovery since 2012, female employment absorption remains relatively low, highlighting the continued challenges women face in accessing stable employment. The overall WPR trends suggest that while workforce engagement has improved, employment quality and gender inclusivity remain critical concerns. Examining the trends from 2000 to 2024, WPR closely follows the trajectory of LFPR but also reflects distinct patterns influenced by employment absorption, economic shifts, and structural transformations in the labour market. In 2000, most Himalayan states recorded higher WPR than the national average, largely due to the strong participation of rural populations in agriculture and informal sectors. However, between 2000 and 2012, WPR declined across most states, mirroring the drop in LFPR. The literature attributes this decline to structural economic shifts, including the decreasing viability of agriculture, limited non-farm employment opportunities, and growing educational aspirations that led many, especially women, to withdraw from the workforce.

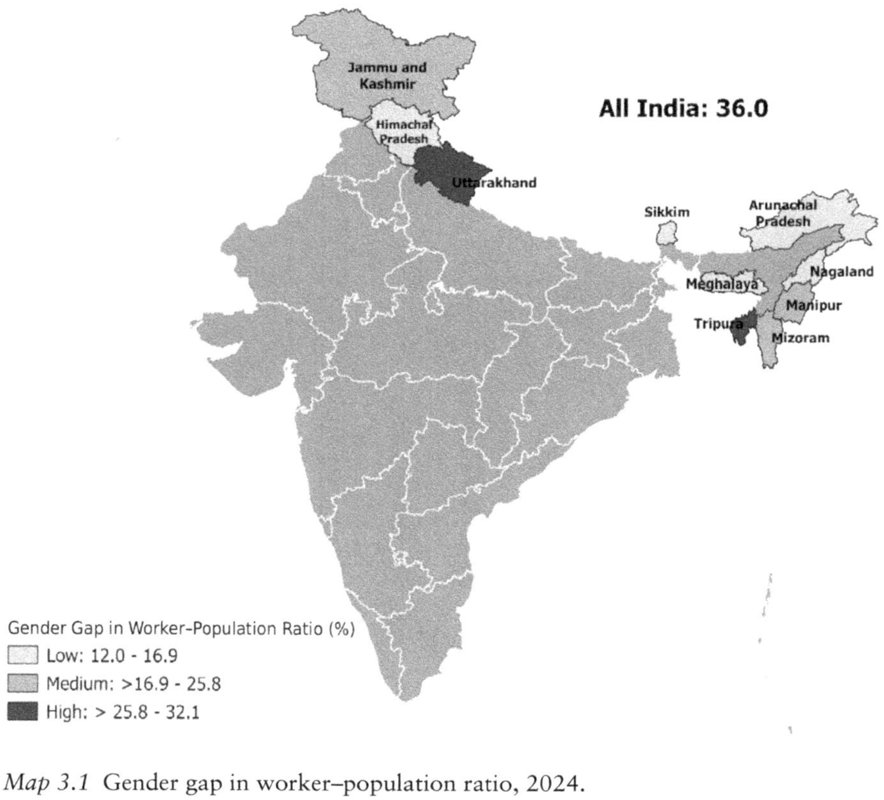

Map 3.1 Gender gap in worker–population ratio, 2024.
Source: PLFS, NSSO.

The recovery observed in 2024 aligns with the resurgence in LFPR, suggesting an improvement in employment opportunities across several Himalayan states. Notably, female WPR has played a significant role in this fluctuation, as states with a sharper increase in female workforce participation, such as Arunachal Pradesh, Meghalaya, and Sikkim, also exhibit higher overall WPR (see Annexure Chapter 3). This pattern indicates that the overall fluctuations in workforce engagement have been largely driven by changes in female employment participation. However, persistent gender disparities in states like Mizoram and Tripura suggest that the quality and stability of employment remain key challenges. Additionally, the rural–urban divide in workforce absorption further reinforces these trends. Rural WPR has historically been higher than urban WPR, driven by the predominance of subsistence agriculture and informal employment. The decline in WPR between 2000 and 2012 was primarily led by rural areas, where economic transitions reduced labour absorption (see Annexure Chapter 3). The resurgence in 2024, particularly in states like Sikkim and Meghalaya, suggests a revival of employment in rural sectors, potentially driven by government initiatives, the expansion of self-employment, and the diversification of rural economies. However, urban WPR trends indicate mixed outcomes, with some states experiencing growth while others, like Mizoram, showing a decline, pointing to challenges in urban employment generation.

Overall, the trends in WPR not only mirror LFPR but also highlight the underlying employment dynamics in the Himalayan states in India. While the workforce participation of women has been a key driver of fluctuations in overall WPR, persistent gender disparities, rural–urban differences, remain crucial factors influencing long-term workforce engagement in the region. In states where LFPR has increased but WPR has not shown a proportionate rise, it indicates higher unemployment or underemployment. For instance, while Mizoram's LFPR was relatively high in 2012, its WPR has declined over time, reflecting reduced employment absorption. Conversely, in states like Sikkim, where both LFPR and WPR have risen consistently, employment generation appears to be stronger.

3.2.3 Unemployment Rate

The unemployment rate in the Himalayan states exhibits considerable variation over time, reflecting economic shifts, structural changes in the labour market, and employment policies. In 2024, unemployment across the Himalayan states highlights significant gender disparities compared to the all-India figure (see Figure 3.5a and Annexure Chapter 3). While national unemployment has increased to 3.2 per cent, some states in the region exhibit much higher unemployment, particularly among women. States like Jammu and Kashmir, Meghalaya, and Nagaland report substantially high unemployment, reflecting persistent job market challenges. On the other hand, Mizoram and Tripura show relatively lower unemployment rates, suggesting more stable labour market conditions.

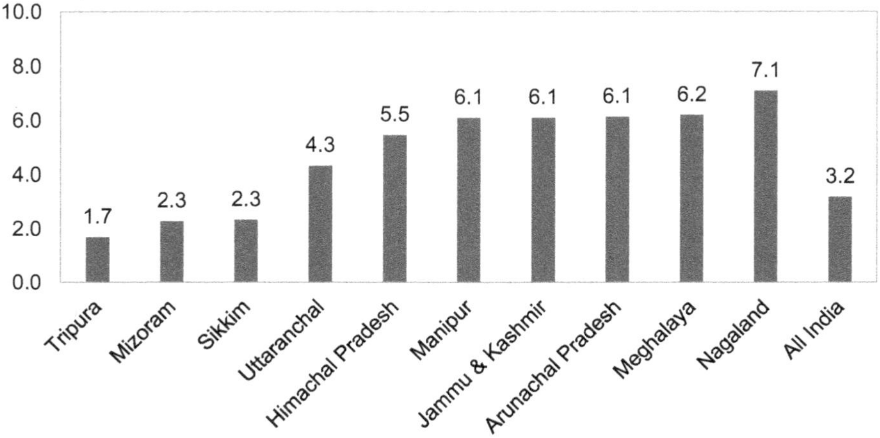

Figure 3.5a Unemployment rate, 2024 (in %).
Source: PLFS, NSSO.

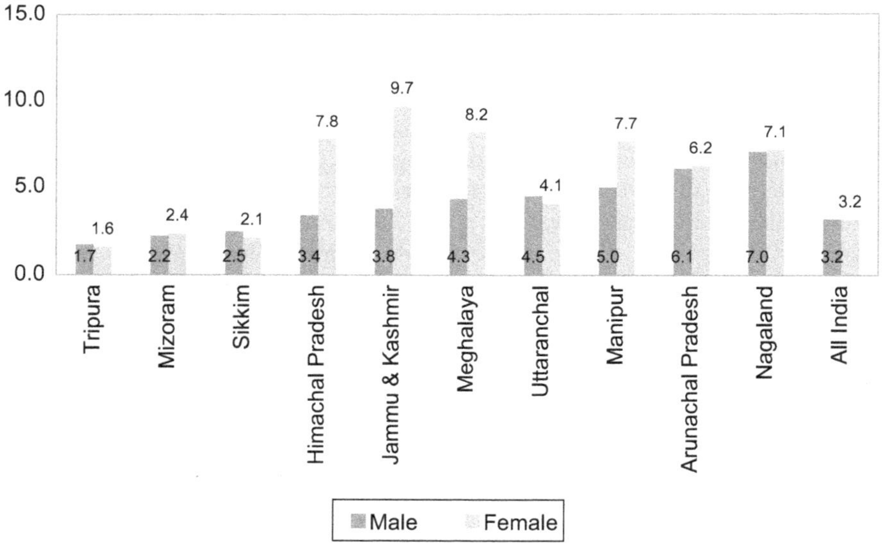

Figure 3.5b Unemployment rate by gender, 2024 (in %).
Source: PLFS, NSSO.

Across most states, female unemployment rate remains higher than male unemployment (see Figure 3.5b), reinforcing the challenges women face in accessing stable employment despite their increasing labour force participation and employment rate. This trend indicates that while women are re-entering the workforce, job creation has not kept pace, leading to rising female unemployment.

The trend from 2000 to 2024 reveals a fluctuating pattern, closely mirroring changes in LFPR and WPR. In 2000, unemployment rate was relatively low across most Himalayan states, often below the national average (see Annexure Chapter 3). However, between 2000 and 2012, joblessness increased in several states, particularly in Nagaland and Tripura, where unemployment surged to alarmingly high levels. This period coincided with structural economic shifts, declining agricultural employment, and limited non-farm opportunities, particularly for women and youth. The literature suggests that the increasing participation of women in education during this period also contributed to lower employment rates, as many women delayed workforce entry (IER, 2024). By 2024, unemployment rate trends exhibit a mixed pattern, with some states experiencing further increases while others witness a decline. Notably, states like Nagaland, which had exceptionally high unemployment in 2012, have seen some recovery, while Meghalaya and Arunachal Pradesh have encountered rising joblessness. This suggests that economic recovery has been uneven, with some regions benefiting from employment growth while others continue to struggle with limited job opportunities.

Further, the fluctuation in unemployment rate appears to be also driven more by rural employment conditions than urban trends, as rural areas have historically had higher WPR but have also been more vulnerable to economic shocks and shifts in labour demand. In rural areas, unemployment rate trends have closely followed fluctuations in LFPR and WPR, reflecting both economic distress and recovery patterns. The decline in agricultural viability, coupled with limited expansion of rural non-farm employment, has contributed to rising rural unemployment in states like Arunachal Pradesh and Meghalaya. Conversely, urban unemployment, while historically higher, has remained relatively stable, with some states experiencing slight improvements due to increasing economic diversification and urban job creation.

These observed unemployment rate trends in the Himalayan states can be attributed to several factors. The region's reliance on agriculture, tourism, and informal employment makes job availability highly seasonal and sensitive to economic fluctuations. States like Himachal Pradesh and Uttarakhand, which have strong tourism-based economies, experienced rising unemployment in 2024, potentially due to pandemic-induced disruptions or changing labour market dynamics. In states like Nagaland and Tripura, the drastic rise and fall in unemployment suggests fluctuations in public sector employment, which has historically been a major employer. The decline in unemployment in Tripura from 12.8 per cent in 2012 to 1.7 per cent in 2024 points to major policy interventions, possibly through employment guarantee schemes or industrial investments. The rural–urban disparity in unemployment highlights the ongoing challenge of job creation in urban areas. With limited industrialisation and a predominantly service-based economy, urban centres in states like Arunachal Pradesh, Meghalaya, and Jammu and Kashmir face a persistent employment crisis. On the other hand, rural unemployment, while lower, is gradually increasing, indicating that traditional agricultural livelihoods are insufficient to sustain the growing workforce.

3.2.3.1 Unemployment Rate Among Youth

Overall unemployment remains relatively low, but the youth (15–29 years) unemployment rate in the Himalayan regions of India presents a critical challenge, and is significantly higher than the overall (15+ years) rate. In 2024, youth unemployment in the Himalayan states presents a concerning picture, with rates significantly higher than the all-India figure (see Table 3.1). While national youth unemployment remains elevated, several Himalayan states face a much more severe crisis, particularly among educated youth and female graduates. The gender disparity is pronounced, as young women continue to experience greater difficulties in securing employment despite increasing educational attainment. This suggests that higher education does not necessarily translate into better job prospects for women, reflecting both structural challenges in the labour market and deep-rooted socio-cultural constraints. Across the Himalayan states, youth unemployment exhibits significant variation. Some states, such as Arunachal Pradesh, Jammu and Kashmir, Nagaland, and Himachal Pradesh, report alarmingly high unemployment rates, especially among highly educated young individuals, indicating a persistent employment crisis. The literature suggests that these trends are linked to a combination of factors, including a lack of decent or quality job creation as desired by educated youth, low public sector employment, and limited

Table 3.1 Unemployment Rate Among Youth, 2024 (%)

States/UTs	*Male*			*Female*			*All*		
	YU	*EDYU*	*GRYU*	*YU*	*EDYU*	*GRYU*	*YU*	*EDYU*	*GRYU*
Jammu and Kashmir	11.8	15.3	24.5	26.7	40.1	65.8	17.4	24.2	43.5
Himachal Pradesh	25.8	29.3	24.3	29.9	35.4	36.2	28.1	32.7	31.3
Uttarakhand	8.3	10.4	10.2	12.3	15.0	23.9	9.8	12.2	16.6
Sikkim	8.3	18.4	24.4	6.8	10.5	14.8	7.7	14.7	20.0
Arunachal Pradesh	21.9	33.8	67.9	19.6	34.3	61.7	20.9	34.0	65.0
Nagaland	27.9	45.1	76.3	26.6	47.4	65.7	27.4	46.0	71.3
Manipur	19.9	23.1	38.8	27.5	33.9	49.7	22.9	27.1	43.4
Mizoram	13.4	25.2	42.2	13.0	30.2	40.3	13.3	26.9	41.4
Tripura	6.8	14.1	20.6	6.7	21.4	26.3	6.8	16.2	22.4
Meghalaya	9.9	17.1	29.7	18.7	30.4	34.0	14.0	24.1	32.1
All India	9.8	13.8	23.5	11.0	19.2	33.7	10.2	15.4	27.0

Note: YU, youth unemployment; EDYU, educated youth unemployment; GRYU, graduate youth unemployment rate (GRYU).

Source: PLFS, NSSO.

industrial development. Furthermore, states with traditionally high youth unemployment have also witnessed significant disparities in employment outcomes between men and women. The trend of higher female unemployment compared to their male counterparts underscores the limited opportunities available for young women, even when they possess higher qualifications.

This suggests that even higher educational attainment does not ensure better employment prospects for women, potentially due to gender-based labour market discrimination and socio-cultural constraints (Sharma & Mehta, 2026). The gap widens for graduate youth unemployment, where female unemployment reaches 23.9 per cent compared to 10.2 per cent among males, suggesting that the lack of employment opportunities remains a significant concern even for highly educated individuals (Chakraborty, 2022d). A similar trend is observed in Manipur, where female unemployment rates (27.5 per cent) exceed those of males (19.9 per cent), emphasising the challenges young women face in securing employment (Devi, 2023). However, the discrepancy appears in educated youth unemployment, where female unemployment rises to 21.4 per cent compared to 14.1 per cent for males. Meghalaya exhibits a different trend, where female youth unemployment (18.7 per cent) is significantly higher than male unemployment (9.9 per cent), reflecting the challenges faced by women in the job market (Goswami, 2023). These statistics indicate that young women, despite achieving higher educational qualifications, continue to face significant barriers to entering the labour market, necessitating urgent policy attention and employment-generation programmes (Sen, 2024).

3.3.4a Quality of Employment: Status of Employment

The employment structure in the Himalayan region states presents a diverse picture influenced by geographical constraints, economic opportunities, and socio-political factors. Compared to all-India employment trends, these states display distinct patterns in self-employment, regular employment, and casual work, with significant variations between rural and urban areas, as well as across gender lines (see Table 3.2 and Annexure Chapter 3). At the national level, self-employment remains the dominant form of employment, accounting for 58.4 per cent of the total workforce. Regular employment constitutes 21.8 per cent, while casual work represents 19.9 per cent. However, in the Himalayan region, the distribution of employment categories varies significantly by state. Arunachal Pradesh exhibits one of the highest self-employment rates (77.9 per cent), with regular employment at 17.7 per cent and casual work at just 4.3 per cent. This indicates a strong dependence on agriculture, small businesses, and traditional livelihoods. In contrast, Meghalaya and Tripura have relatively higher shares of casual workers, at 30.8 per cent and 25.3 per cent, respectively, reflecting a greater reliance on informal and temporary employment arrangements. Some states, such as Himachal Pradesh, Jammu and Kashmir, and Nagaland, have a more

Table 3.2 Unemployment Rate Among Youth, 2012 and 2024 (in %)

States/UTs	*2012*				*2024*			
	SE	*RE*	*CW*	*All*	*SE*	*RE*	*CW*	*All*
Arunachal Pradesh	73.1	19.8	7.0	100	77.9	17.7	4.3	100
Himachal Pradesh	67.6	18.0	14.4	100	66.1	22.7	11.2	100
Jammu and Kashmir	59.2	21.7	19.1	100	66.7	22.1	11.1	100
Manipur	67.4	14.6	18.1	100	72.6	22.4	4.9	100
Meghalaya	65.2	16.8	18.0	100	52.6	16.6	30.8	100
Mizoram	68.8	23.1	8.0	100	68.5	25.5	6.0	100
Nagaland	75.7	22.5	1.8	100	66.3	28.2	5.5	100
Sikkim	69.8	25.5	4.7	100	61.3	31.2	7.5	100
Tripura	40.6	16.5	42.9	100	61.6	13.0	25.3	100
Uttarakhand	68.1	18.8	13.1	100	61.3	26.4	12.3	100
All India	52.2	18.5	29.3	100	58.4	21.8	19.9	100

Note: SE, self-employment; RE, regular employment; CW, casual work.

Source: EUS and PLFS, NSSO.

balanced employment structure, with self-employment ranging between 50 per cent and 70 per cent and regular employment making up around 20 per cent to 30 per cent. These states have a comparatively higher presence of government and private sector jobs, particularly in education, healthcare, and tourism. Sikkim and Uttarakhand also display a relatively stable employment mix, with self-employment at around 61.3 per cent in both states and regular employment at 26.4 per cent and 31.2 per cent, respectively.

Over the years, the employment status in the Himalayan states between 2012 and 2024 shows a shift towards self-employment and regular employment, with a decline in casual labour. Self-employment remains the dominant form of employment across most Himalayan states, but its share has shown varied trends across different states. While states like Arunachal Pradesh (73.1–77.9 per cent) and Manipur (67.4–72.6 per cent) have seen an increase in self-employment, others like Meghalaya (65.2–52.6 per cent), Sikkim (69.8–61.3 per cent), and Nagaland (75.7–66.3 per cent) have experienced a decline. This divergence suggests that in some states, a growing informal sector and lack of wage employment opportunities have pushed individuals towards self-employment, whereas in others, increased opportunities in regular employment have reduced reliance on self-employment.

On the other hand, a positive trend in regular employment is visible across almost all states. The share of regular employment increased in key states like Uttarakhand (18.8–26.4 per cent), Nagaland (22.5–28.2 per cent), and Sikkim (25.5–31.2 per cent), indicating a shift towards more stable and formal employment opportunities. This growth aligns with policies aimed at skill development, tourism promotion, and industrial expansion in these states. However, some states like Tripura (16.5–13.0 per cent) and Arunachal Pradesh (19.8–17.7 per cent) saw a marginal decline in regular employment, possibly due to structural constraints or lack of large-scale employment-generation industries.

In the case of casual labour, a major trend observed is a decline in casual work in most states, indicating a potential improvement in job security and livelihood conditions. For instance, Arunachal Pradesh (7.0–4.3 per cent), Manipur (18.1–4.9 per cent), and Jammu and Kashmir (19.1–11.1 per cent) have witnessed a sharp reduction in casual work. This shift suggests improved access to more stable employment avenues, including government schemes, small enterprises, and self-employment ventures. However, a few states, such as Meghalaya (18.0–30.8 per cent), Tripura (42.9–25.3 per cent), and Sikkim (4.7–7.5 per cent), have shown a rise in casual employment, pointing to ongoing economic distress or dependence on short-term work opportunities. Overall, these trends broadly mirror the national-level pattern of increasing self-employment and regular jobs, alongside a reduction in the share of casual work. In particular, states with strong tourism and service sectors, and with industrial initiatives (such as Uttarakhand and Sikkim), have seen higher growth in regular employment, whereas those with weaker industrial bases or high out-migration (such as Meghalaya and Tripura) continue to rely more on casual work.

3.3.4a.1 Male–Female and Rural–Urban Differences

A clear gender disparity exists in employment patterns across the Himalayan region (see Annexure Chapter 3). Nationally, self-employment is more prevalent among females (67.4 per cent) compared to males (53.6 per cent), largely due to limited formal employment opportunities and social norms restricting women's participation in the salaried workforce. This trend is even more pronounced in states like Arunachal Pradesh and Jammu and Kashmir, where female self-employment stands at 89.5 per cent, significantly higher than the male rate. Himachal Pradesh and Mizoram show relatively better female participation in regular employment (12.6 per cent and 14.1 per cent, respectively), but this remains lower than the male regular employment rates in these states. Casual work among women is minimal in states like Jammu and Kashmir (0.5 per cent) and Mizoram (0.2 per cent), suggesting that women in these states either engage in self-employment or regular employment, avoiding informal and unstable jobs. However, in Meghalaya, and Tripura, female casual work is considerably high (23.5 per cent, 19.8 per cent, and 7.2 per cent, respectively), indicating a greater vulnerability of women in the workforce.

Additionally, the rural–urban differences shows that rural employment in the Himalayan states is overwhelmingly dominated by self-employment, aligning with national trends where 64.7 per cent of the rural workforce is self-employed (see Annexure Chapter 3). States like Arunachal Pradesh (82.1 per cent), Mizoram (76.6 per cent), and Manipur (76.1 per cent) report exceptionally high self-employment rates, emphasising the predominance of agriculture, handloom, and other traditional economic activities. Conversely, urban employment patterns show a significant shift towards regular jobs. Nationally, 47.5 per cent of the urban workforce is in regular employment, a trend reflected in states like Himachal Pradesh (61.5 per cent), Sikkim (48.9 per cent), and Uttarakhand (48.3 per cent). These states benefit from better infrastructure, education, and industrial opportunities, leading to higher absorption in salaried jobs (Mehta, 2023).

However, states like Arunachal Pradesh (44.7 per cent) still have relatively lower urban regular employment rates, suggesting limited job creation in the formal sector. Casual employment is more prevalent in urban areas in certain states, with Meghalaya (19.0 per cent), Tripura (17.2 per cent), witnessing higher levels of informal work. This reflects a dependence on daily wage jobs, construction work, and low-skill service sector employment in urban centres. States like Mizoram and Nagaland, with casual work shares of 6.7 per cent and 7.8 per cent, respectively, indicate a more structured urban labour market with fewer informal jobs.

Overall employment composition in the Himalayan states reflects both similarities and deviations from national employment patterns. While self-employment dominates across all states, it is particularly high in rural areas, driven by agriculture, forestry, and handicrafts. Regular employment is relatively lower in the Himalayan states compared to the national average, except in urban pockets where salaried jobs are more concentrated. The significant variation in casual work highlights economic disparities within the region. Meghalaya and Tripura have high shares of casual labour, indicating weaker labour protections and greater dependence on unstable jobs. In contrast, states like Himachal Pradesh, Sikkim, and Mizoram have lower casual employment rates, suggesting a more formalised labour market.

3.3.4b Quality of Employment: Organised–Unorganised and Formal–Informal Employment

Employment quality in the Himalayan regions is further examined through formal–informal jobs and employment in the organised and unorganised sectors. A large proportion of the workforce in these regions is engaged in informal employment, highlighting the precarious nature of jobs available. Arunachal Pradesh has a high prevalence of informal employment, with 85.5 per cent of the workforce engaged in informal jobs, whereas formal employment remains limited at 14.5 per cent (see Table 3.3). The organised sector employs 18.9 per cent of the workforce, while the unorganised sector accounts for 81.1 per cent. In Himachal Pradesh, 86.5 per cent of employment is informal, with only 13.5 per cent in formal employment. A slightly higher proportion (20.3 per cent) is engaged in organised employment, while 79.7

Table 3.3 Organised–Unorganised and Formal–Informal Employment, 2024 (in %)

States/UTs	*Formal*	*Informal*	*Total*	*Organised*	*Unorganised*	*Total*
Arunachal Pradesh	14.5	85.5	100	18.9	81.1	100
Himachal Pradesh	13.5	86.5	100	20.3	79.7	100
Jammu and Kashmir	11.6	88.4	100	18.0	82.0	100
Ladakh	20.5	79.5	100	20.1	79.9	100
Manipur	16.2	83.8	100	19.3	80.7	100
Meghalaya	9.4	90.6	100	20.5	79.5	100
Mizoram	22.4	77.6	100	26.2	73.8	100
Nagaland	23.7	76.3	100	27.6	72.4	100
Sikkim	13.9	86.1	100	27.6	72.4	100
Tripura	7.2	92.8	100	15.3	84.7	100
Uttarakhand	14.5	85.5	100	19.8	80.2	100
All India	10.1	89.9	100	17.1	82.9	100

Note: Definition adopted from IER (2024).

Source: PLFS, NSSO.

per cent remain in the unorganised sector. Jammu and Kashmir also reflects high informal employment at 88.4 per cent, with formal employment at only 11.6 per cent, while the organised sector comprises 18.0 per cent of employment compared to 82.0 per cent in the unorganised sector. Manipur, Meghalaya, and Mizoram also exhibit high levels of informal employment, at 83.8 per cent, 90.6 per cent, and 77.6 per cent, respectively.

The proportion of formal employment is slightly better in Mizoram (22.4 per cent) compared to Meghalaya (9.4 per cent). The organised sector remains low, with Manipur having 19.3 per cent in the organised sector, Meghalaya at 20.5 per cent, and Mizoram at 26.2 per cent, reflecting a higher degree of employment stability compared to other North-eastern states. Nagaland stands out with the highest proportion of formal employment at 23.7 per cent, while informal employment remains at 76.3 per cent. The organised sector comprises 27.6 per cent of employment, the highest among all states, compared to 72.4 per cent in the unorganised sector.

Even within the organised sector, a significant proportion of workers are in informal employment like All India (see Table 3.4). Arunachal Pradesh has 24.6 per cent of workers in informal employment despite being part of the organised sector, while Himachal Pradesh and Jammu and Kashmir exhibit similar trends, with 34.7 per cent and 37.1 per cent of their organised sector workers being informally employed, indicating persistent job insecurity. In contrast, Ladakh has the lowest percentage of informal employment within the organised sector, with only 3.7 per cent of its workforce in such conditions, suggesting a relatively stable employment environment in the region. Manipur, Mizoram, and Nagaland also maintain lower informal employment

Table 3.4 Formal–Informal Employment with Organised Sector, 2024

States/UTs	*Organised Sector*		
	Formal	*Informal*	*Total*
Arunachal Pradesh	75.4	24.6	100
Himachal Pradesh	65.3	34.7	100
Jammu and Kashmir	62.9	37.1	100
Ladakh	96.3	3.7	100
Manipur	82.3	17.7	100
Meghalaya	44.7	55.3	100
Mizoram	84.8	15.2	100
Nagaland	84.3	15.7	100
Sikkim	49.5	50.5	100
Tripura	46.8	53.2	100
Uttarakhand	70.8	29.2	100
All India	56.8	43.2	100

Note: Definition adopted from IER (2024).

Source: PLFS, NSSO.

rates within their organised sectors, at 17.7 per cent, 15.2 per cent, and 15.7 per cent, respectively, reflecting better job security compared to other states (Goswami, 2023). However, states like Meghalaya, Sikkim, and Tripura exhibit a different picture, with a substantial proportion of informal employment within the organised sector. Meghalaya records the highest rate at 55.3 per cent, followed by Tripura at 53.2 per cent and Sikkim at 50.5 per cent, which is even higher than the national average of 43.2 per cent. This suggests that even within formal or organised sector employment, a significant number of workers lack formal protections and benefits. Uttarakhand, with 29.2 per cent of organised sector workers in informal employment, also highlights the prevalence of insecure job arrangements.

These figures indicate that informal employment remains the predominant mode of employment in the Himalayan regions, where a significant proportion of the workforce continues to work under precarious conditions. The gendered nature of employment within these structures also suggests that women are more likely to be engaged in informal and unorganised employment, further exacerbating their vulnerability in the labour market (Devi, 2023).

3.2.5 *Industrial Structure of Employment*

Employment distribution across broad industries (primary, secondary, and tertiary) in the Himalayan states exhibits distinct variations from the national average, shaped by geographical, economic, and social factors (see Table 3.5 and Annexure Chapter 3).

Table 3.5 Employment by Industrial Sectors, 2012 and 2024

Industry	*Arunachal Pradesh*	*Himachal Pradesh*	*Jammu and Kashmir*	*Manipur*	*Meghalaya*	*Mizoram*	*Nagaland*	*Sikkim*	*Tripura*	*Uttaranchal*	*All India*
2012											
Agriculture, etc.	68.0	58.4	42.3	39.5	56.6	55.3	60.5	61.6	27.1	48.8	48.8
Mining and quarrying	0.1	0.1	0.1	0.3	2.3	0.3	0.1	0.0	0.3	0.0	0.5
Primary	**68.1**	**58.5**	**42.4**	**39.8**	**58.8**	**55.6**	**60.6**	**61.6**	**27.5**	**48.9**	**49.4**
Manufacturing	1.0	6.6	9.6	10.1	2.4	1.8	2.1	3.5	6.4	9.2	12.5
Electricity, gas, and water supply	0.3	1.4	1.2	0.2	0.1	0.4	1.9	2.5	0.0	0.6	0.5
Construction	5.5	14.5	19.1	19.7	7.0	8.1	3.6	6.5	40.1	12.2	10.6
Secondary	**6.8**	**22.6**	**29.9**	**30.1**	**9.5**	**10.3**	**7.5**	**12.6**	**46.5**	**22.0**	**23.6**
Trade, hotel, and restaurants	7.1	5.2	10.2	11.7	13.7	12.3	9.5	7.9	10.9	14.2	11.0
Transport, storage, and communication	1.2	3.6	3.9	3.8	3.5	2.4	2.7	4.2	3.1	5.2	4.9
Finance, business, real estate, etc.	1.9	1.7	1.1	0.7	0.6	0.7	0.8	1.2	0.9	1.3	2.3
Public admin, health, education, etc.	15.0	8.5	12.5	13.9	13.8	18.7	18.8	12.4	11.2	8.5	8.8
Tertiary	**25.1**	**19.0**	**27.7**	**30.1**	**31.6**	**34.1**	**31.9**	**25.8**	**26.0**	**29.1**	**27.0**
Total	100	100	100	100	100	100	100	100	100	100	100

(*Continued*)

Table 3.5 (Continued)

Industry	*Arunachal Pradesh*	*Himachal Pradesh*	*Jammu and Kashmir*	*Manipur*	*Meghalaya*	*Mizoram*	*Nagaland*	*Sikkim*	*Tripura*	*Uttaranchal*	*All India*
2024											
Agriculture, etc.	62.0	58.3	45.7	35.7	47.0	43.1	50.0	45.8	35.6	47.2	45.7
Mining and quarrying	0.1	0.3	0.0	0.3	1.5	0.3	0.1	0.2	0.0	0.0	0.3
Primary	**62.1**	**58.6**	**45.7**	**35.9**	**48.5**	**43.4**	**50.0**	**46.0**	**35.6**	**47.2**	**46.0**
Manufacturing	2.2	6.9	8.4	14.7	2.6	5.4	6.2	3.4	3.1	9.9	11.4
Electricity, gas, and water supply	1.5	1.6	1.2	0.5	0.4	0.2	0.3	2.2	0.0	0.9	0.5
Construction	5.6	8.4	15.9	10.8	17.0	5.3	5.6	9.2	20.5	10.4	13.0
Secondary	**9.3**	**17.0**	**25.5**	**26.0**	**20.0**	**10.9**	**12.1**	**14.8**	**23.7**	**21.3**	**25.0**
Trade, hotel, and restaurants	10.7	7.7	11.5	11.1	11.9	16.1	8.9	11.2	16.4	14.5	12.1
Transport, storage, and communication	2.3	4.6	5.0	5.5	4.6	6.2	4.9	7.0	8.5	4.0	5.4
Finance, business, real estate, etc.	0.3	1.8	1.6	5.7	2.0	7.0	6.9	0.3	3.1	2.3	2.7
Public admin, health, education, etc.	15.3	10.4	10.8	15.7	12.9	16.4	17.2	20.7	12.7	10.7	8.8
Tertiary	**28.6**	**24.4**	**28.8**	**38.0**	**31.5**	**45.7**	**37.9**	**39.2**	**40.7**	**31.5**	**29.0**
Total	100	100	100	100	100	100	100	100	100	100	100

Note: Definition adopted from IER (2024).

Source: EUS and PLFS, NSSO.

3.2.5.1 Primary Sector

The primary sector remains a dominant source of employment in most Himalayan states, though its share has declined over time. In Arunachal Pradesh, employment in agriculture continues to be significant, though it has decreased from 65.9 per cent in 2011–12 to 62.3 per cent in 2023–24, reflecting a gradual shift towards industrialisation and services (Nayak, 2021b; Sharma & Das, 2022c). States such as Himachal Pradesh and Uttarakhand have also seen a decline in agricultural employment, aligning with national trends of structural transformation (Basole, 2022; Rana & Bisht, 2023). In contrast, states like Tripura have experienced an increase in primary sector employment, rising from 24.7 per cent to 43.8 per cent. This countertrend suggests regional economic disparities, where dependency on agriculture persists despite industrialisation efforts (Chakraborty, 2022d; Sharma, 2024). Women remain heavily engaged in the primary sector, particularly in agriculture and allied activities, often due to limited formal employment opportunities and socio-cultural constraints (Baruah & Mohan, 2021).

3.2.5.2 Secondary Sector

The secondary sector, comprising manufacturing, construction, and utilities, has played a crucial role in economic diversification. Meghalaya has seen a rise from 9.7 per cent to 17.3 per cent, indicating industrial expansion (Government of Meghalaya, 2023). However, in states like Jammu and Kashmir and Manipur, secondary sector employment has declined, suggesting limited industrial growth and continued reliance on agriculture and services (Bhat & Lone, 2022a).

Manufacturing employment varies across the region, with states such as Manipur (15.3 per cent) and Uttarakhand (13.1 per cent) surpassing the national average of 11.4 per cent, indicating stronger industrial bases. In contrast, Arunachal Pradesh (3.1 per cent) and Sikkim (3.4 per cent) exhibit lower shares, highlighting limited industrialisation. Construction remains an essential employment generator, particularly in states like Tripura (18.4 per cent) and Jammu and Kashmir (15.0 per cent), where infrastructure projects have provided job opportunities. However, in Nagaland (4.6 per cent) and Mizoram (6.8 per cent), lower employment in construction suggests limited urbanisation and industrial activity.

3.2.5.3 Tertiary Sector

The tertiary sector has seen remarkable growth across the Himalayan region, contributing significantly to employment and economic output. In Mizoram, the share of employment in services increased from 35.6 per cent to 49.7 per cent, reflecting a shift towards a service-driven economy (Lalhriatpuii, 2022b; Aayog, NITI, 2018). Sikkim has experienced a similar trend, with tertiary sector employment rising from 30.7 per cent to 43.9 per cent, primarily due to the expansion of tourism and hospitality industries. Nagaland also saw a sharp rise in tertiary sector employment, reaching 43.7 per cent, driven by public administration, education, and financial services (Das, 2022). Employment in trade, hotels, and restaurants serves as a key indicator of tourism and commercial activity. Mizoram (19.8 per cent) and Uttarakhand (15.0 per cent) report higher engagement, reflecting a thriving tourism industry. In contrast, Arunachal Pradesh (10.0 per cent) and Himachal Pradesh (8.1 per cent) suggest smaller commercial bases and lower urbanisation rates. The public sector continues to be a significant employer, particularly in Sikkim (22.2 per cent), Nagaland (19.5 per cent), and Mizoram (18.0 per cent), where government jobs compensate for the lack of private sector opportunities (Choudhury et al., 2023).

3.2.5.4 Male–Female and Rural–Urban Differences

Gender disparities persist across the Himalayan states, with women primarily engaged in agriculture and informal services. In Arunachal Pradesh, 75.7 per cent of women work in agriculture, compared to 77.8 per cent in Jammu and Kashmir, reflecting limited formal employment opportunities (Bhat & Lone, 2012). Women's participation in manufacturing is significant in Manipur (27.4 per cent), driven by small-scale industries and handloom businesses (Devi & Singh, 2021). Public administration and education also employ a large share of women, particularly in Sikkim (23.5 per cent) and Nagaland (15.6 per cent), where government jobs offer stability and social security (Chaudhury et al., 2023). In addition, stark rural–urban contrasts exist in employment patterns across the Himalayan states. In rural areas, agriculture dominates, with states like Arunachal Pradesh (69.2 per cent) and Meghalaya (57.5 per cent) showing significantly higher shares. In contrast, urban employment patterns indicate a shift towards manufacturing and services. For instance, urban Himachal Pradesh has 30.9 per cent of its workforce engaged in manufacturing, while urban Uttarakhand shows 16.6 per cent in the same sector. The urban workforce in most states is also heavily concentrated in trade, hotels, and public administration, with states like Sikkim (28.5 per cent) and Meghalaya (34.7 per cent) exhibiting high public sector employment.

*3.2.6 **Structural Transformation: Relationship Between Employment and Economic Output (GVA)***

The distribution and trends in employment and economic output (gross value added – GVA) across broad industries – primary, secondary, and tertiary – highlight the structural changes underway in the Himalayan states. These shifts in employment are closely linked to changes in sectoral output, as discussed briefly in the previous chapter (see Table 3.5 and Table 3.6).

Table 3.6 Gross Value Added (GVA) by Broad Industry, 2012 and 2024

States/UTs	*2012*				*2024*			
	Primary	*Secondary*	*Tertiary*	*Total*	*Primary*	*Secondary*	*Tertiary*	*Total*
Arunachal Pradesh	44.1	17.2	38.7	100	26.2	24.2	49.6	100
Himachal Pradesh	17.2	43.8	39.0	100	13.8	46.1	40.1	100
Jammu and Kashmir	17.9	27.6	54.4	100	15.7	26.2	58.1	100
Manipur	19.8	15.4	64.8	100	18.1	11.0	70.8	100
Meghalaya	22.3	33.0	44.7	100	18.1	18.8	63.1	100
Mizoram	20.8	19.8	59.4	100	16.1	29.3	54.6	100
Nagaland	31.4	12.4	56.2	100	25.2	10.5	64.3	100
Sikkim	8.3	62.8	28.8	100	6.5	63.7	29.8	100
Tripura	33.5	14.1	52.4	100	39.5	13.4	47.1	100
Uttaranchal	14.0	52.1	33.9	100	8.9	49.2	41.8	100
All India	21.7	29.3	49.0	100	17.5	28.1	54.4	100

Source: National Statistical Office (2025).

3.2.6.1 Primary Sector

As discussed earlier, employment in the primary sector (agriculture and allied activities) has generally declined across most Himalayan states, reflecting a structural shift away from traditional farming. Arunachal Pradesh, Himachal Pradesh, Meghalaya, Mizoram, and Nagaland all saw a reduction in workforce dependence on agriculture, aligning with national trends. However, in Tripura and Uttarakhand, primary sector employment increased, possibly due to continued reliance on agriculture and rural livelihood schemes. Despite these employment patterns, the primary sector's GVA contribution declined significantly, indicating lower productivity and increased mechanisation.

3.2.6.2 Secondary Sector

The secondary sector (manufacturing, construction, and industry) experienced employment growth in several Himalayan states, particularly Arunachal Pradesh, Himachal Pradesh, and Sikkim, reflecting industrial expansion and infrastructure development. Increased GVA share in the secondary sector across these states suggests rising industrial productivity and diversification. In contrast, some states like Tripura and Uttarakhand saw limited industrial employment growth, indicating slower industrialisation.

3.2.6.3 Tertiary Sector

The tertiary or services sector emerged as the dominant driver of economic growth, with an increasing GVA share across most of the Himalayan states. Jammu and Kashmir, Manipur, Nagaland, and Uttarakhand saw significant gains in both employment and economic output from services, highlighting a shift towards higher-value economic activities. Even in states where primary and secondary sector employment persisted, GVA in services expanded, reflecting higher productivity in trade, tourism, and IT-related sectors.

3.2.6.4 Sectoral Linkages and Structural Shift

The preceding analysis indicates a progressive shift from agriculture to industry and services, with declining employment and output in the primary sector balanced by rising contributions from the secondary and tertiary sectors. This transition reflects economic modernisation, where mechanisation reduces the need for agricultural labour, industrialisation generates new employment, and services become a key driver of economic growth. These trends highlight policy impacts, technological advancements, and sectoral transformations, shaping the evolving economic landscape of Himalayan states.

3.3 Migration

Labour market patterns and trends influence both in-migration and out-migration. Migration has long been an integral aspect of the Himalayan region's socio-economic landscape, driven by a complex interplay of economic, social, and environmental factors. In the Himalayan region, migration patterns reflect unique regional characteristics. Historically, these states have experienced both in-migration and out-migration, influenced by factors such as economic opportunities, political stability, and infrastructure development.

3.3.1 Migration Rate

Migration trends in India have been well documented through national-level surveys such as the Census and PLFS. The Himalayan states exhibit distinct migration patterns compared to the national average due to geographical isolation, economic conditions, and socio-political factors (see Annexure Chapter 3).

3.3.1.1 Long-Term Migration Trends (Census of India, 2011)

Census data provide a long-term view of migration in the Himalayan states. Among these states, Uttarakhand, Arunachal Pradesh, Himachal Pradesh, and Sikkim have consistently recorded higher migration rates (see Table 3.7). In 2011, Uttarakhand reported one of the highest migration rates, exceeding the national average. This trend is largely attributed to economic development in urban centres such as Dehradun and Haridwar, as well as employment opportunities in tourism, education, and the services sector. Himachal Pradesh, characterised by its hilly terrain and reliance on agriculture, has also seen steady migration towards urban and industrialised areas. The Northeastern states display varied migration trends. Arunachal Pradesh recorded a significant increase in migration, from 33.8 per cent in 1991 to 44.0 per cent in 2011, reflecting improved infrastructure and economic opportunities. Sikkim has witnessed increased migration linked to rapid socio-economic development. In contrast, Jammu and Kashmir has historically shown lower

Table 3.7 Migration Rate, 1991, 2001, 2011 (in %)

States/UTs	*1991*	*2001*	*2011*
Arunachal Pradesh	33.8	37.5	44.0
Himachal Pradesh	35.6	36.1	41.3
Jammu and Kashmir	NA	17.8	22.6
Manipur	6.4	17.4	28.8
Meghalaya	15.0	16.4	26.2
Mizoram	15.4	30.3	34.6
Nagaland	10.6	19.1	28.3
Sikkim	30.8	34.6	43.4
Tripura	29.5	30.1	33.6
Uttaranchal	NA	36.2	44.2
All India	27.4	30.6	37.5

Source: Census of India.

migration rates due to political instability and limited industrial growth. The national migration rate increased from 27.4 per cent in 1991 to 37.5 per cent in 2011, while many Himalayan states such as Uttarakhand, Himachal Pradesh, and Arunachal Pradesh surpassed this average. Conversely, states like Jammu and Kashmir reported lower-than-average migration rates, primarily due to security concerns and socio-political instability.

3.3.1.2 Migration Trends (NSS-PLFS Data)

Data from the National Sample Survey (NSS), 2007–08, and Periodic Labour Force Survey (PLFS), 2020–21 highlight a shift in migration patterns in recent years. Arunachal Pradesh witnessed a dramatic increase in migration compared to 2008, owing to infrastructure improvements and greater economic integration (see Table 3.8).

Himachal Pradesh and Uttarakhand, known for historically high migration rates, have seen minor declines in migration, possibly due to better local employment opportunities in tourism and services. Jammu and Kashmir has shown a modest increase in migration, influenced by political stability and employment in security services. Tripura has seen minimal growth in migration, suggesting relatively stable economic conditions. States like Manipur, Mizoram, Nagaland, and Sikkim have exhibited significant reductions in migration rates, possibly due to improved employment opportunities within these states or socio-political factors restricting movement.

3.3.2 Out-Migration Trends

Migration patterns in the Himalayan states reflect both in-migration and out-migration dynamics. Uttarakhand's hill districts have experienced substantial

Table 3.8 Migration Rate, 2021 (in %)

States/UTs	*2007–08*	*2020–21*
Arunachal Pradesh	1.3	24.2
Himachal Pradesh	39.1	38.1
Jammu and Kashmir	17.6	22.1
Manipur	0.9	0.2
Meghalaya	3.5	9.8
Mizoram	15.3	0.8
Nagaland	13.4	0.3
Sikkim	33.6	11.6
Tripura	11.7	12.0
Uttarakhand	37.9	35.0
All India	28.5	28.9

Note: The data for 2021 has some limitations and should be interpreted with caution, as it was collected during the COVID-19 period. Additionally, it is not a special migration-round.

Source: NSS (2007–08) and PLFS (2020–21).

out-migration due to limited economic opportunities, leading to declining populations in several villages. In contrast, its plain districts have seen population growth due to in-migration (Sharma, 2022). The COVID-19 pandemic influenced migration patterns, with a surge in return migration due to economic uncertainty and travel restrictions. Census data (1991–2011) highlights significant variations in out-migration rates across Himalayan states. The national inter-state migration rate increased from 13 per cent in 1991 to 17 per cent in 2011 (see Table 3.9).

Uttarakhand and Himachal Pradesh reported the highest out-migration rates among the Himalayan states (Map 3.2). Although Uttarakhand's out-migration rate has declined marginally over time, it remains much higher than that of Himachal Pradesh and other states, largely due to limited economic opportunities in its hilly districts, as also discussed in Box 3.1.

The North-eastern states exhibit unique migration patterns driven by unemployment, ethnic tensions, and environmental factors. While Nagaland experienced significant out-migration in the 1990s, this trend has moderated in recent years (Goswami & Deka, 2020). Mizoram and Arunachal Pradesh have seen an increasing trend of work-related migration, with many moving to metropolitan cities (Singh, 2019). Sikkim and Meghalaya demonstrate relatively higher in-migration rates, particularly due to employment and business opportunities. Meghalaya's urban centres attract migrants from nearby regions, while Sikkim's economic development has contributed to an influx of workers, as some cases discussed in Box 3.2.

Himachal Pradesh maintained a stable out-migration rate of around 25 per cent, while Arunachal Pradesh reported lower rates of out-migration. Mizoram, which saw a peak in out-migration in 2001 (36 per cent), recorded a decline to 8 per cent in 2011, indicating improved local opportunities.

Table 3.9 Out-Migration Rate (%)

States/UTs	*1991*	*2001*	*2011*
Arunachal Pradesh	20	11	15
Himachal Pradesh	28	25	25
Jammu and Kashmir	NA	11	10
Manipur	9	14	14
Meghalaya	13	8	10
Mizoram	17	36	8
Nagaland	11	16	11
Sikkim	28	11	17
Tripura	10	7	8
Uttaranchal	NA	38	36
All India	13	16	17

Note: NA, not available.

Source: Census of India.

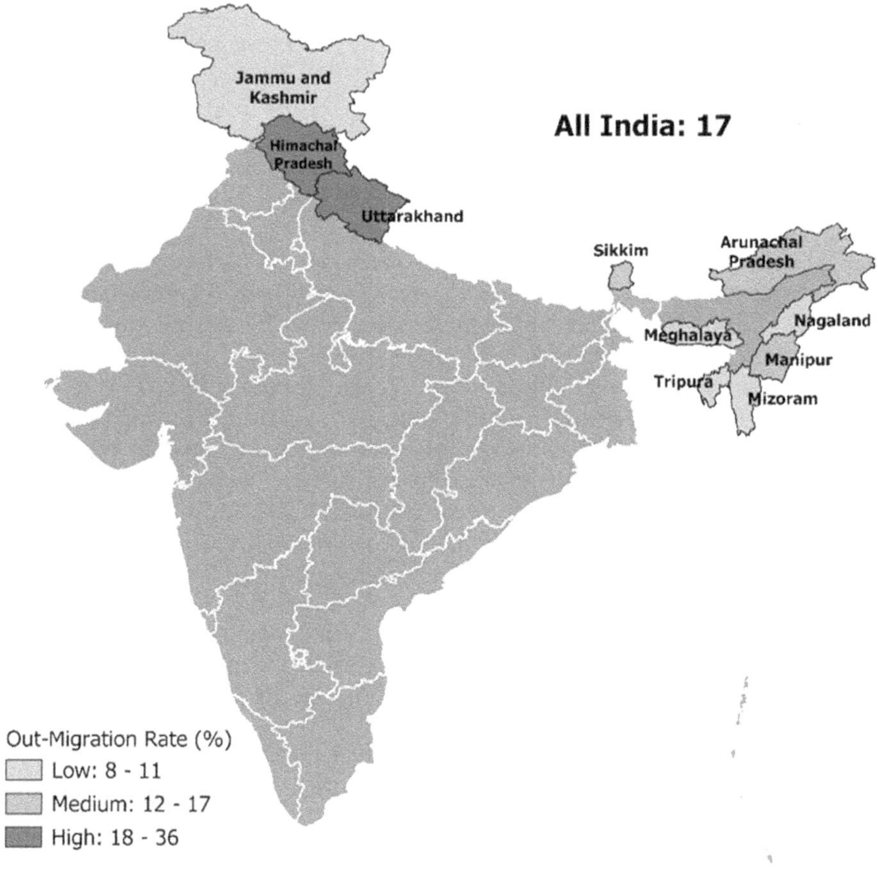

Map 3.2 Out-migration rate (%).

Source: Census of India (2011).

Box 3.1 Out-migration Reasons in Uttarakhand

Case 3.1.1

"Out-migration from the hill districts is taking place primarily because of the low economic base, as well as, lack of adequate employment and income earning opportunities. The migration patterns have been changing fast; people are by and large moving out permanently from the villages not only for earning a livelihood but also for better education for their children and availing improved health facilities. This movement is conspicuous from villages to small towns; even block, tehsil and district

headquarters are experiencing out-migration. It is also increasingly noted that people are settling in urban locations within the state."

Source: Awasthi, I., & Mehta, B. S. (2020). *Forced out-migration from hill regions and return migration during the pandemic: Evidence from Uttarakhand.* Indian Journal of Labour Economics, 63(4), 1107–1124. https://doi.org/10.1007/s41027-020-00291-w.

Case 3.1.2

"Migration has led to depopulation and land abandonment in rural areas, which has severe repercussions on the farming systems. The rate of out-migration has increased mainly after 2000 and has aggravated during recent times. Unemployment is one of the major impediments of out-migration. Since the rural areas are devoid of infrastructural and institutional facilities, augmentation of employment is not possible. Further, the output from traditionally practised subsistence cereal cultivation is not enough to carry livelihood sustainably. These factors have manifested a large out-migration of youth from the region, and if it continues, the out-migration will have severe adverse implications on the rural areas and their economy. Several steps should be raised to minimise out-migration and attract the migrants to come back to their respective villages. Institutions related to development should be set up so that employment can be augmented and granted to the local people. The development of educational institutions may be a strong tool that can restrict the youth to out-migrate for education. Modern technological innovations related to agriculture can enhance the yield of crops and employment opportunities. Therefore, at the community level, the development of agriculture should be ensured. The government should come forward for the development of infrastructural facilities and through it, employment can be augmented."

Source: Vishwambhar Prasad Sati, "Out-migration in Uttarakhand Himalaya: Its Types, Reasons, and Consequences," *Migration Letters*, May 2021, Volume: 18, No: 3, pp. 281–295 ISSN: 1741–8984 (Print) ISSN: 1741–8992 (Online) journals.tplondon.com/ml.

Box 3.2 Out-migration Reasons in North-eastern States

Case 3.2.1

"The eight peripheral Northeast states comprise one of the most underdeveloped regions in the country. The lack of economic development,

infrastructural facilities, employment opportunities and business activity, along with the scarcity of higher educational institutions, are major determinants of out-migration from the region. Migration for economic reasons is common across low-income states, and the NE states are no exception. However, migration for education from the NE states is about double the national average for male migrants and three times the national average for female migrants. This shows a demand-supply mismatch in higher education endowments in the NE region and the NE people's willingness and interest to acquire higher education. The migrant cohort analysis across the major destinations helps us visualise how cultural ties and political unrest/violence can shape migration patterns, as witnessed in the case of the Tripura cohort in West Bengal and the Manipur cohort in Delhi and Maharashtra."

Source: Pinak Sarkar, "Out-Migration from the North-Eastern States of India: Evidence from Census 2011," *Journal of Migration Affairs*, Vol. III(1): 108–118, September 2020, https://doi.org/10.36931/jma.2020.3.1.108-118.

Case 3.2.2

"Migrants from the North East or Eastern IHR, especially Manipur and Nagaland, are usually sought after by the hospitality and cosmetic industries in metropolitan cities like Mumbai and Delhi where a study shows that their labour is in high demand because of their exotic 'un-Indian' look and somewhat fluent English. A large number of women migrant workers also work in the garment industries in Tamil Nadu, and have been facing adversities during the pandemic. Educational aspirations are a major reason for the youth in Darjeeling to migrate to metropolitan cities like Delhi, Mumbai, and Kolkata. Similar patterns is observed among Ladakhi youth who migrate to Chandigarh, Delhi, and Jammu. As a result of political unrest, insurgency, underdevelopment, and alienation from the rest of the country, the out-migration from northeast to Delhi, Bengaluru, Kerala, and other metropolitans has become a common phenomenon (Marchang, 2017; McDuie-Ra, 2012)."

Source: Chitra, Annesha, and the IMN Team, "The Indian Himalayan Region: A Lesser-Known Migration Story," July 6, 2020.

Further, gender-wise analysis of out-migration reveals that female migration often surpasses male migration due to marriage-related movement. Nationally, female migration (19 per cent) is higher than male migration (16 per cent). In Uttarakhand, female migration reached 43 per cent, compared to 29 per cent for males, reflecting both economic and marital migration.

Himachal Pradesh exhibited a similar trend, with female migration at 29 per cent and male migration at 21 per cent. Migration patterns in the Himalayan region of India also exhibit significant rural–urban variations, driven by diverse socio-economic and environmental factors. The availability of employment opportunities, infrastructure development, and socio-political conditions shape these migration trends; some cases and reasons for migration are given in Box 3.3.

Box 3.3 Out-migration Reasons in Himachal Pradesh

Case 3.3.1

"Rural-to-rural migration was the most prevalent among all the four streams of migration. Females outnumbered their male counterparts in this stream of migration. This was because a large part of rural-to-rural migration comprises of female marriage migrants. Urban-to-urban migration was another stream in which females were reported in higher numbers in comparison to males. Rural-to-urban and urban-to-rural streams of migration were male dominated. Migrants of all the four streams were concentrated in semi- hilly areas close to districts located in plain areas of the state. A considerable proportion of urban migrants reported in district Shimla, which is hilly and interior in location, owing to its administrative importance as the capital city and being the only Class I city of Himachal Pradesh."

Source: Archana Sinha, "Changes in Patterns of Migration in Himachal Pradesh Since 1991," *Punjab Geographer*, ISSN-0973-3485, Vol. 13, October 2017.

Case 3.3.2

"As far as change in patterns of in-migration is concerned, unpredictable percent change in volume of inmigrants was reported in districts where either the developmental activities have started of late or industrial growth took place abruptly. Recent exploration of the remote districts namely Kinnaur, Kullu and Lahul & Spiti induced some migration where magnitude of migration used to be almost nil. Magnitude of migration is still quite low in absolute numbers, but change that has been seen over the past census years is incredible. Districts experiencing rapid industrial development were obvious to attract remarkable number of migrants because of unparalleled rise in employability. What can be conjectured is that magnitude of migration in Himachal Pradesh will obviously increase in the times to come but proportion of migrant population in mid and high zone of Himachal Pradesh consisting of

districts Hamirpur, Mandi, Chamba, Kinnaur, Kullu and Lahul & Spiti will remain low. It is quite plausible that some of these districts might experience a negative change in volume of migration. District Shimla lying in mid and high zone is an exception in this regard. This is because of high level of development and the administrative importance of the district. Districts lying in Shivaliks near to the plains of Punjab and Haryana, will continue to experience high migration because they enjoy both locational and physiographic advantages."

Source: Veena Kumari and Paras Verma, "A Geographical Study of Migration in Himachal Pradesh," *International Journal of Advance Research and Innovative Ideas in Education*, Vol. 5, Issue 1, 2019 IJARIIE: ISSN(O)-2395-4396.

Migration in Kashmir enables a segment of the unemployed to secure livelihoods, with three-fourths of migrants leaving Kashmir in pursuit of better job opportunities and higher earnings. Additionally, the desire to escape the ongoing conflict motivates some individuals to migrate. The pattern of in-migration in the Valley reveals that rural migrants tend to settle in rural areas, while urban migrants predominantly choose cities like Srinagar. This highlights distinct rural-to-rural and urban-to-urban migration streams, with rural-to-rural movement being more prevalent, as shown in Box 3.4.

Box 3.4 Out-migration Reasons in Jammu and Kashmir

Case 3.4.1

"While migration helps a section of the unemployed to find livelihoods, three-fourths of migrants leave Kashmir in search of better jobs and earnings. The desire to escape the ongoing conflict also motivates a section of the population to migrate. Data suggest that migrants both at the bottom of earning and the top bracket of earning before migration improved their earnings after migration. Remittances significantly contribute to migrant households' annual incomes. Remittances help them reduce their economic distress, tide over their indebtedness, and increase spending on food, health, education, and other consumption needs. The emerging pattern of remittance utilisation indicates that international migrants, who also come from a better-endowed background, spend more on productive investment, while the majority of inter-state migrants spend more on immediate consumption needs."

Source: Mohd. Aslam Bhat and Tareak A. Rather, "Inter-State and International Migration Out of Kashmir: Trends, Characteristics, and Outcomes," *Journal of Migration Affairs*, Vol. VI (1–2): 75–90, March 2024, https://doi.org/10.36931/jma.2024.6.1-2.75-90.

Case 3.4.2

"The process of in-migration in the Valley shows that rural in-migrants prefer to stay in rural areas, whereas urban in-migrants mostly prefer to stay in cities like Srinagar. This is a clear case of rural–rural and urban–urban stream of migration, with rural–rural stream having dominance. In-migrants were also found in rural–urban and urban to rural categories. It is also important to note here that, in all the four migration streams, female in-migrants were having a majority. The district-level picture reflects that Srinagar was dominated by the urban–urban stream of migration, whereas all other districts were dominated by the rural–rural stream of migration."

Source: Aijaz Ahmad Turrey, "Impact of Conflict on Labour Migrants in Kashmir," *Economic and Political Weekly*, August 12, 2023, Vol. Lviii, No. 32.

3.3.2.1 Male–Female Migration Trends

The Periodic Labour Force Survey (PLFS), 2021, highlights a significantly low rate and a decline in male migration across most states, likely due to economic slowdowns, mobility restrictions, and the impact of COVID-19 lockdowns (see Table 3.10). States such as Arunachal Pradesh (5.2 per cent), Mizoram (0.6 per cent), and Nagaland (0.1 per cent) recorded extremely low male migration rates, signalling a slowdown in employment-driven migration (see Table 3.10). This decline can be attributed to economic uncertainties, industrial stagnation, and return migration due to job losses in urban centres during the pandemic (Srivastava, 2020; Awasthi & Mehta, 2020; Mehta, 2023). Despite these economic challenges, female migration rates remained relatively stable in most Himalayan states, with only a marginal decline in some areas, such as Tripura (20.5 per cent) and Sikkim (13.9 per cent). States such as Himachal Pradesh (62.0 per cent) and Uttarakhand (55.1 per cent) continued to show high female migration, reinforcing the fact that marriage remains the primary driver of female migration and is largely unaffected by economic slowdowns (Tumbe, 2018).

The Census 2011 data reflect long-term structural migration patterns, where male migration is linked to employment, while female migration is primarily marriage-driven. The PLFS 2021 data suggest short-term disruptions in male migration, with significant declines due to economic and

Table 3.10 Migration Rate: Male–Female, 2011 and 2021 (in %)

States/UTs	*(Census, 2011)*		*(PLFS, 2021)*	
	Male	*Female*	*Male*	*Female*
Arunachal Pradesh	40.1	48.2	5.2	45.3
Himachal Pradesh	21.1	62.2	13.8	62.0
Jammu and Kashmir	12.0	34.5	9.0	35.9
Manipur	19.4	38.2	0.1	0.2
Meghalaya	27.4	24.9	11.6	8.2
Mizoram	34.0	35.3	0.6	1.0
Nagaland	27.8	28.8	0.1	0.2
Sikkim	36.6	51.1	9.5	13.9
Tripura	23.3	44.5	3.9	20.5
Uttaranchal	30.0	58.9	16.4	55.1
India	**22.6**	**53.2**	10.7	47.9

Source: Census of India (2011) and PLFS (2021).

pandemic-related factors. However, female migration patterns remained stable, as marriage-driven migration was not significantly affected by these disruptions. The sharp decline in male migration in 2021 across several states indicates reduced labour mobility, particularly among working-age males who returned to their home states due to pandemic-induced job losses. This analysis highlights the need to view Census and PLFS data separately, as they capture migration trends in different timeframes and contexts – the Census reflecting long-term patterns, while the PLFS provides insights into short-term economic and social disruptions affecting migration, based on sample surveys.

3.3.2.2 *Rural–Urban Migration Trends*

Migration from rural to urban areas has historically been higher due to the concentration of employment opportunities in cities (see Table 3.11). In 2011, Census data showed that the highest rural-to-urban migration rates were in Himachal Pradesh (74.6 per cent) and Arunachal Pradesh (63.4 per cent), indicating substantial movement towards urban centres. Conversely, migration from urban to rural areas was much lower, with a few exceptions such as Manipur (90 per cent), Sikkim (37.9 per cent), and Mizoram (30.6 per cent), where some reverse migration trends were observed, likely due to better living conditions in rural areas or return migration.

Overall, Himachal Pradesh and Uttarakhand have significantly higher rural-to-urban migration rates, while states such as Nagaland and Mizoram report much lower migration rates among the Himalayan states. This is influenced by factors such as a lack of local employment opportunities, inadequate infrastructure, river erosion, seasonal agricultural work, and

Table 3.11 Migration Rate: Rural–Urban and Urban–Rural, 2011 (in %)

States/UTs	*Migrated From Urban to Rural Areas*	*Migrated From Rural to Urban Areas*
Arunachal Pradesh	7.7	63.4
Himachal Pradesh	13.5	74.6
Jammu and Kashmir	16.3	66.7
Manipur	90.0	10.5
Meghalaya	20.7	18.9
Mizoram	30.6	32.0
Nagaland	NA	NA
Sikkim	37.9	38.2
Tripura	16.0	57.8
Uttarakhand	23.1	46.8
All India	**15.6**	53.9

Source: Census of India (2011).

movement to urban centres. The low migration rates in Mizoram and Nagaland suggest strong community ties, localised economies, and limited push factors for migration.

3.3.3 *Reasons for Migration*

Migration in the Himalayan states is shaped by a complex interplay of socio-economic, demographic, environmental, and political factors. Data from Census 2011 and the Periodic Labour Force Survey (PLFS), 2020–21 highlight key patterns, including out-migration, rural–urban shifts, and gender-specific migration trends (see Table 3.12a and Table 3.12b and Annexure Chapter 3).

3.3.3.1 *Economic Development and Employment-Driven Migration*

Economic underdevelopment is a major push factor for migration in the Himalayan region (Maithani, 2006). The scarcity of local job opportunities in states like Uttarakhand, Himachal Pradesh, Arunachal Pradesh, and Sikkim compels individuals to seek employment in urban centres such as Delhi, Chandigarh, and Dehradun (Census, 2011). The expansion of tourism and infrastructure projects has also fuelled migration, particularly in Arunachal Pradesh and Sikkim (PLFS, 2020–21). Similarly, Mizoram has witnessed high employment-related migration, driven by a growing service sector and government employment opportunities (PLFS, 2020–21). In contrast, states such as Manipur, and Nagaland report significantly lower employment-driven migration, which may indicate either the availability of local job opportunities or socio-political constraints limiting workforce mobility.

Table 3.12a Reasons for Out-Migration, 2021 (in %)

States/UTs	*Work/ Employment*	*Business*	*Education*	*Marriage*	*Moved After Birth*	*Moved With Household*	*Others*	*Total*
Arunachal Pradesh	18.9	3.0	4.4	16.7	1.5	24.3	31.2	100
Himachal Pradesh	11.2	0.4	1.7	58.2	3.3	13.4	11.7	100
Jammu and Kashmir	4.4	0.7	1.3	51.1	2.0	14.7	25.8	100
Manipur	3.3	1.3	1.7	35.7	2.4	20.5	35.2	100
Meghalaya	7.0	1.3	3.1	22.2	3.1	18.3	45.1	100
Mizoram	16.2	1.9	3.9	9.7	2.5	36.0	29.7	100
Nagaland	20.2	4.0	7.9	12.4	0.9	26.4	28.2	100
Sikkim	18.8	2.0	3.2	29.7	2.7	18.8	24.7	100
Tripura	7.1	1.0	0.9	39.6	0.7	21.4	29.3	100
Uttarakhand	14.3	0.4	2.2	42.1	1.5	25.3	14.3	100
All India	**9.1**	**0.8**	**1.2**	**46.3**	**7.4**	**14.5**	**20.7**	100

Source: PLFS (2021).

Table 3.12b Reasons for Out-Migration, 2011 (in %)

States/UTs	*Work/ Employment*	*Business*	*Education*	*Marriage*	*Moved After Birth*	*Moved With Household*	*Others*	*Total*
Arunachal Pradesh	13.7	1.2	14.9	18.6	1.2	32.9	17.4	100
Himachal Pradesh	22.6	0.8	5.4	26.4	3.8	30.7	10.3	100
Jammu and Kashmir	22.4	1.0	6.1	14.3	2.0	39.8	14.3	100
Manipur	25.8	2.6	19.2	9.9	0.7	28.5	13.2	100
Meghalaya	17.8	2.0	7.9	28.7	1.0	29.7	12.9	100
Mizoram	19.3	1.2	15.7	10.8	1.2	30.1	21.7	100
Nagaland	16.8	2.5	10.1	17.6	1.7	36.1	15.1	100
Sikkim	17.6	1.1	13.1	29.0	1.1	22.2	15.9	100
Tripura	19.3	3.6	6.0	25.3	1.2	31.3	13.3	100
Uttaranchal	23.7	0.5	2.5	29.4	1.6	32.7	9.5	100
All India	**27.6**	**1.1**	**2.2**	**23.8**	**4.4**	**29.8**	**11.0**	**100**

Source: Census (2011).

3.3.3.2 Lack of Higher Education Infrastructure and Education-Driven Migration

Limited access to quality higher education has led to increasing student migration from the Himalayan region. The 1990s and 2000s saw a rise in student migration from North-eastern states to metropolitan cities such as Bangalore, Mumbai, Kolkata, and Delhi (Shimray & Ushadevi, 2009). Migration for education is notably higher in Nagaland and Arunachal Pradesh, where local institutions fail to meet academic demands (PLFS, 2020–21). Conversely, states such as Tripura report lower education-related migration, reflecting the adequacy of local institutions (Census, 2011). Meghalaya stands out as an exception, attracting students from neighbouring states due to institutions such as North-Eastern Hill University (NEHU) (PLFS, 2020–21).

3.3.3.3 Marriage as a Primary Driver of Migration

Marriage remains the dominant reason for migration among women across the Himalayan states, particularly in Himachal Pradesh, Jammu and Kashmir, and Uttarakhand, where over half of female migrants relocate due to marriage (Census, 2011). However, in states such as Mizoram and Meghalaya, which have matrilineal traditions, marriage-related migration is relatively lower, with household movement playing a more significant role (PLFS, 2020–21).

3.3.3.4 Household and Dependent Migration

Household migration, defined as the movement of entire families rather than individual job seekers, is a significant trend in Mizoram, Nagaland, and Meghalaya. High shares of household migration suggest a preference for community-based relocation, possibly due to strong kinship ties and traditional social structures (Census, 2011). Meghalaya also exhibits family-based migration, emphasising a collective approach to economic mobility rather than isolated worker migration (PLFS, 2020–21). The relocation of earning members is particularly high in Uttarakhand, Sikkim, and Mizoram, where migration patterns reflect family movement rather than individual migration (PLFS, 2020–21).

3.3.3.5 Rural–Urban Migration

Out-migration from rural areas is a critical issue in Uttarakhand, Himachal Pradesh, and Arunachal Pradesh, where significant rural depopulation occurs as individuals seek better employment and living conditions in urban areas. This trend reflects a shift from agrarian-based economies to service-oriented urban employment (Census, 2011). Sikkim and Mizoram also exhibit high rural–urban migration, with urban centres developing as employment and educational hubs (PLFS, 2020–21). However, in states such as Nagaland and

Manipur, rural–urban migration remains subdued, likely due to socio-political instability and limited industrialisation (PLFS, 2020–21).

3.3.3.6 Gender-Specific Migration Trends

Migration patterns differ significantly between men and women. Male migration is predominantly employment-driven, with Uttarakhand, Himachal Pradesh, Sikkim, and Arunachal Pradesh reporting high proportions of male migrants moving for work (Census, 2011). Mizoram also reports high male migration for employment, reflecting economic opportunities within the state's urban centres (PLFS, 2020–21). In contrast, states like Manipur and Meghalaya report lower employment-driven migration among men, with household relocation playing a more significant role. For women, migration is overwhelmingly driven by marriage, though with notable regional variations. In Himachal Pradesh and Jammu and Kashmir, over two-thirds of female migrants relocate due to marriage, aligning with national trends (Census, 2011). However, Mizoram and Meghalaya exhibit lower marriage-related migration, reflecting their matrilineal social structures that provide women with greater economic independence (PLFS, 2020–21). Employment-related migration among women is minimal but slightly higher in Mizoram and Sikkim, where service sector opportunities and government employment attract female workers (PLFS, 2020–21).

3.3.3.7 Political Unrest and Security Concerns

Political instability and security concerns significantly influence migration patterns in Jammu and Kashmir and Tripura. Ethnic conflicts, insurgency, and socio-political unrest have led to increased out-migration from these states (PLFS, 2020–21). Manipur, for instance, has been severely affected by political tensions, with frequent strikes disrupting education and employment opportunities, further prompting migration to other parts of the country (Remesh, 2012). Tripura also reports higher migration due to ethnic tensions and security issues (PLFS, 2020–21).

3.3.3.8 Environmental Factors and Climate-Induced Migration

Environmental vulnerabilities contribute to migration in the Himalayan region. Natural disasters, including floods and landslides, have led to displacement in states like Manipur, Himachal Pradesh, and Sikkim (PLFS, 2020–21). Manipur records one of the highest shares of migration due to environmental factors, likely due to frequent landslides and other climate-related challenges. Similarly, Himachal Pradesh and Sikkim report migration linked to extreme weather events, reinforcing the vulnerability of mountain communities to climate-induced displacement (Census, 2011).

3.3.3.9 Post-Retirement and Housing-Related Migration

Post-retirement migration is significant in Himachal Pradesh and Uttarakhand, where many retirees return to their native villages after working in urban centres, reflecting a strong attachment to ancestral homes (Census, 2011). Housing-related migration, on the other hand, is more prominent in Meghalaya and Mizoram, where urban expansion and housing shortages have led to increased intra-state mobility (PLFS, 2020–21) (see Table 3.12a and 3.12b). In Mizoram, real estate investment has emerged as a key driver of migration, indicating changing urban development patterns (PLFS, 2020–21). Overall, migration in the Himalayan region is shaped by a range of economic, social, and environmental factors. While employment and education remain key drivers, marriage and household migration also play a crucial role, particularly among women. Political instability and climate-related displacement further add complexity to migration patterns, reflecting the diverse challenges and opportunities in the region.

Thus, several factors – both economic and non-economic – induce or compel people to migrate from fragile mountain regions. The major drivers include lack of employment and livelihood opportunities, uneconomic landholdings, climate change, and aspirations for better education. Migration from mountain regions is a common phenomenon and has become increasingly visible in recent years. All the mountain states experience both out-migration and in-migration, each presenting its own set of challenges. Out-migration is primarily driven by the search for better livelihood opportunities, as subsistence-based economies in fragile regions offer limited employment. Agriculture continues to sustain a large share of the population, mostly in rain-fed areas, but industrial development is negligible, with only a few small enterprises that often operate with narrow margins.

Educational aspirations also fuel migration, as students leave their home states in search of better higher education and specialized training opportunities elsewhere. Male out-migration is particularly high in states such as Uttarakhand and Himachal Pradesh, leaving women to shoulder increased household and agricultural responsibilities. This shift, however, carries long-term implications, including prolonged family separations and emotional strain. In addition to permanent migration, large numbers of young people move seasonally to the plains, engaging in agriculture, construction, and service-sector jobs. Such patterns affect the local labour market, creating competition between local workers and incoming migrants.

At the same time, large-scale in-migration has altered demographic balances, raising concerns over cultural identity and traditional land ownership. In the North-eastern states, where ethnic identities are deeply rooted, this has generated political resistance to the permanent settlement of outsiders. In Himachal Pradesh's apple belt, migrant workers from Bihar, Jharkhand, and Nepal play a crucial role in the harvest, yet remain socially segregated. Mountain regions are also highly vulnerable to climate change, facing landslides, floods, and other natural disasters. For instance, the 2013 Uttarakhand disaster displaced thousands of people, some permanently, further intensifying migration pressures.

Some clear policy directions emerge to help restrict out-migration from these regions. First, agriculture must be diversified into high-value horticultural products, where these areas hold a natural comparative advantage. Second, development efforts should prioritise improved connectivity, along with support for credit, training, technology, markets, and information flow. Third, greater emphasis is needed on strengthening education and healthcare facilities in these fragile regions.

3.4 Chapter Summary and Conclusion

Employment and migration patterns in the Himalayan states reflect a complex interplay of economic opportunities, social structures, and regional disparities. Worker–population ratio (WPR) trends closely follow labour force participation rates, but persistent gender gaps, rural–urban differences, and sectoral variations significantly affect long-term employment prospects. The WPR varies across states, with women's employment playing a crucial role in shaping overall trends. In several states, such as Mizoram, an increase in LFPR has not translated into a proportional rise in WPR, indicating high levels of unemployment or underemployment. Conversely, states like Sikkim, where both LFPR and WPR have grown, show stronger employment absorption capacity. One of the most pressing concerns is high youth unemployment, particularly among educated and graduate youth. This highlights the need for targeted employment policies, including skill development programmes tailored to local labour markets, investment in emerging industries, and gender-inclusive employment initiatives. Without these interventions, the growing pool of educated but unemployed youth, especially women, will face barriers to economic participation, limiting both individual and regional growth.

Employment status, or job quality, in the Himalayan region broadly mirrors national trends, with an increase in self-employment and regular jobs alongside a decline in casual labour. However, states with strong tourism, service industries, and industrial initiatives – such as Uttarakhand and Sikkim – have seen higher growth in regular employment. In contrast, states with weaker industrial bases and high out-migration – such as Meghalaya and Tripura – continue to rely more on casual work. Another important issue is the growing informality within the formal sector. Even within the organised sector, a large proportion of employment remains informal. For instance, 24.6 per cent of workers in Arunachal Pradesh are in informal jobs within the organised sector. This increasing informalisation of formal employment underscores the need for labour policy reforms and stronger social security measures to improve job quality. To address these challenges, targeted policies are needed to enhance employment opportunities, particularly in rural areas. Expanding non-farm employment, strengthening local industries, and investing in skill development and entrepreneurship can help create sustainable jobs and reduce reliance on low-paid, informal employment.

Migration in the Himalayan states is driven by a mix of economic, social, political, and environmental factors. Some states experience high migration due to employment opportunities, urbanisation, and infrastructure growth, while others face distress migration due to economic stagnation, lack of livelihood options, and socio-political instability. Male migration is primarily employment-driven, with people moving in search of better job opportunities, while female migration is largely influenced by marriage and family-related factors. Student migration is common in states with limited higher education opportunities, pushing young people to move to better-equipped educational hubs. Environmental migration is also a concern, as climate change, deforestation, and natural disasters force communities to relocate. The impact of COVID-19 and wider economic disruptions has also led to reverse migration in several states, highlighting the vulnerabilities of migrant workers. The lack of comprehensive data on migration further limits policymakers' ability to address these challenges effectively.

Addressing employment and migration challenges in the Himalayan region requires a multi-pronged and state-specific approach. Strengthening local economies by promoting sustainable livelihoods in agriculture, horticulture, tourism, and rural industries can help retain the workforce and reduce distress migration. Expanding access to higher education, vocational training, and market-relevant skills will improve employment prospects and reduce youth unemployment. Gender-inclusive employment policies, such as creating equal job opportunities for women and supporting women-led enterprises, are also crucial. Furthermore, improving infrastructure – particularly transport, digital connectivity, and industrial zones – can facilitate regional economic growth and employment generation. A comprehensive national and state-level database on migrant workers is essential for better planning, welfare programmes, and labour market integration. A long-term vision that balances economic growth with environmental sustainability and social equity is vital for the Himalayan region. By learning from successful models, integrating climate adaptation strategies, and fostering local industries, policymakers can create a more resilient and prosperous economy while mitigating the negative effects of distress migration and informal employment.

4 Human Capital: Education and Health in Himalayan Region

4.1 Introduction

This chapter focuses on two fundamental components of human capital: education and health. These elements play a crucial role in determining the economic growth and development of any region, particularly in the unique and often challenging context of Himalayan economies. The first section of this chapter examines the state of education and skill development in Himalayan economies, highlighting key trends, challenges, and policy interventions. Education serves as the foundation for human capital accumulation, enabling individuals to acquire the knowledge and skills necessary for economic productivity and social mobility (Schultz, 1961; Becker, 1993). However, Himalayan regions often face barriers such as limited access to quality education, inadequate infrastructure, and geographical constraints, which hinder educational attainment and skill development. Addressing these challenges is essential for fostering inclusive growth and enhancing workforce competitiveness in the region.

The second section explores the health status of populations in Himalayan economies, emphasising its impact on human capital formation. Good health is a prerequisite for productive engagement in economic activities, as poor health outcomes can significantly reduce an individual's ability to participate effectively in the labour market (Grossman, 1972). The Himalayan region faces unique health challenges, including high maternal and child mortality rates, limited healthcare infrastructure, and the prevalence of diseases linked to harsh climatic conditions and inadequate nutrition. Understanding these issues is critical for designing effective policies that promote better health outcomes and, in turn, enhance overall human capital development. By addressing education and health comprehensively, this chapter underscores their interconnected role in shaping the long-term economic resilience and well-being of Himalayan economies.

4.2 Education and Skill Development in Himalayan States in India

In light of the preceding discussion, this section provides a comprehensive analysis of the education and health landscape in the Himalayan region of India. It examines variations in educational achievements across age

DOI: 10.4324/9781003595410-4

groups, as well as the availability and accessibility of school infrastructure at all levels over the past two decades. The analysis covers enrolment and dropout rates, reasons for dropout, school infrastructure, participation in higher and technical education, vocational skill development, infrastructure for higher education, teacher–student ratios, teacher–school ratios, access to educational institutions and ICT, and expenditure on education. Additionally, this section critically evaluates key government schemes and policies, assessing their impact on school and higher education. This is achieved by drawing upon the latest administrative data and updated information from sources such as the Unified District Information System for Education (UDISE+), government dashboards, and nationwide higher educational surveys. State government evaluation studies and other policy documents are also consulted to gain insights into the education and skilling landscape in the Himalayan states.

Education has increasingly contributed to human development in general and the overall development of individuals in particular. Recognised as the most significant catalyst for socio-economic and political transformation, education has been central to policy debates and decisions aimed at universalising elementary and, subsequently, secondary education. Sustainable human development begins with empowering the masses, for which school education serves as the most crucial instrument. The emphasis on education is reinforced by Sustainable Development Goal (SDG) 4, which advocates for inclusive, equitable, and high-quality education along with lifelong learning opportunities for all (UNESCO, 2023). The Indian education system is structured to ensure accessibility and inclusivity, particularly for marginalised and disadvantaged groups. The National Education Policy (NEP) 2020 reaffirms this commitment by emphasising meaningful and holistic education, bridging socio-economic gaps, and ensuring quality learning experiences for all students (Government of India, 2020).

Despite these efforts, the Himalayan states of India – Jammu and Kashmir, Himachal Pradesh, Uttarakhand, Sikkim, Arunachal Pradesh, Nagaland, Manipur, Mizoram, Tripura, and Meghalaya – face distinct educational challenges due to their unique geographical characteristics. The mountainous terrain, scattered population, and harsh climatic conditions hinder access to educational institutions, particularly at the secondary and higher secondary levels. While primary education has seen notable improvements in enrolment and literacy, dropout rates remain a significant concern, especially in rural and tribal communities.

The North-eastern states have historically faced additional barriers, including armed conflicts, insurgency, and socio-cultural and political challenges, which have adversely affected educational development (NCTE, 2009). These challenges have particularly affected the younger generation, limiting opportunities for the universalisation of secondary education. Furthermore, the region has suffered from inadequate educational infrastructure, particularly at the secondary level. The demand for secondary education has surged due to an increase in transition rates from elementary to secondary education, the implementation of the Rashtriya Madhyamik Shiksha Abhiyan (RMSA) to universalise secondary education, and a reduction in regional migration owing to improved political stability. A thorough analysis of the demand and supply of secondary teachers, teacher educators, and teacher education institutions in the North-eastern states is essential to achieving the goals of RMSA. Given India's multicultural federal structure, the North-eastern region represents a microcosm of national diversity in terms of ethnicity, language, geography, and socio-economic factors, all of which have profound implications for its education system.

The relevance of education is particularly pronounced in the Himalayan regions, where unique geographical and socio-economic challenges influence educational outcomes. These states have implemented various government initiatives to improve educational access, which has led to increased enrolment rates. However, several challenges persist, including teacher shortages, infrastructure gaps, and limited access to digital learning technologies (MHRD, 2021). The education sector in the Himalayan region has witnessed a positive transformation, driven by government initiatives and non-governmental organisation (NGO) interventions that have boosted school enrolment. However, disparities in infrastructure, teacher availability, digital connectivity, and quality of education persist.

Government programmes such as the Sarva Shiksha Abhiyan (SSA), Rashtriya Madhyamik Shiksha Abhiyan (RMSA), and the Samagra Shiksha Abhiyan have been instrumental in improving school infrastructure, providing teacher training, and integrating technology into learning. Despite these efforts, addressing the systemic challenges in the Himalayan states requires continued investment in education policies tailored to the region's unique socio-geographical context. By strengthening infrastructure, expanding digital access, and ensuring the availability of qualified teachers, the government can bridge educational disparities and promote equitable learning outcomes across the Himalayan states.

This part of the chapter provides an in-depth analysis of the education landscape in the Himalayan states of India, highlighting variations in educational achievements across different schooling levels (age groups) and the availability of school infrastructure over the past two decades. It also explores key indicators such as enrolment rates, dropout rates, gender disparities, access to vocational education, and the impact of government policies on the education sector. The analysis is based on data from the Unified District Information System for Education Plus (UDISE+), the education rounds of the National Sample Survey (NSS), the Annual Status of Education Report (ASER), the All India Survey on Higher Education (AISHE), and various policy evaluation reports. The detailed tables are given in the Annexure.

4.2.1 Government Expenditure on Education

Investment in education varies significantly across the Himalayan states, reflecting the distinct socio-economic and geographical challenges of the region.

Most Himalayan states allocate a higher percentage of their gross state domestic product (GSDP) to education compared to the national average of 3.0 per cent (NITI Aayog, 2025). This higher allocation underscores the critical role of education in human capital development in an environment characterised by difficult terrain and limited industrial opportunities.

Jammu and Kashmir and Mizoram allocate the highest proportion of their GSDP to education among the Himalayan states, both at 6.2 per cent, followed by Manipur at 6.1 per cent (World Bank, 2021) (see Annexure Chapter 4). This trend suggests a strong governmental focus on improving education to address socio-economic disparities and create alternative employment opportunities beyond agriculture and traditional crafts. Mizoram's high literacy rates and community-driven education initiatives are attributed to its substantial educational investment (Mizoram Education Report, 2022). Other states such as Arunachal Pradesh (5.1 per cent), Meghalaya (5.6 per cent), and Nagaland (4.8 per cent) also report educational expenditures above the national average. These states face challenges in improving literacy and reducing dropout rates, particularly in rural and tribal areas (Ministry of Education, 2023). In contrast, Himachal Pradesh (4.2 per cent), Sikkim (4.0 per cent), and Tripura (4.4 per cent) allocate relatively lower portions of their GSDP to education. Despite this, Himachal Pradesh consistently ranks high in educational attainment due to effective policy implementation and robust school infrastructure in remote areas (Himachal Pradesh Education Report, 2022).

Uttarakhand, which records the lowest educational expenditure among the Himalayan states at 3.2 per cent, faces unique challenges such as migration and disaster vulnerability (Uttarakhand Human Development Report, 2023). Studies indicate the need for greater investments in vocational training and higher education to reduce out-migration and increase local employment opportunities. While high educational expenditure in many Himalayan states signifies a commitment to human capital development, research suggests that efficient utilisation of resources, teacher training, infrastructure enhancement, and digital learning integration are equally crucial to improving educational outcomes (Azim Premji University, 2022). Increased spending alone is insufficient; targeted interventions in school infrastructure, technology-enabled learning, and vocational education are necessary to ensure that financial investments translate into meaningful educational progress.

4.2.2 Literacy Rates

The literacy rates in the Himalayan states have shown substantial progress over the past two decades, reflecting the concerted efforts of both government and non-governmental initiatives in improving access to education. According to the latest data from the Census of India (2023), the national literacy rate stands at 84.3 per cent, marking a steady increase from 64.8 per cent in 2001 and 73.0 per cent in 2011. Despite these improvements, significant inter-state disparities persist, with some Himalayan states achieving exceptional literacy levels while others lag behind due to socio-economic and geographical constraints (see Annexure Chapters 2 and 4).

Among the best-performing states, Meghalaya (98.2 per cent), Manipur (94.3 per cent), Sikkim (93.7 per cent), Jharkhand (92.1 per cent), and Mizoram (95.8 per cent) have achieved high literacy rates (Northeast India Education Report, 2023). These improvements can be attributed to successful educational policies focused on rural and tribal populations, enhanced school infrastructure, and active community participation in educational initiatives. Himachal Pradesh has also demonstrated a notable upward trend, with its literacy rate increasing from 76.5 per cent in 2001 to 88.9 per cent in 2023–24 (MHRD, 2023). Conversely, Arunachal Pradesh (84.3 per cent), as discussed in Box 4.1, and Jammu and Kashmir (82.2 per cent) have made commendable progress but continue to face challenges in bridging the literacy gap with the national average. Uttarakhand (80.9 per cent) and Tripura (84.0 per cent) exhibit slower progress, indicating a need for more targeted interventions, particularly in remote and disaster-prone areas (Education Policy Review, 2022).

Box 4.1 Education Issues in North-eastern States

"Of course, there are significant variations in the literacy rates among different States with Arunachal Pradesh and Meghalaya below the national average. Even as the average literacy rate in the region is higher than the national average, there are concerns about the quality of education. More importantly, the literacy rate has not translated into higher employability or productivity" (p. 4).

"Creation of education and training facilities for the youth of the region in Information Technology (IT) and Information Technology Enabling Services (ITES) could provide a great impetus in generating a pool of personnel increasing employment opportunities for the youth" (p. 27).

Source: North Eastern Region Vision 2020, General Strategies for the Region, Vol. I, North Eastern Council, Ministry of Development of North Eastern Region.

There are gender disparities in literacy rates across the Himalayan states, which remain a critical concern, particularly in states like Jammu and Kashmir, Sikkim, and Uttarakhand, where female literacy is considerably lower than male literacy. At the national level, the male literacy rate is recorded at 87.1 per cent, while the female literacy rate stands at 74.4 per cent, reflecting a gender gap of 12.7 percentage points (MHRD, 2023). In states like Jammu and Kashmir, Sikkim, and Uttarakhand, the gender literacy gap is as high as 15.8, 10.0, and 13.2 percentage points, respectively. Although Mizoram and Meghalaya exhibit minimal gender disparities, other states require additional efforts to bridge this gap through scholarships, awareness campaigns, and targeted infrastructure development (UNESCO, 2023).

Box 4.2 Education Issues in Uttarakhand

"Primary research indicates an overall preference for education when compared to skill development. As affirmed by the National on Policy Skill Development and Entrepreneurship 2015, nationally there is over emphasis on education when compared to other mediums of employment. In a state like Uttarakhand, this emphasis on education as only means of economic and self-development leads to extra pressure on infrastructure. This pressure has an impact on heavily populated districts like Haridwar, Udham Singh Nagar (recording low literacy rates) and in hilly regions with low connectivity like Bageshwar, Uttarkashi (recording low admission rates in engineering colleges). For skill development, interest of the population in ITIs and Polytechnics needs to be examined, to determine the causes for the decline in admissions. In line with this need, more focus is required on improving distribution of skill training centres, to ensure adequate accessibility for youth in all districts" (pp. 84–85).

Source: Uttarakhand Skill Gap Study: A Study of the Existing Situation of Demand and Supply of Labour, May 11, 2018.

One of the primary reasons for the relatively low literacy rates in certain Himalayan states is the lack of adequate educational infrastructure. This issue is more serious in the hilly regions of the Himalayan states, as the Uttarakhand case is discussed in Box 4.2. Many schools in the region lack basic amenities such as classrooms, furniture, and sanitation facilities, which hampers effective learning. Additionally, the shortage of trained teachers remains a significant challenge, with some areas experiencing a high student–teacher ratio, forcing a single teacher to teach multiple subjects (Azim Premji University, 2022). Access to quality education is also a major concern in remote and mountainous areas, where students often have to travel long distances to attend school. This geographic constraint contributes to high dropout rates, as many children are compelled to leave school early to support their families in agricultural or household work (World Bank, 2021). The dropout rate is particularly high among girls due to socio-cultural factors, early marriages, and economic pressures, further exacerbating gender disparities in literacy (UNESCO, 2023). The cultural diversity of the Himalayan region also plays a significant role in shaping educational outcomes. Many state curricula follow a standardised national model that does not always integrate local culture, traditions, and languages, leading to a disconnect between students and their cultural roots. This lack of cultural relevance in education often results in disengagement and reduced motivation to pursue formal schooling (Northeast India Education Report, 2023).

Despite these challenges, several government initiatives have contributed to improving literacy rates in the Himalayan region. Programmes such as the Sarva Shiksha Abhiyan (SSA) and Rashtriya Madhyamik Shiksha Abhiyan (RMSA) have played a crucial role in enhancing access to education, particularly for marginalised communities. These initiatives aim to provide quality education to all children, improve school infrastructure, and bridge the gap in teacher availability (Government of India, 2020). Furthermore, the National Education Policy (NEP) 2020 underscores the importance of inclusive and equitable education, emphasising localised curriculum development, vocational training, and digital education to cater to the unique needs of Himalayan states (MHRD, 2021). Expanding access to information and communication technology (ICT) in education, along with strengthening teacher training programmes, will be instrumental in further advancing literacy rates in these regions.

Overall, the Himalayan states have made significant strides in literacy. However, continued efforts are required to address the remaining disparities and challenges. Investing in educational infrastructure, increasing teacher availability, promoting gender-inclusive policies, and integrating local cultural elements into the curriculum are essential strategies for sustaining progress. With the right policy interventions and targeted investments, the region can achieve higher literacy rates, bridge socio-economic gaps, and contribute to broader human development.

4.2.3 *Enrolment Rates: Gross and Net Enrolment Ratios*

The gross enrolment ratio (GER) and net enrolment ratio (NER) are crucial indicators for assessing the extent of educational participation across various levels in the Himalayan states. These indicators help in understanding the effectiveness of educational policies, the reach of schooling infrastructure, and the socio-economic barriers affecting student retention and progression.

4.2.3.1 *Gross Enrolment Ratio (GER) Across Educational Levels*

The GER for 2023–24 reveals significant disparities across different schooling levels in the Himalayan states. At the primary level, GER is notably high, with Meghalaya (178.4 per cent), Mizoram (151.8 per cent), and Manipur (136.8 per cent) leading, far exceeding the national GER of 93.0 per cent (UDISE+, 2023) (see Annexure Chapters 2 and 4). Such inflated GER values suggest widespread enrolment of over-age and under-age students, possibly due to late entry into school, high repetition rates, and flexible entry policies (NUEPA, 2022). However, GER declines significantly at the secondary and higher secondary levels. While Himachal Pradesh (100.1 per cent) and Mizoram (98.1 per cent) maintain relatively strong GERs at the secondary level, states such as Nagaland (60.2 per cent), Arunachal Pradesh (67.8 per cent), and Jammu and Kashmir (65.4 per cent) report substantially lower figures, reflecting challenges in school accessibility, socio-economic barriers, and high dropout rates (India Education Statistics, 2023). These trends align with findings from the National Sample Survey (NSS), which attribute declining GER at higher levels to financial constraints, long travel distances to schools, and a preference for vocational activities over formal education (NSSO, 2023).

In the domain of higher education, GER remains below the national average of 28.4 per cent across most Himalayan states, underscoring limited access to tertiary education (Map 4.1). In particular, states like Uttarakhand (41.8 per cent) and Himachal Pradesh (43.1 per cent) show relatively higher enrolment, benefiting from better higher education infrastructure and policy

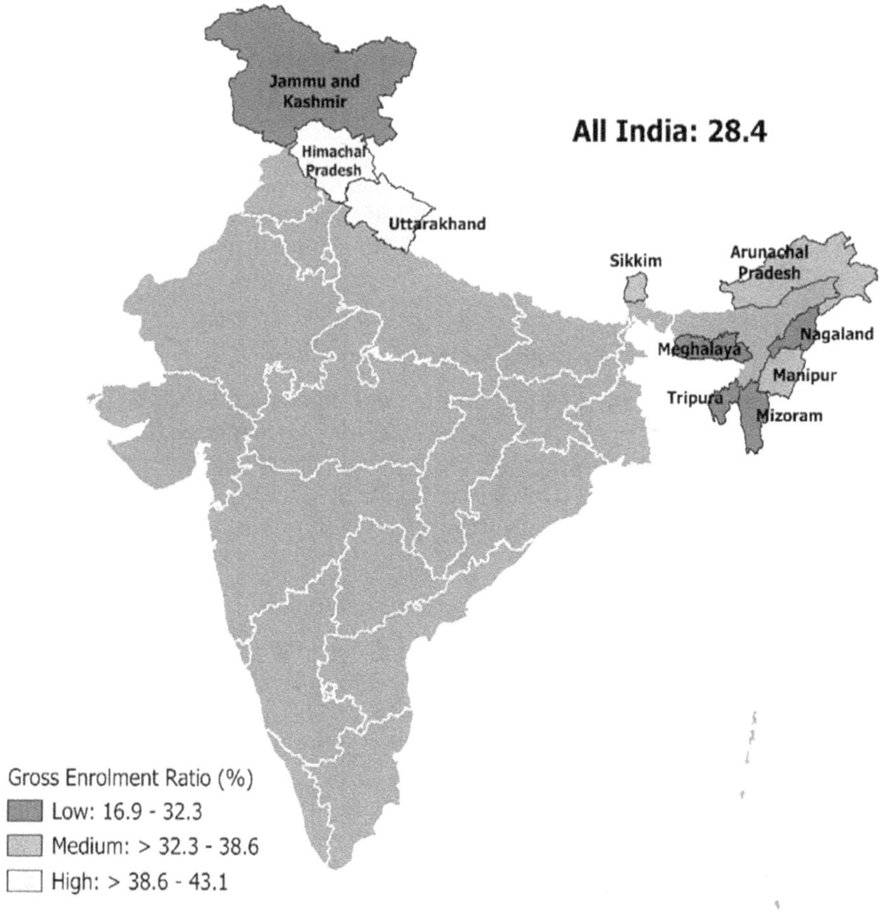

Map 4.1 GER in higher education.
Source: AISHE (2023).

focus on expanding university-level institutions (AISHE, 2023). In contrast, states such as Nagaland (18.8 per cent) and Meghalaya (25.4 per cent) struggle with lower GER, primarily due to the lack of higher education institutions, financial constraints, and cultural factors influencing participation in tertiary education (MHRD, 2023).

4.2.3.2 Net Enrolment Ratio (NER) and Student Participation

While GER provides an overall measure of enrolment, NER offers a more accurate depiction of age-appropriate student participation. The primary-level NER is encouraging in states such as Meghalaya (98.0 per cent) and Jammu and Kashmir (82.8 per cent), indicating successful early education outreach and policy effectiveness (UDISE+, 2023) (see Annexure Chapter 4). However, a significant drop is observed at the secondary level, where Nagaland (39.6 per cent), Jammu and Kashmir (38.8 per cent), and Arunachal Pradesh (41.6 per cent) record some of the lowest NERs in the country. This decline points to systemic issues such as socio-economic constraints, early marriages, limited secondary school availability, and a lack of financial support for continuing education (UNESCO, 2023).

Several factors contribute to the declining enrolment and retention rates in the Himalayan states, which include geographical constraints, as the rugged terrain and scattered settlements make school accessibility a major challenge, particularly at the secondary and higher secondary levels (Singh & Mehta, 2022); socio-economic factors, as many children, especially in tribal and rural areas, leave school early to support household income or engage in agricultural activities (Azim Premji Foundation, 2022); gender disparities, with female enrolment remaining lower in states such as Jammu and Kashmir and Uttarakhand due to traditional socio-cultural norms that prioritise male education over female education (MHRD, 2023); and infrastructure and resource deficiencies, as many schools in remote areas lack basic infrastructure, qualified teachers, and digital learning facilities, which further deter school participation (World Bank, 2021).

4.2.4 Dropout Rates

Dropout rates remain a crucial challenge in the educational landscape of India, particularly in the Himalayan states, where geographical, socio-economic, and infrastructural factors significantly impact student retention. Understanding dropout trends at different educational levels is essential to formulating effective policy interventions.

4.2.4.1 Dropout Rates at the Primary Level

At the primary level, India's overall dropout rate remains relatively low at 1.9 per cent, with a slight gender disparity – 2.1 per cent for boys and 1.7 per cent for girls (see Annexure Chapter 4). However, certain Himalayan states exhibit considerably higher dropout rates. Meghalaya records the highest primary-level dropout rate at 7.5 per cent, followed by Arunachal Pradesh (5.4 per cent). Gender disparities in dropout rates are also evident, with boys in Meghalaya dropping out at a rate of 8.3 per cent, compared to 6.8 per cent for girls. Key factors contributing to high dropout rates include economic hardship, inadequate educational infrastructure, and the need for children to assist in agricultural and household labour (UNESCO, 2021). Conversely, some states demonstrate remarkable success in student retention. Himachal Pradesh (0.0 per cent), Uttarakhand (0.1 per cent), and Tripura (0.5 per cent) report negligible dropout rates at the primary level. The effectiveness of policies such as the Mid-Day Meal Scheme, community-driven education initiatives, and school retention programmes in these states has played a pivotal role in sustaining student enrolment (NUEPA, 2021).

4.2.4.2 Dropout Rates at the Upper Primary Level

Dropout rates see a significant increase at the upper primary level. Nationally, the dropout rate rises to 5.2 per cent, with boys and girls showing similar trends (see Annexure Chapter 4). However, the problem is more pronounced in certain Himalayan states. Meghalaya, for example, has an alarmingly high dropout rate of 12.4 per cent, followed by Arunachal Pradesh (6.8 per cent). Meghalaya's dropout rate escalates to 13.9 per cent for boys and 11.1 per cent for girls, underscoring the impact of limited access to secondary education, economic constraints, and traditional gender roles that discourage female education beyond the primary level (World Bank, 2020). Comparatively, states such as Himachal Pradesh (0.6 per cent), Jammu and Kashmir (3.2 per cent), Uttarakhand (2.3 per cent), and Tripura (4.1 per cent) perform better than the national average, but dropout issues, especially among girls, remain a major concern in the case of Jammu and Kashmir, as discussed in Box 4.3. Sikkim (4.9 per cent) reports moderate dropout rates, indicating the need for improved educational access and infrastructure in remote areas (NUEPA, 2021).

4.2.4.3 Dropout Rates at the Secondary Level

Dropout rates peak at the secondary level, where the national average stands at 14.1 per cent, with 15.5 per cent for boys and 12.6 per cent for girls (see Annexure Chapter 4). The Himalayan states experience even higher rates, largely due to factors such as inadequate secondary school infrastructure, financial barriers, early marriages, and domestic responsibilities. Meghalaya (22.0 per cent) and Arunachal Pradesh (19.3 per cent) recorded the highest dropout rates, highlighting systemic challenges that impede student progression beyond primary education (UNESCO, 2021). On the other hand, Himachal Pradesh (4.9 per cent), Uttarakhand

(7.0 per cent), and Tripura (10.4 per cent) have relatively lower dropout rates, reflecting stronger school retention policies, better infrastructure, and government-led scholarship programmes. States such as Nagaland (11.6 per cent) and Mizoram (14.8 per cent) perform slightly better than the national average but still require targeted interventions to reduce dropout rates further (Ministry of Education, 2021).

Several interrelated factors contribute to high dropout rates in the Himalayan states: (1) *Economic hardship.* Many families in these states rely on subsistence agriculture and informal labour markets, making it difficult to prioritise education over immediate economic survival (World Bank, 2020). (2) *Inadequate educational infrastructure.* Many remote areas lack sufficient secondary schools, forcing students to travel long distances, which increases dropout probabilities, particularly for girls (UNESCO, 2021). (3) *Gender disparities.* In several Himalayan states, societal norms and responsibilities placed on girls, such as early marriage and household duties, result in lower educational attainment for females (ASER, 2022). (4) *Quality of education.* Shortage of trained teachers, lack of digital learning tools, and outdated curricula also contribute to students disengaging from formal education (NUEPA, 2021). (5) *Migration and displacement.* Seasonal migration due to economic distress and natural disasters forces children to drop out of school at a higher rate than the national average (Ministry of Education, 2021).

Box 4.3 Dropout Issues in Jammu and Kashmir

"Gender disparities persist in Jammu and Kashmir, resulting in higher dropout rates among girls, particularly between the age of 15–16 years. Socio-cultural norms, economic constraints, and ignorance of parents serve as major obstacles to achieving gender equality in education. Moreover, the region's education system grapples with unique challenges deeply rooted in its history of political instability. Decades of political unrest and tensions have disrupted normal life, including educational institutions, leading to frequent closures, curfews, and disruptions in academic calendars. To sum up, the educational landscape of Jammu & Kashmir faces multifaceted challenges, ranging from long-standing conflicts to infrastructural deficiencies, inadequacy of trained teachers, and gender disparities. Addressing these challenges demands concerted attention and effort."

Source: "Learning Deficit in Kashmir's Education system: Insights from ASER Reports," *J&K Policy Institute: Advocating for Sustainability*, by Neha Aggarwal, March 26, 2024, ASER survey titled "Beyond Basics," 2023.

4.2.5 *Transition Rates*

Transition rates in education serve as crucial indicators of student progression across different levels of schooling, reflecting the effectiveness of educational policies, infrastructure availability, and socio-economic factors influencing student retention. A high transition rate signifies a well-functioning education system, while a decline indicates barriers such as economic hardship, inadequate school facilities, and socio-cultural constraints.

4.2.5.1 *Primary-to-Upper-Primary Transition*

The transition rate from primary to upper primary levels remains relatively high across India, with the national average at 88.8 per cent (see Annexure Chapter 4). In the Himalayan states, the transition rate varies significantly. Himachal Pradesh (98.8 per cent) and Ladakh (95.2 per cent) outperform the national average, indicating strong educational continuity and policy effectiveness in ensuring students' progress beyond primary education. These states benefit from well-implemented mid-day meal schemes, community engagement in education, and better school infrastructure (World Bank, 2020). Conversely, Meghalaya (74.2 per cent) and Manipur (83.1 per cent) lag behind, reflecting significant challenges related to educational access, socio-economic constraints, and high dropout rates. The lower transition rates in these states are often attributed to factors such as poor road connectivity in remote areas, lack of secondary schools within accessible distances, and financial barriers, leading students – especially those from tribal and economically weaker backgrounds – to drop out early (ASER, 2022).

4.2.5.2 *Secondary-to-Higher-Secondary Transition*

The transition rate from secondary to higher secondary levels declines sharply across the country, with the national average at 71.5 per cent. This drop highlights increasing dropout rates at higher educational levels due to economic pressures, lack of higher secondary schools, and limited parental awareness regarding the benefits of continued education, particularly for girls (NUEPA, 2021). Among the Himalayan states, Tripura (85.7 per cent), Uttarakhand (86.1 per cent), and Nagaland (78.3 per cent) exhibit relatively high transition rates, suggesting stronger policy interventions aimed at improving secondary education access. These states have benefited from programmes such as the Rashtriya Madhyamik Shiksha Abhiyan (RMSA) and state-specific scholarship initiatives that help students, particularly girls and marginalised communities, transition to higher education (Ministry of Education, 2021). However, states such as Ladakh (50.5 per cent) and Meghalaya (42.8 per cent) report alarmingly low transition rates, underscoring the severe challenges students face in continuing education beyond the secondary level. The decline can be attributed to a combination of factors, including financial constraints, the expectation of early workforce participation, and socio-cultural norms discouraging higher education for girls (UNESCO, 2021).

4.2.6 Reasons for Non-Enrolment and Dropout

The reasons for non-enrolment and discontinuation of education vary significantly across genders, socio-economic backgrounds, and geographic regions in India. In the Himalayan states, these factors are further compounded by issues such as limited infrastructure, economic hardship, and cultural expectations.

4.2.6.1 Factors Affecting Boys' Non-Enrolment and Dropout Rates

Nationally, boys tend to drop out of school due to reasons such as lack of interest in education (11 per cent), engagement in domestic activities (19.3 per cent), and economic pressures requiring them Ministry of Education (MoE, 2024). The situation in the Himalayan states follows similar trends but is exacerbated by the difficult terrain and limited employment opportunities that push children into the informal labour sector. (1) *Disinterest in education.* In states like Arunachal Pradesh (15.8 per cent), Jammu and Kashmir (10.4 per cent), and Nagaland (9.1 per cent), a significant percentage of boys cite disinterest in formal education as the main reason for dropping out (MHRD, 2020). This highlights a pressing need for curriculum reforms that align education with local needs, including vocational training and skill development programmes tailored to the region's economic landscape. (2) *Economic constraints and early workforce participation.* Many boys from lower-income families in Meghalaya and Ladakh drop out to work in agriculture, tourism, or small-scale industries to support their families. Seasonal migration for work, particularly in Ladakh and Uttarakhand, also disrupts education, as children often accompany their parents to temporary job locations, leading to discontinuation (NUEPA, 2021). (3) *Lack of secondary schools and poor infrastructure.* In remote districts of Arunachal Pradesh, Manipur, and Sikkim, the absence of nearby secondary schools' forces students to travel long distances, discouraging many from continuing education beyond the primary level. Poor road connectivity and harsh weather conditions further contribute to the high dropout rates (World Bank, 2020).

4.2.6.2 Factors Affecting Girls' Non-Enrolment and Dropout Rates

For girls, non-enrolment and dropout rates are primarily driven by gender-based socio-cultural norms, economic constraints, and early marriage. (1) *Household responsibilities and gender roles.* A striking 42.1 per cent of girls in Sikkim drop out due to domestic responsibilities, one of the highest rates in the country. Similarly, in Nagaland (19.9 per cent) and Meghalaya (20.5 per cent), young girls are often required to take care of younger siblings, assist in household chores, and participate in agricultural labour, limiting their access to education (see Annexure Chapter 4). (2) *Early marriage and social expectations.* In Jammu and Kashmir and Arunachal Pradesh, traditional expectations around marriage and domestic responsibilities lead to high dropout rates among adolescent girls. Early marriage remains a major barrier to education, particularly in rural communities, where girls are expected to prioritise family over schooling (UNESCO, 2021). (3) *Financial constraints and lack of sanitary facilities.* The cost of education, including school fees, uniforms, and transportation, disproportionately affects girls' schooling. In addition, the lack of gender-friendly sanitation facilities in schools, especially in Arunachal Pradesh and Meghalaya, contributes to high dropout rates among adolescent girls, particularly after puberty (Ministry of Education, 2021).

4.2.7 Teacher–Student Ratio

The teacher–student ratio is a critical determinant of education quality, influencing student learning outcomes, classroom engagement, and individual attention. Lower teacher–student ratios often correlate with better academic performance, improved student–teacher interactions, and enhanced learning environments (UNESCO, 2021). Conversely, high teacher–student ratios can lead to overcrowded classrooms, reduced instructional quality, and increased dropout rates.

At the primary level, India maintains a national average teacher–student ratio of 21:1, which aligns with global recommendations (Ministry of Education, 2024). However, significant regional disparities exist, particularly in the Himalayan states: (1) *States with low teacher–student ratios.* Sikkim (6:1) and Ladakh (6:1) report exceptionally low ratios, suggesting better student engagement and personalised learning opportunities (see Annexure Chapter 4). This may be attributed to smaller school sizes, government policies promoting recruitment, and lower student enrolment in sparsely populated areas (NUEPA, 2022). Himachal Pradesh (14:1) and Arunachal Pradesh (15:1) also maintain favourable ratios, reflecting strong recruitment policies and efforts to improve primary education accessibility (World Bank, 2023).

(2) *States with high teacher–student ratios.* At the higher secondary level, the ratios increase significantly, indicating a shortage of specialised teachers and infrastructural challenges. Tripura (40:1) and Jammu and Kashmir (35:1) exceed the national average, suggesting an urgent need for trained educators, particularly in science, mathematics, and vocational subjects (Ministry of Education, 2021). Uttarakhand (30:1) also report high ratios, reflecting resource constraints and recruitment gaps in secondary education.

4.2.7.1 Impact of Teacher–Student Ratios on Educational Outcomes

- *Learning outcomes and academic performance.* Research suggests that smaller class sizes contribute to better academic performance, as students receive more individualised attention, feedback, and interactive learning experiences (ASER, 2022). States like Sikkim and Ladakh, with their lower ratios, report higher literacy rates and better foundational learning outcomes compared to states with overcrowded classrooms (NUEPA, 2022).

- *Teacher workload and instructional quality.* In states with high teacher–student ratios, overburdened teachers struggle to provide effective instruction, leading to lower student engagement and reduced learning efficiency. Studies indicate that in Tripura and Jammu and Kashmir, where secondary-level ratios exceed 35:1, teachers face higher workloads, negatively impacting student motivation and retention rates (World Bank, 2023).
- *Dropout rates and student retention.* High teacher–student ratios at the secondary level correlate with increased dropout rates, as students receive less personalised support (UNESCO, 2021). In states like Tripura and Jammu and Kashmir, where secondary education ratios exceed the national average, dropout rates remain high due to lack of engagement and limited access to quality instruction (Ministry of Education, 2021).
- *Gender disparities and inclusive education.* Studies show that girls in high-ratio classrooms are more likely to discontinue education due to limited teacher support, lack of remedial teaching, and socio-cultural barriers (ASER, 2022). Ensuring gender-responsive teaching strategies and recruitment of more female educators can enhance girl's retention and participation in secondary education (UNESCO, 2021).

Teacher–student ratios play a pivotal role in shaping education quality. While low ratios in Sikkim and Ladakh enable better student engagement, overcrowded classrooms in Tripura and Jammu and Kashmir hinder learning outcomes. Addressing regional disparities, expanding teacher recruitment, and investing in professional training are crucial to ensuring equitable, high-quality education in the Himalayan states.

4.2.8 *Vocational Education and Skill Development*

Vocational education and skill development are crucial for addressing the education–employment gap, particularly in the Himalayan states, where traditional employment opportunities are scarce due to geographical constraints and limited industrialisation. Skill development programmes aim to equip youth with industry-specific competencies, improving their employability in sectors such as agriculture, tourism, information technology (IT), and handicrafts – all of which are vital to the region's economy (NSDC, 2023).

4.2.8.1 *Initiatives and Regional Disparities in Skill Development*

The National Skill Development Corporation (NSDC) and various state governments have launched several initiatives to promote vocational training. Pradhan Mantri Kaushal Vikas Yojana (PMKVY) and Skill India Mission have played significant roles in integrating vocational education into the mainstream education system, particularly in states like Himachal Pradesh and Uttarakhand, where technical education infrastructure has expanded in recent years (Ministry of Skill Development and Entrepreneurship, 2023b).

However, despite progress, states such as Arunachal Pradesh and Nagaland continue to struggle with limited access to vocational training centres. The lack of well-equipped training institutes, inadequate funding, and low awareness of vocational career opportunities hinder skill development efforts in these states. Investment in technical education infrastructure remains a key challenge, requiring greater policy intervention and financial support (World Bank, 2023).

4.2.8.2 State-Wise Trends in Vocational Training Participation

Vocational training participation varies significantly across the Himalayan states, influenced by gender disparities, infrastructure availability, and policy emphasis. At the national level, vocational training participation stands at 34.4 per cent, with 44.6 per cent of males and 24.1 per cent of females receiving some form of vocational education (PLFS, 2023–24) (see Annexure Chapter 4). However, state-level data reveal distinct trends: (1) *High vocational training participation.* Himachal Pradesh (64.3 per cent), Meghalaya (63.5 per cent), and Manipur (56.5 per cent) exceed the national average in vocational training participation, reflecting successful state-level skilling programmes and strong community engagement. These states have actively promoted training programmes in hospitality, tourism, agriculture, and traditional handicrafts, aligning vocational education with local employment opportunities (NSDC, 2023). (2) *Low vocational training participation.* Nagaland (17.0 per cent), Sikkim (20.2 per cent), and Uttarakhand (21.4 per cent) report significantly lower participation rates. The lack of awareness, financial barriers, and cultural attitudes towards vocational careers contribute to low engagement in these states. Expanding vocational training outreach, particularly in rural districts, is necessary to bridge the skill gap (World Bank, 2023).

Gender disparities are evident in vocational training participation. While nationally, male participation (44.6 per cent) is significantly higher than female participation (24.1 per cent), some Himalayan states defy this trend: Nagaland leads in formal vocational training participation, with a total of 49.6 per cent, surpassing the national average. Notably, female participation (57.8 per cent) is higher than male participation (45.7 per cent), making Nagaland a unique case in gender representation in skill development (NSO, 2023). This trend can be attributed to targeted government programmes aimed at empowering women in traditionally male-dominated sectors, such as IT and entrepreneurship. In contrast, states such as Manipur (8.7 per cent) and Meghalaya (11.3 per cent) have lower formal vocational training participation rates, indicating the need for stronger institutional support and policy intervention to encourage both male and female students to enrol in skill-based programmes (Ministry of Skill Development and Entrepreneurship, 2023).

Despite progress, several challenges persist in integrating vocational education effectively across the Himalayan region: (1) *Limited institutional capacity.* The shortage of well-equipped training institutes in remote areas reduces access to skill development programmes. Expanding infrastructure, particularly in Arunachal Pradesh, Sikkim, and Nagaland, is crucial (World Bank, 2023). (2) *Societal perceptions of vocational careers.* Many students and parents perceive vocational training as inferior to formal education. Awareness campaigns emphasising the benefits of skill-based careers are needed (NSDC, 2023). (3) *Lack of industry linkages.* Many vocational training programmes do not have strong industry linkages, leading to low employability. Public–private partnerships with industries in tourism, IT, and agribusiness can enhance job placements (Ministry of Skill Development and Entrepreneurship, 2023). (4) *Financial barriers.* Many students from low-income backgrounds cannot afford vocational courses, and scholarship schemes should be expanded, particularly for women and marginalised groups (NSO, 2023).

Overall, the vocational education and skill development play a vital role in bridging the employment gap in the Himalayan states, where traditional job opportunities are scarce. While some states, such as Himachal Pradesh and Meghalaya, have successfully integrated vocational training, others, including Arunachal Pradesh and Nagaland, require stronger infrastructure, policy support, and financial investment. Expanding gender-inclusive vocational training, strengthening industry partnerships, and promoting skill-based education as a viable career pathway can help enhance employability and economic growth in the region.

4.2.9 Types of Educational Institutions

The distribution of educational institutions in the Himalayan states of India highlights the dominance of government institutions at the school level, with a more balanced mix of government and private institutions in higher education. This distribution is influenced by geographical constraints, economic disparities, population density, and state policies that determine the accessibility and affordability of education. Analysing these trends provides insights into the equity and efficiency of educational provisions in the region (Ministry of Education, 2022).

4.2.9.1 School Education: Dominance of Government Schools

At the school level, India's national average indicates that 74.6 per cent of schools are government-managed, while 25.4 per cent are private institutions (see Annexure Chapter 4). The Himalayan states largely exceed this percentage, reflecting a greater reliance on public education due to challenging geography, lower urbanisation, and limited private sector involvement (NUEPA, 2022). The highest proportion of government schools is found in: Tripura (86.9 per cent), Himachal Pradesh (85.4 per cent), and Arunachal Pradesh (83.6 per cent), where strong state intervention ensures educational access in remote regions. Meghalaya (81.8 per cent), Jammu and Kashmir (77.3 per cent), and Manipur (75.7 per cent) also have a high share of public schools, aligning closely with the national trend (World Bank, 2023).

States with a higher proportion of private schools: Mizoram (71.5 per cent), Nagaland (71.6 per cent), and Sikkim (70.2 per cent) show a relatively larger private sector presence in school education. Uttarakhand (74.6 per cent) matches the national average but has a higher percentage of private schools (25.4 per cent), reflecting greater urban and semi-urban private sector engagement (Ministry of Education, 2022). These figures emphasise public funding's crucial role in ensuring universal access to education in the geographically remote Himalayan region, where private investment remains comparatively limited.

4.2.9.2 Higher Education: Variation in Government and Private Colleges

Unlike school education, higher education institutions in the Himalayan states show greater variation in the proportion of government and private colleges. Several Himalayan states have a higher proportion of government colleges than the national average of 21.5 per cent, reflecting strong public sector involvement in higher education: Sikkim (80.0 per cent), Tripura (79.6 per cent), and Mizoram (77.5 per cent) also have significant public sector participation, ensuring affordable and accessible education (see Annexure Chapter 4). Conversely, some states have a greater proportion of private colleges than the national average, highlighting higher private sector involvement: Nagaland (69.1 per cent), Uttarakhand (59.7 per cent), and Meghalaya (58.0 per cent) have more than half of their higher education institutions privately managed, suggesting higher private investment in infrastructure. Himachal Pradesh (52.9 per cent) and Arunachal Pradesh (44.2 per cent) show a more balanced distribution between government and private colleges. Jammu and Kashmir (43.9 per cent) and Manipur (43.7 per cent) lean towards government-managed institutions, though the private sector has a notable presence (Ministry of Education, 2022). This variation in higher education highlights regional disparities in educational accessibility and affordability, with some states relying more on private institutions while others maintain strong public-sector dominance.

4.2.9.3 University-Level Institutions: Government vs Private Universities

At the university level, India's national distribution comprises 696 government universities (59.6 per cent) and 472 private universities (40.4 per cent). The Himalayan states follow different trends, depending on state policies and private sector participation (ASER, 2023). The states with complete government control over universities include Jammu and Kashmir (16 government, 0 private), Arunachal Pradesh (10 government, 0 private), and Ladakh (100 per cent government universities). These states have no private universities, reinforcing strong public-sector control over higher education. Some states exhibit a relatively equal distribution between government and private universities, which include Himachal Pradesh (13 government, 17 private), and Uttarakhand (18 government, 20 private). This trend indicates a growing role of private universities in higher education expansion (NUEPA, 2022). On the other hand, some states with a limited private university presence include Manipur (8 government, 2 private), Mizoram (2 government, 1 private), Nagaland (2 government, 4 private), and Tripura (4 government, 1 private). These states have fewer private universities, maintaining a dominantly government-driven higher education system.

Challenges and policy implications include these: (1) *Geographical and infrastructure challenges.* Remote locations hinder private investment in education. States with rugged terrains (e.g. Arunachal Pradesh, Ladakh) rely entirely on government-funded institutions (World Bank, 2023). (2) *Equitable access to higher education.* High reliance on government institutions ensures affordable education, but limited infrastructure restricts access, especially in rural areas. States with higher private sector participation (e.g. Nagaland, Uttarakhand) show better educational expansion, but affordability concerns persist (ASER, 2023). (3) *Need for strengthening public–private partnerships.* Expanding private investment in school and higher education can bridge infrastructure gaps. Encouraging collaborations between government and private institutions can improve education quality and accessibility (Ministry of Education, 2022).

Overall, the distribution of educational institutions in the Himalayan states reflects strong public sector dominance, particularly in school and higher education. While government schools remain the backbone of school education, private institutions play an increasing role in higher education. States with balanced public–private partnerships show greater expansion in higher education, while others rely solely on government funding. Strengthening private sector participation, improving infrastructure, and ensuring affordable access are crucial for bridging educational gaps in the Himalayan region.

4.2.10 School Infrastructure and Educational Resources

School infrastructure is a crucial determinant of educational quality and learning outcomes, influencing student retention, attendance, and overall academic performance (UNESCO, 2022). In the Himalayan states of India, the availability of key school infrastructure such as electricity, drinking water, sanitation, and digital resources varies significantly across regions. While some states have achieved near-universal access to basic facilities, others continue to struggle due to geographical constraints, resource limitations, and policy gaps (World Bank, 2023).

4.2.10.1 Electricity Availability

Access to electricity in schools is essential for ensuring effective teaching–learning environments, particularly in an era of digital education. Across the Himalayan states, electricity availability varies widely, with some states achieving near-universal access, while others face major infrastructure gaps.

States with high electricity access: Himachal Pradesh (99.2 per cent), Sikkim (97.0 per cent), and Uttarakhand (90.2 per cent) surpass the national average (89.7 per cent), ensuring almost-universal access to electricity in schools (see Annexure Chapter 4). These states have effectively integrated energy access policies, benefiting from state-sponsored electrification programmes and renewable energy initiatives to power schools in remote areas (NUEPA, 2022). *States with poor electricity access:* Meghalaya (26.8 per cent) and Arunachal Pradesh (58.0 per cent) lag significantly behind, indicating serious infrastructure gaps that hinder classroom operations, digital learning, and school safety (World Bank, 2023). The low electricity access in these states is primarily due to challenging terrains, inadequate grid connectivity, and lack of investment in off-grid solutions (ASER, 2023).

4.2.10.2 Access to Drinking Water

Access to safe drinking water is critical for student health, hygiene, and school attendance. While some Himalayan states have achieved near-total coverage, others still struggle with water accessibility, particularly in remote and tribal areas. *States with high drinking water coverage:* Himachal Pradesh (100 per cent), Sikkim (98.9 per cent), and Manipur (99.4 per cent) ensure near-universal access to safe drinking water in schools, exceeding the national average (see Annexure Chapter 4). These states have benefitted from government programmes such as Jal Jeevan Mission, which has successfully expanded water access in schools (World Bank, 2023). *States with limited drinking water access:* Meghalaya (49.3 per cent) and Nagaland (66.5 per cent) report significantly lower access to drinking water in schools, reflecting infrastructural deficits and groundwater scarcity in certain regions (NUEPA, 2022). Schools in these states often depend on rainwater harvesting or water supplied from distant sources, leading to irregular access and hygiene concerns (ASER, 2023).

4.2.10.3 Toilet Facilities and Sanitation

Adequate sanitation in schools is a key factor in improving student retention, particularly for girls. While some states have achieved high sanitation standards, others still struggle with functional toilet availability. *States with high toilet availability:* Himachal Pradesh (99.9 per cent), Sikkim (99.8 per cent), and Uttarakhand (98.6 per cent) have ensured almost universal coverage of school toilets, reflecting strong policy efforts under programmes like Swachh Vidyalaya Abhiyan (see Annexure Chapter 4). *Challenges in sanitation infrastructure:* Arunachal Pradesh (70.1 per cent) lags behind in providing functional girls' toilets, impacting female student retention and attendance (World Bank, 2023). The lack of separate and well-maintained toilets in some schools discourages girls from attending classes, especially during adolescence (ASER, 2023). Despite improvements in sanitation infrastructure, maintenance of toilets remains a challenge, with reports of non-functional or poorly maintained facilities in some states (NUEPA, 2022).

4.2.10.4 Digital Infrastructure and Internet Connectivity

With the growing shift towards digital education, the availability of digital infrastructure, computers, and internet connectivity in schools has become a critical indicator of educational quality. However, there are significant disparities across the Himalayan states in terms of digital access. *Digitally well-equipped states:* Uttarakhand (68.5 per cent with internet; 86.6 per cent with computers) and Sikkim (46.8 per cent with internet; 91.9 per cent with computers) are among the best-performing states in terms of digital infrastructure in schools (see Annexure Chapter 4). These states have seen substantial investment in ICT (information and communication technology) education, benefiting from programmes such as Digital India and PM e-Vidya (World Bank, 2023). *States with poor digital infrastructure:* Meghalaya (24.5 per cent with internet; 18.8 per cent with computers) has the poorest digital infrastructure, indicating a major digital divide that restricts e-learning opportunities (ASER, 2023). The lack of access to computers and internet connectivity is a significant barrier to online education, particularly in tribal and remote regions (NUEPA, 2022). The COVID-19 pandemic further highlighted these disparities, as students in digitally under-equipped states faced major disruptions in learning due to the absence of online education facilities (World Bank, 2023). The availability of school infrastructure in the Himalayan states varies widely, with some states achieving near-universal access to electricity, drinking water, and sanitation, while others struggle with digital infrastructure and school facilities. Addressing these infrastructure gaps is essential for ensuring equitable access to quality education across the Himalayan region.

4.2.11 Performance and Quality of Education

The quality of education in the Himalayan states of India exhibits significant variation both in comparison to the all-India average and across different states, particularly in rural areas. While some states have shown strong educational performance, others continue to struggle with foundational learning outcomes, school retention, and dropout rates. These disparities underscore structural challenges related to teacher availability, infrastructure, pedagogical approaches, and socio-economic factors (ASER, 2023; UNESCO, 2022).

4.2.11.1 Foundational Learning Outcomes: Literacy and Numeracy

The early-grade literacy and numeracy skills in the Himalayan states reveal considerable disparities. *Reading comprehension in grade 3:* The percentage of third-grade children who can read a second-grade-level text is highest in

Himachal Pradesh (50.6 per cent) and Mizoram (29.6 per cent), both exceeding the national average (27.0 per cent). However, states like Jammu and Kashmir (16.6 per cent) perform significantly below the national average, indicating early literacy challenges (ASER, 2023) (see Annexure Chapter 4). *Numeracy skills in grade 3:* Early arithmetic skills follow a mixed pattern, with Mizoram (57.2 per cent) and Himachal Pradesh (57.9 per cent) performing much better than the national average (33.7 per cent). On the other hand, Meghalaya (22.8 per cent) report weaker foundational numeracy, highlighting gaps in early mathematical education (World Bank, 2023). By grade 5, reading ability continues to show strong variations across states: Himachal Pradesh (71.3 per cent) and Mizoram (67.5 per cent) outperform the national average (48.7 per cent), indicating stronger literacy initiatives in these regions. Jammu and Kashmir (37.7 per cent) remain below the national benchmark, necessitating urgent interventions to improve reading proficiency (UNESCO, 2022). In terms of mathematical competencies, the ability to perform division in grade 5 also reflects a similar trend. Himachal Pradesh (50.5 per cent) and Mizoram (44.7 per cent) report better performance than the all-India figure (30.7 per cent), while Meghalaya (16.0 per cent) continue to struggle with foundational numeracy (ASER, 2023).

4.2.11.2 Learning Outcomes at the Secondary Level (Grade 8)

At the eighth-grade level, learning outcomes continue to display regional disparities, particularly in reading comprehension and mathematical skills. *Reading comprehension in grade 8:* Himachal Pradesh (88.3 per cent), Mizoram (90.7 per cent), and Uttarakhand (82.2 per cent) exceed the national average (71.1 per cent), demonstrating strong language proficiency among students (see Annexure Chapter 4). However, Jammu and Kashmir (58.5 per cent) remain behind, indicating the need for strengthened literacy programmes (NUEPA, 2022). *Mathematical proficiency (division in grade 8):* Mizoram (60.9 per cent), Himachal Pradesh (54.4 per cent), and Uttarakhand (52.5 per cent) perform above the national average (45.7 per cent), showing better mathematical competencies. In contrast, Meghalaya (19.2 per cent) continues to show poor performance in division, suggesting deficiencies in numeracy instruction (World Bank, 2023).

4.2.12 Summing Up

The education landscape in the Himalayan states of India presents a mixed picture of progress and challenges. While literacy rates and primary education enrolment have significantly improved over the years, concerns remain regarding dropout rates in secondary and higher education, disparities in infrastructure, and teacher availability (ASER, 2023; NUEPA, 2022). Government policies and interventions have played a crucial role in shaping educational outcomes, but additional targeted efforts are needed to address regional disparities, gender gaps, and skill development (Ministry of Education, 2022; World Bank, 2023). A holistic approach is required to ensure that children across rural and remote areas have equitable access to quality education. Key focus areas include strengthening school infrastructure, improving teacher–student ratios, expanding digital education, and promoting vocational training to enhance employability and regional development (UNESCO, 2022).

4.2.12.1 *Public and Private Education: A Shifting Balance*

The Himalayan region follows a structured public-sector-driven system at the school level, which transitions into a mixed governance model in higher education. However, in recent years, there has been a surge in private unaided schools across the region. These institutions are often credited with improving education quality by offering better infrastructure, trained teachers, and enhanced learning resources (Ministry of Education, 2022). While private schools may provide higher-quality education, they remain inaccessible to many children from low-income families due to high tuition costs. This creates a socio-economic divide, where affluent families opt for private schooling while economically disadvantaged students rely on government schools, which often struggle with funding constraints, teacher shortages, and outdated pedagogical approaches (World Bank, 2023). Therefore, policymakers must ensure that both public and private education systems work in synergy, emphasising affordable and quality education across all socio-economic groups. Bridging the public–private divide will be essential in achieving sustainable educational equity in Himalayan states (UNESCO, 2022).

4.2.12.2 *The Educational Crisis: Persistent Challenges and a Need for Contextual Evaluation*

The Himalayan states, despite their rich cultural and geographical diversity, continue to struggle with significant educational challenges. The Performance Grading Index (PGI) 2.0 (2021–22) ranked Arunachal Pradesh, Meghalaya, and Mizoram among the worst-performing states in school education, reflecting low learning outcomes, teacher shortages, and weak infrastructure (Ministry of Education, 2022). Furthermore, states like Himachal Pradesh and Tripura, which showed notable improvements in 2020–21, have experienced a decline in performance in 2021–22, signalling systemic issues in education delivery (NUEPA, 2022). These trends indicate that the challenges in the regions require a tailored evaluation approach, rather than being compared with national-level standards.

4.2.12.3 *Key Factors Hindering Educational Progress in the Himalayan States*

- *Inadequate infrastructure and resources.* Many schools lack basic facilities, including electricity, drinking water, and functional toilets. Access to digital learning tools and internet connectivity remains limited, particularly in rural and remote areas (World Bank, 2023).

- *Shortage of trained teachers.* A high percentage of teachers in government schools are on contractual terms, often lacking professional training. The absence of continuous professional development programmes affects teaching quality and student engagement (UNESCO, 2022).
- *Funding constraints and policy variability.* Since education is a concurrent subject under the Indian Constitution, state governments play a critical role in fund allocation and policy prioritisation. Budgetary limitations have impacted the expansion of secondary education, vocational training, and digital learning initiatives (Ministry of Education, 2022).
- *Geographical and socio-economic barriers.* The hilly terrain and dispersed population make school access difficult, leading to high dropout rates in secondary education. Economic constraints force many children to leave school early and enter the workforce (ASER, 2023). There are regional disparities in internet connectivity and digital learning access (World Bank, 2023).

4.3 Health and Healthcare Services in Himalayan Economies

Access to quality healthcare services is a crucial determinant of human development, significantly influencing economic growth, productivity, and overall well-being. The burden of morbidity and mortality not only affects individual health outcomes but also has far-reaching socio-economic consequences, particularly in regions where healthcare infrastructure is weak. Within the framework of the Sustainable Development Goals (SDGs), health holds a central position, particularly under Goal 3, which emphasises ensuring good health and well-being for all (United Nations, 2015). The role of healthcare extends beyond individual well-being, serving as the foundation for sustainable economic progress and social equity.

India's National Health Policy (NHP) of 2017 is aligned with global commitments to strengthen health systems and achieve universal health coverage (UHC). The policy prioritises affordable, accessible, and high-quality healthcare services, emphasising preventive and promotive care (Ministry of Health and Family Welfare, 2017). However, the Himalayan states of India face distinct geographical and infrastructural challenges, which exacerbate disparities in healthcare access and outcomes. The rugged terrain, extreme weather conditions, and scattered population settlements pose logistical difficulties in establishing healthcare facilities, deploying healthcare professionals, and ensuring continuous medical supplies (WHO, 2021). These barriers disproportionately affect marginalised communities, limiting their ability to access even basic healthcare services (NFHS-5, 2019–21).

The healthcare infrastructure in Himalayan states is characterised by low health facility density, inadequate human resources, and limited financial investments, resulting in disparities in healthcare access and utilisation. According to the National Family Health Survey (NFHS-5, 2019–21), states such as Arunachal Pradesh and Meghalaya report significantly lower institutional delivery rates compared to national averages, indicating gaps in maternal healthcare utilisation (IIPS & MoHFW, 2021). The prevalence of home deliveries, often due to long distances to healthcare facilities and cultural preferences, contributes to higher maternal and neonatal mortality rates in these states (UNICEF, 2022). A critical issue in the Himalayan region is the disproportionate burden of communicable and non-communicable diseases (NCDs). While infectious diseases such as tuberculosis, respiratory infections, and vector-borne diseases continue to pose challenges, there is a growing prevalence of NCDs such as hypertension, diabetes, and cardiovascular diseases, exacerbated by changing lifestyles, dietary patterns, and limited access to preventive healthcare (World Bank, 2023). The epidemiological transition has placed additional strain on the fragile healthcare system, necessitating a dual focus on disease prevention and treatment (WHO, 2021).

Overall, the healthcare system in the Himalayan economies must be redesigned to be more resilient, inclusive, and responsive to the unique challenges of the region. Addressing healthcare inequities, improving service delivery, and strengthening health financing mechanisms will be crucial in ensuring that these states achieve better health outcomes and align with the broader goals of universal health coverage and sustainable development. In this context, this section focuses on analysing the health and healthcare system in Himalayan regions in India to understand progress and challenges. For this analysis, data has been sourced from the National Family Health Surveys (NFHS), health rounds of the National Sample Surveys (NSS), the National Health Profile (NHP) by the Central Bureau of Health Intelligence (CBHI), the Sample Registration System (SRS) of the Office of the Registrar General and Census Commissioner, and other relevant reports and publications from state governments, the Ministry of Health and Family Welfare (MoHFW), the National Health Mission (NHM), and other associated agencies. The detailed tables are given in the Annexure.

4.3.1 Health Financing and Expenditure

Effective health financing and expenditure are critical determinants of equitable healthcare access, service delivery, and health outcomes. Government health expenditure (GHE) and out-of-pocket (OOP) expenditure significantly influence the affordability and quality of healthcare services, particularly in resource-constrained regions such as the Himalayan states of India. The proportion of public health spending relative to gross state domestic product (GSDP) varies significantly across these states, highlighting disparities in healthcare investment and fiscal prioritisation.

4.3.1.1 Government Health Expenditure (GHE)

Public health spending as a percentage of GSDP is a key indicator of government commitment to healthcare. Among the Himalayan states, Arunachal

Pradesh and Mizoram allocate the highest share of their GSDP to health, at 3.4 per cent, underscoring their strong commitment to public healthcare investment (Ministry of Health and Family Welfare, 2022b). Meghalaya follows with 2.7 per cent, while Manipur (2.2 per cent) and Nagaland (2.3 per cent) also demonstrate relatively high public spending. These figures suggest that these states recognise the necessity of robust health financing, particularly given their geographical constraints and dispersed populations, which require higher per capita investment to ensure healthcare access. Conversely, Uttarakhand (1.1 per cent) and Jammu and Kashmir (1.2 per cent) allocate the lowest share of GSDP to healthcare, indicating potential underinvestment despite the challenges posed by their mountainous terrain and climatic adversities (Ministry of Health and Family Welfare, 2022a). Lower GHE often correlates with increased financial burdens on households, forcing individuals to seek private healthcare services, which further exacerbates healthcare inequities (NITI Aayog, 2022a). The disparities in GHE across the Himalayan states emphasise the need for region-specific policy interventions to bridge funding gaps and ensure universal healthcare access.

4.3.1.2 Out-of-Pocket Expenditure (OOP)

High out-of-pocket (OOP) healthcare expenses remain a pressing concern, particularly in the Himalayan states, where limited public health infrastructure compels many individuals to seek private healthcare services. At the national level, OOP expenditure has declined from 47.1 per cent in 2019–20 to 39.4 per cent in 2021–22, reflecting increased public health investments and expanded government-funded health schemes (NHSRC, MoHFW, 2023) (see Annexure Chapter 4). Among the Himalayan states, Jammu and Kashmir recorded the most significant reduction in OOP expenditure, decreasing from 46.6 per cent to 25.9 per cent, largely due to enhanced coverage under government health schemes, including Ayushman Bharat and state-sponsored health insurance programmes (NHSRC, MoHFW, 2023). This decline indicates that improvements in public health financing can effectively reduce the financial burden on households, leading to better healthcare utilisation and lower economic distress due to medical expenses. However, Himachal Pradesh continues to report relatively high OOP spending, suggesting a persistent reliance on private healthcare services, possibly due to insufficient availability of specialised care in public health facilities (NITI Aayog, 2022d).

4.3.2 Child Health and Nutrition

Ensuring optimal child health and nutrition is crucial for improving overall human development indicators, particularly in the Himalayan states, where geographical isolation and socio-economic disparities pose unique challenges. Malnutrition in children manifests in various forms, including stunting (low height-for-age), wasting (low weight-for-height), and underweight (low weight-for-age), which are key indicators of nutritional deficiencies and poor public health interventions. Despite several government programmes aimed at addressing child malnutrition, significant disparities persist across the Himalayan region, reflecting varying levels of healthcare access, food security, and maternal health awareness.

4.3.2.1 Stunting

Stunting, a chronic form of malnutrition that results from prolonged nutritional deficiencies and recurrent infections during early childhood, remains a severe public health issue in many Himalayan states. According to the National Family Health Survey (IIPS & MoHFW, 2021), Meghalaya recorded the highest stunting rate at 46.5 per cent, significantly exceeding the national average of 35.5 per cent (see Annexure Chapter 4). This suggests that food insecurity, inadequate maternal nutrition, poor sanitation, and limited healthcare access continue to hinder children's physical development in the state. In addition, Arunachal Pradesh (34.9 per cent) also reports high stunting prevalence, emphasising the need for enhanced nutritional interventions and improved maternal and child healthcare services. Conversely, Sikkim (22.3 per cent) and Manipur (23.4 per cent) report the lowest stunting rates in the region, indicating relatively effective maternal and child health programmes, higher literacy levels among mothers, and better access to nutrition-focused interventions (IIPS & MoHFW, 2021). These findings highlight that stunting is not merely a result of food scarcity but is also linked to healthcare accessibility, socio-economic conditions, and hygiene practices.

4.3.2.2 Wasting

Wasting, a more acute form of malnutrition characterised by low weight-for-height, is a critical concern in the Himalayan states. According to IIPS & MoHFW (2021), Nagaland (19.1 per cent) reports significantly higher wasting rates compared to the national average, reflecting ongoing food insecurity and inadequate dietary diversity among children (see Annexure Chapter 4). High wasting rates are often linked to poor maternal health, inadequate breastfeeding practices, and infectious diseases, all of which contribute to sudden weight loss and increased mortality risk among young children. However, some states have shown remarkable progress in reducing wasting prevalence. Meghalaya (12.1 per cent) and Arunachal Pradesh (13.1 per cent) have reported notable improvements, largely attributed to targeted nutritional programmes such as the Integrated Child Development Services (ICDS), the Mid-Day Meal Scheme, and state-specific supplementary nutrition initiatives (IIPS & MoHFW, 2021). These states have benefited from community-based nutrition awareness programmes and health system strengthening, underscoring the importance of multi-sectoral approaches in tackling child malnutrition.

4.3.2.3 Underweight

The underweight indicator, which reflects both chronic and acute malnutrition, varies widely across the Himalayan region. Tripura (25.6 per cent) reports significantly higher underweight prevalence, pointing to continued nutritional deficiencies, food insecurity, and gaps in maternal healthcare (see Annexure Chapter 4) (IIPS & MoHFW, 2021). These figures indicate the urgent need for improved maternal nutrition, fortified food distribution, and early childhood feeding practices to combat malnutrition effectively. On the other hand, Ladakh (9.1 per cent) and Mizoram (12.7 per cent) exhibit significantly lower underweight rates, reflecting better access to food security programmes, higher maternal education levels, and more effective public health interventions (IIPS & MoHFW, 2021). The success of these states underscores the role of comprehensive, community-based approaches, including enhanced prenatal and postnatal care, increased breastfeeding promotion, and expanded maternal health education programmes in reducing childhood undernutrition.

4.3.2.4 Infant Mortality Rate (IMR)

The infant mortality rate (IMR), defined as the number of infant deaths per 1,000 live births, is a critical indicator of healthcare effectiveness, maternal health conditions, and overall socio-economic development. A declining IMR reflects improvements in maternal and child healthcare services, enhanced public health interventions, and better healthcare accessibility. However, significant disparities exist across the Himalayan states, influenced by geographical remoteness, healthcare infrastructure, and socio-economic inequalities. According to the National Family Health Survey (NFHS-5, 2019–21), the national IMR stood at 35.2, marking a decline from 40.7 in NFHS-4 (2015–16), indicating steady progress in infant healthcare and neonatal survival rates (IIPS, 2021) (see Annexure Chapter 4). Among the Himalayan states, Sikkim (11.2), Arunachal Pradesh (12.9), and Jammu and Kashmir (16.3) reported the lowest IMRs, reflecting strong healthcare interventions, high institutional delivery rates, and improved neonatal care facilities. The availability of skilled birth attendants, early breastfeeding practices, and expanded immunisation coverage in these states has contributed to better infant survival rates.

In contrast, Tripura (37.6) and Uttarakhand (39.1) reported higher IMRs, surpassing the national average, highlighting gaps in healthcare access, limited availability of emergency obstetric care, and disparities in healthcare service utilisation. Additionally, Meghalaya (32.3) also exhibited relatively high IMRs, largely attributed to difficult terrain, inadequate healthcare infrastructure, and challenges in reaching remote tribal populations. The persistence of malnutrition, high prevalence of low-birth-weight infants, and delays in seeking postnatal care further exacerbate infant mortality in these states. Other Himalayan states, including Mizoram (21.3), Nagaland

(23.4), Manipur (25.0), and Himachal Pradesh (25.6), recorded moderate IMRs, indicating gradual improvements but the need for sustained efforts in strengthening neonatal healthcare (IIPS & MoHFW, 2021). Access to quality maternal healthcare, promotion of exclusive breastfeeding, and targeted community-based interventions have played a crucial role in reducing infant mortality rates across these states.

A historical analysis of IMR trends between NFHS-3 (2005–06) and NFHS-5 (2019–21) reveals notable progress in reducing infant mortality across all Himalayan states, albeit at varying rates. Arunachal Pradesh recorded a remarkable drop from 60.7 to 12.9, demonstrating the effectiveness of improved healthcare outreach and public health programmes. Similarly, Sikkim witnessed a significant decline from 33.7 to 11.2, reflecting successful maternal and neonatal health policies. Jammu and Kashmir also made substantial progress, reducing IMR from 44.7 to 16.3, attributed to expansion in institutional deliveries, maternal nutrition programmes, and improved neonatal intensive care services.

Despite these improvements, some states continue to face challenges in sustaining progress. Mizoram showed an unusual trend, with IMR initially rising from 34.1 in NFHS-3 to 40.1 in NFHS-4 before declining significantly to 21.3 in NFHS-5, indicating improved healthcare infrastructure and targeted child survival programmes in recent years. However, Tripura and Uttarakhand exhibited slower progress in reducing infant mortality, with Tripura's IMR increasing from 26.7 in NFHS-4 to 37.6 in NFHS-5, possibly due to healthcare accessibility challenges and maternal undernutrition. Uttarakhand, on the other hand, only marginally improved from 41.9 in NFHS-3 to 39.1 in NFHS-5, emphasising the need for targeted interventions in remote and hilly regions.

4.3.2.5 Under-Five Mortality Rate (U5MR)

The under-five mortality rate (U5MR), defined as the number of deaths of children under 5 years per 1,000 live births, serves as a broader indicator of child health, nutrition, and overall healthcare system efficiency. A decline in U5MR typically reflects improvements in child immunisation, management of childhood illnesses, maternal nutrition, and neonatal healthcare services.

As per NFHS-5 (2019–21), India's national under-five mortality rate (U5MR) stood at 41.9, a decline from 49.7 in NFHS-4 (2015–16), showcasing steady national progress in reducing child mortality (IIPS, 2021) (see Annexure Chapter 4). Within the Himalayan states, Sikkim (11.2), Jammu and Kashmir (18.5), and Arunachal Pradesh (18.8) reported the lowest U5MRs, indicative of strong neonatal and child healthcare services, effective immunisation programmes, and improved healthcare access in these regions. These states have demonstrated success in reducing child mortality through expanded primary healthcare facilities, community health interventions, and better maternal and child nutrition programmes. However, Tripura (43.3) and Meghalaya (40.0) recorded the highest U5MRs among the Himalayan states, exceeding the national average. These figures highlight persistent healthcare access challenges, inadequate neonatal care, and high incidences of preventable childhood diseases such as diarrhoea and pneumonia, which remain major causes of child mortality in these regions. In addition, malnutrition and poor maternal health status further exacerbate the risk of child mortality, making it imperative to enhance maternal and child healthcare services in these states. Uttarakhand reported the highest U5MR at 45.6, underscoring the urgent need to strengthen healthcare delivery, improve immunisation coverage, and enhance early childhood healthcare services in remote and mountainous regions (IIPS & MoHFW, 2021). The lack of adequate paediatric healthcare facilities, limited availability of skilled healthcare workers, and poor sanitation and hygiene conditions contribute to high child mortality rates in these areas.

4.3.3 Maternal Health in the Himalayan States

Maternal health is a fundamental determinant of child mortality and overall public health outcomes, encompassing fertility trends, institutional deliveries, and nutritional status.

4.3.3.1 Total Fertility Rate (TFR)

The total fertility rate (TFR), a critical demographic indicator reflecting the average number of children a woman is expected to have during her reproductive years, has exhibited a consistent decline across the Himalayan states, mirroring national trends. According to the National Family Health Survey (NFHS-5, 2019–21) (see Annexure Chapter 4), India's TFR stood at 1.8, falling below the replacement level of 2.1, signalling progress towards population stabilisation and improved reproductive health services (IIPS, 2021). This decline is attributed to increased access to family planning services, better female education, and improved maternal healthcare. Among the Himalayan states, Sikkim reported the lowest TFR at 1.1, followed by Jammu and Kashmir at 1.4 and Himachal Pradesh at 1.7, demonstrating the effectiveness of widespread contraceptive use, delayed marriages, and improved socio-economic conditions. However, certain states, such as Meghalaya (2.9) and Manipur (2.2), recorded TFRs above the national average, indicating persistent challenges in reproductive health awareness, contraceptive accessibility, and socio-cultural norms that encourage higher fertility rates.

4.3.3.2 Nutritional Challenges and Anaemia Prevalence

Anaemia remains a severe public health challenge among children and women in the Himalayan region, significantly impacting overall health, cognitive development, and economic productivity. According to the National

Family Health Survey (NFHS-5, 2019–21), anaemia prevalence among children aged 6–59 months in India surged to 67.1 per cent, up from 58.6 per cent in NFHS-4, reflecting deteriorating nutritional status and inadequate iron intake (IIPS, 2021) (see Annexure Chapter 4). Several Himalayan states reported anaemia levels exceeding the national average, including Jammu and Kashmir (72.7 per cent) and Tripura (64.3 per cent), indicating persistent micronutrient deficiencies and dietary inadequacies. Although Meghalaya (45.1 per cent), Manipur (42.8 per cent), Mizoram (46.4 per cent), and Nagaland (42.7 per cent) recorded relatively lower anaemia rates, these states still showed an upward trend compared to NFHS-4, suggesting the need for continued interventions to prevent further deterioration.

Among women aged 15–49 years, anaemia prevalence rose from 53.0 per cent in NFHS-4 to 57.0 per cent in NFHS-5 at the national level, highlighting widespread nutritional challenges, inadequate access to iron-rich foods, and gaps in public health interventions. Within the Himalayan states, Tripura (67.2 per cent) reported alarmingly high anaemia rates, pointing to deficiencies in maternal nutrition, reproductive health issues, and limited access to fortified foods. Conversely, Mizoram (34.8 per cent), Nagaland (28.9 per cent), and Manipur (29.4 per cent) had the lowest anaemia prevalence in the region, likely due to better dietary habits, higher consumption of iron-rich traditional foods, and relatively improved maternal healthcare services.

4.3.3.3 Maternal Mortality Rates

The maternal mortality rate (MMR) serves as a critical indicator of maternal health and the overall effectiveness of healthcare systems. According to the Sample Registration System (SRS) 2018–20, India's MMR stands at 97 per 100,000 live births, showing significant regional disparities, particularly in the Himalayan states (Registrar General of India, 2022) (see Annexure Chapter 4). Among these states, Mizoram (19) and Tripura (21) report the lowest MMRs, well below the national average. This success can be attributed to strong maternal healthcare services, high institutional delivery rates, comprehensive antenatal and postnatal care, and government-led programmes such as Janani Suraksha Yojana (JSY) and Janani Shishu Suraksha Karyakram (JSSK) that promote safe motherhood (MoHFW, 2022b). Similarly, Himachal Pradesh (55) maintains a lower-than-average MMR, reflecting well-developed healthcare infrastructure, improved road connectivity, and a high percentage of deliveries conducted in health facilities.

However, several Himalayan states continue to experience alarmingly high maternal mortality rates, significantly exceeding the national average. Arunachal Pradesh (284) and Manipur (282) report some of the highest MMRs in the country, highlighting persistent healthcare gaps and systemic challenges in maternal care. These states struggle with poor maternal health outcomes due to inadequate access to healthcare in rural areas, delayed emergency obstetric care, and socio-economic barriers such as poverty and low female literacy rates (MoHFW, 2022c). Arunachal Pradesh and Manipur face additional challenges, including difficult terrain, scattered populations, and limited access to specialised maternal healthcare services, which result in lower institutional delivery rates and higher incidences of home births, often without skilled birth attendants.

Meghalaya (266) and Sikkim (228) also exhibit high MMRs, reflecting limited emergency obstetric care, high prevalence of home deliveries, and socio-cultural barriers that prevent timely maternal health interventions. In these states, traditional practices and a preference for home births continue to impact maternal survival rates, necessitating targeted public health initiatives to improve institutional deliveries and enhance healthcare access. Furthermore, the shortage of skilled birth attendants, insufficient referral mechanisms for high-risk pregnancies, and the lack of comprehensive maternal nutrition programmes exacerbate maternal health risks in these high-MMR states (IIPS, 2021).

4.3.3.4 Institutional Deliveries

The proportion of institutional deliveries in the Himalayan region has witnessed a significant increase over the years, largely due to targeted government interventions aimed at improving maternal healthcare access and reducing maternal and neonatal mortality. Programmes such as the Janani Suraksha Yojana (JSY) and Janani Shishu Suraksha Karyakram (JSSK) have played a crucial role in promoting safe deliveries by providing financial incentives, free medical services, and transportation support to pregnant women, particularly in rural and remote areas (MoHFW, 2022c). According to the National Family Health Survey (NFHS-5, 2019–21), India's overall institutional delivery rate has risen to 88.6 per cent, reflecting the success of these initiatives (see Annexure Chapter 4).

Among the Himalayan states, Sikkim (94.7 per cent), Jammu and Kashmir (92.4 per cent), and Himachal Pradesh (88.2 per cent) report institutional delivery rates above the national average, indicating robust healthcare infrastructure, increased awareness of maternal health benefits, and effective implementation of government programmes. The high rates in these states are attributed to improved access to public health facilities, higher literacy levels among women, and strong community health networks that encourage facility-based childbirth (IIPS, 2021).

Despite this progress, institutional delivery rates remain significantly lower in some Himalayan states, particularly in Nagaland (45.7 per cent) and Meghalaya (58.1 per cent), where cultural preferences for home births, geographical constraints, and inadequate healthcare infrastructure continue to hinder progress (IIPS & MoHFW, 2021). Traditional childbirth practices, reliance on untrained birth attendants, and a lack of adequate transportation facilities in remote areas contribute to lower hospital delivery rates in these states. In addition, healthcare access is further constrained by a shortage of skilled medical personnel, poor road connectivity, and limited emergency obstetric care services, particularly in rural and tribal-dominated areas (WHO, 2023b).

4.3.3 Life Expectancy

Life expectancy is a fundamental indicator of a region's overall health, socio-economic progress, and the effectiveness of healthcare systems. Over the past few decades, the Himalayan states of India have experienced notable improvements in life expectancy, largely attributed to advancements in public health infrastructure, better access to medical care, improved nutrition, sanitation, and targeted government health interventions (MoHFW, 2022a). However, despite these positive trends, significant regional and gender-based disparities persist, influenced by factors such as disease burden, healthcare accessibility, and socio-economic conditions.

According to estimates from 2016–20, India's overall life expectancy at birth stood at 70.0 years, with males averaging 68.6 years and females 71.4 years, reflecting the persistent gender gap in mortality trends (Registrar General of India, 2022) (see Annexure Chapter 4). Among the Himalayan states, Jammu and Kashmir (74.3 years) and Himachal Pradesh (73.5 years) reported the highest life expectancies, surpassing the national average. These states have benefited from higher healthcare accessibility, reduced maternal and child mortality rates, and better immunisation coverage, contributing to longer life spans (IIPS, 2021). In contrast, Uttarakhand (70.6 years) reported a life expectancy slightly above the national average, but disparities remain between urban and rural populations due to limited healthcare access in hilly terrains, migration-related challenges, and a high burden of lifestyle diseases (MoHFW, 2023b).

The variations in life expectancy across the Himalayan states underscore the need for targeted healthcare policies, improved last-mile healthcare delivery, and enhanced preventive healthcare measures. Strengthening primary healthcare services, increasing investments in disease control programmes, addressing environmental and occupational health hazards, and improving healthcare infrastructure in remote regions are crucial for further enhancing life expectancy and reducing regional disparities. Additionally, health awareness campaigns, promotion of healthy lifestyles, and greater integration of digital health services can contribute to better health outcomes in states lagging behind (WHO, 2023a, 2023b; MoHFW, 2023b).

A consistent demographic trend observed across all Himalayan states is that females outlive males, a pattern that mirrors national life expectancy trends. This gender disparity is primarily attributed to lower engagement in high-risk occupations, reduced exposure to lifestyle-related diseases, and improvements in maternal healthcare (MoHFW, 2022a). For instance, in Jammu and Kashmir, female life expectancy stands at 76.3 years, significantly higher than 72.6 years for males, indicating better maternal health services and a lower disease burden among women (RGI, 2022). Similarly,

Himachal Pradesh demonstrates a sharp contrast in life expectancy, with females living an average of 77.5 years, while males have a shorter lifespan of 70.3 years, largely due to lower rates of cardiovascular diseases and other lifestyle-related illnesses among women (IIPS, 2021).

In contrast, Uttarakhand presents a more concerning picture, with both male (67.5 years) and female (73.9 years) life expectancies falling below the national average. This disparity suggests significant healthcare inequalities, environmental stressors, and limited healthcare accessibility in remote areas, which collectively impact longevity (MoHFW, 2023b). Among the Himalayan states, Assam (representing North-eastern Himalayan states) records the lowest life expectancy rates, with males at 67.3 years and females at 68.6 years, highlighting persisting health challenges such as high maternal and infant mortality rates, malnutrition, and inadequate healthcare access (RGI, 2022; WHO, 2023b).

4.3.4 Health Infrastructure

Healthcare infrastructure is a critical determinant of public health outcomes, particularly in geographically challenging regions such as the Himalayan states. These states face unique challenges, including difficult terrain, low population density, and logistical constraints in healthcare service delivery. The availability of doctors, specialists, hospitals, and hospital beds per 100,000 population is a key indicator of healthcare accessibility and quality. The following analysis examines the state-wise healthcare infrastructure in the Himalayan region, comparing it to the national average and highlighting disparities.

4.3.4.1 Availability of Doctors and Specialists

The number of doctors and specialists per 100,000 population varies significantly across the Himalayan states. Himachal Pradesh has the highest availability, with 14 doctors per 100,000 people, nearly seven times the national average of two doctors per 100,000 (see Annexure Chapter 4). This reflects the state's emphasis on expanding medical education and healthcare services. Arunachal Pradesh also performs relatively well, with nine doctors per 100,000, indicating a stronger healthcare workforce relative to other North-eastern states. In contrast, Jammu and Kashmir, Mizoram, and Uttarakhand each report only four doctors per 100,000 population, which aligns with the national average but is insufficient considering the geographical and demographic challenges in these regions. This shortage often results in an increased patient load per doctor, longer wait times, and reliance on traditional or informal healthcare providers, particularly in remote districts. States like Manipur (7), Meghalaya (5), Nagaland (6), Sikkim (5), and Tripura (6) fall within a moderate range but still require significant improvements in workforce distribution, particularly in rural and tribal areas where access to specialist care remains limited.

4.3.4.2 *Availability of Hospitals*

The density of hospitals per 100,000 population provides insight into healthcare accessibility. Jammu and Kashmir (13), Arunachal Pradesh (12), and Himachal Pradesh (11) lead the Himalayan region, reflecting a stronger healthcare network in terms of hospital infrastructure (see Annexure Chapter 4). These figures are significantly higher than the national average of three hospitals per 100,000 population, indicating that these states have made notable investments in expanding medical facilities. On the other hand, states such as Manipur (0 hospitals per 100,000) and Uttarakhand (6 hospitals per 100,000) report lower availability, highlighting critical gaps in infrastructure. Manipur's figure suggests that while healthcare services exist, they may be concentrated in a few urban centres, necessitating significant improvements in rural healthcare coverage. Mizoram (8), Nagaland (8), Meghalaya (5), Sikkim (5), and Tripura (4) also fall behind in hospital density, necessitating policy interventions to expand healthcare infrastructure. The low hospital density in these states often forces patients to travel long distances for treatment, increasing the burden on urban healthcare centres.

4.3.4.3 *Availability of Hospital Beds*

Hospital bed availability is a key indicator of healthcare system preparedness, particularly in the context of handling medical emergencies, pandemics, and routine inpatient care. Sikkim (267 hospital beds per 100,000 population) has the highest hospital bed availability among the Himalayan states, significantly surpassing the national average of 62 beds per 100,000 population (see Annexure Chapter 4). This reflects the state's strong emphasis on hospital-based healthcare services. Himachal Pradesh (224 beds per 100,000) and Arunachal Pradesh (174 beds per 100,000) also perform well, indicating better healthcare capacity in these states. Meghalaya (138), Tripura (131), Mizoram (163), and Manipur (78) have moderate hospital bed density, but they still exceed the national average. In contrast, Jammu and Kashmir (74), Nagaland (86), and Uttarakhand (74) have bed availability closer to the national average but insufficient considering their geographical challenges. Low hospital bed availability in these states often leads to overcrowding in government hospitals, increased referral rates to tertiary care centres in neighbouring states, and greater reliance on private healthcare facilities.

Overall, the healthcare infrastructure in the Himalayan states presents a mixed picture, with some states like Himachal Pradesh and Sikkim outperforming the national average, while others like Manipur and Uttarakhand require urgent improvements in medical staffing, hospital density, and bed availability. The disparities across states call for targeted policy interventions, increased healthcare funding, and innovative healthcare delivery models to ensure equitable access to quality healthcare services across the region.

4.4 Role of Education and Health Policies and Interventions

The Himalayan states face unique challenges in healthcare and education due to their difficult terrain, dispersed populations, and socio-economic vulnerabilities. In response, the Government of India has implemented comprehensive policies and interventions aimed at improving public health, education, and skill development in these regions. These initiatives not only address immediate healthcare and learning needs but also contribute to long-term socio-economic development.

4.4.1 *Strengthening Healthcare and Nutrition*

To combat malnutrition and improve healthcare access, various national programmes have been introduced. The Ayushman Bharat Scheme, through the Pradhan Mantri Jan Arogya Yojana (PMJAY), provides free secondary and tertiary healthcare to economically disadvantaged families. In addition, Health and Wellness Centres (HWCs) have been established to deliver comprehensive primary healthcare, particularly in maternal and child health. The National Health Mission (NHM), integrating both rural and urban healthcare initiatives, has played a vital role in expanding healthcare infrastructure, reducing child mortality, and improving immunisation coverage.

Programmes like the Integrated Child Development Services (ICDS) and the Mid-Day Meal Scheme have had a transformative impact on child nutrition and early education. ICDS provides supplementary nutrition, preschool education, and immunisation services to children under six, while the Mid-Day Meal Scheme has improved child nutrition and school attendance in remote areas. These efforts have significantly enhanced child health outcomes and learning capacities. Despite these interventions, challenges persist in ensuring equitable access to healthcare, improving dietary diversity, and addressing socio-economic determinants of malnutrition. Moving forward, a more integrated and community-driven approach is needed to comprehensively address these issues.

4.4.2 *Expanding Educational Access and Quality*

Education initiatives in the Himalayan states have focused on improving accessibility, quality, and inclusivity. The National Education Policy (NEP) 2020 is a major reform aimed at holistic learning, foundational literacy, and teacher training. Complementing this, the Right to Education (RTE) Act, 2009 continues to guarantee free and compulsory education for children aged 6–14, helping bridge educational gaps in these regions. The Samagra Shiksha programme and PM SHRI Schools have enhanced school infrastructure, teacher training, and learning methodologies, ensuring better educational outcomes. In addition, experiential learning programmes like PRERNA and literacy initiatives like ULLAS have empowered both students and marginalised communities. Digital education platforms such as DIKSHA and SWAYAM Plus have further enabled access to quality learning resources, while the NISHTHA programme has significantly upskilled educators. Higher education support has also been strengthened through financial assistance initiatives like the PM-Vidyalaxmi Scheme, ensuring meritorious students from economically weaker backgrounds can pursue their academic goals. Increased funding for Kendriya Vidyalayas, Navodaya Vidyalayas, and higher education institutions has reinforced the government's commitment to expanding quality education in these regions.

4.4.3 Enhancing Skill Development and Employment

Recognising the need for skill-based education and employment generation, the government has launched various skill development programmes. The Skill India Mission, along with Pradhan Mantri Kaushal Vikas Yojana (PMKVY) and Deen Dayal Upadhyaya Grameen Kaushalya Yojana (DDU-GKY), has provided vocational training and entrepreneurship opportunities to youth in the Himalayan states. In addition, the National Apprenticeship Promotion Scheme (NAPS) and Start-up India/Stand Up India have encouraged industrial apprenticeships and self-employment. State-specific initiatives have also been instrumental in addressing local employment needs. The Uttarakhand Skill Development Mission (UKSDM) has emphasised tourism and disaster management, while Himachal Pradesh Kaushal Vikas Nigam (HPKVN) and skill development projects sponsored by ADB and other organisations have provided various skill trainings for youth in the state, as discussed in Box 4.4. Sikkim's programmes have strengthened skills in the green economy and sustainable tourism.

Box 4.4 Skill Development Projects in Himachal Pradesh

"Despite constraints such as its hilly terrain, poor connectivity, and predominantly rural population (90%), the state's economic, poverty, education, and health indicators have improved significantly since 2000 owing to the efforts of the Government of Himachal Pradesh (GOHP) to improve infrastructure and delivery of basic public services. While the government has successfully increased school and college enrolments over the past decade, it now faces the 'second-generation challenge of providing relevant and good quality technical and vocational education and training (TVET) opportunities to its youth to prepare them for the changing needs of the labour market. The project will assist GOHP in reforming and modernising its TVET institutions and programs to boost the employability of Himachal Pradesh's youth and improve their employment prospects."

Source: "India: Himachal Pradesh Skills Development Project," Sovereign Project | 49108–002; Asian Development Bank https://www.adb.org › projects.

4.5 Chapter Summary and Conclusion

The analysis in this chapter highlights key insights and concluding observations on education and health in the Himalayan states.

In education, enhancing the gross enrolment ratio (GER) and net enrolment ratio (NER) requires a comprehensive approach that addresses infrastructural, financial, and social barriers. Expanding secondary and higher secondary schools, particularly in remote areas, is crucial to reducing travel distances and improving accessibility (NITI Aayog, 2022c). In addition, targeted financial incentives, such as scholarships and financial aid for economically disadvantaged groups – especially girls and tribal communities – can significantly boost retention rates (Government of India, 2023b; Ministry of Education, 2023). Improving learning outcomes necessitates well-equipped schools with digital classrooms, sanitation facilities, and a sufficient number of qualified teachers (MHRD, 2023). Community-driven initiatives involving parents and local stakeholders can further promote awareness and increase participation in education (UNESCO, 2023). A holistic implementation of these interventions will lead to sustained enrolment, improved retention, and overall educational advancement, ultimately contributing to socio-economic growth in the region.

Reducing dropout rates and strengthening vocational training are essential to addressing high dropout rates in the Himalayan states, and require targeted policy interventions. Strengthening secondary school infrastructure in remote areas is critical to ensuring accessibility and minimising dropouts. Financial support mechanisms such as conditional cash transfers and scholarships provide economic relief to low-income families, enabling children to continue their education. Community participation in school governance has proven effective in improving retention rates, especially among female students. Integrating vocational training and skill development into school curricula can make education more relevant to local employment needs, thus encouraging students to stay in school. The incorporation of livelihood-based skills such as eco-tourism, agriculture, and handicrafts can create direct employment opportunities for students. In addition, continuous professional development programmes for teachers can enhance student engagement and learning outcomes, ultimately leading to higher retention rates (World Bank, 2023).

Improving transition rates and educational infrastructure is vital to ensuring smooth educational progression across different levels. Strengthening school infrastructure in remote and rural areas, along with providing financial support and scholarships – particularly for girls and tribal students – can encourage continued education. The integration of vocational and skill-based education offers students practical skills, enhancing their motivation to pursue higher studies. Community engagement programmes that educate parents on the long-term benefits of education can help reduce early dropouts and improve transition rates. These efforts will contribute to higher literacy rates, better employability, and overall socio-economic development in the Himalayan region.

Addressing disparities in teacher–student ratios and improving education quality require targeted recruitment of specialised teachers, particularly for secondary and higher secondary education. States like Tripura and Jammu and Kashmir, which face high teacher–student ratios, need focused recruitment drives to accommodate growing student populations (NUEPA, 2022). Strengthening teacher training programmes and professional development initiatives will equip educators with modern pedagogical techniques, thereby improving education quality in high-ratio classrooms (World Bank, 2023). Digital learning platforms and e-classrooms can supplement teacher shortages, particularly in remote areas (Ministry of Education, 2021).

Addressing infrastructure gaps, including poor road connectivity, limited electricity, and inadequate sanitation facilities, is crucial to improving educational access. Expanding off-grid renewable energy solutions, such as solar power, can enhance electricity access in schools (UNESCO, 2022). Bridging the digital divide by expanding internet connectivity and providing computer access is essential for promoting digital education. Government initiatives like PM e-Vidya and Digi-Education should prioritise underprivileged and remote areas (ASER, 2023). Additionally, well-maintained sanitation facilities, particularly for girls, should be a policy priority, with increased funding for initiatives like the Jal Jeevan Mission and Swachh Vidyalaya Abhiyan (World Bank, 2023).

In health and the healthcare system, strengthening healthcare in the Himalayan states requires a multi-pronged strategy that improves primary healthcare networks, expands telemedicine initiatives, increases financial investments in health infrastructure, and ensures an equitable distribution of healthcare professionals (UNDP, 2023). Integrating indigenous and traditional healthcare practices with modern medical systems can offer complementary benefits, particularly in states where Ayurveda, Sowa-Rigpa, and traditional tribal medicine play a significant role in community health (WHO, 2022).

The National Rural Health Mission (NRHM) and the National Urban Health Mission (NUHM), now integrated under Ayushman Bharat, have played a crucial role in strengthening primary healthcare infrastructure and financial protection (Ministry of Health and Family Welfare, 2022b). However, health financing gaps persist, with out-of-pocket expenditures (OOPE) remaining high, particularly in rural and tribal communities. Public health expenditure as a percentage of GDP in many Himalayan states remains below the recommended benchmark, underscoring the need for increased financial commitment to public health (NITI Aayog, 2022a).

Addressing healthcare workforce shortages and expanding access is critical, as a shortage of trained healthcare professionals exacerbates the healthcare access crisis. Many district hospitals and primary health centres (PHCs) lack specialists, particularly gynaecologists, paediatricians, and anaesthetists, which negatively impacts maternal and child health services (Ministry of Health and Family Welfare, 2022c). The doctor-to-population ratio in several Himalayan states remains below the WHO-recommended threshold of 1:1,000, putting additional strain on the healthcare system (WHO, 2021). Innovative approaches such as telemedicine, mobile health units, and community health worker programmes have shown promise in bridging accessibility gaps, but their sustainability requires stronger policy interventions and funding (World Bank, 2023).

Improving maternal and child health outcomes remains a priority, as disparities persist in infant mortality rate (IMR) and under-five mortality rate (U5MR) across the Himalayan states. Enhancing public health investments, expanding neonatal and paediatric care facilities, and strengthening maternal health interventions are critical to ensuring equitable healthcare access. Community-based health initiatives, nutritional support programmes, and targeted healthcare interventions for marginalised populations will be essential in improving child health outcomes in the region.

Tackling the rising anaemia burden in the Himalayan states requires comprehensive nutrition programmes, strengthened iron and folic acid supplementation initiatives, and policies promoting dietary diversification. Government interventions such as the Anaemia Mukt Bharat (AMB) campaign, the Mid-Day Meal Scheme, and food fortification programmes must be reinforced, particularly in high-burden states. Raising awareness about iron absorption enhancers (such as vitamin C-rich foods) and reducing inhibitors (such as excessive tea consumption) can help combat anaemia effectively (MoHFW, 2022c; WHO, 2023d).

Enhancing maternal healthcare and institutional deliveries is essential to reducing maternal mortality in the Himalayan region. This requires expanding healthcare infrastructure, improving transportation networks for timely medical referrals, and enhancing maternal nutrition programmes. Strengthening initiatives such as the Pradhan Mantri Surakshit Matritva Abhiyan (PMSMA), which provides free antenatal checkups, and ensuring emergency obstetric care in remote regions are crucial steps towards improving maternal health outcomes. Community-based maternal health awareness programmes, mobile health units, and digital health technologies can further enhance healthcare accessibility (WHO, 2023a).

Institutional delivery rates vary significantly across the Himalayan states, necessitating region-specific strategies to address logistical and socio-cultural barriers. Expanding mobile health clinics, improving last-mile connectivity, and strengthening maternal health awareness programmes are essential steps towards increasing institutional deliveries. Public–private partnerships to establish well-equipped birthing facilities in remote regions and leveraging telemedicine for antenatal care can significantly improve maternal and neonatal health outcomes (MoHFW, 2023b).

By addressing regional disparities and fostering inclusive growth, sustained policy focus on digital education, remote healthcare services, and localised skill development will be crucial in bridging existing gaps and ensuring long-term socio-economic stability in the Himalayan states.

5 Poverty and Inequality in Himalayan Economies

5.1 Introduction

The issue of poverty and inequality continues to attract significant attention from policymakers, economists, and development practitioners, especially in the context of the Sustainable Development Goals (SDGs), where SDG 1 targets the eradication of poverty and SDG 10 seeks to reduce inequality within and among countries. These dual objectives highlight the intricate linkage between poverty and inequality – two interrelated challenges that must be tackled simultaneously to achieve inclusive and sustainable development (UNDP, 2020; World Bank, 2022). While governments have initiated a variety of anti-poverty programmes over the past decades, assessing their impact necessitates continuous and nuanced measurement of poverty and inequality. Traditionally, poverty has been assessed by examining income or consumption below a fixed threshold, whereas inequality metrics look at the distribution of income or wealth across the entire population, capturing both relative and absolute disparities (Deaton & Drèze, 2002; Sen, 1997). Understanding inequality is thus not merely complementary but essential to reducing poverty sustainably, as a highly unequal society may experience slower poverty reduction even during periods of growth.

Recent studies and empirical evidence suggest a gradual decline in both poverty and inequality across many of India's Himalayan states, driven by targeted policy interventions, improved access to services, and expanded social protection schemes. However, substantial disparities persist between and within these states, particularly between their hilly and plain regions, tribal and non-tribal populations, and rural and urban settlements (Bhattacharya & Patel, 2020; OPHI, 2021). This spatial and social heterogeneity warrants a closer, disaggregated analysis to fully comprehend the regional dynamics of deprivation. In this context, the chapter explores the multiple dimensions of poverty and inequality in the Himalayan states of India, identifying them not only as statistical indicators but also as manifestations of deeper socio-economic and institutional asymmetries that hinder inclusive growth.

DOI: 10.4324/9781003595410-5

To investigate these dynamics, the chapter employs both traditional and alternative approaches to poverty and inequality measurement. The conventional method uses income or consumption-based indicators such as monthly per capita expenditure (MPCE), headcount ratios, and distributional analysis to estimate the magnitude and depth of poverty across rural and urban areas. The analysis also incorporates tools such as Engel curves to understand shifts in expenditure patterns over time and across income groups. Alongside this, the chapter adopts a multidimensional lens, drawing upon the Multidimensional Poverty Index (MPI), which considers deprivations in key areas like health, education, and living standards. Developed by the Oxford Poverty and Human Development Initiative (OPHI) and later adopted by the Government of India through NITI Aayog, the MPI provides a more holistic perspective on well-being and offers valuable insights into the overlapping disadvantages that shape poverty in these mountainous regions (Alkire & Santos, 2014; NITI Aayog, 2021a).

In parallel, the chapter also examines the extent and structure of inequality through tools such as the Gini coefficient and fractile-based income ratios. These measures allow for an in-depth analysis of disparities across income groups, particularly by comparing the expenditure levels of the top and bottom income fractiles. Such analysis reveals the degree to which economic gains have been equitably distributed, especially in states with complex topography and socio-ethnic diversity. Furthermore, the use of fractile ratios across time helps in assessing whether inequality is widening or narrowing, thereby aiding in the evaluation of the inclusiveness of growth trajectories in these states (Chatterjee & Ray, 2019; Himanshu, 2019b).

Data for this analysis have been drawn from a wide range of national sources, including the National Sample Survey (NSS) consumption surveys, National Family Health Surveys (NFHS), and other government data portals such as the SDG India Index and State Dashboards. These are further supplemented by secondary literature including policy briefs, peer-reviewed journal articles, evaluation reports, departmental publications, and academic books. Together, this comprehensive dataset enables a multi-layered understanding of poverty and inequality, helping to contextualise quantitative trends within broader socio-economic processes and policy environments.

The chapter is structured as follows: The first section presents the levels and trends of poverty in the Himalayan region using both MPCE and MPI indicators; the second section focuses on patterns of inequality through fractile analysis and Gini estimates; and the third part outlines key anti-poverty schemes implemented in these states, evaluating their scope, effectiveness, and reach. The concluding section synthesises the findings and reflects on the implications for policy, emphasising the need for geographically tailored, socially inclusive, and multidimensional strategies to address poverty and inequality in these ecologically and culturally unique regions.

5.2 Level of Poverty

5.2.1 *Poverty Headcount and Number of Poor*

The headcount ratio (HCR), which measures the percentage of the population living below the poverty line, reveals substantial improvements across the Himalayan states between 2011–12 and 2022–23 (see Table 5.1a). The most significant declines are seen in Manipur (–30.8 percentage points) and Arunachal Pradesh (–29.1), suggesting that these states have benefited considerably from targeted poverty alleviation programmes, enhanced public infrastructure, and greater inclusion in central development schemes. Initiatives such as the Pradhan Mantri Awas Yojana, expanded food security through the National Food Security Act (NFSA), and increased rural employment opportunities under MGNREGA may have collectively contributed to this transformation (Planning Commission, 2014; NITI Aayog, 2021b). Despite their geographical isolation and lower baseline economic indicators, these North-eastern states demonstrate that focused social spending, improved connectivity, and better institutional mechanisms can yield impactful poverty reduction outcomes (Baruah, 2020; Nayyar & Sharma, 2020).

In contrast, states like Himachal Pradesh, Sikkim, and Jammu and Kashmir had relatively lower initial poverty levels, and while their absolute declines in HCR were smaller – Himachal (–5.9), Sikkim (–6.6), J&K (–7.6) – these represent significant progress in already better-performing states. Himachal Pradesh's success is often attributed to its strong investments in human development indicators, such as education and healthcare, as well as a high degree of female participation in development initiatives (Dev & Ravi, 2019). Sikkim has adopted innovative models of sustainable development, including organic farming, universal healthcare, and rural infrastructure, which have improved livelihoods while preserving ecological balance (UNDP, 2023). Jammu and Kashmir, with support from central transfers and special status until 2019,

Table 5.1a Headcount Ratio, 2011–12 to 2022–23 (in %)[1]

	2011–12	*2022–23*	*% Change*
Arunachal Pradesh	34.7	5.59	–29.1
Himachal Pradesh	8.1	2.16	–5.9
Jammu and Kashmir	10.4	2.73	–7.6
Manipur	36.9	6.08	–30.8
Meghalaya	11.9	6.55	–5.3
Mizoram	20.4	2.49	–17.9
Nagaland	18.9	9.41	–9.5
Sikkim	8.2	1.64	–6.6
Tripura	14.1	1.89	–12.2
Uttarakhand	11.3	2.65	–8.6
All India	**21.9**	**5.27**	**–16.7**

Source: Household Consumption Survey (2011–12 and 2022–23), and NITI Aayog (2024).

also witnessed welfare improvements, despite facing persistent political and economic instability. Meanwhile, the modest declines in Meghalaya (–5.3) and Nagaland (–9.5) highlight ongoing development gaps, possibly linked to limited diversification of livelihoods, higher dependency on subsistence agriculture, and weaker state capacity in service delivery (Verghese, 2023).

When compared with the all-India average, which saw a reduction in HCR from 21.9 per cent in 2011–12 to 5.27 per cent in 2022–23 (a decline of –16.7 percentage points), most Himalayan states performed well, with many exceeding the national average in terms of poverty reduction. This trend is notable, especially given the region's challenging topography, conflict zones, and lower levels of industrialisation. The data indicates that regional disparities in poverty are narrowing to some extent, reflecting better fiscal decentralisation, strengthened safety nets, and perhaps rising remittance flows from out-migrating workers (World Bank, 2022; Chand & Singh, 2021). However, the disparities in the pace of poverty decline across these states also underscore the need for state-specific strategies – focusing on inclusive growth, climate resilience, and employment generation – to sustain the gains made so far. As the country moves toward multidimensional poverty assessments, continuing investments in education, health, and gender equity will be critical in ensuring that poverty alleviation translates into long-term human development improvements in the Himalayan region (UNDP, 2023; World Bank, 2022).

The number of poor people, measured in absolute terms, has declined significantly across the Himalayan states from 2011–12 to 2022–23, mirroring broader national trends in poverty reduction (see Table 5.1a). The significant reductions in the number of poor were recorded in Arunachal Pradesh (–404,000), Manipur (–827,000), and Jammu and Kashmir (–955,000), demonstrating the success of targeted development policies and central assistance programmes like the Pradhan Mantri Awas Yojana, PMGSY (rural roads), and Direct Benefit Transfers (Planning Commission, 2014; Dev & Ravi, 2019; World Bank, 2022; NITI Aayog, 2021a). The consistent efforts in expanding basic services, food security coverage, and rural employment schemes helped reduce the vulnerability of populations in remote and conflict-affected regions.

However, states like Meghalaya and Nagaland witnessed relatively modest reductions in the number of poor – only 142,000 and 166,000, respectively. This comparatively slower progress could be attributed to various structural challenges, including limited economic diversification, high dependency on traditional agriculture, and weaker institutional delivery mechanisms (Verghese, 2023). Despite being geographically part of the resource-rich North-east, these states have struggled to integrate into national economic flows due to weaker connectivity and fragile law and order situations in certain districts. Furthermore, the lack of large-scale industrial or service-sector opportunities restricts income mobility, particularly for youth and women, reinforcing a cycle of persistent poverty. In contrast, states like Himachal

Table 5.1b Number of Poor (in 000), 2011–12 to 2022–23

	2011–12	*2022–23*	*Change*
Arunachal Pradesh	491	87	-404
Himachal Pradesh	559	161	-398
Jammu and Kashmir	1,326	371	-955
Manipur	1,023	196	-827
Meghalaya	361	219	-142
Mizoram	228	31	-197
Nagaland	376	210	-166
Sikkim	51	11	-40
Tripura	524	78	-446
Uttarakhand	1,160	309	-851
All India	**2,69,783**	**75,291**	**-1,94,492**

Source: Household Consumption Survey (2011–12 and 2022–23).

Pradesh and Sikkim – though having smaller populations – saw commendable reductions relative to their size, due to long-term investments in education, healthcare, women's participation, and decentralised governance (Chand & Singh, 2021; UNDP, 2023).

At the all-India level, the number of poor declined dramatically by approximately 194 million, dropping from 269.8 million in 2011–12 to 75.3 million in 2022–23 (Table 5.1b). This trend indicates substantial progress driven by economic growth, improved social safety nets, and the scaling up of anti-poverty programmes across the country. Many Himalayan states outperformed or kept pace with the national trend in proportional terms, demonstrating that even geographically challenging and demographically diverse regions can achieve significant poverty reduction with the right mix of policy interventions and governance reforms (Nayyar & Sharma, 2020; World Bank, 2022). However, the variation in the extent of reduction across these states also highlights the importance of tailored, context-specific approaches to poverty alleviation. Going forward, sustaining this momentum will require greater focus on inclusive economic opportunities, addressing regional disparities, and ensuring that gains in poverty reduction are complemented by progress in health, education, and climate resilience (UNDP, 2023; Dev & Ravi, 2019).

5.2.2 Poverty Headcount and Number of Poor: Rural–Urban Differences

The headcount ratio (HCR) by rural and urban sectors across Himalayan states from 2011–12 to 2022–23 reveals a substantial decline in poverty, particularly in rural areas. States such as Mizoram (Table 5.2a), Arunachal Pradesh, and Manipur witnessed remarkable reductions in rural poverty, with Mizoram recording a drop from 35.4 per cent to 2.96 per cent (–32.5 percentage points), Arunachal Pradesh from 38.9 per cent to 6.8 per cent (–32.1), and Manipur from 38.8 per cent to 7.57 per cent (–31.2). These

Table 5.2a Headcount Ratio by Sector, 2011–12 to 2022–23 (in %)

	Rural		*Urban*		*% Change*	
	2011–12	*2022–23*	*2011–12*	*2022–23*	*Rural*	*Urban*
Arunachal Pradesh	38.9	6.8	20.3	2.07	−32.1	−18.3
Himachal Pradesh	8.5	2.13	4.3	2.45	−6.4	−1.9
Jammu and Kashmir	11.5	2.85	7.2	2.46	−8.7	−4.7
Manipur	38.8	7.57	32.6	2.99	−31.2	−29.6
Meghalaya	12.5	6.71	9.3	5.91	−5.8	−3.4
Mizoram	35.4	2.96	6.4	2.11	−32.5	−4.3
Nagaland	19.9	15.35	16.5	2.4	−4.6	−14.1
Sikkim	9.9	1.75	3.7	1.51	−8.1	−2.2
Tripura	16.5	2.05	7.4	1.64	−14.5	−5.8
Uttarakhand	11.6	2.55	10.5	2.84	−9.1	−7.6
All India	25.7	6.85	13.7	2.78	−18.9	−10.9

Source: Household Consumption Survey (2011–12 and 2022–23).

trends suggest a significant improvement in rural livelihoods, likely driven by increased public investment in rural infrastructure, improved access to basic services, and stronger implementation of welfare schemes like MGNREGA, rural electrification, and rural health initiatives (NITI Aayog, 2021b; Dev & Ravi, 2019). In addition, enhanced connectivity and the development of agro-based enterprises may have supported income diversification in rural Himalayan economies, leading to a significant upliftment of rural households (World Bank, 2022). In contrast, states like Nagaland and Meghalaya saw relatively modest rural poverty reductions, pointing to continued structural challenges in achieving inclusive rural growth (Verghese, 2023).

Urban poverty in the Himalayan states also saw notable reductions, though at a slower pace compared to rural areas. For instance, urban poverty in Manipur fell sharply from 32.6 per cent to 2.99 per cent (−29.6 percentage points), and in Arunachal Pradesh from 20.3 per cent to 2.07 per cent (−18.3), reflecting effective urban poverty mitigation through schemes like the National Urban Livelihoods Mission (NULM), improved access to affordable housing under PMAY-Urban, and expanded urban employment through skill development programmes (UNDP, 2023; MoHUA, 2022). However, in some states such as Nagaland and Meghalaya, the decline in urban poverty was relatively modest – at −14.1 and −3.4 percentage points, respectively – suggesting limitations in urban economic absorption capacity and a persistent lack of formal employment opportunities in smaller urban centres. Himachal Pradesh and Sikkim exhibited very low urban poverty levels to begin with, and their marginal changes over time indicate near-universal access to urban services and stronger human development indicators, including education and health (Dev & Ravi, 2019; Chand & Singh, 2021).

At the all-India level, rural poverty declined from 25.7 per cent in 2011–12 to 6.85 per cent in 2022–23, and urban poverty fell from 13.7 per cent to 2.78 per cent, marking percentage point reductions of –18.9 and –10.9, respectively. This shows that the Himalayan states, particularly in rural areas, outperformed the national average in poverty reduction, underscoring the effectiveness of geographically targeted policies and welfare programmes. The narrowing rural–urban poverty gap in several of these states also reflects improvements in rural infrastructure, decentralised governance, and enhanced state capacity to implement centrally sponsored schemes effectively (Planning Commission, 2014; Nayyar & Sharma, 2020). Nonetheless, the heterogeneity in performance across states suggests the need for continued monitoring of both sectoral and regional dimensions of poverty. Moving forward, strengthening local institutions, promoting sustainable employment generation, and aligning poverty reduction strategies with climate resilience and inclusive urbanisation will be crucial in sustaining and deepening these gains across the Himalayan belt (World Bank, 2022; UNDP, 2023).

The sector-wise distribution of the number of poor in the Himalayan states between 2011–12 and 2022–23 highlights a substantial reduction in rural poverty, which has been a central focus of India's poverty alleviation efforts over the past decade (Table 5.2b). Uttarakhand (–635,000) witnessed the most dramatic decline in the rural poor, followed by Arunachal Pradesh (–346,000), and Manipur (–580,000). These reductions point towards the positive impact of key rural development initiatives such as the Mahatma Gandhi National Rural Employment Guarantee Act (MGNREGA), rural electrification under Saubhagya, and the expansion of rural housing through PMAY-Gramin

Table 5.2b Number of Poor (in 000) by Sector, 2011–12 to 2022–23

	Rural		*Urban*		*Change*	
	2011–12	*2022–23*	*2011–12*	*2022–23*	*Rural*	*Urban*
Arunachal Pradesh	425	79	66	8	-346	-58
Himachal Pradesh	529	142	30	19	-387	-11
Jammu and Kashmir	1,073	269	253	102	-804	-151
Manipur	745	165	278	31	-580	-247
Meghalaya	304	178	57	41	-126	-16
Mizoram	191	17	37	14	-174	-23
Nagaland	276	186	100	25	-90	-75
Sikkim	45	6	6	5	-39	-1
Tripura	449	52	75	27	-397	-48
Uttarakhand	825	190	335	119	-635	-216
All India	2,16,658	61,772	53,125	13,519	-1,54,886	-39,606

Source: Household Consumption Survey (2011–12 and 2022–23).

(World Bank, 2022; NITI Aayog, 2021a). Moreover, greater access to financial services through the Jan Dhan Yojana and better implementation of the Public Distribution System (PDS) have enhanced economic resilience in rural areas. Himachal Pradesh and Sikkim, already low in rural poverty in 2011–12, made further strides due to their strong investment in rural education, health, and local governance institutions (Chand & Singh, 2021).

Urban poverty in these states also declined, albeit at a slower pace and lower base compared to rural areas. For example, Manipur saw a sharp fall in its urban poor population, from 278,000 to just 31,000 (a reduction of 247,000), indicating a significant improvement in urban livelihoods and service access. Similarly, Jammu and Kashmir reduced their urban poor populations by 151,000 and 775,000, respectively. These outcomes can be attributed to the implementation of urban poverty reduction schemes such as the National Urban Livelihoods Mission (NULM), Pradhan Mantri Awas Yojana-Urban, and improved municipal governance in tier-II and tier-III cities (MoHUA, 2022; UNDP, 2023). However, in some states like Meghalaya and Sikkim, reductions in urban poverty were modest, possibly due to the already small urban poor base or limited urbanisation. These findings align with broader trends showing that while urban poverty is numerically smaller in the Himalayan region compared to rural poverty, addressing it requires continued focus on inclusive urban development, housing, and employment-generation in urban informal sectors (Nayyar & Sharma, 2020).

At the national level, the number of poor declined sharply in both rural and urban areas – by approximately 154.9 million in rural India and 39.6 million in urban India – highlighting a broad-based decline in poverty across India during the period. When compared to this national trend, several Himalayan states – particularly Arunachal Pradesh, Manipur, and Uttarakhand – exhibited performance either on par or exceeding the national rate of reduction in both sectors. This reflects successful alignment of state policies with centrally sponsored schemes, effective last-mile delivery, and socio-economic improvements at the grassroots level (Planning Commission, 2014; Dev & Ravi, 2019). Nevertheless, the persistence of relatively higher poverty in states like Nagaland and Meghalaya underscores the importance of deepening institutional capacity, enhancing human capital, and addressing state-specific challenges such as ethnic conflict, infrastructural gaps, and market access barriers (Verghese, 2023). Going forward, sustaining poverty reduction in both rural and urban settings will require more integrated development planning that incorporates climate resilience, digital inclusion, and gender-responsive economic strategies (World Bank, 2022; UNDP, 2023).

5.2.3 Changes in Average Monthly Per Capita Expenditure

The growth in real average monthly per capita expenditure (MPCE) between 2011–12 and 2023–24 in the Himalayan states reveals substantial improvements in living standards, with notable rural–urban variations (see Table 5.3). States such as Sikkim, Tripura, and Arunachal Pradesh recorded particularly high rural MPCE growth rates – 11.5 per cent, 9.3 per cent, and 6.3 per cent, respectively – outpacing the all-India rural growth rate of 5.0 per cent. These figures indicate enhanced rural livelihoods, improved access to public goods, and rising income levels in remote regions. This is consistent with findings that the expansion of rural infrastructure, social protection programmes like MGNREGA, and agricultural diversification have significantly contributed to raising rural consumption in these states (Dev & Ravi, 2019; Chand et al., 2021). Sikkim's robust growth, for instance, is often attributed to its successful organic farming initiative, high human development indicators, and sustained government investment in rural health and education (NITI Aayog, 2021b). In contrast, Nagaland (3.8 per cent) and Meghalaya (4.0 per cent) recorded relatively slower rural MPCE growth, suggesting persistent challenges related to market access, conflict, and governance capacity (Verghese, 2023).

In urban areas, MPCE growth has generally been stronger than, or on a par with, rural areas, particularly in states like Sikkim (10.3 per cent), Manipur (7.7 per cent), Tripura (7.1 per cent), and Arunachal Pradesh (7.0 per cent), indicating a significant rise in urban consumption patterns. This trend reflects the growing role of urbanisation in driving economic development in these states, with enhanced access to services, job opportunities in the informal and public sectors, and improved infrastructure (MoHUA, 2022; UNDP,

Table 5.3 Growth Rate in Real Average MPCE (in Rs.) by Sector (at 2011–12 prices)

	Rural		*Urban*		*ACGR*	
	2011–12	*2023–24*	*2011–12*	*2023–24*	*Rural*	*Urban*
Arunachal Pradesh	1782	3,710	2654	5,968	6.3	7.0
Himachal Pradesh	2034	3,544	3259	5,577	4.7	4.6
Jammu and Kashmir	1743	2,974	2485	3,852	4.6	3.7
Manipur	1502	2,790	1483	3,628	5.3	7.7
Meghalaya	1475	2,369	2436	4,747	4.0	5.7
Mizoram	1644	3,623	2568	5,262	6.8	6.2
Nagaland	2059	3,209	2284	4,916	3.8	6.6
Sikkim	1565	5,756	2608	8,438	11.5	10.3
Tripura	1334	3,869	2144	4,905	9.3	7.1
Uttarakhand	1726	3,112	2339	4,560	5.0	5.7
All-India	1430	2,580	2630	4,277	5.0	4.1

Note: To convert nominal values into real values, CPI-Rural and CPI-Urban are used.

ACGR, annual compound growth rate.

Source: Household Consumption Survey (2011–12 and 2022–24).

2023). Rapid urban growth in smaller cities and towns in the North-east has also benefited from increased central and state transfers under schemes like AMRUT and PMAY-Urban. However, states such as Jammu and Kashmir (3.7 per cent) and Himachal Pradesh (4.6 per cent) registered lower urban MPCE growth, potentially due to economic disruptions such as conflict, slower private investment, and a limited industrial base. The data aligns with broader literature emphasising that while urban consumption is generally higher, it remains vulnerable to inequality and informality, which can temper growth outcomes (Nayyar & Sharma, 2020).

Comparatively, the all-India figures for MPCE growth – 5.0 per cent in rural and 4.1 per cent in urban areas – suggest that many of the Himalayan states, particularly the smaller North-eastern ones, have outperformed national averages. This indicates the relative success of targeted policies and region-specific development strategies aimed at overcoming geographic and socio-political constraints (Planning Commission, 2014; World Bank, 2022). Nonetheless, disparities persist both within and across states. For example, despite strong growth in MPCE, states like Manipur and Mizoram still face structural issues such as limited formal employment and vulnerability to climate shocks, necessitating more resilient economic planning. Overall, the rise in MPCE reflects an encouraging trend of improved purchasing power and living standards across the Himalayan region, but sustaining this momentum will require addressing gaps in employment, connectivity, and sustainable livelihoods (Chand & Singh, 2021; UNDP, 2023).

5.2.4 Food and Non-Food Expenditure (Engel Curve)

The changing pattern of food and non-food expenditure across Himalayan states, as reflected in Table 5.4, aligns closely with Engel's Law, which posits that as household incomes rise, the proportion of income spent on food tends to decline, while the share of non-food expenditure rises. The rural sector in most Himalayan states shows a clear decline in the food-to-non-food expenditure ratio from 2011–12 to 2023–24, indicating a shift in consumption priorities consistent with rising income levels and improved living standards. For instance, Tripura's rural ratio declined significantly from 1.35 to 0.87. This trend implies that while food remains a vital part of rural household budgets, increased disposable incomes have enabled greater spending on non-food essentials like education, health, transportation, and communication (Dev & Ravi, 2019; Chand & Singh, 2021). The exceptions, like Arunachal Pradesh and Sikkim where the ratio remained relatively stable, may reflect a more balanced or slower transition due to their unique demographic and geographical conditions.

In urban areas, the Engel curve dynamic is even more prominent. All states show a decline or relative stabilisation in the food-to-non-food expenditure ratio between 2011–12 and 2023–24. For example, Jammu and Kashmir

Table 5.4 Changes in Food and Non-Food Expenditure Ratio

	Rural		*Urban*	
	2011–12	*2023–24*	*2011–12*	*2023–24*
Arunachal Pradesh	1.09	1.01	0.75	0.79
Himachal Pradesh	0.90	0.81	0.74	0.61
Jammu and Kashmir	1.24	1.05	0.92	0.74
Manipur	1.18	0.95	1.10	0.77
Meghalaya	1.14	1.01	0.73	0.65
Mizoram	1.20	0.89	0.93	0.70
Nagaland	1.14	0.86	1.03	0.83
Sikkim	1.10	1.01	0.79	0.86
Tripura	1.35	0.87	1.02	0.77
Uttarakhand	0.98	0.78	0.86	0.62
All-India	1.12	0.76	0.74	0.64

Source: Household Consumption Survey (2023–24).

saw a drop from 0.92 to 0.74, while Himachal Pradesh declined from 0.74 to 0.61. This shift signifies an increasing urban preference for non-food consumption such as housing, healthcare, digital services, and lifestyle-related expenditures. This trend also corresponds with urbanisation and rising educational attainment, which drive more diversified and aspirational spending habits (Nayyar & Sharma, 2020; World Bank, 2022). In some states like Sikkim and Arunachal Pradesh, urban non-food expenditure has surpassed food expenditure, showing a reversal in traditional spending behaviour, which is often observed in more developed and urbanised economies. This reflects a maturing consumption pattern, characteristic of higher living standards and greater economic diversification.

At the all-India level, the decline in the food-to-non-food expenditure ratio – from 1.12 to 0.76 in rural areas and from 0.74 to 0.64 in urban areas – confirms a broad structural transformation in household consumption across the country. The Himalayan states largely mirror this national trend, albeit with varying degrees. The ongoing reduction in food expenditure ratios highlights a movement away from subsistence toward improved quality of life, made possible by rising incomes, targeted public transfers, and enhanced access to goods and services (Planning Commission, 2014; UNDP, 2023). This change has policy implications, particularly for rural development and food security strategies, which must now account for evolving expenditure priorities and the growing role of services in household budgets. Furthermore, as households move toward greater non-food spending, the demand for better infrastructure, health, and education services in remote regions becomes more pressing (Chand et al., 2021). Overall, the shift observed through Engel curve analysis illustrates both economic progress and changing social aspirations in the Himalayan states.

5.2.5 Multidimensional Poverty

The Multidimensional Poverty Index (MPI) is a comprehensive measure that captures the multiple deprivations experienced by individuals across three critical dimensions – health, education, and standard of living. Unlike income-based poverty metrics, the MPI reflects the interlinked nature of disadvantages that impede human well-being. Developed by the Oxford Poverty and Human Development Initiative (OPHI) and the United Nations Development Programme (UNDP), the MPI incorporates two key components: the headcount ratio (H) and the intensity of poverty (A). The headcount ratio (H) denotes the proportion of the population classified as multidimensionally poor. It is calculated by dividing the number of poor individuals by the total population. The intensity of poverty (A), on the other hand, reflects the average percentage of weighted indicators in which poor individuals are deprived. The MPI value is derived by multiplying these two components:

$$MPI = H \times AMPI = H \times AMPI = H \times A$$

This measure provides both the incidence and the depth of poverty, enabling a nuanced understanding of poverty dynamics (Alkire & Santos, 2014). The MPI framework used in this study is based on the baseline report released by NITI Aayog in 2021, which draws from the National Family Health Survey, round 5 (NFHS-5, 2019–21) as detail given in Table 5.5.

Headcount ratio. In the Himalayan states, between NFHS-4 (2015–16) and NFHS-5 (2019–21), most regions witnessed significant reductions in the headcount ratio. For example, Arunachal Pradesh saw a drop from 24.23 per cent to 13.76 per cent, indicating improved access to education, health, and standard of living (Alkire & Santos, 2014; OPHI, 2021). These reductions in multidimensional poverty, particularly in the North-eastern states, align with expanded access to social sector schemes like PMAY-G, Ujjwala Yojana, and rural electrification initiatives (NITI Aayog, 2021b). However, despite the reduction in headcount poverty, several North-eastern states – Meghalaya, Nagaland, Arunachal, and Tripura – still have much higher poverty rate than other Himalayan states (Table 5.5 and Map 5.1).

Intensity of poverty. The intensity of poverty, however, has shown relatively less variation across survey rounds, indicating that while fewer people are poor, those who remain poor continue to suffer from substantial deprivations. Meghalaya, for instance, recorded a very small change in intensity – from 48.08 per cent to 48.01 per cent – even though the headcount ratio dropped from 32.54 per cent to 27.79 per cent. This suggests persistent challenges in improving the depth of deprivation among the poorest, particularly in tribal and remote regions (Drèze & Khera, 2017). In contrast, states like Mizoram and Uttarakhand experienced not only reduced headcounts but also noticeable improvements in intensity, highlighting

Table 5.5 Headcount Ratio Intensity and MPI Score

States	*NFHS-4 (2015–16)*			*NFHS-5 (2019–21)*		
	Headcount Ratio (Per Cent)	*Intensity (Per Cent)*	*MPI*	*Headcount Ratio (Per Cent)*	*Intensity (Per Cent)*	*MPI*
Arunachal Pradesh	24.23	47.25	0.115	13.76	43.04	0.059
Himachal Pradesh	7.59	39.44	0.030	4.93	40.22	0.020
Manipur	16.96	44.61	0.076	8.10	41.91	0.034
Meghalaya	32.54	48.08	0.156	27.79	48.01	0.133
Mizoram	9.78	47.42	0.046	5.30	45.62	0.024
Nagaland	25.16	46.29	0.116	15.43	42.61	0.066
Sikkim	3.82	41.20	0.016	2.60	41.02	0.011
Tripura	16.62	45.03	0.075	13.11	42.68	0.056
Uttarakhand	17.67	44.35	0.078	9.67	41.99	0.041
Jammu and Kashmir	12.56	44.17	0.055	4.80	42.11	0.020
All India	24.85	47.14	0.117	14.96	44.39	0.066

Source: NFHS (2015–16 and 2019–21).

successful targeting and delivery of entitlements in states with stronger administrative capacity and better health infrastructure (World Bank, 2022).

MPI scores. This combines headcount and intensity, where we see a consistent trend of reduction across all Himalayan states, reflecting an overall improvement in multidimensional well-being. Mizoram and Sikkim report particularly low MPI scores in NFHS-5 (0.024 and 0.011, respectively), suggesting that these states have been relatively successful in eradicating multidimensional poverty. In contrast, Meghalaya continues to have a higher MPI (0.133), above the all-India average of 0.066, underlining the need for targeted interventions, particularly in maternal and child health, sanitation, and education (UNDP & OPHDI, 2021). These variations across the Himalayan belt point to structural inequalities and geographic isolation, which can impede the delivery of social programmes.

Comparing these trends with all-India averages, the Himalayan states are, in general, outperforming the national figures in the recent period, especially states like Himachal Pradesh, Sikkim, and Jammu and Kashmir. India's headcount ratio fell from 24.85 per cent to 14.96 per cent, while the MPI fell from 0.117 to 0.066. Several Himalayan states performed significantly better than this average in both rounds. For instance, Sikkim's MPI in 2019–21 (0.011) was six times lower than the national average. These positive outcomes are likely due to a combination of sustained investments in public health, inclusive education systems, and livelihood programmes that reach into rural and tribal areas (UNDP, 2022).

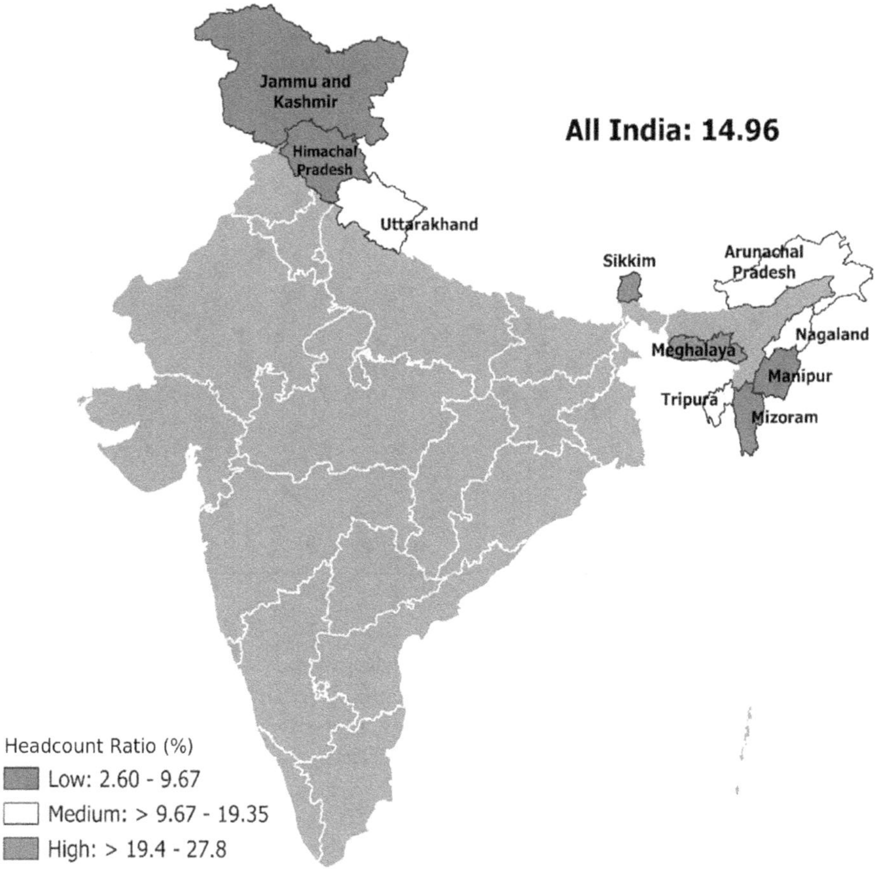

Map 5.1 Headcount ratio.
Source: NFHS (2019–21).

It is also critical to note the variations within the Himalayan region. While Himachal Pradesh and Sikkim have MPI scores far below the national average, states like Meghalaya, and Nagaland continue to record relatively high scores, highlighting persistent disparities within the region. These differences underscore the importance of localised policy responses, especially in states facing constraints like difficult terrain, poor connectivity, and higher tribal populations, which affect programme delivery (Bhattacharya & Patel, 2020). Moreover, the resilience of intensity levels in some states suggests that surface-level improvements may not always reflect deeper structural shifts in access to quality services and opportunities.

5.3 Level of Inequality

5.3.1 *Gini Coefficient*

The Gini coefficient, a widely used measure of income or consumption inequality, reveals notable trends in the Himalayan states over the period 2011–12 to 2023–24 (see Table 5.6). In rural areas, most Himalayan states experienced a decline in inequality, with states like Arunachal Pradesh showing a sharp drop from 0.361 to 0.226, and Himachal Pradesh from 0.301 to 0.226. These reductions align with improvements in rural income distribution due to expanded social protection schemes, rural employment programmes, and better access to basic services, which have collectively supported inclusive rural development (Dev & Ravi, 2019; Mehrotra, 2021). At the all-India level, rural inequality also declined significantly, from a Gini coefficient of 0.306 to 0.230, indicating that rural inequality reduction is not unique to the Himalayan region but part of a broader national trend catalysed by welfare interventions such as PM-KISAN, MGNREGA, and targeted PDS expansions (Planning Commission, 2014; World Bank, 2022). Urban areas in the Himalayan states similarly saw a decline in inequality in most cases, though the extent varied. Uttarakhand and Tripura recorded substantial decreases in the urban Gini coefficient, with Uttarakhand falling from 0.372 to 0.266 and Tripura from 0.302 to 0.199.

These improvements may reflect more balanced urban growth, better access to services, and expanded livelihoods in peri-urban and secondary cities. However, exceptions exist, such as Sikkim and Meghalaya, where urban inequality slightly increased (Gini rising from 0.232 to 0.260 and 0.236 to

Table 5.6 Consumption (MPCE) Inequality (Gini Coefficient) in Rural and Urban Areas

	Rural			*Urban*		
	2011–12	*2023–24*	*% Change*	*2011–12*	*2023–24*	*% Change*
Arunachal Pradesh	0.361	0.226	-0.135	0.334	0.247	-0.087
Himachal Pradesh	0.301	0.226	-0.075	0.350	0.266	-0.084
Jammu and Kashmir	0.264	0.214	-0.050	0.317	0.244	-0.073
Manipur	0.211	0.177	-0.034	0.211	0.189	-0.022
Meghalaya	0.190	0.187	-0.003	0.236	0.238	0.002
Mizoram	0.247	0.220	-0.027	0.259	0.200	-0.059
Nagaland	0.197	0.197	0.000	0.233	0.184	-0.049
Sikkim	0.223	0.246	0.023	0.232	0.26	0.028
Tripura	0.225	0.182	-0.043	0.302	0.199	-0.103
Uttarakhand	0.272	0.21	-0.062	0.372	0.266	-0.106
All-India	0.3060	0.23	-0.076	0.390	0.279	-0.111

Source: Author's own calculations.

0.238, respectively). These outliers may point to structural disparities between fast-growing urban elites and slower income gains among the working poor or migrants (Jha & Gaiha, 2015; UNDP, 2023). At the all-India level, urban inequality also decreased – from 0.390 to 0.279 – demonstrating progress toward more equitable consumption patterns, though urban inequality still remains higher than rural inequality overall, due to greater heterogeneity in job quality and access to assets in cities (Nayyar & Sharma, 2020).

Overall, the decline in Gini coefficients across most Himalayan states and the country as a whole reflects a positive shift in income and consumption distribution, particularly in rural areas. The narrowing inequality can be attributed to enhanced state capacity, social safety nets, and inclusive growth strategies, including rural electrification, improved education access, and digital financial inclusion (Chand et al., 2021; World Bank, 2022). However, persistent or rising urban inequality in certain regions like Sikkim suggests that policies must continue to target vulnerabilities in the urban informal sector and address regional disparities. The Gini trends, especially when seen in conjunction with poverty reduction and rising MPCE, point to the importance of sustaining broad-based growth and redistributive policies that ensure the gains of economic development reach all segments of the population.

5.3.2 Inequality: Average MPCE Fractile Ratio, 2023–24

The MPCE (monthly per capita expenditure) fractile ratio is an important tool to assess consumption inequality across various population segments.[2] The F12/F1 ratio indicates the disparity in average consumption between the richest (12th) and poorest (1st) fractile classes, while F6/F1 and F12/F6 represent inequalities in the middle and upper halves of the population, and the combined ratio of top three to bottom three fractiles ((F10+F11+F12)/(F1+F2+F3)) captures broader consumption inequality (see Tables 5.7a–5.7c and Annexure Chapter 5). Among the Himalayan states in 2023–24, Sikkim recorded the highest F12/F1 ratio at 6.9, followed by Arunachal Pradesh at 6.0, which is equal to the all-India average (see Table 5.7a). This indicates a significant gap in consumption between the top and bottom segments in these regions, reflecting skewed income distribution and unequal access to resources and opportunities in certain parts of the Himalayas (Mehrotra & Parida, 2021; Chand et al., 2021). In contrast, states like Manipur (4.0) showed relatively lower inequality, suggesting a more compressed consumption distribution, possibly due to strong community-based redistribution mechanisms or more homogeneous economic structures (UNDP, 2023).

Examining the F6/F1 and F12/F6 ratios reveals deeper nuances of inequality. Most Himalayan states showed a consistent pattern with F6/F1 values between 1.8 and 2.2 and F12/F6 between 2.1 and 2.7, indicating that while the gap between the middle and lower classes is modest, the upper-middle to rich class exhibits greater divergence. For example, in Mizoram and Himachal Pradesh, both F12/F1 and F12/F6 ratios hover around 5.2–5.3 and 2.6–2.7,

Table 5.7a Inequality in Average MPCE Over 12 Fractile Classes: MPCE Fractile Ratios in 2023–24 (Rural Area)

	F12/F1	*F6/F1*	*F12/F6*	*(F10 + F11 + F12)/ (F1 + F2 + F3)*
Arunachal Pradesh	6.0	2.2	2.7	3.6
Himachal Pradesh	5.3	1.9	2.7	3.4
Jammu and Kashmir	4.9	1.9	2.6	3.3
Manipur	4.0	1.9	2.1	2.7
Meghalaya	4.3	2.0	2.2	2.9
Mizoram	5.2	2.0	2.6	3.3
Nagaland	5.0	2.1	2.4	3.1
Sikkim	6.9	2.6	2.7	4.1
Tripura	4.4	1.8	2.4	2.8
Uttarakhand	5.3	1.9	2.7	3.3
All-India	**6.0**	**2.1**	**2.9**	**3.6**

Note: F, average MPCE fractile.

Source: Household Consumption Survey (2023–24).

Table 5.7b Inequality in Average MPCE Over 12 Fractile Classes: MPCE Fractile Ratios in 2023–24 (Urban Area)

	F12/F1	*F6/F1*	*F12/F6*	*(F10 + F11 + F12)/ (F1 + F2 + F3)*
Arunachal Pradesh	6.9	2.5	2.8	4.0
Himachal Pradesh	6.9	2.1	3.2	4.2
Jammu and Kashmir	5.9	1.9	3.0	3.8
Manipur	4.5	2.0	2.3	2.9
Meghalaya	6.0	2.0	3.0	3.7
Mizoram	4.7	1.8	2.6	3.0
Nagaland	4.3	1.8	2.3	2.8
Sikkim	6.8	2.1	3.2	4.1
Tripura	4.6	1.7	2.7	3.0
Uttarakhand	7.2	2.2	3.2	4.3
All-India	8.5	2.4	3.6	4.7

Source: Household Consumption Survey (2023–24).

respectively, suggesting that inequality is more pronounced at the upper end of the distribution. These patterns echo findings from national studies indicating that growth in recent years has been disproportionately captured by the upper fractiles of the population, especially in urbanised or rapidly developing regions (Dev & Ravi, 2019; World Bank, 2022). The persistence of such trends despite poverty reduction indicates that while absolute deprivation may be decreasing, relative disparities remain a concern.

Table 5.7c Changes in Inequality in Average MPCE Over 12 Fractile Classes: Ratios (2011–12 and 2023–24) (Rural Areas)

	F12/F1	*F6/F1*	*F12/F6*	*(F10 + F11 + F12)/(F1 + F2 + F3)*
Arunachal Pradesh	-4.0	0.1	-1.9	-2.6
Himachal Pradesh	-3.2	-0.1	-1.4	-1.1
Jammu and Kashmir	-1.6	-0.2	-0.5	-0.3
Manipur	-0.7	0.2	-0.6	-0.5
Meghalaya	-0.1	0.1	-0.2	0.1
Mizoram	-0.7	-0.1	-0.2	-0.3
Nagaland	0.8	0.5	-0.3	0.3
Sikkim	2.8	1.1	-0.1	1.3
Tripura	-0.7	-0.1	-0.3	-0.5
Uttarakhand	-1.0	0.2	-0.8	-0.4
All-India	-2.6	-0.1	-1.0	-1.0

Source: Household Consumption Survey (2011–12 and 2023–24).

The combined top three to bottom three consumption ratio provides a composite measure of inequality. In Sikkim, this ratio is 4.1, higher than the all-India average of 3.6, suggesting deeper consumption divides, possibly driven by rapid economic development in select sectors such as tourism and hydropower that benefit a limited section of the population. States like Manipur (2.7) and Tripura (2.8) exhibit more equitable consumption patterns. These findings align with Engel's law, which states that as income rises, the proportion of income spent on food declines, leading to diversified consumption patterns for richer households and increasing non-food expenditures (Engel, 1857; Sen & Himanshu, 2004). This divergence in expenditure trends further fuels inequality in the upper fractiles, as the richer groups consume more services and durable goods, widening the gap from lower-income households. Hence, despite broad poverty reduction, these MPCE fractile ratios highlight that inequality remains entrenched in the structure of rural economies in the Himalayan states.

The inequality in urban monthly per capita expenditure (MPCE), measured through fractile ratios in the Himalayan states for 2023–24, reveals notable disparities when compared with the all-India averages. The F12/F1 ratio, which compares the average consumption of the richest and poorest fractile groups, is highest in Uttarakhand (7.2), Arunachal Pradesh and Himachal Pradesh (6.9 each), and Sikkim (6.8). While these states show significant inequality, their F12/F1 values are still below the national urban average of 8.5. This suggests that urban inequality, though pronounced, is relatively less extreme in these Himalayan regions than at the national level, perhaps due to more uniform levels of development or smaller urban populations (Dev & Ravi, 2019; World Bank, 2022). States like Nagaland (4.3), Mizoram (4.7), and Manipur (4.5) report lower inequality, reflecting either limited urban economic stratification or a higher degree of income homogeneity among urban residents.

The mid-fractile comparisons – F6/F1 and F12/F6 – offer insights into the inequality within the lower and upper halves of the consumption distribution. While the F6/F1 ratio varies from 1.7 in Tripura to 2.5 in Arunachal Pradesh, the F12/F6 ratios are consistently above 2.3 across most Himalayan states, peaking at 3.2 in Uttarakhand, Sikkim, and Himachal Pradesh. This pattern indicates that the wealthiest segments are pulling away from both the middle and lower classes, driving a widening consumption gap in urban areas. These trends are consistent with findings from the literature that urban inequality in India has been increasingly shaped by unequal access to high-paying formal jobs, digital services, and real estate gains that benefit the top fractiles, while the lower and middle-income urban households remain tied to stagnant or informal sectors (Mehrotra & Parida, 2021; Himanshu, 2019a). Furthermore, urbanisation in the Himalayan states is still evolving, and emerging divides may intensify if policy responses to inclusive development lag behind.

The composite measure – (F10 + F11 + F12)/(F1 + F2 + F3) – reinforces these observations, with values ranging from 2.8 in Nagaland to 4.3 in Uttarakhand and 4.2 in Himachal Pradesh, compared to 4.7 for all-India. This ratio captures the broader polarisation between the top and bottom thirds of the consumption distribution. In states like Sikkim (4.1), and Jammu and Kashmir (3.8), the data indicates a marked shift in expenditure concentration toward the top fractiles. These patterns resonate with Engel's Law, where higher-income households increase their share of non-food spending, driving inequality in overall MPCE as the affluent diversify their consumption basket significantly more than the poor (Engel, 1857; Sen & Himanshu, 2004). As urban economies in the Himalayan states transition, ensuring access to quality education, healthcare, housing, and skilling for lower-income groups will be crucial to mitigating widening inequalities in consumption and well-being.

The changes in rural consumption inequality across Himalayan states, as measured by MPCE fractile ratios between 2011–12 and 2023–24, suggest a general decline in disparity, with some state-specific deviations. The F12/F1 ratio, which compares the consumption of the richest (12th fractile) to the poorest (1st fractile), declined most sharply in Arunachal Pradesh (−4.0), Himachal Pradesh (−3.2), and all-India (−2.6), indicating a notable narrowing of the consumption gap between the top and bottom income groups in rural areas. This decline may be attributed to improved access to social protection schemes, rural infrastructure, and livelihood support, especially through employment programmes like MGNREGA and targeted subsidies (Dev, 2020; Mahajan, 2022). In contrast, states like Sikkim (+2.8) and Nagaland (+0.8) saw an increase in this ratio, pointing toward rising inequality likely driven by uneven benefits from tourism, remittances, or localised growth hubs, reflecting the differentiated impacts of rural development across the region (World Bank, 2022).

Examining the F6/F1 and F12/F6 ratios, which reflect inequality between the middle and lower class and between the upper and middle class, respectively, further clarifies these dynamics. For most Himalayan states, the F6/F1 ratio remained relatively stable or experienced marginal changes, suggesting that the lower-middle segment has not diverged significantly from the poorest group. However, the F12/F6 ratio declined across all states except Meghalaya and Nagaland, indicating that the upper class's expenditure growth slowed compared to that of the middle class. This trend aligns with recent findings that rural consumption patterns have become more compressed due to food price stabilisation, expansion of rural connectivity, and increased penetration of welfare delivery systems, which have benefited the lower and middle fractiles more uniformly than before (Himanshu, 2019b; Mehrotra & Parida, 2021). Arunachal Pradesh and Himachal Pradesh experienced some of the sharpest contractions in this upper-middle gap, which may reflect more equitable rural development efforts in these states.

The final inequality metric – (F10 + F11 + F12)/(F1 + F2 + F3) – also shows a decline in most states, with Arunachal Pradesh (–2.6), Himachal Pradesh (–1.1), and all-India (–1.0) showing the strongest reductions. This implies a shrinking divide between the richest and poorest terciles in rural consumption, consistent with the broader pattern of rural convergence. Notably, Sikkim and Nagaland report positive changes in this ratio, further underscoring rising inequality in select geographies. Such divergence can be linked to the unique structural features of their rural economies, such as dependence on high-value horticulture or government employment that disproportionately benefits upper-income rural households (Chatterjee et al., 2021). The general reduction in rural inequality across most Himalayan states, in line with national trends, reflects the evolving shape of India's rural Engel curve, where food expenditure shares have declined and non-food items such as education, healthcare, and consumer durables have risen more uniformly, aiding in consumption smoothing and reducing extreme disparities.

The changes in urban consumption inequality across the Himalayan states from 2011–12 to 2023–24, as reflected in the MPCE fractile ratios, indicate a broadly favourable trend toward reduced disparities, with notable variation across regions. The most striking declines are observed in Arunachal Pradesh (F12/F1: -6.5) and all-India (–6.1), suggesting a sharp contraction in the gap between the top and the bottom urban income fractiles. This trend indicates that urban consumption growth among lower-income groups has outpaced or kept pace with that of the wealthier segments. Improved access to urban employment, enhanced financial inclusion, and expanded social welfare provisioning, such as urban affordable housing, PDS reforms, and DBT mechanisms, likely played roles in this compression of inequality (Dev, 2020; Mehrotra & Parida, 2021). States like Jammu and Kashmir and Tripura also show strong reductions in F12/F1 ratios, highlighting the success of targeted regional development strategies and post-conflict reconstruction efforts in enhancing inclusivity (World Bank, 2022).

Looking at the F6/F1 and F12/F6 ratios helps understand inequality within the lower-middle and upper-middle income groups. Most states report relatively stable or slightly declining F6/F1 ratios, implying little movement in inequality between the middle and bottom fractiles. However, a marked reduction in F12/F6 is observed in many states, such as Arunachal Pradesh (–1.7), and all-India (–1.8), indicating slower growth of upper-class consumption relative to the middle class. These shifts align with Engel's law, where rising urban incomes lead to a declining share of food expenditures and a convergence in non-food consumption patterns, such as education, communication, and mobility, particularly due to increasing urban penetration of digital goods and services (Chatterjee et al., 2021; Himanshu, 2019a). States like Sikkim, however, saw increases in all fractile ratios, suggesting widening inequality likely driven by regional economic shifts like the expansion of tourism and green industrial development that may have disproportionately benefited wealthier urban households.

Finally, the composite metric – (F10 + F11 + F12)/(F1 + F2 + F3) – which reflects the overall urban consumption inequality between the richest and poorest terciles, decreased in most states, supporting the narrative of a broader narrowing of disparities (Table 5.7d). Arunachal Pradesh (–3.7), and all-India (–2.4) report substantial reductions, indicating that urban growth and welfare programmes have helped rebalance consumption patterns. However, a few exceptions remain: Meghalaya, Mizoram, and Sikkim show either stability or marginal increases in inequality, potentially linked to region-specific developments such as uneven infrastructure gains or the role of informal economies that benefit certain strata disproportionately. Overall, the evidence confirms a progressive shift toward urban consumption equity in most Himalayan states, in tandem with national trends, possibly driven by the structural transformation of urban economies, changes in the Engel curve, and policy-led inclusion mechanisms (Mahajan, 2022; World Bank, 2022).

Table 5.7d Changes in Inequality in Average MPCE Over 12 Fractile Classes: Ratios (2011–12 and 2023–24) (Urban Areas)

	F12/F1	*F6/F1*	*F12/F6*	*(F10 + F11 + F12)/ (F1 + F2 + F3)*
Arunachal Pradesh	–6.5	–0.5	–1.7	–3.7
Himachal Pradesh	–2.3	–0.5	–0.3	–0.8
Jammu and Kashmir	–3.1	–0.4	–0.9	–1.4
Manipur	–0.2	0.1	–0.3	–0.4
Meghalaya	0.0	–0.3	0.4	–0.1
Mizoram	–0.6	–0.4	0.2	–0.7
Nagaland	–0.4	–0.2	0.0	–0.7
Sikkim	1.6	0.1	0.7	0.9
Tripura	–3.5	–0.4	–1.1	–1.8
Uttarakhand	–2.7	–0.3	–0.6	–1.2
All-India	–6.1	–0.3	–1.8	–2.4

Source: Household Consumption Survey (2011–12 and 2023–24).

5.4 Anti-Poverty Schemes

The Himalayan states, including the North-eastern region, Uttarakhand, Himachal Pradesh, and Jammu and Kashmir, have witnessed notable progress in the implementation of anti-poverty schemes, especially in the last decade. The Mahatma Gandhi National Rural Employment Guarantee Scheme (MGNREGS) has played a critical role in offering employment and reducing rural poverty in these geographically challenging areas. Studies have shown that in states like Sikkim, Arunachal Pradesh, and Himachal Pradesh, MGNREGS has improved household incomes, reduced distress migration, and enhanced rural infrastructure (Kapur et al., 2023). The scheme's gender-inclusive provisions have further benefitted women, particularly in states like Nagaland and Meghalaya, by increasing their participation in the workforce and enhancing their decision-making power within households (Singh & Choudhary, 2022). However, challenges related to delayed wage payments, limited administrative capacity, and difficult terrain persist in many remote districts, constraining the full potential of the scheme in reducing poverty sustainably (Government of India, 2024).

The Deendayal Antyodaya Yojana – National Rural Livelihoods Mission (DAY-NRLM) has also gained momentum in the Himalayan region, focusing on mobilising women into self-help groups (SHGs), promoting financial inclusion, and supporting livelihoods. The programme has demonstrated significant success in enhancing women's empowerment and creating sustainable income-generating activities in the North-eastern states and Uttarakhand, where traditional handicrafts, handlooms, and agri-based microenterprises have been supported under NRLM initiatives (Das & Sharma, 2021). In Jammu and Kashmir, the UMEED scheme, a regional adaptation of DAY-NRLM, has emerged as a strong vehicle for poverty reduction, particularly among conflict-affected and economically marginalised women (Khan, 2022). Despite these achievements, barriers such as limited access to markets, poor connectivity, and climate vulnerability pose ongoing challenges to the scaling up and sustainability of livelihood interventions in remote Himalayan regions (Economic Survey, 2024).

The Pradhan Mantri Awas Yojana-Gramin (PMAY-G) has contributed to improving living standards by providing pucca housing to the rural poor in fragile mountain environments. In Himachal Pradesh and Uttarakhand, PMAY-G has facilitated improved access to sanitation, drinking water, and energy in rural households, thereby reducing multidimensional poverty (NITI Aayog, 2023). In the North-eastern states, although progress has been made, implementation has been uneven due to land tenure complexities, extreme weather events, and logistical hurdles (Lalnunmawia et al., 2023). In addition, schemes such as the National Social Assistance Programme (NSAP) and the Public Distribution System (PDS) have provided essential social safety nets to vulnerable populations, especially the elderly, single women, and tribal communities in these regions; one such case is discussed for Jammu and Kashmir in Box 5.1. While the convergence of multiple schemes has enhanced the poverty reduction framework in the Himalayan belt, further efforts are required to address systemic bottlenecks, strengthen local institutions, and ensure inclusive development in ecologically sensitive and socio-politically diverse contexts (Government of India, 2024).

Box 5.1 Food Entitlement Scheme in Jammu and Kashmir

"It is a matter of concern that the poverty ratio of Jammu & Kashmir increased from 9.4% to 10.4% between 2009 and 2013 (Planning Commission, 2014). Also, the multidimensional poverty index report revealed that 12.58% of the population in J&K is multidimensionally poor (NITI Aayog, 2023), which indicates that more people are now food insecure and covered under welfare schemes like the public distribution system (PDS) in the state" (p. 36).

"Since more than one million people live BPL in J&K, these people are economically unable to access sufficient foodgrains. Thus, an insufficient allocation of PDS foodgrains will directly push them into the severe condition of food insecurity" (p. 37).

Source: "Evaluation of Household Awareness and Utilisation of Jammu and Kashmir Food Entitlement Scheme by Khurshid Ahmad Rather," *Economic and Political Weekly*, Vol. 59, Issue No. 5, February 3, 2024.

Over the years, the Government of India has introduced a wide range of anti-poverty programmes, mainly livelihood schemes, which aim to alleviate poverty, enhance employment opportunities, and improve the overall quality of life for economically disadvantaged groups. Prominent among these initiatives are the Mahatma Gandhi National Rural Employment Guarantee Scheme (MGNREGS), Pradhan Mantri Awas Yojana – Gramin (PMAY-G), Pradhan Mantri Gram Sadak Yojana (PMGSY), Deendayal Antyodaya Yojana – National Rural Livelihoods Mission (DAY-NRLM), Garib Kalyan Rozgar Abhiyan (GKRA), the Food for Work Programme, and the Prime Minister's Rozgar Yojana, among others, as discussed in the case of North-eastern states and Uttarakhand in Box 5.2 and Box 5.3.

Box 5.2 Livelihood Projects in North-east Region

"Financial inclusion of rural communities was one of the strategic mechanisms employed by the North East Rural Livelihood Project (NERLP) to enhance the incomes and livelihood opportunities of the

poor and address the wide gap in financial inclusion between the North East Region (NER) of India and the rest of the country" (p. 3).

"In the mountainous terrain of the North Eastern Region (NER), the presence of bottom-up community led institutions is a critical step towards social and financial inclusion of the rural poor and marginalised. Six of 10 most financially excluded states and more than half of the bottom 100 districts that are least financially linked in India are in the NER. For a meaningful, targeted and effective financial inclusion of the poorest of the poor, a bottom-up approach must be tailored to the regional context. In the NER, where strong local financial institutions are scarce, SHGs are perfectly poised to become the vehicle of economic development and empowerment, so that community members may have a voice in determining and improving their own future" (p. 9).

Source: "South Asia Agriculture and Rural Growth Discussion Note Series," January 2021, the North East Rural Livelihood Project: https://documents1.worldbank.org › curated › pd.

These programmes have played a crucial role in mitigating poverty through the creation of employment opportunities, development of rural infrastructure, provision of affordable housing, promotion of entrepreneurship, and expansion of access to vital services such as healthcare, sanitation, and safe drinking water. Furthermore, they have contributed significantly to the development of sustainable livelihoods and the socio-economic empowerment of rural populations, particularly women and marginalised groups.

Nevertheless, despite these positive outcomes, several of these initiatives have faced persistent challenges in implementation and outreach. Obstacles such as limited awareness among beneficiaries, bureaucratic inefficiencies, infrastructural constraints, and shortcomings in beneficiary identification and targeting have, at times, limited the overall effectiveness of these schemes. Strengthening institutional capacity, enhancing transparency, and fostering greater community engagement are essential steps toward improving the efficacy and long-term impact of India's anti-poverty efforts.

Several independent studies have examined the impact of anti-poverty programmes across various Himalayan regions and have emphasised the need for better and more holistic management of these initiatives. The selected references are presented in the following boxes.

Box 5.3 Livelihood Scheme in Uttarakhand

"In Uttarakhand, the poverty is low, but there is concern about generating livelihood for people in the hills, who tend to get by-passed

by the growth process. The strategy to provide sustainable livelihoods to all people of Uttarakhand, in the hills and in plains will rely primarily on two growth-driver sectors. Transforming hill agriculture with emphasis on horticulture, including aromatic and medicinal plants, for improving productivity and creating livelihood, along with promotion of state-wide tourism, both carried out on a Mission Mode, will help the state in generating the necessary livelihood options. The Micro, Small and Medium Enterprises (MSME) is a cross-cutting sector which will link up to the growth-driver sectors to help generate further employment downstream. Simultaneous efforts to develop renewable energy in the form of small hydro-power and expansion of Information Technology to all parts of the state economy will make the growth plan sustainable and make its fundamentals stronger" (p. 6).

Source: Uttarakhand Vision 2030, Institute for Human Development (2018) for the Department of Planning, Government of Uttarakhand.

5.5 Chapter Summary and Conclusion

To conclude, Himalayan states have made remarkable strides in reducing consumption or income poverty and multidimensional poverty over the past decade, reflecting the impact of targeted welfare schemes, improved service delivery, and strengthened rural development initiatives. The decline in both the incidence and, in several cases, the intensity of poverty suggests that people are not only moving above the poverty threshold but also experiencing better quality of life. States such as Sikkim, Himachal Pradesh, and Arunachal Pradesh illustrate that concerted policy action, even in geographically challenging environments, can lead to meaningful outcomes. However, disparities persist across the region, with states like Meghalaya and Nagaland continuing to grapple with deep-rooted deprivations, indicating that the fight against poverty is far from over.

When it comes to inequality, the picture is more nuanced. While rural inequality has declined significantly across most states, pointing to the success of redistributive schemes and inclusive development models, urban inequality remains a concern. Urban areas continue to witness stark consumption and income divides, particularly in states such as Sikkim, where the gains from economic growth have not been equitably shared. The fractile analysis further reveals a widening gap between the richest and the rest, especially among the upper income brackets. These findings underscore the need to sustain efforts towards reducing inequality, not just through income transfers, but also by expanding opportunities and assets for the disadvantaged across both rural and urban spaces.

In light of these findings, future policy interventions must prioritise geographically sensitive, inclusive development strategies that account for the unique needs of Himalayan states. Enhancing last-mile delivery of services, investing in quality education and healthcare, and ensuring that tribal and remote populations are not left behind will be critical. The integration of climate resilience into poverty reduction efforts is equally important, given the environmental fragility of the region. States that have achieved substantial progress offer useful models, but scaling these successes requires greater decentralisation, inter-sectoral coordination, and adaptive governance tailored to local contexts.

Going forward, narrowing both poverty and inequality will depend on sustaining momentum through innovation in public service delivery, better data systems for monitoring multidimensional deprivation, and enhanced fiscal and institutional capacities in lagging states. Policy focus should shift from short-term poverty relief to long-term human development, with attention to decent employment generation, gender equity, and climate-adaptive infrastructure. A more spatially differentiated approach, anchored in evidence and local realities, will help translate national successes into comprehensive regional gains, ensuring that the path toward prosperity in the Himalayan states is both inclusive and sustainable.

Notes

1 Several scholars question the comparability of HCES 2022–23 with earlier CES rounds and argue that other evidences don't support a steep poverty decline (Anand, 2024; Himanshu et al., 2025; Kishore & Jha, 2024; Ghatak & Kumar, 2024; Mehrotra & Kumar, 2024). Even so, tracking poverty and headcount ratios over time remains useful; independent studies also show low poverty in 2023–24 – just not as low as official government estimates.

2 A fractile class of MPCE (monthly per capita expenditure) refers to a segment of the population that falls between two specific percentiles. The population is ranked in ascending order based on MPCE and divided into 12 fractile classes, each representing a fixed share (typically 5% per cent) of the estimated population – for example, "0–5 per cent," "5–10 per cent," "10–20 per cent," . . ., "95–100 per cent."

6 Sustainability and Disasters in Himalayan Economies

6.1 Introduction

The global mountain agenda traces its origins to the 1992 UN Conference on Environment and Development, commonly known as the "Earth Summit," held in Rio de Janeiro, Brazil. During this summit, mountains received significant attention through "Agenda 21," the adopted plan of action, which included an entire chapter dedicated to them: *Chapter 13: Managing Fragile Ecosystems – Sustainable Mountain Development*. The United Nations Conference on Environment and Development (UNCED) also led to the creation of the UN Commission on Sustainable Development. However, sustainable development is an ongoing process that seeks to meet present needs while ensuring the long-term availability and responsible use of natural and other resources. It also considers the well-being of future generations (Price, 2004). The 2010 *Global Change and the World's Mountains* conference, held in Perth, Scotland, provided a valuable platform to assess the current state of mountain research, evaluate its progress, and explore its contributions to sustainable mountain development. Another key milestone was the designation of 2002 as the International Year of Mountains, which led to the establishment of the International Partnership for Sustainable Development of Mountain Regions. The International Year of Sustainable Mountain Development 2022 presents a valuable opportunity to highlight the importance of mountains and mountain communities in global sustainability efforts, their role in maintaining ecological balance, and their contribution to achieving the Sustainable Development Goals.[1]

The Sustainable Development Goals (SDGs), approved by the United Nations, represent a set of global objectives and strategies designed to eradicate poverty, safeguard the environment, and ensure that, by 2030, every person can experience peace and prosperity. Within these SDGs, Sustainable Development Goal 13, known as "Climate Action," seeks to take immediate steps to address climate change and its consequences. SDG 13 comprises five specific targets.

These targets encompass enhancing resilience and adaptability concerning climate-induced disasters (Target 13.1), integrating climate change

DOI: 10.4324/ 9781003595410-6

considerations into policymaking and planning (Target 13.2), developing knowledge and capacities to tackle climate change (Target 13.3), implementing the United Nations Framework Convention on Climate Change (UNFCCC) (Target 13.a), and promoting mechanisms that bolster capacity in planning and management (Target 13.b). Each of these targets incorporates one or more metrics that assist in assessing and overseeing progress.

The UNFCCC establishes the legal framework and principles for international cooperation for addressing climate change, with the overarching goal of stabilising greenhouse gas concentrations in order to prevent "dangerous anthropogenic interference with the climate system." The Kyoto Protocol, adopted in December 1997, builds on the UNFCCC by requiring industrialised countries and those in transition to market economies to set specific emissions reduction targets for a group of six greenhouse gases (GHGs), thus aiming to enhance the effectiveness of global climate change mitigation efforts.

Mountains are prone to earthquakes, volcanic eruptions, and natural hazards like landslides, floods, and avalanches due to steep slopes and high precipitation. Climate change worsens these risks by altering rainfall, snowfall, and temperature patterns, leading to more extreme events, including wildfires and earlier snowmelt (UNEP, 2002; Klein et al., 2019). Mountain communities traditionally relied on local ecosystems, but external forces have driven change in recent decades. Development projects, market pressures, and commercialisation have often had negative impacts. Key threats include agricultural expansion, infrastructure development, deforestation, resource extraction, tourism, and conflicts (Byers, 1995).

Climate change has significantly affected human well-being and livelihood, primarily manifesting through extreme weather events such as heatwaves, droughts, floods, and cyclones. These events have exacerbated issues related to water resource management, reduced agricultural output and increased food insecurity, raised health hazards, damaged vital infrastructure, and disrupted essential services such as water supply, sanitation, education, energy, and transportation.

This chapter underscores the vital need for a mountain-specific development framework to foster sustainable and inclusive growth in India's hill and Himalayan regions. Such a framework aims to align environmental preservation with socio-economic progress, taking into account the distinct vulnerabilities and development potential of mountain ecosystems. The failure to incorporate a mountain perspective into mainstream development planning has led to adverse consequences, including ecological degradation, biodiversity loss, and the erosion of livelihoods for mountain communities. This neglect has also contributed to the growing frequency and intensity of natural disasters – such as landslides, earthquakes, and floods – causing widespread harm to both human and animal life, along with long-term socio-economic disruptions (Awasthi, 2024).

Building on this premise, the chapter is organised into four key sections: Section 2 explores the ecological fragility and socio-economic vulnerability of mountain ecosystems, Section 3 examines the occurrence and impact of natural disasters across the Himalayan region, Section 4 addresses the mounting risks posed by climate change-induced disasters, and Section 5 concludes with a synthesis of key insights and policy recommendations to support resilient, inclusive, and ecologically sound development in mountain regions.

6.2 Vulnerability of Mountain Ecosystems

Mountain economies are particularly vulnerable to disasters due to their unique geographical and ecological characteristics. Their inherent fragility makes them prone to natural calamities and environmental degradation, often stemming from overexploitation of resources and a lack of sustainable resource management. This fragility adversely affects land and forest ecosystems. Common disasters such as floods, landslides, and earthquakes frequently result in substantial loss of life, property, and natural resources. Many mountain regions have endured multiple natural and human-induced disasters, which have severely impacted human well-being (Awasthi et al., 2014).

The mountainous ecosystems around the world, as outlined, exhibit common bioclimatic characteristics and shared concerns. Whether we look at the mountainous regions of the European Alps, the Andes mountain ranges in South America (comprising Venezuela, Colombia, Ecuador, Peru, Bolivia, Chile, and Argentina), or the countries in the Hindu Kush Himalayan (HKH) region of South Asia (including Afghanistan, Pakistan, India, China, Nepal, Bhutan, Bangladesh, and Myanmar), a primary issue they face is a changing mountain environment due to resource degradation caused by excessive exploitation. This has led to a decrease in biomass production, marginalisation, and diminished human well-being.

Many of these mountain regions are susceptible to various natural hazards such as landslides, earthquakes, avalanches, and diseases (Li Tianchi et al., 2001), and they are also often plagued by human conflicts and wars, particularly in economically disadvantaged areas (Libiszewski & Bachler, 1997), which further increases the vulnerability of mountain-dwelling populations. In some of these mountain areas, minority communities not only bear the brunt of resource exploitation but also face issues related to ethnic conflicts, violence, and warfare (Ives et al., 1997). However, there are significant differences in the economic development trajectories of mountainous regions in developed European countries as compared to those in the Andean and HKH regions.

In Europe and Central Asia, the focal point of climate change impacts and climate-driven weather events is the mountainous regions. These events include droughts, floods, mudslides, and landslides. When combined with unsustainable land use practices such as overgrazing or deforestation, these impacts pose a significant threat not only to natural landscapes but also to agricultural lands, residences, and transportation infrastructure such as roads and bridges. In addition, rising temperatures and the melting of glaciers in mountainous areas put the water supply for millions of people in valleys throughout Europe and Central Asia at risk (World Bank Blogs, 2021).

The Andean region faces a significant threat from both natural disasters and the impacts of climate change. Within this relatively compact area, various events such as earthquakes, tsunamis, landslides, volcanic eruptions, forest fires, and floods frequently occur. This proximity provides an opportunity to study intricate interconnections. For instance, intense rainfall can trigger a landslide that obstructs a river, subsequently resulting in flooding (Andes – Laboratory for Natural Hazards, 2018).

The HKH region is known for being highly susceptible to disasters such as floods, landslides, avalanches, and earthquakes, leading to significant negative consequences for both people's lives and their means of making a living. According to estimates, the four most extensive floods between 2000 and 2013 in this area resulted in the loss of over 10,000 lives and the displacement of more than 50 million people (GRID-Arendal, 2018). Such substantial rainfall greatly increases the likelihood of floods and landslides. In China, some 59,000 homes collapsed and 150,000 others were damaged due to record rainfall around the country's capital in August 2023.

There is a significant lack of institutional frameworks and capacity to effectively manage multi-hazard environments and cascading disasters. Such environments are prevalent across many countries in the Hindu Kush Himalaya (HKH) region. Among the most vulnerable populations are women, who face additional risks due to gender-based norms and systemic barriers (Vaidya et al., 2019).

6.3 Disasters in Himalayan Regions of India

Himalayan states, although possessing comparable biophysical traits, exhibit diverse development trends. These regions are susceptible to numerous natural calamities, with frequent heavy rains, avalanches, soil erosion, landslides, and floods, thereby causing huge losses in terms of lives and livelihoods. Disasters caused by natural hazards like earthquakes, floods, cyclones, and droughts are referred to as natural disasters.

Although State Climate Action Plans (SCAPs) have been prepared to address vulnerabilities such as landslides, flash floods, glacial lake outbursts, and shifting agro-ecological zones, localised vulnerability assessments remain vital. Uttarakhand uses GIS mapping for landslide and flood risks, while Sikkim has developed glacier monitoring systems. Many states have adopted ecosystem-based adaptation in their climate plans – Meghalaya through community forest management, Arunachal Pradesh via catchment restoration, and Himachal Pradesh with an integrated cross-sector approach. States like Sikkim, Nagaland, and Himachal Pradesh involved communities, NGOs, and experts, with Sikkim aligning its SCAP with overall state development strategies.

However, much remains to be done. Many SCAPs lack clear baselines, targets, and timelines, rely heavily on consultancy reports, and show weak budgetary integration. Vulnerability mapping is still insufficiently localized, capacity building remains limited, and departmental coordination is weak, with most working in silos.

Disasters in Indian mountain regions are discussed to underscore the critical need for comprehensive disaster preparedness and mitigation strategies.

6.3.1 *Jammu and Kashmir (J&K) and Ladakh*

The Jammu and Kashmir (J&K) and Ladakh regions are among the most severely affected by natural disasters. Characterised by young mountain ranges with fragile rock formations, these areas are highly vulnerable to debris, mud, and rock flows triggered by disruptions in slope stability. Their geographical features and extreme climatic variations contribute to a wide range of natural hazards. The region has witnessed major floods, devastating earthquakes, and recurring avalanches and landslides. Significant disasters in its recent history include the 2005 earthquake, the flash floods and landslides of 2010, and the extensive flooding in 2014 (Patel et al., 2020).

6.3.1.1 *Landslides*

Most areas in Jammu and Kashmir are prone to landslides, with districts such as Bandipora, Kargil, Anantnag, Kishtwar, Pulwama, and Shopian being particularly vulnerable (SDMP, 2017). According to a report by RMSI, a global leader in geospatial and engineering solutions, Jammu and Kashmir experienced 80 landslide events between 1982 and 2018, resulting in approximately 333 casualties. Landslides frequently occur in specific locations, including Banihal, Ramban, Doda, Rajouri, Kishtwar, and Udhampur, particularly along the national highway (Kumar & Tyagi, 2021). Notable landslide-prone areas include the Bali, Samroli, and Narsoo areas, as documented by various researchers (Pandey, 2018).

In 2010, the Ladakh region experienced one of its most devastating landslides caused by a cloudburst. The intense rainfall triggered multiple landslides and flash floods, resulting in 234 fatalities, with foreign nationals comprising approximately 10 per cent of the casualties (Gupta et al., 2012).

On April 29, 2024, the Jammu–Srinagar National Highway was shut down due to multiple landslides triggered by heavy rainfall across various parts of Jammu and Kashmir. This highway, the only all-weather road connecting Kashmir to the rest of the country, was obstructed by landslides at Mehar, Gangroo, Mom Passi, and Kishtwari Pather in the Ramban district.

On August 14, 2025, a powerful cloudburst hit a remote hamlet in the Kishtwar region of the Chenab Valley, triggering sudden, torrential rainfall. The disaster claimed many lives, with hundreds more injured and missing. Raging torrents of water mixed with debris tore through the settlement, demolishing homes, sweeping away livestock, and inflicting severe damage on infrastructure. The intensity of the deluge left a trail of devastation, severing road links and severely hindering urgent rescue and relief efforts. A deadly cloudburst struck Jammu and Kashmir's Kathua district on August 17, 2025, claiming about a dozen lives and unleashing landslides and flash floods. The torrential waters swept away roads, damaged houses, and disrupted train services along the Jammu–Pathankot line. At least 117 people lost their lives between August 14 and August 30, 2025.

The hills surrounding the Jammu–Srinagar highway are predominantly rocky and barren, making them highly susceptible to disturbances, whether natural or man-made. In recent years, the frequency of landslides has increased, largely due to ongoing construction activities and the expansion of the highway and tunnels. The region is highly susceptible to floods, as major rivers like the Jhelum, Chenab, and Indus flow through densely populated areas (SDMP, 2017). The bowl-shaped topography of the Kashmir Valley, with significant altitude variations, increases the flood risk in its low-lying areas. In addition, in the region's two major urban centres – Jammu and Srinagar – the decline in wetlands, including lakes and ponds that serve as natural sponges, has led to frequent urban flooding (Gupta, 2014).

An exceptionally heavy rainfall event in September 2014 triggered one of the most severe and widespread cases of flooding in the region. This flooding had a severe impact on 10 out of the 22 districts in the area, particularly affecting districts in the southern part of Kashmir. Approximately 30 per cent of the urban areas in the region were submerged, and the floods affected 2,600 villages, with 400 of them being completely inundated. The impacts of floods and avalanches have had severe effects on the lives and livelihoods of people.

6.3.1.2 Earthquakes

Located adjacent to the Himalayas, the J&K and Ladakh region lies within a mountain-building geological zone, making it prone to frequent seismic activity (Hassan, 2014). The region has witnessed several earthquakes throughout its long history. During the period from 1889 to 1990, a total of 170 earthquakes were reported in the area (Hassan, 2014). One of the most devastating earthquakes to hit the region occurred in 1885, and its impact was widespread, resulting in the loss of at least 3,081 lives, affecting areas from Srinagar to Gilgit and even reaching as far as Shimla in the neighbouring state of Himachal Pradesh (Anees & Bhat, 2016). The October 2005 earthquake in Kashmir was one of the most severe natural disasters in South Asia, with a magnitude of 7.6. It claimed at least 1,350 lives and left 6,266 injured in the state of Jammu and Kashmir. Among the most devastating quakes in the region's history, it struck on October 8, 2005. More recently, two consecutive earthquakes on August 20, 2024, with magnitudes of 4.9 and 4.8, and their epicentre in Baramulla, highlight the region's significant seismic vulnerability.

6.3.2 Disasters in Uttarakhand

Uttarakhand has a long-standing history of natural disasters, particularly earthquakes and landslides, which have caused significant loss of life and extensive damage to infrastructure and property (Awasthi et al., 2014). Over the past century, the region has repeatedly faced such calamities. The state has been severely affected by earthquakes, cloudbursts, flash floods, and intense rainfall, all of which have taken a heavy toll on both human and animal lives. These disasters have led to considerable destruction of homes, roads, public infrastructure, forests, plantations, and agricultural land, severely impacting livelihoods and well-being. The biggest flash flood in mid-June 2013 took over 10,000 lives and caused heavy damage to property. It is a dismal reflection of the insensitivity of the government while chalking out the development trajectory for this region.

In recent times, heavy construction activities have crossed the bearing capacity of the region, thereby damaging the ecosystem of the already fragile region. These challenges have been further exacerbated by the proliferation of hydroelectric projects, dam construction, unchecked urban development, tunnel excavations, extensive blasting, the building of ropeways and mountain railways, as well as indiscriminate mining and quarrying. Collectively, these activities have significantly disrupted the fragile ecosystem of the hill region.

6.3.2.1 Landslides

Uttarakhand is among the most landslide-prone regions in the world. Extensive research on landslides has been conducted by environmentalists, geographers, geologists, and scholars at local, national, and international levels. Valdiya (1985) examined the causes, consequences, and mitigation strategies for accelerated erosion and landslide-prone zones in the Himalayas. Gupta and Joshi (1990) developed the Landslide Nominal Risk Factor (LNRF) index for hazard zoning in a section of the Ramganga catchment, incorporating factors such as land use, lithology, proximity to tectonic features, and azimuth direction. Saha et al. (2002) introduced a GIS-based statistical approach for landslide susceptibility zonation, with a case study in the Himalayas. Remote sensing and GIS have proven highly effective in database preparation, data integration, and analysis. Mathew et al. (2007) utilised binary logistic regression to estimate the coefficients of predictor variables, enabling the calculation of landslide susceptibility across the study area within a GIS framework.

Earthquakes, cloudbursts, flash floods, and heavy rainfall are recurring disasters in Uttarakhand, causing severe loss of human and animal lives, destruction of property, and disruption of livelihoods. The state has experienced significant casualties and extensive damage to houses, roads, buildings, forests, plantations, and agricultural fields. In recent years, rapid and intensive construction has exceeded the region's carrying capacity, further destabilising its already fragile ecosystem. This situation has been exacerbated by the development of hydroelectric projects, large-scale construction of dams, roads, tunnels, buildings, towers, ropeways, and public utility structures, along with rampant mining and quarrying. These activities have severely disrupted the natural balance of the hill region, leading to unprecedented environmental consequences.

One of the most devastating landslides in Uttarakhand occurred on September 18, 1880 – the Sher ka Danda landslide in Nainital – triggered by excessive rainfall, which claimed 151 lives, including 43 Europeans and Eurasians (DMMC, 2011). During the 1990s, the region experienced four major landslides: in 1990, 1998, and 1999, collectively resulting in over 460 fatalities and extensive property damage. The early 2000s also witnessed severe landslides, notably in 2002 and 2009, which claimed 72 lives, wiped out several villages, and served as grim precursors to the catastrophic June 2013 disaster. The 2013 calamity led to massive destruction, with an estimated death toll exceeding 10,000, although official figures report a significantly lower number. The preliminary assessment revealed enormous losses, underscoring the scale of the challenge ahead. The United Nations Disaster Management Team (UNDMT) played a crucial role in evaluating the initial damage in affected districts, assisting local administrations in developing social sector recovery plans encompassing health, education, food security, livelihood, and shelter. Additionally, UNDMT coordinated response and rehabilitation efforts, with district reports proving instrumental in assessing damage and guiding recovery initiatives undertaken by various stakeholders. (http://dmmc.uk.gov.in/pages/display/57-reports-published).

The land subsidence witnessed in Joshimath in January 2023 serves as a sombre recall of the events that unfolded in Kedarnath in June 2013 (Awasthi, 2023). The haphazard and unchecked developmental activities in Joshimath resulted in land subsidence, causing numerous homes and roads to develop cracks and instilling fear among local residents. Similarly, the recent tunnel collapse in Uttarkashi in November 2023, with 41 workers trapped inside, stands as yet another stark reminder of the intersection between development and disaster. Other towns in the region may eventually face similar challenges in these fragile mountain areas unless development is guided by a mountain-sensitive perspective that prioritises sustainability. The most recent flash flood occurred on August 5, 2025, when a cloudburst in Uttarkashi's Dharali region triggered massive surges of water, engulfing everything in their path, including people and homes. Hundreds were rescued, while dozens remained trapped beneath a massive flow of sludge that buried scores of houses, roads, trees, and vehicles.

In recent years, construction activities have surged beyond the region's carrying capacity, further destabilising its already fragile ecosystem. This strain has been compounded by the expansion of hydroelectric projects and the large-scale development of dams, roads, tunnels, buildings, towers, ropeways, water tanks, and other infrastructure. Additionally, unregulated mining and quarrying have severely disrupted the ecological balance of the hill region – creating a situation previously unseen in its history.

6.3.2.2 *Earthquakes*

Earthquakes are considered the most devastating of all natural disasters due to their unpredictable and sudden nature. The Himalayas, which experience frequent and severe earthquakes, are an active seismic region resulting from the ongoing collision between the Indian and Asian tectonic plates. The study of earthquake technology in India and internationally gained significant attention after the 1967 Koyna earthquake. In the Himalayas, a few scholars have also undertaken research related to earthquakes.

Much of the large-scale ground movement in this region is concentrated along faults – fractures in the Earth's crust – with the Himalayan belt in Uttarakhand being a notable example. Earthquakes occur when movement along these faults releases energy suddenly. The North-eastern part of the Uttarakhand Himalayas, particularly the Dharchula–Kapkot belt, and adjoining north-western Nepal (Bajang) frequently experience earthquakes with magnitudes ranging from 5 to 6. The quantitative seismicity map of the Himalaya, as presented by Kalia and Narain in 1976, indicates that this part of the Himalaya exhibits the highest seismic activity within the Himalayan arc, with values exceeding 6.

Moreover, not only have earthquakes become more frequent in the Bajang–Dharchula region, but their focal depths are also relatively greater, ranging between 33 and 60 kilometres. This area is crisscrossed by several transverse and oblique faults, including one along the Gori River from Baram to Baikot and another near Baluwakot in the Kali valley. Significantly, this region aligns with the active Moradabad–Dataganj faults located in the basement of the Ganga Basin – the source of the December 1966 earthquake that originated in the Dharchula area. This earthquake severely affected the townships of Moradabad and Pilibhit. Earthquakes occur less frequently in the outer Himalayan belt, but they tend to have higher magnitudes, with movement being primarily dip-slip in this region.

The seismic activity in the Himalayan region is also associated with strike-slip movement along certain transverse faults in the litho-tectonic provinces, as noted by Valdiya in 1976.

All the districts in Uttarakhand are situated in an active seismic zone, and the region experiences earthquakes of varying magnitudes almost every year. In its recorded history, one major earthquake struck on September 1, 1803, resulting in the loss of hundreds of lives. In recent times, Uttarakhand has faced two major earthquakes, one with a magnitude of 6.6 in the Pilang-Bhatwari (Uttarkashi-Chamoli) region on October 20, 1991, and another with a magnitude of 6.8 in the Chamoli-Pipalkoti region on March 29, 1999. These earthquakes led to more than 850 casualties, over 5,000 injuries, and the destruction of 68,000 houses and buildings. Nearly 3,000 villages were affected by these earthquakes, which caused extensive damage to infrastructure, agriculture, and the economy. The frequency and intensity of disasters vary across the districts, and the frequency of landslides was reported to be the highest, followed by flash floods and rock falls (Sati, 2023).

In addition to landslides, earthquakes, forest fires, flash floods, cloudbursts, and droughts, the region is also susceptible to other disasters such as avalanches, environmental degradation, wildfires, hailstorms, road accidents, industrial fires, and chemical hazards. Among these, forest fires are the most prevalent, having existed for as long as forests themselves. They pose a significant threat not only to forest resources but also to the entire ecosystem, severely impacting biodiversity and ecological balance. A notable study on forest fire planning, management, and fire prevention principles was conducted by Shafi (1950), emphasising the crucial role of forests in the national economy and highlighting the need for effective forest utilisation planning. In addition, Ballabh and Singh (1988) explored community participation in forest management through the Van Panchayat system in Uttarakhand.

6.3.3 *Disasters in Himachal Pradesh*

6.3.3.1 *Landslides*

Landslides have a long-recorded history in the state. The gazetteer of the Shimla Hill has mentioned numerous landslides since 1803. A massive landslide buried an entire village near the north of Kullu town (Kahlon et al., 2014). Records show that in the 1905 Kangra earthquake, numerous landslides were induced in the Beas River valley between Kullu and Manali. The 1950s and 1960s also witnessed massive landslides on the Kalka-Shimla highway and the Bilaspur-Chandigarh highway at Gambhar in Bilaspur, respectively. In 1989, Matiana on the Hindustan-Tibet (HT) highway in Shimla district, and Luggar-Bhatti in Kullu district in 1995, witnessed devastating landslides, resulting in the loss of many lives (Kahlon et al., 2014). This trend continued in the 2000s in several places. In later years, the intensity increased due to heightened cloudburst and flash flood activities in the state.

Extremely high rainfall in July–August 2023 resulted in the loss of 400 lives; over 10,000 livestock perished, and numerous houses and properties were damaged or destroyed. This was one of the worst disasters in the past 100 years. Since July 31, 2024, heavy rainfall has led to multiple landslides and cloudbursts across several districts, including Shimla, Kullu, and Mandi, causing severe loss of life, displacement of communities, and widespread infrastructure damage.

On August 26, 2025, Himachal Pradesh witnessed a series of flash floods as the Beas River surged with strong currents, causing massive destruction in Manali, Kullu district. By the night of August 25, 2025, a total of 795 roads across the state had been closed, while around 956 power transformers and

517 water supply schemes were disrupted. Between June 20 and August 25, at least 156 people lost their lives in rain-related incidents in Himachal Pradesh, with over three dozen people remaining missing.

6.3.3.2 *Earthquakes*

Himachal Pradesh has a historical susceptibility to seismic threats, being situated in a highly seismic zone. Over the past century, earthquakes have claimed the lives of more than 25,000 individuals in the region. The devastating 1905 Kangra earthquake, centred in the Kangra Valley, resulted in the loss of 20,000 lives, the demise of over 50,000 domestic animals, and the destruction of 100,000 houses. The 1975 Kinnaur earthquake, with a magnitude of 6.8, struck Himachal Pradesh in northern India, causing extensive damage and resulting in 47 casualties. The state has a prolonged history of seismic activity, with many incidents proving particularly lethal. Comprehensive documentation of seismicity in the area is available in historical records, as highlighted (Chandel et al., 2010).

Construction activity has been characterised by negligence, with a significant disregard for the seismic risks involved. Regions sensitive to seismic activity, including Chamba, Shimla, Kullu–Manali, Kinnaur, and northern Kangra, attract a substantial influx of tourists throughout the year. Furthermore, these areas have become significant hydropower generation zones, with numerous power projects at different stages of construction. In this context, the susceptibility of the human population and the potential economic losses in the event of an earthquake would be notably high (Chandel et al., 2010).

Himachal Pradesh experiences an average of five low-intensity earthquakes each month. Situated in the high-intensity seismic zones IV and V, the state recorded 87 earthquakes between October 2021 and March 2023, according to data from the National Centre for Seismology (NCS). In 2020, a relatively high number of earthquakes were recorded near Himachal Pradesh, with a total of 25 earthquakes of magnitude 4 or higher. The strongest earthquake that year had a magnitude of 5. The most significant earthquake in the past decade near Himachal Pradesh occurred on June 13, 2023, with a magnitude of 5.2, located north–north-west of Shimla at a depth of 10 kilometres. Similarly, on April 4, 2024, an earthquake of magnitude 5.3 struck the Chamba district, Himachal Pradesh. All this had a devastating effect on the region, resulting in the loss of lives, livelihoods, and infrastructure.

6.3.4 *Disasters in North-eastern Region*

Three primary natural hazards – floods, earthquakes, and landslides – impact North-east India. Among these, earthquakes are particularly challenging due to their unpredictable nature.

6.3.4.1 *Floods and Landslides*

Landslides and floods are common disasters in the North-east region during the June–September monsoon season. India, particularly Assam, is considered one of the world's most vulnerable regions to climate change due to increasingly intense rainfall and flooding. While the North-eastern states experience numerous landslides each year, their socio-economic vulnerability remains relatively lower due to sparse population density and vast unoccupied mountainous areas. In 2022, a total of 145 landslide incidents were recorded across various states in the region, with most triggered by heavy rainfall. In addition, 41 casualties were reported, including ten in Arunachal Pradesh, 11 in Assam, eight in Manipur, and 12 in Meghalaya (North Eastern Space Applications Centre, 2022).

The North-east part of India is hit by floods almost every year. Since 1950, there have been around 20 major floods. Major floods are caused by the Brahmaputra river system spread across the North-eastern area. The Brahmaputra basin is one of the largest river basins in the North-east region, covering Assam and neighbouring areas. A large part of the flat land lies in the floodplains of the Brahmaputra and Barak rivers, and their numerous tributaries are highly flood-prone, causing substantial damage to crops and the economy, and bringing untold misery for inhabitants. It has been reported that floods occurred due to high monsoon rainfall in the years 1988, 1989, 1993, 1995, and 1999 (Dhar & Nandargi, 2000). Assam has experienced numerous devastating floods throughout its history, with catastrophic flooding becoming a recurring phenomenon after the 1950 earthquake. Major flood events were recorded in the years 1954, 1962, 1972, 1977, 1984, 1988, 1998, 2002, 2004, 2012, 2019, 2020, and 2022.

Devastating floods in the North-east have struck repeatedly for nearly a decade, resulting in huge loss of lives and livelihoods, and widespread dislocation. In 2022, Assam and Meghalaya, along with some other states, faced one of their worst floods. Roads and bridges were washed away, submerging thousands of villages and displacing hundreds of thousands of people from their homes. In Assam alone, floods and accompanying landslides impacted over 3 million people, with several fatalities reported. Estimates suggest that more than 3.7 million individuals across 30 districts were affected by these calamities. In 2023, reports indicated that approximately 1.2 lakh people across 20 districts in Assam were impacted by floods.

6.3.4.2 *Earthquakes*

The North-east region has been placed in the highest level of seismic hazard potential (zone V). Two powerful earthquakes occurred in 1897 in Shillong. Another powerful earthquake struck the entire Assam region in North-eastern India in 1950, leading to significant changes in the course and bed levels of numerous rivers. The Brahmaputra, for instance, experienced a sudden increase in bed levels at locations such as Dibrugarh and several others. This abrupt elevation was caused by the earthquake dislodging a substantial amount of debris, which ultimately altered the river's morphology. Other major earthquakes in the region include Cachar (January 10, 1869), Srimangal (July 8, 1918), Dhubri (July 2, 1930), and Manipur (August 6, 1988). An earthquake of magnitude 5.4 occurred in August 2023, affecting Assam and Meghalaya. Another earthquake of magnitude 5.4 occurred in Assam on October 2, 2023. It has also been reported that, in recent times, the region experienced 30 minor and light tremors between January 1 and March 14, 2023.

6.4 Climate Change–Induced Natural Disasters

Mountainous areas are prone to various natural disasters, including earthquakes, landslides, wildfires, droughts, floods, and epidemics, mainly due to their biophysical characteristics and vulnerability. Unfortunately, these mountain regions are often overlooked during the planning and execution of development programmes, with many projects designed without considering the unique challenges of mountainous terrain. The Planning Commission has explicitly acknowledged the fragile geomorphology of the Himalayan region, highlighting its crucial role in providing ecosystem services to the nation, particularly to those living in the Indo-Gangetic Plain. Therefore, it is imperative to prioritise sustainable development in this region to strike a balance between environmental preservation and economic growth, as emphasised in the Twelfth Plan document (Planning Commission, 2013). Despite the acknowledged interdependence of the environment and development, the region continues to suffer from the adverse effects of seemingly indiscriminate development activities, resulting in significant losses.

Typically, mountainous regions have predominantly embraced a development model that overlooks the distinctive characteristics of these areas, which differ markedly from flat terrains. The primary causes for this oversight of mountain perspectives can be traced to the failure to explicitly or implicitly consider the specific conditions and features of mountainous terrain during the conceptualisation, design, execution, and evaluation of interventions in these regions, as highlighted by Jodha et al. (1992). Compelling evidence indicates that significant infrastructure projects, such as dams, hydropower facilities, and mineral exploration, have occurred in the region without adequate consideration for the fragility of the environment and associated environmental risks.

Whenever the mountain perspective is overlooked in the planning and implementation of development projects and programmes, it has grave consequences for the ecology, environment, and the livelihoods of the local population in these mountainous areas. The frequent occurrence of landslides, earthquakes, and floods, and their subsequent impacts – including the loss of human and animal lives and the disruption of livelihoods – clearly indicate the development trajectory being pursued in mountain regions.

Successive governments have repeatedly overlooked the recommendations put forth by scientists, geologists, environmentalists, and expert panels. Despite numerous warnings, both central and state authorities persisted with large-scale projects and unregulated, haphazard construction activities (Chopra, 2014). Although institutional mechanisms are in place from the national level down to the district and sub-district level for the management of disasters, there are severe lacunae in these mechanisms when viewed from a holistic perspective.

Disasters have a volatile and sudden occurrence, causing large-scale property and livestock losses which have a profound bearing on socio-economic factors, institutions, and structures (Parasuraman & Acharya, 2000). The impacts of disasters, particularly in rural economies, are immense; the erosion of crops, livelihoods, and livestock is formidable. The psychological impacts of disasters are often profound but frequently overlooked by relief agencies, resulting in mental healthcare needs being largely excluded from disaster management plans (Pande et al., 2000). However, the mental health dimensions of disasters are increasingly acknowledged and studied globally, including in India. Key principles for mental health care have been identified, highlighting the need for targeted interventions across various phases of disaster response (Murthy, 2000).

6.5 Chapter Summary and Conclusion[2]

The disaster framework typically encompasses four distinct phases: risk reduction, relief, early recovery, and recovery and reconstruction. *Risk reduction* involves activities such as risk assessment, prevention, preparedness, and early warning. *Relief measures* primarily focus on life-saving interventions, including search and rescue, medical care, and meeting basic needs. *Early recovery* entails the restoration of essential facilities like health and education, while *recovery and reconstruction* address infrastructure, livelihoods, and other fundamental necessities (Goyet, 2008).

It is crucial to establish an information system for disasters in each phase with an aim to collect data at disaggregated levels. This data collection is indispensable for improved disaster management and an effective policy response. Technology plays an important role in forecasting, accessing, and sharing information related to disaster data. The presence of well-functioning institutional and community-based organisations is often critical in mitigating disasters at various levels (Tolia, 2013).

It has been observed that even low-income countries have effectively reduced disaster-related fatalities – for instance, during the severe cyclone in Bangladesh in 2007 – while some developed nations, such as the United States during Hurricane Katrina in 2005, have struggled with efficient disaster management. To bridge the gap between intentions and actual outcomes, it is essential to implement a robust system for monitoring and evaluation within disaster management frameworks.

Disasters have a profound impact on human lives, with colossal consequences in terms of human casualties, loss of animals, livelihoods, property, and various infrastructures, including land and forest resources. The aftermath of such natural calamities inflicts insurmountable losses on individuals and communities, which requires an extended period for recovery from nature's rage. However, it is contended that prevention is often both feasible and cost-effective, with effective prevention requiring a proactive role from governments and institutions (World Bank, 2010).

Despite the establishment of State Disaster Management Authorities (SDMAs), the overall performance of states in addressing natural disasters and preventing their recurrence has been generally unsatisfactory. Consequently, there is a clear need to integrate disaster management into the development agenda of the states.

Rehabilitation and reconstruction are the principal tasks as part of bringing relief to the people. These efforts require short-, medium-, and long-term strategies and corresponding action plans. Short-term measures focus on urgent relief efforts, such as evacuating people to safer areas and ensuring access to food, medicines, and other essential supplies. Medium-term strategies involve restoring livelihoods and facilitating the relocation of affected communities. Long-term measures emphasise sustainable development, aiming to balance environmental conservation with social and economic progress.

6.5.1 Short-Term Measures

Immediate actions such as evacuating individuals to safer locations and promptly supplying essential necessities like food, water, and medicines are crucial for preserving lives. In numerous instances, delays in immediate relief efforts have resulted in significant loss of lives, both human and animal, which could have been prevented with the timely provision of assistance. The challenge in providing immediate relief arises because catastrophes of this nature occur without warning, and there is a lack of appropriate technological tools for advanced disaster assessment. Delays in rescue and relief measures during such disastrous situations are often attributed to human factors, which can be overcome with an efficient administrative set-up and institutional mechanisms.

However, the hilly terrain and inaccessibility make it somewhat difficult to promptly reach distant disaster-affected locations. This situation necessitates a serious action plan to develop medium and long-term strategies within the framework of a mountain economy.

6.5.2 Medium-Term Measures

Disasters result in considerable loss of livelihoods, entitlements, and income sources in the affected areas, rendering people threatened and vulnerable.

The extensive loss, coupled with the destruction of infrastructure, leaves individuals incapacitated and permanently affected.

6.5.2.1 *Restoration of Infrastructure*

The restoration of infrastructure, encompassing houses, roads, culverts, bridges, irrigation channels, schools, health centres, community buildings, communication infrastructure, and cultivable land, is essential. Due to the specific characteristics of hilly terrain, infrastructure serves as the lifeline for hill communities, and without its rebuilding and restoration, providing livelihoods for the people remains an unattainable goal. Consequently, the medium-term development strategy must prioritise the restoration of infrastructure. It is crucial to employ technology and materials that align with the unique nature of the hill region, given its fragility.

For example, the construction of eco-friendly and disaster-resistant housing and other infrastructure should be undertaken while respecting bioclimatic specificities. Innovations such as constructing green buildings and using cold mix technology for green roads, as witnessed in Assam, represent valuable experiences. This technology proves particularly beneficial in addressing challenges related to road connectivity, especially in the face of heavy rainfall that often hampers road construction and maintenance (Papola, 2014c).

6.5.2.2 *Provision of Livelihood*

Mountainous regions are characterised by subsistence agriculture, often carried out on terraced fields, which inherently faces limitations in expanding its land-based activities. Hill agriculture is an integrated endeavour that combines elements of animal husbandry with the utilisation of land and forest resources. The catastrophe results in the extensive loss of cultivable lands and a significant reduction in the animal population, creating a scarcity of livelihood options. Given the colossal devastation and the prolonged time required for normalisation, it is unlikely to swiftly restore the substantial livelihood losses.

Therefore, there is a crucial need to focus on restoring and generating livelihoods in both the agriculture and non-agriculture sectors in the medium term. When cultivable lands are washed away, and livestock perishes, the immediate restoration of cultivation and animal husbandry activities becomes extremely challenging. An effective medium-term strategy is essential to revitalise such activities, whether by bringing more land under cultivation in the original locations or by relocating people to areas where cultivable land is available for cultivation.

6.5.3 *Long-Term Measures*

The extensive destruction caused by disasters severely disrupts the social and economic infrastructure, which is vital for the recovery of agriculture, industry, and services. Efforts to revive economic activity often rely on conventional development models that fail to account for the distinctive regional attributes (Papola, 2014d; Chopra, 2013). Long-term recovery requires adopting a mountain-specific development framework that integrates environmental sustainability with social and economic progress. This is essential due to the consistent neglect of mountain perspectives – defined as the explicit or implicit consideration of unique mountain conditions and their practical implications during the planning, execution, and evaluation of interventions in these regions (Jodha et al., 1992a).

6.5.3.1 Utilisation and Management of Natural Resources

The Himalayan states are often regarded as having significant potential in hydroelectric power, forest resources, horticulture, tourism, and a range of hill-specific products such as fruits, vegetables, flowers, medicinal plants, and seeds. However, the full development of these sectors has been largely constrained by the lack of a coherent and context-specific development strategy. In many instances, unregulated exploitation of forests, mining, and water resources has led to serious ecological and environmental repercussions. Government policies, large-scale infrastructure projects, and commercial ventures have frequently been pursued without adequate environmental safeguards, further accelerating degradation. These developments have posed major threats to both environmental sustainability and the livelihoods of mountain communities. The region continues to face a range of disasters – including landslides, earthquakes, flash floods, cloudbursts, and droughts – that are closely tied to ecological imbalances and have severe impacts on human well-being.

Therefore, it is argued that community involvement is crucial for optimal resource management, considering conservation, management, and recycling aspects to achieve sustainable development and resource use, even with lower productivity and returns. There is a pressing need for capacity building within the community and local governance bodies, supported by a robust institutional foundation for resource utilisation, conservation, and regeneration. Simultaneously, an effective environmental monitoring mechanism should be developed and consistently implemented for each project and programme.

6.5.3.2 Environment-Friendly Infrastructure Build-up

There is growing evidence that major infrastructural developments – such as dams, hydroelectric projects, and mineral exploration – are being introduced in the region without sufficient attention to its ecological fragility and the environmental hazards associated with such activities. Moreover, these projects often lack integration with local economies, resulting in limited ancillary benefits. The primary advantages – such as water, irrigation, and electricity – tend to flow toward lowland areas, while highland agriculture and related non-farm sectors see minimal improvements. Unsustainable logging practices, including the indiscriminate felling of trees for commercial use by private contractors, traders, and at times even state agencies, have severely depleted forest cover. This rampant deforestation in upstream areas has triggered environmental degradation downstream, contributing to the increasing frequency and severity of floods.

Mountain regions are now experiencing a surge in natural hazards such as flash floods, landslides, cloudbursts, excessive rainfall, earthquakes, forest fires, and other disasters. Much of this is exacerbated by large-scale, unplanned construction that fails to account for the unique environmental and geological conditions of mountainous terrain. Infrastructure built without a mountain-sensitive approach has significant environmental costs. Government policies and commercial undertakings that disregard ecological concerns have further deepened environmental degradation (Chopra, 2014), threatening both sustainability and the livelihoods of hill communities. As Papola (2014; 2014b) notes, the critical balance between economic development and environmental integrity lies at the core of sustainable progress.

As emphasised earlier, infrastructure development in mountain regions must respect their ecological complexity. This includes adopting green technologies – from eco-friendly roads and buildings to disaster-resilient housing – and ensuring that hydro and other large-scale projects are designed with environmental sensitivity. Mandatory environmental impact assessments should be enforced for all proposed projects to prevent long-term ecological damage and preserve biodiversity.

6.5.3.3 Agro-climatic Suitability for Industrial Activities

Numerous development opportunities exist, particularly in specialised segments where the state possesses comparative advantages and agro-climatic suitability, such as tourism, power generation, and the cultivation of horticultural, medicinal plants, and herbs. Enterprise-based activities play a crucial role in sustainable employment generation and income enhancement, contributing to the improvement of people's living standards. However, various factors, including typical hill specificities like inaccessibility, fragility, and marginality, as well as a limited and thinly spread resource base, insufficient infrastructural facilities, distant markets, a low entrepreneurial base, and a lack of appropriate policy support, severely constrain enterprise-based activities in the hilly region. Ecological and environmental considerations further limit large-scale enterprise development, concentrating entrepreneurial activities mainly in plain districts that lack the handicaps associated with the hilly region.

In the context of hill regions, enterprise-based activities can take various forms, ranging from diversification from cereal-based products to high-value horticultural products, simple processing, and other activities such as livestock, non-timber forest products, artisanal work, and tourism services. Additionally, pollution-free and precision-based enterprises, such as electronics, can contribute to hill development. A strategy that accommodates the hill perspective in promoting enterprise-based activities is crucial for sustainable development. This approach not only safeguards against a reduction in biomass production and the occurrence of natural disasters but also protects against marginalisation and ensures higher human welfare.

6.5.4 Policy Response

UN Sustainable Development Goal 13 clearly specifies the climate actions which are imperative for global sustainability and environmental well-being. This is especially pertinent for vulnerable mountain economies that endure numerous and frequent natural hazards.

Policies impacting mountain systems are often formulated by external actors who may have limited understanding of the dynamics of local mountain social-ecological systems. To address this challenge, it is essential to involve local stakeholders in decision-making processes to enhance resilience and drive adaptive transformations (Klein et al., 2019; Ives, 2022).

Mountain regions have typically experienced a development trajectory that overlooks their unique characteristics. Development activities often adhere to 'normative' strategies, neglecting regional or mountain-specific considerations (Papola, 2014a; Chopra, 2013). Viewing development through the lens of mountain regions involves the "explicit or implicit consideration of specific mountain conditions and characteristics and their operational implications while conceiving, designing, implementing, and assessing interventions in mountain areas" (Jodha et al., 1992). Instances abound where large infrastructural projects have been implemented in the Himalayan region, disregarding its fragility and associated environmental hazards. When the mountain perspective is overlooked in development planning, it results in harmful consequences for the region's ecology, environment, and the livelihoods of its people. The increasing occurrence of landslides, earthquakes, floods, and their devastating impacts on both human and animal lives – as well as the disruption of livelihoods – reflects the unsustainable trajectory of current development practices. These recurring disasters underscore how the exclusion of mountain-specific considerations inevitably leads to heightened vulnerability and ecological instability in such fragile regions.

State Climate Action Plans (SCAPs) in mountain states address hazards like landslides, flash floods, GLOFs, and agro-ecological shifts. Some states show progress: Uttarakhand uses GIS-based hazard mapping, Sikkim monitors glaciers and links SCAP with development strategies, Meghalaya promotes community forestry, Arunachal restores catchments, and Himachal adopts cross-departmental approaches. Multi-stakeholder consultations are also evident in Sikkim, Nagaland, and Himachal. Yet major gaps remain: vague targets, reliance on consultancy reports, weak budgetary integration, inadequate disaggregated vulnerability mapping, poor capacity for advanced technologies, and limited inter-departmental coordination.

The failures and the recurrence of frequent disasters and catastrophes can be attributed to the indifference of successive governments that advocate for indiscriminate development, leading to such disasters. As Ravi Chopra aptly mentioned, it is a "refusal to pay heed to warnings from nature, science, and people" (Chopra, 2023). Indeed, the foundation of sustainable development lies in the integration of economic development, social development, and environmental protection – three mutually reinforcing pillars for mountain economies.

Notes

1 A part of this chapter is drawn from the author's paper (Awasthi, 2024).
2 Some part of this chapter has been drawn from author's earlier work (Awasthi et al., 2014).

7 Replicating Success Stories Across Himalayan States

The Indian Himalayan states present several success stories, within and across the region, that offer replicable models for other Himalayan states. These experiences – ranging across areas like sustainable tourism, community-led natural resource management, decentralised governance, and climate-resilient agriculture – demonstrate the scalability and adaptability of locally developed strategies to different socio-cultural and ecological contexts across the Himalayan expanse.

Several remarkable success stories from across the Himalayan states showcase innovative approaches that have delivered concrete socio-economic and environmental gains. These cases underscore the creativity and resilience of mountain communities while offering tested models that can be adapted and replicated elsewhere in the Himalayan region to tackle comparable challenges.

7.1 Himachal Pradesh

Himachal Pradesh stands out as a consistent performer in economic and social advancement. Its journey – from spearheading a horticultural revolution to achieving near-universal electrification – demonstrates how mountain economies can thrive when development strategies leverage local strengths, foster community participation, and place environmental sustainability at the forefront (Chauhan, 2014). Himachal Pradesh's notable successes that serve as guiding lessons for other Himalayan states include:

1. Apple cultivation and diversification in horticulture
2. Hydropower for regional prosperity
3. Village tourism for livelihoods
4. Public investment in basic services
5. Local institutions and governance

7.1.1 Apple Cultivation and Horticultural Diversification

One of Himachal Pradesh's most striking economic transformations is the "Apple Revolution," which marked a shift from subsistence grain farming,

DOI: 10.4324/ 9781003595410-7

often defined by low productivity and high susceptibility to climatic variations. The introduction of high-yield apple varieties, inspired by the pioneering efforts of American missionary Samuel Evans Stokes, fundamentally reshaped the state's economy (Sharma, 2011). In the decades that followed, investments in road connectivity, cold storage infrastructure, and cooperative marketing systems enabled farmers to tap into national markets (World Bank, 2014; Government of Himachal Pradesh, 2016). The transformation extended beyond apple production to the creation of a robust value chain encompassing nurseries, transport, packaging, and processing, which generated employment throughout the year (Chauhan, 2014; Sharma & Partap, 1993). Building on this success, farmers diversified into other high-value horticultural crops such as cherries, kiwis, and pears. The experience demonstrates that niche, climate-appropriate crops can outperform traditional agriculture in mountain economies – a lesson equally relevant for other Himalayan states like Arunachal Pradesh (kiwis, oranges) and Sikkim (cardamom, organic vegetables) (Chauhan, 2014). Himachal's apple boom transformed steep slopes into cash generators, supported by orchard roads, nurseries, plant health services, cold storage, and strong cooperatives. As warming pushed climate zones upward, farmers diversified into cherries, kiwi, stone fruits, vegetables, and floriculture. Rural homestays brought steady income and jobs, while hydropower – paired with royalty sharing and local works – funded education, health, and roads. The takeaway: build full value chains, link tourism to villages, and secure upfront, predictable community benefits from large infrastructure to invest back into the valleys that host it (PeepulTree, 2018; HP General Studies, 2019).

7.1.2 Hydropower for Regional Prosperity

Himachal Pradesh's numerous rivers, sustained by glaciers and seasonal snowmelt, provide the state with substantial hydropower potential. By strategically harnessing this resource, the state has developed an installed capacity exceeding 10,000 MW, generating electricity for both domestic consumption and export to other states (Government of Himachal Pradesh, 2023; CEA, 2022). Hydropower has emerged as a critical revenue source, enabling the financing of social welfare programmes while keeping public debt at manageable levels (World Bank, 2015; Government of India, 2024).

A distinctive feature of Himachal's hydropower development is its emphasis on sharing benefits with local communities. Many projects generate local employment, enhance infrastructure such as roads and bridges, and contribute to the establishment of community development funds (Himachal Pradesh State Electricity Board, 2021). Environmental clearance processes have been reinforced, placing greater emphasis on compensatory afforestation and well-structured resettlement and rehabilitation plans (MoEFCC, 2020).

Other Himalayan states – particularly Uttarakhand and Arunachal Pradesh, with their vast untapped hydropower potential – can draw on Himachal's experience. This experience underscores the importance of balancing energy generation with environmental safeguards and adopting participatory approaches that deliver tangible benefits to local communities (World Bank, 2015; CEA, 2022; Government of India, Rajya Sabha, 2024).

7.1.3 Village Tourism for Livelihoods

Tourism has become another sector in Himachal Pradesh that has achieved significant success. Beyond its established hill stations such as Shimla and Manali, the state has actively promoted rural and eco-tourism through community-based homestay programmes (Department of Tourism and Civil Aviation, Himachal Pradesh, 2019; World Bank, 2015). Supported by enabling state policies, these initiatives allow visitors to stay with local families, enjoy traditional cuisine, and participate in cultural activities, thereby offering authentic, place-based experiences.

For rural households, homestays generate supplementary income without requiring substantial capital investment. Women frequently assume key roles in managing guest accommodations, preparing meals, and organising cultural events, contributing to enhanced female economic participation (Sharma, 2018). Additionally, the model fosters the preservation of intangible cultural heritage, as tourists are often drawn to communities that maintain traditional practices (UNWTO, 2019).

Several other Himalayan states – such as Meghalaya, Sikkim, and Ladakh – have initiated similar approaches, yet Himachal Pradesh's experience underscores the importance of sustained policy support, host training, and integration with local transport networks and guide services (Department of Tourism & Civil Aviation, Himachal Pradesh, 2019; UNWTO, 2019; Planning Dept., Govt. of HP, 2023).

7.1.4 Public Investment in Basic Services

Himachal Pradesh consistently performs strongly on human development indicators, achieving near-universal literacy, high female school enrolment, and extensive rural health coverage (Government of Himachal Pradesh, 2023; NITI Aayog, 2021). These achievements are the result of sustained public investment in basic services, including in geographically remote and difficult-to-access areas (World Bank, 2015).

Education policies – such as the provision of free and subsidised schooling, the Mid-Day Meal Scheme, and targeted initiatives to promote girls' education – have contributed to narrowing gender disparities (Ministry of Education, 2020). In the health sector, a network of primary health centres, sub-centres, and mobile medical units has expanded rural service delivery, resulting in improved maternal and child health indicators (National Health Mission, 2022). In addition, subsidies for electricity, cooking gas, and public transport have helped raise living standards, particularly for low-income households (Government of Himachal Pradesh, 2023; IJCRT, 2024).

The Himachal experience demonstrates that strong social outcomes are achievable despite inherent biophysical constraints. Other Himalayan states, such as Arunachal Pradesh and Nagaland, could benefit from adopting similar strategies, including incentives for teachers in remote areas and mobile healthcare services for underserved communities (NITI Aayog, 2021).

7.1.5 Local Institutions and Governance

Himachal Pradesh has been a pioneer in institutionalising Panchayati Raj Institutions (PRIs) for decentralised governance, empowering local bodies to implement development plans and deliver services at the grassroots level (Government of Himachal Pradesh, 2022). Women's participation has grown significantly, with statutory reservations of one-third of Panchayat seats for women – later increased to 50 per cent in several districts.

This governance model enables communities to actively shape development priorities according to local needs. Gram Panchayats, for example, independently decide on infrastructure projects, drinking water schemes, and village-level tourism initiatives, resulting in tangible development outcomes.

Other Himalayan states can draw lessons from Himachal Pradesh's experience by strengthening their own PRIs through robust capacity-building programmes, granting fiscal autonomy, and instituting community-based accountability mechanisms – thereby making decentralised governance more effective and inclusive.

7.2 Jammu and Kashmir: GI Orchards With Cold-Chain Reach

Jammu and Kashmir's development success is rooted in the remarkable transformation of its high-value horticulture sector, now a major engine of the region's rural economy.

This shift has driven the cultivation and commercialisation of apples, walnuts, almonds, cherries, and the famed Kashmiri saffron. Traditionally, farming in the region was largely subsistence-based, with most holdings small in size and market linkages underdeveloped. In recent years, however, Jammu and Kashmir has evolved into a thriving horticultural economy, generating significant economic opportunities for farmers and local communities alike. This transformation was propelled by three mutually reinforcing developments. First, farmers gained greater access to improved planting material, which substantially enhanced fruit yields and quality. This was further strengthened by the adoption of scientific orchard management practices designed to minimise environmental impacts. Together, these measures fostered on-farm practices that boosted both the quantity and quality of horticultural output (IBEF, 2020; India PR Distribution, 2020).

Second, concerted efforts were undertaken to upgrade and modernise post-harvest infrastructure. This made it possible to sort fruits more effectively by quality and grade, improve packaging, and process produce so that only the finest products reached premium markets. These facilities ensured that the value of high-quality produce was preserved throughout the supply chain.

Third, the introduction of Geographical Indication (GI) tags for Kashmiri saffron and apples played a vital role in strengthening brand recognition and consumer trust. These tags, as a form of intellectual property, link products to their geographical origin and distinctive qualities in international markets. GI status enabled producers to command higher prices and gain access to niche markets, giving farmers and traders a strong incentive to uphold high standards in order to secure premium returns for their products (Krishi Jagran, 2022).

The expansion of horticulture has also created strong spillover effects in off-farm sectors, generating substantial employment opportunities. These benefits are evident in areas such as transportation, cold storage logistics, packaging, sorting, retail, and agro-processing. This diversification has significantly enhanced the livelihoods and incomes of the rural population.

In addition, pashmina – an iconic product of Jammu and Kashmir – has witnessed a strong revival. This resurgence was driven by high quality standards, cooperative procurement, and management systems that enabled small artisans to access raw materials at fair prices, thereby supporting their craftsmanship. These initiatives have revitalised artisan livelihoods, preserved traditional weaving skills, and enhanced the wellbeing of pashmina-producing communities.

Clearly, the success story of Jammu and Kashmir is replicable in other mountain states and offers important lessons. First, it is essential to identify climate-appropriate, high-value crops suitable for cultivation. This requires a strategy focused on quality enhancement through improved planting material and the adoption of technologies that support integrated pest management, ensuring sustained high productivity while preserving the environmental ecosystem.

Second, mountain horticulture faces unique challenges, making it essential to establish cold-chain hubs and agro-logistics infrastructure close to production centres to minimise post-harvest losses. Equally important is empowering farmers by reducing dependence on exploitative intermediaries, improving market access, and ensuring fair prices for their produce.

Third, leveraging technologies such as Geographical Indication tags alongside modern digital traceability systems can strengthen brand protection and boost consumer confidence. By ensuring product authenticity and safeguarding quality, these measures enable producers to command premium prices.

7.3 Ladakh: Green Energy, Water Smarts, and Eco-Tourism

Ladakh is characterised by intense climatic conditions and scarce natural resources. It has successfully demonstrated how a sustainable and inclusive growth trajectory can be achieved by leveraging its unique natural and social strengths. This high-altitude region enjoys abundant sunshine throughout the year and breathtaking landscapes in an ecologically fragile setting. It also possesses a rich heritage of deeply rooted community resilience and traditional knowledge. These strengths have been thoughtfully harnessed to address the region's challenges while promoting long-term economic and environmental sustainability.

One of the most notable successes has been Ladakh's innovative use of solar energy. The region has invested significantly in solar micro-grids that power remote villages, schools, health centres, and public facilities. As a result, households have greatly reduced their dependence on polluting diesel generators. This has provided a more reliable, affordable, and clean source of energy, enabling community services to remain functional throughout the severe winter season, when cold conditions are at their harshest (UNDP, 2024).

Water scarcity has been addressed through a series of locally proven solutions. Traditional wisdom and modern knowledge converge in methods such as snow fencing, which slows snowmelt and enhances groundwater recharge. Artificial glaciers, or ice stupas, are built during the winter to store excess water as frozen reservoirs. As temperatures rise in spring, these ice structures melt gradually, providing early-season irrigation for crops – particularly barley, vegetables, and other staples. This innovative water storage technique effectively extends the agricultural growing season in a region where water availability is scarce.

Another important niche sector is tourism, a key economic driver that has undergone a significant transformation – unlike the unsustainable mass tourism seen in many fragile hill stations. In Ladakh, tourism has been developed through an approach that directly benefits local communities. Homestays, guided trekking routes, and heritage-based tourism circuits, as part of eco-tourism, have emerged as new models that strengthen village economies. Tourism development has prioritised environmental concerns, ecological fragility, and the preservation of cultural ethos. This approach has significantly empowered and benefited local communities (Krishi Jagran, 2022).

Ladakh's experience offers a clear and actionable roadmap for other similar Himalayan regions. First, decentralised energy systems have directly benefited homes, schools, and community centres. This has been accompanied by local capacity-building in operation and maintenance training, ensuring that these systems are managed efficiently.

Second, innovative watershed restoration schemes, adapted to local techniques and climatic conditions, help store snow and ice melt. This has increased water availability for both domestic use and cultivation.

Third, the strength of Ladakh's tourism policy lies in its ability to balance economic benefits with environmental protection. To achieve this, several measures have been implemented, including strict tourist management regulations that align economic interests with environmental conservation.

The strength of Ladakh's sustainable development initiatives lies in their small-scale, locally managed, and environmentally inclusive nature. These efforts prioritise community well-being, drawing on local knowledge and wisdom, supported by modern technology, and guided by inclusive institutions (UNDP, 2024).

7.4 Uttarakhand: Community Forestry, Herbal Trade, and Spring Revival

Uttarakhand's enduring strength is deeply rooted in a long-standing tradition of community stewardship over its precious forests and water resources. For generations, local institutions such as the Van Panchayats – community forest councils – and women's collectives have played a central role in sustainably managing common property resources. These bodies operate through locally designed, context-specific rules based on customary norms and a sense of community ownership. They help conserve biodiversity and also support rural livelihoods in vulnerable mountain environments (WWF-India, 2012; Tripathi et al., 2016).

Climate change and rising water stress have underscored the urgency of reviving and conserving natural springs, which serve as vital sources of drinking water and sustain hill agriculture. Acknowledging their significance, government agencies have launched ridge-to-valley watershed restoration programmes that include slope stabilisation through bioengineering methods, reforestation, and the construction of contour trenches and check dams to curb runoff and soil erosion. These measures have helped rejuvenate spring flows and improve groundwater recharge (Jal Jeevan Mission, 2021).

On the livelihoods front, Uttarakhand has developed niche products and promising value chains, such as the harvesting and cultivation of herbal and aromatic plants. Species such as lemongrass, rosemary, tulsi (holy basil), and rhododendron have been linked to expanding markets for Ayurvedic medicines, herbal teas, essential oils, and natural wellness products. This has helped generate additional household incomes and has been complemented by off-season vegetables and floriculture. Such diversification into niche agricultural products helps reduce dependence on traditional staples and enhances income security.

Eco-tourism has become a significant source of livelihood and income generation, with homestays fostering sustainable tourism models that strengthen village economies. These initiatives have also promoted cultural preservation and environmental protection, creating strong and mutually beneficial linkages with local communities. Uttarakhand's experience offers clear, practical lessons for other mountain economies. A key takeaway is the empowerment of local communities through strong legal provisions that enable them to manage and protect natural assets. This fosters a sense of ownership, accountability, and sustainable resource use. Equally important is the adoption of locally developed hydrological and conservation techniques that are both affordable and well-suited to local conditions (CSIR-IHBT, 2020).

Another key lesson is the promotion of small-scale processing and value addition units for herbs, aromatic plants, and vegetables. Such units generate local employment, retain greater value within mountain economies, support sustainable livelihoods, and help reduce distress-driven out-migration. Government investment in schools, healthcare services, rural road networks, and reliable electricity has strengthened both livelihoods and overall quality of life, helping to curb out-migration to some extent.

Uttarakhand's experience clearly shows that when communities are empowered to manage resources and lead development initiatives – backed by supportive government policies – it fosters inclusive and sustainable mountain development, benefiting both people and ecosystems in the long run.

7.5 Sikkim: Organic Pioneer With Branding Edge

Sikkim's prominent initiative was to eliminate chemical inputs and empower its farmers, making it the first fully organic state in India. Farmers were equipped with the knowledge, skills, and resources needed for sustainable cultivation, ensuring that produce came from pristine mountain environments free from synthetic chemicals. This ambitious transformation earned Sikkim global recognition as a leader in sustainable agriculture.

This achievement was possible through sustained efforts involving close coordination among government departments, farmer organisations, and private sector partners. The state gave overriding priority to strengthening agricultural extension services, which reached farmers even in remote mountain villages. These services introduced the basics of organic farming techniques, emphasising practices without chemical use. Practical training guided farmers in preparing and using bio-inputs such as neem extracts and locally sourced pest repellents. On-farm demonstrations provided hands-on learning platforms where farmers could witness the benefits of organic practices and adapt them to local agro-climatic conditions. Alongside this, the state focused on quality assurance by establishing rigorous certification protocols to ensure produce met strict organic standards and gained consumer trust.

The *Sikkim organic model* is built on a comprehensive approach to sustainable development. The tourism sector is aligned with clean and green towns, while prioritising biodiversity, cultural heritage, and eco-friendly shelters. To promote eco-friendly tourism, product diversification has been adopted with a focus on niche products. The state has encouraged the cultivation of orchids, floriculture, and high-value spices, all of which have rising domestic and international demand. Sikkim's success serves as an inspiring example for other Himalayan states. The organic model effectively combines biodiversity, culture, and emerging market opportunities. GI-protected products from the state stand out for their uniqueness, high quality, and authenticity (Press Information Bureau, 2023; Business Standard, 2018).

Appropriate policy measures that promote the green organic model add tangible value to mountain agricultural products, making them well-suited to fragile mountain ecosystems while supporting sustainable livelihoods. This policy has strengthened Sikkim's mountain economy and serves as an inspiration for other mountain states.

7.6 Arunachal Pradesh: Forests, Kiwis, and Market Links

Arunachal Pradesh has rich biodiversity, and local communities have taken the lead in carefully managing forest resources, balancing livelihood needs with conservation. Traditional tribal village institutions play a crucial role in ensuring sustainable harvesting of non-timber forest products while preserving biodiversity. This optimal use supports both subsistence and commercial needs. The approach has also transformed agriculture, as farmers blend indigenous knowledge with modern practices to cultivate high-value horticultural crops like kiwi, oranges, and spices. This shift towards quality and market-driven products has significantly enhanced household incomes and diversified livelihoods even in remote, fragile regions.

Improved post-harvest facilities and supply chains have been pivotal in driving this agricultural transformation. They have reduced the significant wastage of perishable horticultural produce while enabling farmers to properly grade and package fruits and spices according to quality standards, thereby fetching higher prices in both national and international markets. Enhanced connectivity has further boosted economic activity by lowering transportation costs, increasing market access, and linking farmers to national supply chains. Alongside this, the rapid spread of digital payment systems has facilitated timely transactions between farmers and buyers, eliminating middlemen and ensuring better remunerative prices. Together, improved connectivity and technology adoption have gradually transformed Arunachal Pradesh's frontier from a subsistence-based agricultural economy into one producing modern, diversified agricultural products (Pharma Innovation Journal, 2021; NCDC, 2020).

Arunachal Pradesh's experience offers clear replicable lessons. First, invest in community-based institutions by building capacity and strengthening local conservation systems that balance biodiversity with people's needs. Second, promote horticulture and high-value crops with assured procurement or buy-back arrangements. Third, ensure fast connectivity that supports farm-to-market linkages, including cold storage facilities, extension services, and market information centres. This comprehensive policy approach – combining community-led conservation, horticulture promotion, infrastructure development, and digital innovation – demonstrates a replicable model of sustainable mountain development that both conserves biodiversity and improves livelihoods (Deccan Herald, 2024).

7.7 Nagaland: Conservation, Culture, and Amur Falcons

Nagaland's most important lesson comes from community conserved areas (CCAs) – village-managed forest zones where local rules have helped protect wildlife and restore biodiversity. Another remarkable achievement is the protection of migrating Amur falcons, once heavily hunted, which are now safeguarded and have become symbols of environmental leadership. Conservation in Nagaland is also deeply intertwined with cultural revival. The Hornbill Festival, a flagship annual event, has woven together the state's many tribes through music, dance, food, and crafts. It has become a national attraction, drawing visitors into homestays, boosting sales of traditional weaves, and projecting a positive, unified image of Nagaland to the rest of India and beyond. On the economic front, farmer groups have built niche value chains around distinctive products – such as the GI-tagged Naga king chilli, smoked meats, and wild honey – moving them into curated, premium markets while retaining their cultural identity (ICCA Consortium/ TERI, 2018).

For other states, the replicable strategies are clear. First, provide a legal framework and modest, flexible budgets that empower communities to create and manage CCAs. Second, develop one or two marquee cultural or natural heritage events that serve as annual "market magnets," attracting tourism and trade. Third, professionalise the packaging, branding, and food-safety compliance of indigenous foods so they can enter mainstream retail channels without losing authenticity or story value. In Nagaland's case, conservation, culture, and commerce work together – each reinforcing the other (Scroll, 2018; Mongabay-India, 2018).

7.8 Manipur: Female Market Leadership, Pineapple, and Loktak

Manipur's most distinctive and inspiring development story is deeply rooted in the vibrant heart of its capital city, Imphal, where the renowned all-women's market, Ima Keithel – literally meaning "mothers' market" – stands as a powerful symbol of cultural heritage and economic empowerment. This centuries-old institution is unique not only for being run entirely by women but also for anchoring the petty trade economy across a diverse range of goods, from fresh vegetables and indigenous spices to traditional textiles, handlooms, and handicrafts. Ima Keithel functions as an economic engine that provides women with daily cash income, thereby enhancing their financial independence and strengthening their bargaining power both within their households and in the wider market. More than a marketplace, it sustains a vibrant micro-economy that has proven remarkably resilient through decades of political upheaval, social change, and economic shifts, making it a beacon of women-led economic resilience in the region.

In agriculture, Manipur has cultivated competitive niches by focusing on select high-potential clusters that capitalise on the state's agro-climatic advantages. Pineapple cultivation has emerged as an important crop with strong market demand. Alongside this, lemongrass oil extraction and ginger cultivation have gained prominence due to their wide use in pharmaceuticals, cosmetics, and culinary markets. These activities have preserved product quality and enhanced value addition, largely operated through farmer cooperatives that enable producers to access better markets and secure higher prices.

Loktak, the largest freshwater lake, provides livelihoods while supporting ecological conservation. It is a critical habitat for many endangered species, including the Sangai deer, Manipur's state animal. To balance livelihoods with conservation, local communities have developed eco-friendly enterprises such as homestays, canoe-guiding, and birdwatching tours that attract eco-tourists and nature enthusiasts. These initiatives not only generate supplementary household income but also encourage protection of the lake's fragile ecosystem (Loktak Development Authority, 2024).

Manipur's experience offers valuable lessons for achieving sustainable development and enhancing livelihood opportunities in fragile regions. First, design public spaces, licensing frameworks, and market policies that actively privilege and empower women's enterprises. This means creating accessible and secure market venues, simplifying licensing procedures, providing targeted training and credit access, and nurturing women's leadership in trade and micro-retailing sectors. Second, concentrate development support on a few carefully selected, high-potential horticulture clusters, pairing these with affordable and decentralised processing technologies. Support structures like farmer cooperatives, contract farming, or producer companies can then enable collective marketing, quality control, and brand building, allowing producers to scale up and access premium markets while maintaining local ownership of the value chain. Third, manage lake and wetland tourism with stringent environmental safeguards to preserve fragile ecosystems, but ensure that local communities capture the majority of visitor spending by owning and operating tourism services and experiences. Empowering communities to be custodians and beneficiaries of their natural heritage fosters sustainable stewardship and equitable development.

In Manipur's case, this unique formula blends women's market leadership through Ima Keithel, value-added agriculture based on select specialty crops, and eco-conscious tourism around Loktak Lake into an integrated model where livelihoods and cultural heritage reinforce one another. Together, they demonstrate how economic empowerment, ecological conservation, and social resilience can work in harmony to advance inclusive mountain development.

7.9 Mizoram: Bamboo, Farming Shifts, and Literacy

Mizoram has the highest literacy rate in India. This remarkable achievement has empowered its people to innovate, adapt to new economic challenges, and at the same time preserve strong social cohesion and cultural identity. The state has gradually shifted away from traditional, shifting agriculture towards market-driven horticultural products. Farming has diversified into high-value crops, such as broom grass, turmeric, ginger, and oranges, which enjoy strong market demand and provide better incomes. The slash-and-burn cycles have been phased out, and modern cultivation practices adopted, ensuring improved livelihoods, higher incomes, and greater environmental sustainability (DIPR Mizoram, 2025; TOI, 2025).

Bamboo is a niche product in Mizoram that is now widely used in flooring, furniture, handicrafts, and incense sticks, supporting numerous microenterprises and women's self-help groups across the state. These enterprises have generated rural employment and income, particularly for women and marginalised groups. To sustain and scale these value chains, the government has introduced initiatives such as kiln-drying facilities to improve product durability and guaranteed offtake agreements that ensure producers receive fair returns for their produce. Mizoram's experience offers two key lessons. First, while Jhum cultivation persisted for centuries, development interventions provided culturally respectful alternatives that enabled farmers to transition smoothly while preserving social cohesion – truly a transformative and successful experience. Second, bamboo and other NTFPs have been managed professionally, with value addition and access to broader markets at remunerative prices.

The four eastern Himalayan hill states – Arunachal Pradesh, Nagaland, Manipur, and Mizoram – have witnessed some of their most significant development successes, where community institutions have played a vital role in harnessing market potential. Village councils, in particular, have been critical in regulating grazing patterns, controlling forest access, and maintaining biodiversity. This conservation success, in turn, creates a strong, trustworthy foundation for eco-tourism and other nature-based enterprises that directly benefit local communities, generating alternative sources of income while protecting fragile ecosystems.

Similarly, when women's groups take charge of managing markets, trade spaces, and local enterprises, household incomes become more stable, and youth unemployment declines as new service and entrepreneurial opportunities emerge. These community-driven economic models foster social inclusion and reinforce gender equity, contributing to broader sustainable development outcomes. Governments that recognise and respect this dynamic relationship between customary institutions and market forces can catalyse positive change by providing small but flexible grants, offering paralegal and technical support to strengthen community rights over land and resources, and committing to patient, ongoing extension services tailored to local contexts. Such enabling environments build confidence among private buyers and investors, encouraging them to engage directly and transparently with local producers, thereby shortening supply chains and improving value capture for communities.

For Himalayan states eager to replicate these gains, the lessons are clear: integrate community and local bodies into the development planning process and give them a sense of ownership. This approach has strengthened local governance and social accountability, while also creating livelihoods, fostering ecological balance, and promoting inclusive development in difficult mountain regions.

7.10 Meghalaya: Forests, Turmeric, and Water Innovation

Meghalaya's sacred groves, conserved and protected by local communities, have played a vital role in preserving biodiversity. These groves are not only sources of ecological and economic value but also deeply rooted in cultural identity and customary law. Traditionally revered as abodes of deities, they embody a strong cultural ethos that has safeguarded biodiversity and nurtured rich flora and fauna, thereby sustaining vital ecosystems (IHD, 2024).

This age-old practice has been complemented by modern value chain innovations that link traditional knowledge with emerging market opportunities. A prime example is Lakadong turmeric, native to Meghalaya and renowned for its exceptional medicinal properties. Its growing prominence in wider markets has encouraged the establishment of local processing units, adding value to the product while generating rural employment opportunities.

Meghalaya has undertaken pioneering work in springshed management, aimed at restoring natural catchment areas that feed springs – an essential water source for many towns and villages. Due to the hilly terrain, communities largely depend on springs, which are often located at considerable distances. Through extensive scientific mapping of water resources, combined with active community participation, Meghalaya has identified aquifers and spring recharge zones for community use. This initiative has significantly improved the availability of spring water, ensuring reliable supply for domestic needs as well as agricultural purposes.

Meghalaya's experience offers a replicable model and valuable lessons for other mountain regions. First, it highlighted the importance of community-led conservation, backed by legal recognition of community rights. This has empowered local communities to safeguard their biodiversity. Second, the promotion of Lakadong turmeric through value addition and branding has created a distinct identity for the product. This initiative has not only enhanced rural incomes but also helped preserve traditional agricultural biodiversity. Third, springshed management must be integrated with ecological restoration, community ownership, and biodiversity conservation to ensure its effectiveness. Meghalaya thus offers a replicable model of sustainable mountain development by combining community-rooted conservation with modern value chain innovations and integrated water resource management.

7.11 Tripura: Rubber, Bamboo, and Border Trade

Tripura shares several features typical of hill economies, such as hilly terrain, fragile ecosystems, and a high dependence on agriculture and forest resources. The state's development experiences also offer valuable lessons for other mountain regions.

The success story of Tripura has two key features. First, the development of smallholder natural rubber cultivation was supported by a comprehensive system for farmers. The Rubber Board's extension services played a crucial role in providing technical knowledge on improved practices for planting, tapping, and maintaining rubber trees. This was complemented by the government's assured procurement at minimum support prices, which ensured farmers a steady and sustainable income. Second, the integration of tribal culture with improved returns from rubber and other niche products fostered both confidence and livelihood security among local communities.

The second success is the bamboo sector, which has transformed into more structured and market-oriented enterprises. Driven by changing market demand, the sector diversified its products, enabling better incomes for those engaged in small enterprises. It has also boosted cross-border trade with Bangladesh, thereby expanding its markets (Department of Industries and Commerce, Tripura; The Hans India, 2025).

Tripura's success story demonstrates that development interventions aligned with local cultural ethos and ecological realities can transform traditional livelihoods into more productive and remunerative enterprises. This approach offers a replicable model that promotes both social inclusion and environmental sustainability.

7.12 Sikkim and Darjeeling: GI Products and Heritage Tourism

Sikkim has promoted unique Geographical Indication (GI) products deeply rooted in its biodiversity, cultural heritage, and traditional knowledge. Prime products such as Dalle Khursani (red hot chilli), Temi Tea, and Sikkim Mandarin have received GI recognition, enabling farmers and local entrepreneurs to fetch remunerative prices. These high-value products are supported by branding and organic certification, reinforcing Sikkim's identity as India's first fully organic state.

Another important sector is heritage tourism, centred around Buddhist monasteries, traditional festivals, and distinctive Himalayan architecture. It attracts both domestic and international tourists. The combination of ecotourism and GI-linked local products has strengthened rural livelihoods while preserving the unique cultural identity of Sikkim.

The neighbouring Darjeeling tea, with its renowned GI tag, offers a notable parallel, having elevated its reputation in both domestic and international markets. Similarly, heritage tourism plays a vital role in Sikkim's economy, with village homestays – often surrounded by orchid gardens – drawing significant visitor interest. In addition, Kalimpong's floriculture sector has emerged as another destination with a thriving export market (WIPO, 2024b).

7.13 Chapter Summary and Conclusion

This chapter compiles transferable models from across the Indian Himalaya that align market opportunity with ecological and institutional realities.

Himachal's horticulture-plus model shows how niche, climate-fit crops and full value chains – supported by roads, storage, logistics, and cooperatives – can lift rural incomes; its homestay policy demonstrates how tourism can be dispersed and community-owned. Jammu and Kashmir illustrates how upgrading post-harvest systems and deploying GI and traceability strengthens returns for speciality horticulture. Ladakh's micro-grids and water innovations (ice stupas) reveal the power of decentralised, small-scale technology matched to high-altitude constraints, while Uttarakhand underscores the centrality of community institutions (Van Panchayats) and springshed restoration in sustaining livelihoods.

Across the eastern Himalaya, Arunachal's kiwi value chain and newly registered GIs, Nagaland's CCAs and Amur falcon turnaround, Manipur's women-run markets with eco-tourism around Loktak, and Mizoram's bamboo-based enterprises and high literacy together highlight how culture, conservation, and commerce can reinforce one another. Meghalaya's sacred-grove traditions paired with Lakadong turmeric branding and springshed work, and Tripura's rubber and bamboo clusters integrated with cross-border trade, further demonstrate how tailored policy, local ownership, and modest but well-targeted public spending generate robust, locally retained gains.

8 Conclusion and Way Forward

A Strategic Vision for Himalayan Region

Himalayan regions across the world, including those in India, face a distinctive set of development challenges shaped by geography, climate, and socio-economic conditions. These regions are increasingly vulnerable to the consequences of climate change – rising temperatures, melting glaciers, erratic weather patterns, and frequent natural disasters such as floods, landslides, and droughts. These challenges are not unique to the Indian Himalayan region, as mountain economies globally – from the Andes to the Alps – face similar existential and developmental threats. However, mountain regions also possess unique advantages, including abundant natural resources, rich biodiversity, water reserves, and immense potential for tourism, which can be strategically leveraged for sustainable growth. This book has explored these themes in seven preceding chapters through a focused lens on the Indian Himalayan states, combining empirical insights with a thematic and comparative framework. Each chapter has highlighted critical issues and provided valuable policy lessons. This concluding section draws on those insights to propose a coherent strategic vision for inclusive, resilient, and sustainable development in the Himalayan region in India.

The following sections of this concluding chapter outline ten key aspects of a people-centred, inclusive, and sustainable vision for the region, drawing from the analyses across the seven preceding chapters and incorporating global best practices, local insights, and policy innovations.

8.1 Rethinking Development for Mountain Economies

The conventional development paradigms, rooted in the experiences of the plains and urban centres, often prove inadequate and even counterproductive when applied to India's Himalayan region. These approaches tend to overlook the unique topographical, ecological, and socio-economic contexts that define the mountain economies of Jammu and Kashmir, Himachal Pradesh, Uttarakhand, and the North-eastern states. The challenges in these regions are multifaceted: fragile ecosystems, disaster-prone geographies, sparse populations, limited connectivity, and ecological limits to resource extraction. As a result, a shift is needed towards a mountain-specific development model

DOI: 10.4324/ 9781003595410-8

that reflects both the vulnerabilities and the distinct opportunities of highland regions.

The first aspect of rethinking development involves tailoring policies to local contexts. Jammu and Kashmir, with its rugged terrains and political sensitivities, requires policies that prioritise decentralisation, ecological sensitivity, and sustainable livelihoods rooted in the cultural identity of the region. In contrast, Himachal Pradesh has pioneered localised development efforts with significant investment in education, health, and horticulture, yet still faces the challenge of stabilising out-migration and diversifying its economy. Uttarakhand, often affected by flash floods and landslides, underscores the need for disaster-resilient infrastructure, watershed-based planning, and careful land-use regulations that reflect the carrying capacity of mountain slopes.

In the North-eastern region – including Arunachal Pradesh, Nagaland, Manipur, Mizoram, Tripura, Meghalaya, Assam, and Sikkim – diverse tribal cultures coexist within complex ecological zones. These states face chronic issues of isolation, connectivity, and, often, a mismatch between development interventions and local needs. For instance, large dams or extensive highways may have unintended consequences in ecologically sensitive zones. Development strategies must, therefore, integrate traditional knowledge systems, community-led planning, and ecological safeguards.

A second pillar of the mountain-specific model must be the integration of ecological preservation into every facet of planning. Mountains are ecological treasures that provide water, forest resources, and biodiversity vital not only to their residents but also to the entire Indian subcontinent. Development cannot be pursued at the cost of ecological degradation. This is particularly urgent in regions like Uttarakhand and Sikkim, where unregulated tourism, real estate speculation, and hydropower expansion have led to soil erosion, biodiversity loss, and increased disaster vulnerability. States like Himachal Pradesh and Sikkim have made progress through bans on plastics, the promotion of organic farming, and afforestation drives, but these efforts need to be deepened and replicated elsewhere.

The third critical dimension is ensuring equity, resilience, and long-term sustainability. In mountain regions, standard economic scale models often do not apply. High transportation costs, sparse markets, and low returns often deter private investment. A sustainability-driven development paradigm must focus on building adaptive capacities, diversifying livelihoods, and reducing vulnerabilities. Jammu and Kashmir, for example, requires peace-linked development strategies that focus on skill-building for youth, support for local crafts, and agri-based value chains that reduce dependence on conflict-sensitive sectors like tourism. Similarly, states like Nagaland and Mizoram, with their community ownership of land, offer a unique opportunity to implement bottom-up, inclusive models of development that mainstream gender equality and cultural preservation.

Empowering local communities through participatory governance is also essential. The traditional top–down policy structures need to be replaced by frameworks that involve Panchayati Raj institutions, women's collectives, and tribal councils. Sikkim's success in organic farming is closely tied to local participation, community education, and strong political will. Likewise, Meghalaya's Sixth Schedule institutions provide a legal basis for community self-rule, which should be leveraged for participatory environmental governance. Mountain development must not treat communities as passive beneficiaries but as active architects of their future.

Finally, this reimagined development model must align with the UN Sustainable Development Goals (SDGs), particularly SDG 1 (No Poverty), SDG 13 (Climate Action), and SDG 15 (Life on Land). Bridging regional inequalities while preserving the fragile Himalayan ecosystem is not only a national priority but a global imperative. India must evolve a national mountain development policy that supports decentralised planning, enables inter-state collaboration across Himalayan states, and provides dedicated funding for climate adaptation and ecological infrastructure.

By adopting this comprehensive, mountain-specific approach, India's Himalayan region can unlock a new paradigm of development that is resilient, inclusive, and sustainable – anchored in the realities of the hills and powered by the aspirations of their people.

8.2 Building Resilient, Green, and Inclusive Economies

The economies of India's Himalayan states remain underdeveloped compared to national averages, primarily due to their difficult terrain, ecological sensitivity, and historical neglect in industrial planning. However, these regions possess immense potential for green, inclusive, and locally anchored economic transformation. The future of these economies lies not in imitating industrial models of the plains but in innovating around their own comparative advantages – ecological wealth, biodiversity, cultural diversity, and vibrant community institutions.

Tourism is one such domain. But it must be reframed not as mass tourism, which strains resources and disrupts communities, but as eco-tourism and cultural tourism that directly benefits local populations. Jammu and Kashmir, known for its scenic beauty and cultural richness, has suffered from an overreliance on traditional tourism models vulnerable to political disruption. A pivot toward community-managed eco-tourism, homestays, cultural treks, and nature conservancies can ensure stable incomes while protecting cultural heritage. Uttarakhand and Himachal Pradesh are also seeing increasing potential in this sector, but require investment in training, local entrepreneurship, and infrastructure that respects carrying capacities.

In the North-east, states like Nagaland and Arunachal Pradesh possess unique tribal cultures, biodiversity hotspots, and unexplored trekking routes. Carefully designed tourism circuits, guided by environmental norms and managed by local communities, could offer sustainable revenue streams. Sikkim has already demonstrated success by promoting eco-tourism alongside strict environmental regulations and community-based tourism boards.

The second major area of opportunity is renewable energy. With abundant hydropower potential, high solar exposure, and biomass reserves, mountain states can lead India's green energy transition. Himachal Pradesh and Sikkim have successfully implemented small hydropower projects that are not only sustainable but often managed by local panchayats or cooperatives. Micro-hydro projects in Arunachal Pradesh or solar farms in Ladakh can similarly serve off-grid communities, create local jobs, and reduce dependence on diesel or coal. A green economy strategy must prioritise distributed renewable energy with community ownership and local employment linkages.

Third, high-value agriculture must become the backbone of resilient mountain economies. Limited arable land and high costs make large-scale monoculture farming unviable. Instead, the focus should be on horticulture (e.g. apples, plums, cherries in Himachal Pradesh and Kashmir), floriculture (e.g. orchids in Sikkim and Mizoram), and medicinal plant cultivation (e.g. rhododendrons and herbs in Uttarakhand and Meghalaya). These sectors offer higher returns per hectare and lower ecological footprints and can be integrated with agri-tourism or organic certification schemes to fetch premium markets. Local processing, packaging, and value addition must be supported through rural enterprise clusters and farmer-producer organisations.

Sikkim's success as an entirely organic state serves as a model worth emulating. Mizoram's New Land Use Policy (NLUP), which promoted shifting from jhum cultivation to sustainable alternatives, can be further improved to include agroforestry, bamboo-based value chains, and carbon credit schemes. In Jammu and Kashmir, saffron cultivation, apple orchards, and walnut farming have great potential, but require support through cold-chain infrastructure, branding, and access to export markets.

Another promising avenue is the growth of Micro, Small, and Medium Enterprises (MSMEs). These businesses, when tailored to local conditions – handicrafts in Nagaland, woollen textiles in Himachal, or bamboo processing in Tripura – can become engines of inclusive growth. Special support must be extended to women entrepreneurs, tribal artisans, and youth-led start-ups through access to finance, incubation centres, and e-commerce linkages. Digital platforms can allow even the most remote artisans to reach national and global markets.

In addition, public employment programmes like MGNREGA and skilling missions should be redesigned to support green livelihoods: watershed restoration, organic composting, sustainable forestry, and renewable energy installation. Uttarakhand and Assam, for example, can combine these programmes with disaster-resilient infrastructure creation, offering both short-term employment and long-term ecological dividends.

In sum, India's mountain economies must not be seen as lagging regions in need of charity, but as future-ready green frontiers that require investment, innovation, and institutional support. A resilient, green, and inclusive economic strategy must be based on participatory planning, ecological limits, and the empowerment of local communities. The Himalayan states, with their diversity and dynamism, are poised to lead India's transition to a sustainable future – provided they are supported with the right vision, resources, and policy frameworks.

8.3 Fixing Labour Market Gaps and Reducing Out-migration

Labour market challenges in the Indian Himalayan region are stark and intensifying, marked by high rates of youth unemployment, pervasive underemployment, and rising patterns of distress-driven out-migration. These issues are especially visible in states like Uttarakhand, Jammu and Kashmir, and many parts of North-east India. Entire villages in regions such as Pauri Garhwal in Uttarakhand and remote districts of Arunachal Pradesh are turning into "ghost villages" as working-age populations move in search of better opportunities. These trends are symptomatic of deeper structural issues in the regional economies, including the lack of diverse employment opportunities, inadequate skilling infrastructure, and weak local markets.

A new approach to labour market planning in the mountains must begin by acknowledging the unique socio-economic geography of the region. The narrow focus on agriculture or low-end government jobs must give way to a broader, integrated strategy for promoting rural non-farm employment. In Himachal Pradesh, the expansion of agro-based industries like apple processing, dairy, and floriculture has begun to absorb rural labour more effectively. These models should be scaled and adapted across the Himalayan belt. For instance, Uttarakhand's traditional crafts and food processing sectors – like the processing of millets and herbs – could be supported by rural food parks, digital marketplaces, and logistics infrastructure.

In Jammu and Kashmir, there is significant potential in reviving artisanal crafts such as Pashmina weaving, wood carving, and papier-mâché through cluster-based approaches and e-commerce integration. Similarly, the North-east has unique comparative advantages in sectors like bamboo crafts (Assam and Mizoram), wellness tourism (Meghalaya), and music and media (Nagaland and Manipur). These creative sectors can become engines of youth employment if combined with targeted investment in digital infrastructure and entrepreneurship ecosystems. Public–private partnerships can play a catalytic role here, especially through rural incubation centres and digital skill hubs.

Moreover, the promotion of gender-inclusive employment strategies is critical. Women in the Himalayan region face multiple barriers to labour market entry – including poor access to childcare, unsafe travel options, and exclusion from credit and land rights. Addressing these requires deliberate gender-responsive planning. For example, self-help groups (SHGs) in Sikkim and Himachal Pradesh have shown how women-led cooperatives in dairy, mushroom cultivation, and eco-tourism can create sustainable local livelihoods. The replication of such models across the region, especially in the tribal belts of Arunachal Pradesh and Nagaland, could greatly expand women's participation in the workforce.

Additionally, a comprehensive strategy for skill development is essential. The region needs climate-resilient, tech-enabled, and remote-friendly skillsets. This includes training youth in areas such as remote service delivery (tele-health, e-learning), digital platforms, green jobs (solar panel installation, waste management), and nature-based services (eco-guiding, conservation jobs). Vocational education linked with demand-driven sectors – especially MSMEs, handicrafts, wellness services, and food processing – can reduce out-migration by making local economies more dynamic and inclusive.

Migration governance must also be strengthened. States like Uttarakhand and Manipur have seen large numbers of youth migrating to urban centres and Gulf countries as informal labour. These migrants are often vulnerable to exploitation and have little access to social security. A comprehensive migration monitoring and support system can ensure that migrant workers remain connected to their home states through welfare portability (e.g. ration cards, health benefits), grievance redressal mechanisms, and returnee reintegration policies. Skill certification and job matching for returnees can create pathways for entrepreneurship or re-entry into the local economy.

Taken together, a labour market strategy for the Himalayas must be localised, inclusive, and forward-looking. By investing in non-farm employment, promoting women's participation, building skills for a green and digital economy, and safeguarding migrants' rights, India can transform the Himalayan workforce from a source of distress migration to a pillar of regional development.

8.4 Strengthening Human Capital: Education and Health for All

Human capital development in the Indian Himalayan region remains uneven and constrained by geography, infrastructure, and social exclusion. While some progress has been made in expanding school enrolment and health coverage, significant disparities remain, especially in remote tribal and high-altitude regions. The combined challenges of teacher and doctor shortages, poor physical connectivity, weak institutional infrastructure, and limited access to digital services have constrained outcomes in both education and health.

In Jammu and Kashmir, including Ladakh, difficult terrain and conflict-related disruptions have led to frequent school closures and reduced access to health services. Many schools in border districts function without regular teachers, and specialist doctors are hard to retain in remote hospitals. Similar patterns are evident in parts of Arunachal Pradesh and Mizoram, where primary schools often lack functional toilets or basic teaching aids. Strengthening the physical infrastructure – by building climate-resilient schools and health centres – is an immediate need. Innovative models like mobile schools or solar-powered clinics could offer feasible alternatives in areas that are hard to reach by conventional means.

The integration of vocational education and digital literacy in secondary schools can be a game-changer in these states. For example, Sikkim has made efforts to integrate vocational training in tourism and hospitality at the school level, equipping youth for local employment opportunities. Similar initiatives could be launched in Uttarakhand and Himachal Pradesh, focusing on eco-tourism, paramedical services, or digital services. In the North-east, combining school curricula with skill modules in bamboo craft, music production, or environmental conservation can link education with cultural identity and local livelihoods.

On the health front, technology must be harnessed to close the last-mile service delivery gap. Telemedicine has seen early success in Sikkim and Himachal Pradesh, where state-run health portals connect district hospitals with remote clinics. Such digital health infrastructure, if scaled, can transform healthcare access in distant areas of Arunachal Pradesh and Nagaland. Mobile health vans equipped with diagnostic tools and satellite connectivity can help bring maternal and child health services to tribal districts like Dima Hasao in Assam or Pangi in Himachal.

Nutrition remains a major challenge across the region. High levels of stunting and anaemia among children and women persist in many districts due to poor dietary diversity, low public health outreach, and poverty. Strengthening the Integrated Child Development Services (ICDS), promoting local food diversity (e.g. millet, pulses, herbs), and linking school meals with horticulture missions can address both nutrition and livelihoods. In this context, the North-east offers potential for integrating indigenous knowledge systems and community farming models for nutrition-sensitive agriculture.

Mental health, often ignored in development planning, is a rising concern, especially among youth and women. The sense of isolation, lack of employment prospects, and exposure to natural disasters contribute to psychological distress. States must scale up community-based mental health programmes and counselling services, with special focus on vulnerable groups such as migrants, adolescents, and the elderly. Partnerships with NGOs and mental health professionals can help design culturally sensitive interventions, especially in conflict-affected or disaster-prone areas.

Special attention must also be paid to girls' education. Early marriage, long travel distances to schools, and lack of menstrual hygiene infrastructure continue to restrict female enrolment and retention. Investments in hostels, gender-sensitive school design, menstrual hygiene products, and safe transportation can boost enrolment, especially in states like Meghalaya, Nagaland, and rural Kashmir. Furthermore, gender-responsive budgeting in health and education can help prioritize resources for women and girls across the region.

Finally, with rising geopolitical and regional interest, select states in the Himalayan belt – like Manipur, Assam, and even Himachal Pradesh – could become hubs for educational and medical tourism. Proximity to South-east Asia, natural healing traditions, and affordable medical services could be leveraged to attract students and patients, provided infrastructure, regulation, and service quality are improved.

In sum, human capital development in the Himalayas must be reimagined as a foundational pillar of inclusive and resilient regional transformation. By expanding equitable access to quality education and healthcare, integrating vocational and digital skills, investing in girls and youth, and harnessing technology, India can unlock the full potential of its mountain populations and break the cycle of out-migration and poverty.

8.5 Tackling Poverty and Inequality in India's Himalayan Regions

Despite visible improvements in headline poverty rates in some Indian Himalayan region states such as Himachal Pradesh and Uttarakhand, poverty and inequality remain deeply entrenched across the mountain belt, particularly in remote, tribal, and border areas. The North-east states and Jammu and Kashmir face a dual burden of economic deprivation and spatial exclusion. Factors such as difficult terrain, conflict histories, marginalisation of tribal communities, and climate-induced vulnerabilities have perpetuated multidimensional poverty in these regions. A reorientation of development strategy is required – one that transitions from a narrow focus on welfare subsidies to a broader vision of asset-building, economic inclusion, and resilience.

In Jammu and Kashmir, border and high-altitude districts such as Kargil, Kupwara, and Poonch suffer from poor connectivity, limited economic opportunities, and conflict-related disruptions. Here, poverty intersects with security vulnerabilities, creating a distinct challenge that needs tailored interventions. Asset-based strategies such as expanding secure land rights, increasing access to financial services, and promoting off-farm employment in sectors like handicrafts and horticulture are critical. Jammu and Kashmir also requires special efforts to ensure that centrally sponsored schemes like PM Awas Yojana and PM Kisan reach border villages with appropriate customisation.

Himachal Pradesh has shown success in reducing poverty through inclusive development in agriculture, education, and healthcare. However, inequality persists in tribal areas such as Lahaul-Spiti and Pangi, where people remain cut off from the mainstream economy due to climatic isolation and inadequate infrastructure. Here, building all-weather connectivity, providing portable social protection systems (such as digital ration and pension portability), and supporting women's self-help groups in tourism, dairy, and value-added agriculture can empower local communities. The success of apple cultivation and horticulture in the mid-Himalayas should be extended to these high-altitude tribal areas with localised policy and technological support.

Uttarakhand presents a complex case, with poverty declining in urban and plain districts but persisting in hilly and remote blocks. Out-migration from villages has led to economic stagnation and feminisation of agriculture.

A poverty-reduction strategy must focus on asset creation through secure housing, access to forest-based livelihoods, and diversification of income sources via eco-tourism and renewable energy. Reviving the Van Panchayat model and enhancing community rights over minor forest produce (MFP) can bolster the economic base of marginalised communities.

In the North-east, the poverty challenge is particularly acute in tribal-majority states such as Nagaland, Arunachal Pradesh, and Meghalaya. Inequality between urban hubs like Guwahati and rural interiors is stark. Land tenure insecurity and limited access to formal credit are key bottlenecks. Providing land titles through community-driven mapping, increasing access to microfinance, and investing in housing under schemes like PMAY-G can help uplift vulnerable households. In tribal areas of Manipur and Mizoram, localised climate-resilient housing and sustainable agriculture practices – including agroforestry, millet cultivation, and organic farming – can insulate communities from environmental shocks while enhancing income security.

Portable social protection is critical for mobile and migratory populations, especially seasonal migrants from Arunachal Pradesh, Nagaland, and Uttarakhand. Linking schemes such as Ayushman Bharat, pensions, and ration distribution to Aadhaar and mobile platforms can ensure continuity of benefits across geographies. Moreover, poverty programmes must integrate disaster resilience, especially in states like Sikkim and Assam, where floods and landslides often erode development gains. By integrating social protection with climate adaptation and livelihood diversification, Indian Himalayan region states can create a sustainable anti-poverty architecture.

Overall, tackling poverty and inequality in the Himalayas requires decentralisation, tribal empowerment, climate resilience, and robust last-mile delivery. The emphasis must shift from income transfers to building community capabilities, ownership of resources, and future-oriented economic pathways that honour ecological and cultural sensitivities.

8.6 Climate Resilience and Disaster Risk Reduction

The Indian Himalayan region is on the frontlines of climate change. It faces a unique convergence of risks: glacial melt, extreme rainfall, floods, landslides, forest fires, and rising temperatures. Human-induced activities like unregulated construction, mining, deforestation, and unchecked tourism have intensified ecosystem degradation, leading to more frequent and severe natural disasters. Building climate resilience and reducing disaster risk is thus not only an environmental imperative but a developmental necessity for the mountain states.

Jammu and Kashmir has witnessed increasing instances of floods, avalanches, and glacial lake outburst floods (GLOFs), particularly in regions like Kashmir Valley and Ladakh. These risks are amplified by haphazard urbanisation and changing snowfall patterns. The region must prioritise scientific mapping of glacial lakes, invest in early warning systems, and promote community-based disaster preparedness. Further, ecological restoration efforts like reforestation of degraded slopes and wetland revival around Dal and Wular Lakes can serve as buffers against extreme weather events.

In Himachal Pradesh, monsoon-triggered landslides and cloudbursts have become more frequent, as seen in Kullu and Mandi. Infrastructure development must be regulated through participatory and rigorous environmental impact assessments (EIAs), especially in fragile areas. Integrating slope stabilization measures, enforcing no-construction zones, and promoting nature-based solutions like bioengineering and vegetation belts are critical. Moreover, the revival of traditional water harvesting structures and forest conservation practices can strengthen local water security and resilience.

Uttarakhand's vulnerability to disasters was starkly highlighted in the 2013 Kedarnath floods and subsequent landslides. The proliferation of hydropower projects and road widening under the Char Dham initiative has disrupted fragile ecological balances. A climate resilience strategy must include limits on high-altitude infrastructure, river basin-based planning, and relocation of critical facilities from high-risk zones. Community-led afforestation drives, catchment area treatment, and local climate risk mapping can empower residents to become proactive agents of resilience.

In the North-eastern states, the ecological importance and vulnerability of biodiversity hotspots like Arunachal Pradesh and Meghalaya are well documented. These states are seeing a rise in deforestation, biodiversity loss, and soil erosion due to shifting cultivation, infrastructure expansion, and climate variability. States like Arunachal can lead with conservation-based tourism models that promote sustainable livelihoods while preserving natural capital. Wetland conservation in Assam, reforestation in Nagaland, and peatland protection in Manipur are essential nature-based solutions that also generate jobs.

Disaster preparedness remains weak in many North-eastern states due to limited forecasting infrastructure and poor institutional capacity. Investments are needed in community-based disaster risk reduction programmes, school-level disaster drills, and training of local first responders. Expanding the coverage of Doppler radar systems, deploying drone-based monitoring, and building resilient housing in flood-prone and landslide-prone zones will reduce vulnerabilities.

All Himalayan states should be encouraged to formulate or update State Climate Action Plans (SCAPs) that align with India's updated Nationally Determined Contributions (NDCs) under the Paris Agreement. These plans should be gender-sensitive, youth-inclusive, and focused on green job creation. Promoting youth and women-led climate enterprises – such as bamboo product start-ups in Tripura or solar panel businesses in Sikkim – can align economic growth with ecological sustainability.

In sum, strengthening climate resilience and disaster risk reduction in the Himalayas demands an integrated, ecosystem-based, and community-led approach. By valuing nature as infrastructure, incorporating indigenous knowledge systems, and building local capacities, the mountain states can transition from vulnerability to resilience and lead India's climate transition from the frontlines.

8.7 Governance and Institutional Innovation

Governance structures in the Indian Himalayan region (IHR) face distinct challenges that stem from the region's complex topography, ecological fragility, and socio-cultural diversity. These challenges are compounded by fragmented institutional arrangements, limited local autonomy, and weak administrative capacities. Traditional top-down approaches to development planning have proven inadequate in these settings, as they often fail to reflect ground realities or adapt to the dynamic needs of mountain communities. A transformative shift in governance architecture is urgently needed to drive sustainable and inclusive development across Jammu and Kashmir, Himachal Pradesh, Uttarakhand, and the North-eastern states.

In Jammu and Kashmir, administrative disruptions post-reorganization have resulted in gaps in local governance and planning. Empowering Panchayati Raj Institutions (PRIs) with greater financial and functional autonomy can significantly enhance local service delivery and participation. Furthermore, there is a pressing need to build a cadre of skilled local bureaucrats familiar with the region's developmental and environmental challenges.

Himachal Pradesh has demonstrated relative governance stability and success in decentralised planning, particularly in sectors like horticulture and renewable energy. However, institutional fragmentation still exists, especially between departments handling forestry, agriculture, and disaster management. Integrated planning across departments and digital governance tools can ensure better coordination and transparency. The state can also benefit from expanding fiscal devolution to local governments to allow village councils to manage their natural resources more effectively.

In Uttarakhand, many remote hill districts suffer from inadequate administrative capacity, leading to delays in implementation and poor utilisation of funds. Strengthening district planning committees, hiring more technical staff, and setting up local data monitoring units can improve execution. The state must also prioritise participatory governance through gram sabhas and user groups in water management, forest protection, and tourism.

The North-eastern states face even more acute governance challenges due to ethnic diversity, tribal autonomy provisions, and difficult terrain. States like Nagaland and Mizoram have community-based institutions that play a central role in governance, but their integration with formal state systems remains weak. Strengthening coordination between traditional councils and state institutions, while ensuring that customary rights are preserved, is essential. In states like Arunachal Pradesh, where administrative outreach is limited, mobile governance units and digital grievance redress platforms can enhance citizen engagement.

To bridge governance gaps across the Indian Himalayan region, the establishment of a National Mountain Development Agency is imperative. Such an agency could coordinate policy, provide technical assistance, and allocate targeted climate and development finance. It should work in close collaboration with state governments, PRIs, and civil society organisations. This agency must also push for mainstreaming mountain concerns in national flagship programmes such as the Jal Jeevan Mission, National Health Mission, and the Skill India initiative.

Inter-state coordination must be enhanced through institutional mechanisms focused on shared resources like rivers, forests, and cross-border trade routes. For example, coordinated flood management in the Teesta basin or the joint conservation of Himalayan biodiversity corridors requires regional planning frameworks. Similarly, disaster risk management must be regionally aligned to enable rapid response and mutual support.

Investments in data systems are critical to improving governance outcomes. A Himalayan Data Observatory platform, integrating satellite, administrative, and citizen-sourced data, can enable real-time monitoring and evidence-based policymaking. This will also improve accountability in welfare delivery, infrastructure development, and environmental management.

In the North-east, while laws like the Inner Line Permit (ILP) are crucial for protecting indigenous communities, they must be balanced with investor-friendly policies. Innovative models such as community-led investment zones, where local ownership is protected while enabling responsible business entry, can offer a middle path. Governance reform in the IHR is not just about state capacity – it is about creating institutions that are inclusive, accountable, and adaptive to mountain realities.

8.8 Accelerating Inclusive Development in the North-east

The North-east region of India is a treasure trove of biodiversity, culture, and strategic geopolitical relevance. Yet it remains one of the most underdeveloped regions in the country. Historical neglect, difficult terrain, socio-political unrest, and security-centric governance have hindered the region's integration with national and global economies. To unlock the full potential of the North-eastern states – including Assam, Arunachal Pradesh, Manipur, Meghalaya, Mizoram, Nagaland, Sikkim, and Tripura – a region-specific development strategy focused on inclusion, connectivity, and sustainability must be adopted.

One of the key avenues for inclusive growth in the region is the development of micro, small, and medium enterprises (MSMEs). The region's rich bamboo resources, horticultural products, and traditional crafts offer immense potential. In Mizoram and Tripura, bamboo-based industries can be scaled with better market access and design innovation. Similarly, floriculture and organic farming in Sikkim and Arunachal Pradesh can attract niche global markets if supported by cold chain logistics and certification systems.

Youth unemployment remains a critical challenge across the North-east. Leveraging the region's strong cultural capital is essential. Music, wellness tourism, indigenous cuisine, and gaming are emerging sectors where youth have comparative advantages. States like Nagaland and Manipur have vibrant music scenes that can be formalised into industries through policy support, training hubs, and incubation centres. Moreover, the wellness and traditional healing practices of Meghalaya and Sikkim can be promoted globally through certification and export facilitation.

Investment in connectivity is foundational to inclusive development. The Kaladan Multi-Modal Transit Transport Project, the India–Myanmar–Thailand Trilateral Highway, and the extension of railway and air connectivity across remote districts must be fast-tracked. Enhanced logistics infrastructure will reduce the region's economic isolation and link producers to national and ASEAN markets.

Reopening transnational trade routes such as the Stilwell Road and promoting economic diplomacy with Bangladesh and Myanmar can position the North-east as a trade and cultural gateway to South-east Asia. Assam and Manipur, with their educational institutions and healthcare infrastructure, can emerge as regional service hubs. Investments to expand medical colleges and private healthcare in Guwahati and Imphal will not only serve local populations but also attract medical tourism from neighbouring countries.

Peace and development must go hand in hand. A shift from security-focused governance to development-focused governance is essential. Programmes like the North East Special Infrastructure Development Scheme (NESIDS) must focus not just on roads and bridges but also on soft infrastructure like skill development, education, and healthcare.

Inclusive development must also prioritise women, tribal communities, and remote populations. Special economic zones for tribal artisans, credit schemes for women entrepreneurs, and mobile health and education units for border villages must be scaled. Government programmes should be co-designed with local communities to ensure ownership and cultural relevance.

The future of North-east India lies in a transnational vision. Embedded in India's Act East Policy, the region must serve as a corridor of cooperation, not conflict. Digital diplomacy, cultural exchange, and people-to-people ties with South-east Asian nations can foster regional identity and peace. With the right investments and institutional reforms, the North-east can transition from the margins to the mainstream of India's development story.

8.9 Regional Blueprints: State-Level Priorities

The Indian Himalayan region states cannot be approached with a one-size-fits-all strategy. Each state within the Himalayan belt presents its own distinct social fabric, ecological landscape, and economic potential. Recognising this diversity is the foundation for developing meaningful regional blueprints that align with local aspirations and capacities. From the apple orchards of

Himachal Pradesh to the vibrant tribal cultures of the North-east, the future of development in the Indian Himalayan region lies in contextualised, state-level planning rooted in equity, sustainability, and resilience.

Uttarakhand is grappling with the twin challenges of rural–urban disparities and climate-sensitive geographies. While cities like Dehradun and Haldwani are witnessing growth, many remote hill villages are experiencing depopulation due to out-migration. To revitalise these areas, sustainable hill economies must be promoted through diversified livelihoods. Eco-tourism offers a transformative opportunity in districts like Chamoli, Tehri, and Pithoragarh, provided it is community-led and environmentally regulated. Reviving traditional crafts such as wool weaving and wood carving, along with promoting climate-resilient agriculture like millets and medicinal herbs, can generate local income. In the mid-hills and high-altitude zones, targeted investments in youth skill development, digital education, and women-led cooperatives can foster entrepreneurship and stem migration. Special economic incentives and connectivity enhancements are essential to integrate these regions into broader markets while preserving their ecological integrity.

Himachal Pradesh presents a relatively successful model in harnessing its natural endowments for development. The horticulture sector, especially apple cultivation, has transformed rural economies in districts like Shimla, Kullu, and Kinnaur. The expansion of horticultural value chains through cold storage facilities, processing units, and cooperative marketing can further enhance farmers' incomes. Moreover, the state has made significant strides in clean energy, particularly in hydroelectricity. Community-owned renewable energy initiatives, including small solar and wind projects, can provide decentralised power and employment. Community-based tourism is another emerging area, with rural homestays gaining popularity. Supporting these initiatives with organic certification and branding of niche products like Chamba woollen textiles, Kangra tea, and herbal cosmetics can open export avenues. At the same time, Himachal must strengthen its disaster preparedness and early warning systems, given its susceptibility to landslides, flash floods, and glacial lake outbursts. Mountain-specific climate adaptation plans must be integrated into district-level planning.

Jammu and Kashmir remains one of the most sensitive and strategically important regions within the Indian Himalayan region. Persistent unemployment and alienation, particularly among youth, have led to significant socio-economic challenges. A development blueprint for the Union Territory must focus on inclusive economic revival. Agro-based clusters centred around saffron (in Pampore), apples (in Baramulla and Shopian), and traditional handicrafts like Pashmina and papier-mâché can create employment and promote regional identity. Supporting these clusters with design innovation, market linkages, and credit access is critical. Reviving tourism in a responsible and community-oriented manner, especially in places like Gulmarg and Pahalgam, can provide livelihoods and foster integration. Peacebuilding initiatives, combined with decentralised governance and better service delivery in remote areas such as Kupwara and Kargil, are essential to bridge trust deficits. Youth-focused skilling programmes, cultural exchange initiatives, and digital connectivity must be prioritised as part of the broader peace and development agenda.

The eight North-eastern states – Arunachal Pradesh, Assam, Manipur, Meghalaya, Mizoram, Nagaland, Tripura, and Sikkim – constitute a region rich in biodiversity, cultural diversity, and geostrategic importance. Yet decades of isolation, conflict, and underinvestment have constrained development. A regional blueprint for the North-east must prioritise connectivity, peacebuilding, and participatory planning. Strengthening road, rail, and air links – especially through Bangladesh and Myanmar – is essential to unlock economic potential. Bamboo-based industries, organic farming, floriculture, and eco-tourism can become growth sectors with proper value chain support. Cultural industries – ranging from music and martial arts to wellness and gaming – offer employment avenues for youth. Community-driven development through self-help groups (SHGs), start-up incubators, and cooperative models must be expanded. States like Sikkim and Mizoram, which have pioneered organic farming and decentralised governance, respectively, can serve as role models. Strengthening regional planning bodies, cross-border trade mechanisms, and local governance systems will be critical for long-term transformation.

8.10 A Vision for the Future: Sustainable, Inclusive, and Equitable Development

The Indian Himalayan region is standing at a crossroads. As India envisions its developmental journey towards 2047 – the centenary of its independence – the Himalayas represent both a frontline of ecological vulnerability and a reservoir of untapped potential. The challenges of out-migration, ecological degradation, infrastructural deficits, and socio-political fragility must be addressed through a future-ready vision grounded in sustainability, inclusion, and equity.

8.10.1 Ecological Stewardship Over Extractive Development

The Himalayan states must reject unsustainable models of development based on resource extraction, haphazard tourism, and top-down infrastructure projects. Instead, ecological stewardship should guide all planning efforts. Mountain ecosystems are fragile and vital to India's hydrological and biodiversity systems. Investments in forest regeneration, river basin management, and green infrastructure must be prioritised. Traditional knowledge and indigenous conservation practices, especially among tribal communities in the North-east and Himachal Pradesh, should be mainstreamed into policy frameworks. Payment for ecosystem services (PES) and carbon credit markets can provide new income streams for communities protecting nature.

8.10.2 People-First Governance

A shift towards people-centric governance is essential. Strengthening Panchayati Raj institutions, Autonomous District Councils in the North-east, and urban local bodies in hill towns must be a priority. Local bodies need financial autonomy, trained human resources, and data systems to deliver services effectively. Participatory planning that involves women, youth, and marginalised communities must be institutionalised. Public services like health, education, and social protection should be delivered through decentralised, tech-enabled systems. Investments in digital infrastructure, mobile service units, and local grievance redressal mechanisms can ensure governance reaches the last mile.

8.10.3 Green and Knowledge-Based Economic Diversification

The Himalayan economies must diversify beyond subsistence agriculture and state-led employment. High-value sectors such as renewable energy, organic farming, medicinal plants, eco-tourism, and cultural industries can drive job creation. Emphasis must be placed on promoting climate-resilient enterprises led by youth and women. Research and innovation hubs focused on mountain technologies, biodiversity, and disaster resilience can transform the region into a knowledge-based economy. Universities and technical institutes in states like Uttarakhand, Sikkim, and Assam must be upgraded as centres of excellence linked to global research networks.

8.10.4 Regional and International Cooperation

Development in the Indian Himalayan region cannot be insular. Strengthening regional cooperation among Himalayan states is crucial to address transboundary issues such as river sharing, biodiversity corridors, and disaster risks. Platforms for inter-state dialogue and joint planning must be institutionalised. At the international level, India must anchor the Himalayas within its "Act East" and climate diplomacy strategies. Cross-border economic corridors, conservation initiatives, and knowledge exchange with countries like Nepal, Bhutan, Bangladesh, and Myanmar must be actively pursued. The Himalayas can become a beacon of regional peace, ecological resilience, and cultural harmony if anchored in cooperative frameworks.

8.10.4.1 Learn and Replicate Successful Practices Across Himalayan States

Himalayan states can grow faster by learning from each other. The idea is simple: find what already works in one state, adapt it to local needs in another, and scale it with strong community ownership and care for the environment. What can be shared? Climate-fit farming with cold-chain infrastructure (like apples, kiwis, citrus), homestays and eco-tourism, spring and watershed revival, organic farming with GI/traceability, community forestry, small solar micro-grids, women-led markets, bamboo and other NTFP value chains, and fair, benefit-sharing models in hydropower.

How do we make it happen? Set up a "Himalayan Solutions Exchange" to shortlist proven ideas and publish simple step-by-step guides. Pair states through twinning and short expert exchanges. Fund quick 100-day pilots with a pooled replication fund. Make local bodies – PRIs, Van Panchayats, village councils, women's groups – co-owners from day one, with clear benefit-sharing and maintenance roles. Build skills and safeguards together. Use common training for officials and community leaders. Set basic standards for quality, certification, and branding. Keep tourism within carrying capacity, protect rivers in hydropower projects, and use fair resettlement rules. Track progress on open dashboards – income gains, service uptime, spring flows, women's enterprise – backed by social audits and easy grievance redress.

Move in stages. In 0–6 months, launch the exchange, pick 8–10 ideas, sign twinning MoUs, and set up the fund. In 6–18 months, run pilots – cold-chain infrastructure, springshed work, micro-grids, GI/organic cohorts – and refine what works. In 18–36 months, scale the best pilots to more districts and bake the safeguards into state rules. The result can be: better farmer prices, year-round rural jobs, reliable water and power, more women-owned enterprises, and healthier forests and rivers. Don't copy projects blindly – replicate the design principles. Start small, learn fast, share openly, and scale only with community consent and strong ecological guardrails.

In conclusion, the future of the Himalayas is not just a regional concern – it is a national imperative and a global responsibility. Sustainable, inclusive, and equitable development in the IHR will ensure India's environmental security, economic well-being, and geopolitical stature. The time to act is now, with courage, compassion, and clarity of purpose.

References

Chapter 1

Allan, N. J. R., Knapp, G. W., & Stadel, C. (eds.) (1988). *Human impacts on mountains*. Rowman & Littlefield.

Awasthi, I. C., Mehta, G. S., & Mamgain, R. P. (2014). Uttarakhand disaster: Lessons and way forward, Occasional Paper-6, Giri Institute of Development Studies, Lucknow, November.

Banskota, M. (2000). The Hindukush Himalayas: Searching for visible socio-economic and environmental options. In Banskota et al. (eds.), *Growth in poverty alleviation and sustainable resource management in the mountain areas of South Asia*. ICIMOD.

Bätzing, W., Perlik, M., & Dekleva, M. (1996). Urbanization and depopulation in the Alps: An analysis of current socio-economic structural changes. *Mountain Research and Development*, *16*(3), 335–350.

Bhadra, B. (2000). *The Hindu Kush-Himalaya, Alpin forum: Moving towards worldwide*. News Letter, (2), Bergamo.

Bhati, U. N. (1990). *Desertification in the Thar: Processes, problems and prospects*. Rawat Publications.

Brundtland, G. H. (1987). *Our common future: The world commission on environment and development*. Oxford University Press.

Byers, A. C. (2000). *The Appalachians, Alpin forum: Moving towards worldwide*. Newsletter (2), 2000, Bergamo.

Chakrabarti, A., & Patra, S. (2019). Borderland livelihoods and development: A case study from India's Northeast. *Economic & Political Weekly*, *54*(9), 45–53.

Chambers, R., & Conway, G. (1992). *Sustainable rural livelihoods: Practical concepts for the 21st century* (IDS Discussion Paper No. 296). Institute of Development Studies.

Chand, P., Gurung, G. B., & Sherchan, D. P. (1992). *The Pakhribas agricultural centre: Research and development for hill farming systems in Eastern Nepal*. Pakhribas Agricultural Centre.

Christaller, W. (1933). *Die zentralen Orte in Süddeutschland*. Gustav Fischer.

CLIENT II. (2018). Andes – Laboratory for natural hazards. *German Federal Ministry of Education and Research (BMBF)*. bmbf-client.de or https://www.fona.de/en/andes-laboratory-for-natural-hazards

Costanza, R., et al. (1997). The value of the world's ecosystem services and natural capital. *Nature*, *387*(6630), 253–260.

Debarbieux, B., & Price, M. F. (2010). *Mountain regions: A global common good?* Mountain Research and Development (MRD), Supplement Issue, Keynotes, Perth.

Denniston, D. (1995). Sustaining mountain people and environments. In *The state of the world*, World Watch Institute Report on Progress Towards a Sustainable Society, WW Norton Company, New York.

Dutta, P. (2016). Ethnicity, insurgency, and development in Northeast India. *Strategic Analysis*, *40*(5), 427–440.

Earth Summit in Rio de Janeiro. (1992). *Managing fragile ecosystems: Sustainable mountain development*. Agenda 21, Chapter 13.

European Commission. (2001). *Unity, solidarity, diversity for Europe, its people and its territory*. Second Report on Economic and Social Cohesion, European Commission, Brussels.

Flint, C. G. (2016, November 4). Framing the human dimensions of mountain systems: Integrating social science paradigms for a global network of mountain observatories. *Mountain Research and Development (MRD)*, *36*, 528–536. http://dx.doi.org/10.1659/MRD-JOURNAL-D-15-00110.1.

Food and Agriculture Organization. (2019). *Key messages | International Mountain Day*. https://www.fao.org › 2019-mountains-matter-for-youth

Food and Agriculture Organization. (2024). https://www.fao.org › mountain-partnership› members

Frank, A. G. (1967). *Capitalism and underdevelopment in Latin America*. Monthly Review Press.

Gereffi, G., Humphrey, J., & Sturgeon, T. (2005). The governance of global value chains. *Review of International Political Economy*, *12*(1), 78–104.

Gichuki, F. N. (2000). *The African mountains and highlands, Alpin forum: Moving towards worldwide*. Newsletter 2000 (2), Bergamo.

Goodrich, C. G., Udas, P. B., & Larrington-Spencer, H. (2019, September). Conceptualizing gendered vulnerability to climate change in the Hindu Kush Himalaya: Contextual conditions and drivers of change. *Environmental Development*, *31*, 9–18.

Greenwood, G. (2013). Mountain research initiative seeks to break new ground in second decade. *Mountain Research and Development*, *33*(4), 473–476.

GRID-Arendal. (2018). *Mountain adaptation outlook series – outlook on climate change adaptation in the Hindu Kush Himalaya*. https://www.grida.no›resources

Holling, C. S. (1973). Resilience and stability of ecological systems. *Annual Review of Ecology and Systematics*, *4*(1), 1–23.

Huddleston, B., Ataman, E., SDRN, de Salvo, P., Zanetti, M., Bloise, M., Bel, J., & Franceschini, G., & Fé d'Ostiani, L. (2003). *Towards a GIS-based analysis of mountain environments and populations*. FAO.

Husain, A. (1992). *The Aga Khan rural support programme in Pakistan: A second interim evaluation*. Aga Khan Rural Support Programme.

Hussain, M. (2013). Borderlands, security, and development: A case of India's Northeast. *Asian Affairs*, *44*(3), 100–118.

ICIMOD. (2012). Sustainable Mountain Development in the Hindu Kush – Himalaya From Rio 1992 to Rio 2012 and beyond, Rio+20 Assessment Report for the Hindu Kush Himalayan Region, ICIMOD, Kathmandu, Nepal, February.

International Centre for Integrated Mountain Development. (2015). *Mountain products initiative: Promoting high-value products for sustainable mountain livelihoods*. International Centre for Integrated Mountain Development.

ICIMOD. (2019). *A compendium of case studies, understanding mountain peoples*, Approach and Practices to Combating Climate Change in the Indian Himalayan Region: Research to Renewal and Reforms 2017–19.

Ives, D. J. (1997). *Comparative inequalities – mountain communities and mountain families in mountains of the world: A global priority*, (B. Messerli & J. D. Ives, eds.). The Parthenon Publishing Group.

Ives, J. D. (2022). *Sustainable mountain development: Getting the facts right*, 2nd ed. Springer Nature.

Ives, J. D., & Messerli, B. (1989b). *The Himalayan dilemma: Reconciling development and conservation*. The United Nations University, Routledge.
Ives, J. D., Messerli, B., & Rhoades, R. E. (1997). *Agenda for sustainable mountain development, in mountains of the world: A global priority* (B. Messerli & J. D. Ives, eds.). Parthenon Publishing Group.
Jodha, N. S. (1992a). Mountain perspective and sustainability: A framework for development strategies. In Jodha et al. (eds.), *Sustainable mountain agriculture: Perspectives and issues*, Vol. 1, International Centre for Integrated Mountain Development (ICIMOD), Oxford & IBH.
Jodha, N. S. (2000). Poverty alleviation and sustainable development in mountain areas: Role of highland-lowland links in the context of rapid globalisation. In Banskota et al. (eds.), *Growth in poverty alleviation and sustainable resource management in the mountain areas of South Asia*. ICIMOD.
Jodha, N. S., Pratap, T., & Banskota, M. (eds.) (1992). *Sustainable mountain agriculture: Perspectives and issues*, Vol. 1, International Centre for Integrated Mountain Development (ICIMOD), Oxford & IBH.
Kapos, V., Rhind, J., Edwards, M., Price, M. F., & Ravilious, C. (2000). Developing a map of the world's mountain forests. In M. F. Price & N. Butt (eds.), *Forests in sustainable mountain development report for 2000* (pp. 4–9). CAB International.
Libiszewski, S., & Bachler, G. (1997). Conflicts in mountain area – a predicament for sustainable development. In B. Messerli & J. D. Ives (eds.), *Mountains of the world: A global priority*. The Pantheon Publishing Group.
Li Tianchi, S., Chalise, R., & Upreti, B. N. (eds.) (2001). *Landslide hazard mitigation in the Hindu Kush-Himalayas*. ICIMOD.
Mountain Areas in Europe – Final Report. (2004). Analysis of Mountain Areas in EU Member States, Acceding and other European Countries, Conclusions from the National Interviews and Reports (Chapter 9), Nordregio Report 2004.
Myrdal, G. (1957). *Economic theory and underdeveloped regions*. Duckworth.
Narpat S. Jodha (1992a). Mountain perspective and sustainability: A framework for development strategies. In Narpat S. Jodha, Mahesh Banskota, & Tej Partap (Eds.), Sustainable mountain agriculture (pp. 41–82). Oxford & IBH Publishing Co. Pvt. Ltd..
Organisation for Economic Co-operation and Development (OECD). (2001). *Policies to enhance sustainable development*. OECD.
Papola, T. S. (2002). *Poverty in mountain areas of the Hindu Kush – Himalayas: Some basic issues in measurement, diagnosis and alleviation*. ICIMOD.
Perroux, F. (1950). Economic space: Theory and applications. *Quarterly Journal of Economics*, *64*(1), 89–104.
Pound, B., Snapp, S., McDougall, C., & Braun, A. (1992). *Managing natural resources for sustainable livelihoods: Uniting science and participation*. International Institute for Environment and Development.
Price, L. W. (1981). *Mountain and man: A study of process and environment*. University of California.
Ramamonjisoa-Amma, J. (2000). *South West Indian Ocean, Alpin forum: Moving towards worldwide*. Newsletter 2000 (2), Bergamo.
Rasul, G., & Molden, D. (2014). The global social and economic value of mountain water. *Water Resources Research*, *50*(5), 3641–3659.
Ray, C. (1998). Culture, intellectual property and territorial rural development. *Sociologia Ruralis*, *38*(1), 3–20.
RESOLVE sarl. (2023, March). Assessing the foundations for delivering a sustainable blue economy in the South West Indian Ocean, report compiled by RESOLVE sarl

Ivandry business centre Rue Velo Rainimangalahy. *Ivandry – Antananarivo, 101*, Madagascar.
Rieder, P., & Wyder, J. (1997). Economic and political framework for sustainability of mountain areas. In B. Messerli & J. D. Ives (eds.), *Mountains of the world: A global priority*. Parthenon Publishing Group.
Romeo, R., Sara, M., & Abear, S. (2022, July 29). The international year of sustainable mountain development 2022: An opportunity to promote action for mountains. *Frontiers Type Opinion*. https://doi.org/10.3389/fsufs.2022.933080
Sarmiento, F. O. (2000). *The Latin American Mountains, Alpin forum: Moving towards worldwide*. Newsletter 2000 (2), Bergamo.
Singh, S. (2018). Borders, security and development in the Himalayan frontier. *India Quarterly*, *74*(3), 275–293.
Tucker, C. M., Alc'antara-Ayala, I., Gunya, A., Jimenez, E., Klein, J. A., Xu, J., & Bigler, S. L. (2021, May). Challenges for governing mountains sustainably: Insights from a global survey. *Mountain Research and Development*, *41*(2), R10–R20.
Tulachan, P. M. (2000). Mountain agriculture in the Hindu Kush Himalaya: Trends and sustainability. In T. S. Papola et al. (eds.), *Growth in poverty alleviation and sustainable resource management in the mountain areas of South Asia*. ICIMOD.
Wester, P., Mishra, A., Mukherji, A., & Shrestha, A. B. (eds.) (2019). *The Hindu Kush Himalaya assessment mountains, climate change, sustainability and people, ICIMOD*. Published for the Hindu Kush Himalayan Monitoring and Assessment Programme (HIMAP), Springer.
World Bank Blogs. (2021, December 15). From the Alps to the Pamirs: Investing in mountain economies to make people and places more resilient. *3*(9). https://blogs.worldbank.org europeandcentralasia›inv . . .
WSSD. (2002, June 3). International Partnership for Sustainable Development in Mountain Regions, World Summit on Sustainable Development, Bali.
Wymann von Dach, S., Ott, C., Kläy, A., & Stillhardt, B. (2006). Will international pursuit of the millennium development goals alleviate poverty in mountains? *Mountain Research and Development*, *26*, 4–8.
Zhaoguang, G., et al. (1992). *Rural industry and the peasant economy in Western Sichuan*. Sichuan University Press.

Chapter 2

Awasthi, I. C. (2012). *Livelihood diversities in mountain economy, constraints and opportunities*. Concept Publishing Company.
Chopra, R. (2013, August 10). Restoring normalcy in Uttarakhand. *Economic & Political Weekly*, *XLVIIL*(32).
Jodha, N. S. (2000). Strategies for the sustainable development of mountain agriculture: An overview. In N. S. Jodha, M. Banskota, & T. Partap (eds.), *Sustainable mountain agriculture*. Oxford & IBH Publishing Co. Pvt. Ltd.
Jodha, N. S., Banskota, M., & Pratap, T. (eds.) (1992). *Sustainable mountain agriculture: Perspectives and issues*, Vol. 1. International Centre for Integrated Mountain Development (ICIMOD), Oxford & IBH.
Mishra, D. K. & Upadhyay, V. (eds.) (2017). *Rethinking economic development in Northeast India: The emerging dynamics*. Routledge India.
National Education Policy. (2020). Ministry of Human Resource Development Government of India.
NITI Aayog. (2018). *SDG India Index – Baseline Report (2018), NITI Aayog*. Government of India.

Papola, T. S. (1982). *Rural industrialisation: Approaches and potential*. Himalaya Publishing House.

Papola, T. S., et al. (eds.) (2014). Uttarakhand disaster–beyond rescue and relief: Some lessons for reconstruction and long-term development. In *Lessons & learning from disasters: Uttarakhand state commentary*. CHEA.

Chapter 3

Aayog, NITI. (2018). *Contributing to sustainable development in the Indian Himalayan region*. NITI Aayog.

Awasthi, I. C., & Mehta, B. S. (2020). Forced out-migration from hill regions and return migration during the pandemic: Evidence from Uttarakhand. *Indian Journal of Labour Economics*, *63*(4), 1107–1124. https://doi.org/10.1007/s41027-020-00291-w

Awasthi, I., & Mehta, B. S. (2020). *Forced out-migration from hill regions and return migration during the pandemic: Evidence from Uttarakhand*. Indian Journal of Labour Economics, 63(4), 1107–1124. https://doi.org/10.1007/s41027-020-00291-w

Awasthi, I. C., & Mehta, B. S. (2022). Migration in Uttarakhand during COVID–19. *Indian Journal of Labour Economics*.

Baruah, A., & Mohan, M. G. (2021). Women farmers' awareness of government agricultural schemes in the North Eastern Region of India. *Journal of Extension Education*, *33*(1), 6558–6565. https://doi.org/10.26725/JEE.2021.1.33.6558-6565

Basole, A. (2022). Structural transformation and employment generation in India: Past performance and the way forward. *The Indian Journal of Labour Economics*, *65*(2), 295–320. https://doi.org/10.1007/s41027-022-00380-y

Bhat, R., & Lone, A. (2012). *Labour force participation and employment trends in Jammu & Kashmir: A sectoral analysis. Journal of Economic Studies*, 39(2), 112–129.

Bhat, A. G., & Lone, S. A. (2022a). Status and Structure of Employment in Jammu and Kashmir. ResearchGate. https://www.researchgate.net/publication/386737943_Status_and_Structure_of_Employment_in_Jammu_and_Kashmir

Bhat, F., & Lone, M. (2022b). *Women's employment and economic output in Jammu & Kashmir*. Springer.

Census. (2001). Office of the Registrar General & Census Commissioner, India. *Census of India 2001*. Ministry of Home Affairs, Government of India. (Detailed tables, especially D-series, available on Census of India website.)

Census. (2011). Office of the Registrar General & Census Commissioner, India. *Census of India 2011*. Ministry of Home Affairs, Government of India. (Migration data accessible via D-Series tables.)

Chakraborty, S. (2022). Labour force projections in India until 2060 and implications for the demographic dividend. *Social Indicators Research*, *164*(2), 795–821.

Choudhury, G., Choudhury, D., & Sharma, P. (2023). Sustainable development and livelihood opportunities in the Himalayan region of Eastern India. In *SDGs in the Asia and Pacific region* (pp. 1–33). Springer International Publishing.

Das, P. (2022). Challenges to the development of the Northeast through the Act East policy. *Strategic Analysis*, *46*(5), 473–493.

Deshingkar, P., & Akter, S. (2009). Migration and human development in India. *Human Development Research Paper 2009/13*, United Nations Development Programme.

Devi, L. (2023). Gender disparities in the Northeast. *Social Science Research*.

Devi, S., & Singh, P. (2021). Gender and employment in Manipur: Examining informal networks. *Asian Labour Journal*, *9*(3), 76–94.

Goswami, A., & Deka, P. (2020). Migration trends in Assam: An analysis. *Economic & Political Weekly*, *55*(42), 78–86.

Goswami, K. (2023). Employment challenges in Meghalaya. *Assam Economic Review*.

Government of Meghalaya. (2023). *Meghalaya industrial investment promotion policy (Draft)*. Directorate of Industries, Government of Meghalaya.

Harris, J. R., & Todaro, M. P. (1970). Migration, unemployment, and development: A two-sector analysis. *American Economic Review*, *60*(1), 126–142.

India Employment Report (IER). (2024). *Youth Employment, Education and Skills, Institute for Human Development (IHD) and International Labour Organization (ILO)*, New Delhi.

Lalhriatpuii, H. (2022a). *Mizoram's transition to a service economy*. Routledge.

Lalhriatpuii, H. (2022b). Service sector expansion and employment in Mizoram: An analysis. *North-East Development Journal*, *17*(4), 56–71.

Maithani, B. P. (2006). *Migration and urban development in India*. Rawat Publications.

Marchang, R. (2017). Being Ladakhi, being Indian. *The Economic and Political Weekly (EPW)*, *52*(14), April 8.

McDuie-Ra, D. (2012). *Northeast migrants in Delhi: Race, refuge and retail*. Amsterdam University Press.

Mehta, B. S. (2023). Migration in Uttarakhand. *Human Development Journal*, *53*(1), 34–56.

National Statistical Office (NSO). (2025). National accounts statistics (GDP data). *Ministry of Statistics and Programme Implementation*. https://esankhyiki.mospi.gov.in

Nayak, P. (2021). *Economic transitions in the Northeast: A sectoral analysis*. Oxford University Press.

Periodic Labour Force Survey (PLFS). (July 2021–June 2022). *National Statistical Office, Ministry of Statistics and Programme Implementation (MoSPI)*. Government of India.

Rana, J. C., & Bisht, I. S. (2023). Reviving smallholder hill farming by involving rural youth in food system transformation: A case of Uttarakhand. *Sustainability*, *15*(11), 8816. https://doi.org/10.3390/su15118816

Remesh, B. P. (2012). Political unrest and migration in Manipur. *Economic and Political Weekly*, *47*(4), 27–32.

Sen, A. (2024). National unemployment and gender inequality. *Economic & Social Research Review*.

Sharma, A. (2024). *Middlemen and a faraway market: Tripura's livelihoods challenges*. India Development Review (IDR).

Sharma, R. (2022). Out-migration and livelihood challenges in Uttarakhand. *Indian Journal of Regional Studies*, *48*(2), 112–130.

Sharma, A. N., & Mehta, B. S. (2026). Trend and pattern of women's work in India, 1983–2024. In *Women and work in India: Challenges, opportunities and perspectives for policy* (pp. 179–208). Springer Nature Singapore.

Sharma, R., & Das, K. (2022a). Employment trends and gender dimensions in Assam's labour market. *Labour Market Review*, *12*(1), 150–169.

Sharma, R., & Das, A. (2022b). Industrial growth and employment shifts in Assam. *Economic & Political Weekly*, *57*(4), 45–58.

Sharma, R., & Das, S. (2022c). Employment dynamics and sectoral shifts in Arunachal Pradesh. *Journal of North Eastern Development Studies*, *14*(2).

Shimray, U. A., & Ushadevi, P. (2009). Migration trends among youth in North-East India. *Social Change*, *39*(1), 91–112.

Singh, N. (2019). Migration and employment in Northeast India. *Journal of Labour Economics*, *61*(3), 215–240.

Srivastava, R. (2020). Labour migration, vulnerability, and development policy: The pandemic as inflexion point. *The Indian Journal of Labour Economics, Springer; The Indian Society of Labour Economics (ISLE)*, *63*(4), 859–883.

Tumbe, C. (2018). *India moving: A history of migration, penguin viking*. Penguin Random House India.

United Nations. (2015). *Transforming our world: The 2030 agenda for sustainable development*. United Nations General Assembly.

Chapter 4

AISHE. (2023). All India Survey on Higher Education 2023. Ministry of Education, Government of India.

ASER. (2022). Annual Status of Education Report 2022: Learning Outcomes and School Quality in India. Pratham Education Foundation.

ASER. (2023). Annual Status of Education Report 2023: Educational Access and Equity in India. Pratham.

Azim Premji Foundation. (2022). Educational Access and Retention in Rural India. Bangalore, India.

Azim Premji University. (2022). Enhancing Educational Outcomes through Effective Resource Utilisation.

Becker, G. S. (1993). *Human capital: A theoretical and empirical analysis, with special reference to education*. University of Chicago Press.

Census of India. (2023). Provisional Population Totals: Literacy and Education. Government of India.

Education Policy Review. (2022). A Review of Educational Reforms in Indian States. New Delhi: NITI Aayog.

Government of India. (2020). National Education Policy 2020. Ministry of Human Resource Development.

Government of India. (2023a). Healthcare initiatives in North East India. Ministry of Health and Family Welfare.

Government of India. (2023b). Mid-Day Meal Scheme: Annual Report on Nutritional Impact in Schools. Ministry of Education.

Grossman, M. (1972). On the concept of health capital and the demand for health. *Journal of Political Economy*, *80*(2), 223–255.

Himachal Pradesh Education Report. (2022). Assessing Educational Performance in Himachal Pradesh.

India Education Statistics. (2023). Ministry of Education, Government of India.

International Institute for Population Sciences (IIPS). (2021). National Family Health Survey (NFHS-5), 2019–21. Ministry of Health and Family Welfare, Government of India.

International Institute for Population Sciences (IIPS) & Ministry of Health and Family Welfare (MoHFW). (2021). *National family health survey (NFHS-5), 2019–21: India report*. IIPS.

Ministry of Education. (2021). Education Statistics in India 2021. Government of India.

Ministry of Education. (2022). National Education Performance and Learning Levels: A State-Wise Analysis. Government of India.

Ministry of Education. (2023). State-Wise Educational Expenditure and Literacy Trends.

Ministry of Education (MoE). (2024). *UDISE+ 2022–23: School education in India*. Department of School Education & Literacy, Government of India.

Ministry of Education (formerly Ministry of Human Resource Development (MHRD). (2023). Department of School Education & Literacy, Ministry of Education, Government of India.

Ministry of Health and Family Welfare. (2017). National Health Policy 2017. Government of India.

Ministry of Health and Family Welfare. (2022a). Ayushman Bharat: Strengthening Primary Healthcare Systems in India. Government of India.

Ministry of Health and Family Welfare. (2022b). Health Expenditure and Financing in Indian States: Trends and Challenges. Government of India.

Ministry of Health and Family Welfare. (2022c). *Rural health statistics 2021–22*. Government of India.

Ministry of Health and Family Welfare. (2023a). Ayushman Bharat: Transforming Healthcare in India. National Health Portal.

Ministry of Health and Family Welfare. (2023b). State Health Progress Report. Government of India.

Ministry of Human Resource Development (MHRD). (2020). *Educational statistics at a glance*. Department of School Education & Literacy, Government of India.

Ministry of Human Resource Development/Department of School Education & Literacy (MHRD). (2021). *Year-End Review 2021 – Department of School Education & Literacy, Ministry of Education*. Government of India.

Ministry of Skill Development and Entrepreneurship. (2023). *Annual report 2022–23*. Government of India.

Mizoram Education Report. (2022). Community Participation and Literacy Development in Mizoram.

National Council for Teacher Education (NCTE). (2009). National Curriculum Framework for Teacher Education (NCFTE-2009): Towards Preparing Professional and Humane Teacher.

National Health Systems Resource Centre (NHSRC), Ministry of Health and Family Welfare (MoHFW). (2023). *National health accounts estimates for India (2021–22)*. Government of India.

National Institute of Educational Planning and Administration (NIEPA) (formerly National University of Educational Planning and Administration, NUEPA). (2021). *UDISE+ 2019–20/2020–21: School education in India*. Ministry of Education, Government of India.

National Skill Development Corporation (NSDC). (2023). Vocational Education and Employment Trends in India. NSDC Publications.

National Statistical Office (NSO). (2023). Periodic Labour Force Survey: Education and Skill Development Trends. Government of India.

National University of Educational Planning and Administration (NUEPA). (2021). *Educational statistics at a glance/unified district information system for education (UDISE+) 2020–21*. Ministry of Education, Government of India.

NITI Aayog. (2022a). Health Sector Performance in India: A State-Wise Analysis. Government of India.

NITI Aayog. (2022b). Policy Recommendations for Improving School Education in India.

NITI Aayog. (2022c). State-Wise Analysis of Education Investment.

NITI Aayog. (2022d). *Health Index 2020–21: Progress Report*. Government of India.

NITI Aayog. (2025). *Expanding quality of higher education through States and State public universities*. Government of India.

Northeast India Education Report. (2023). Trends in Literacy and Education in Northeast India. New Delhi: National Institute of Educational Planning and Administration.

NSSO. (2023). Household Survey on Education. National Sample Survey Office, Government of India.

NUEPA. (2022). Status of School Education in India. National University of Educational Planning and Administration.

Registrar General of India. (2022). Sample Registration System (SRS) 2018–20. Government of India.

Schultz, T. W. (1961). Investment in human capital. *The American Economic Review*, *51*(1), 1–17.

Singh, B., & Mehta, R. (2022). Challenges in school education in the Himalayan states. *Journal of Educational Development*, *18*(3), 45–62.
UDISE+. (2023). Unified District Information System for Education. Ministry of Education, Government of India.
UNDP. (2023). *Strengthening health systems for equitable access in developing regions*. UNDP Publications.
UNESCO. (2021). *Education for all: The role of teacher-student ratios in learning outcomes*. United Nations Educational, Scientific and Cultural Organization.
UNESCO. (2022). *Global education monitoring report: Infrastructure and equity in schools*. UNESCO Publishing.
UNESCO. (2023). *Global education monitoring report: Gender disparities in literacy*. UNESCO.
UNICEF. (2022). Maternal and Neonatal Health in India: Challenges and Progress. UNICEF.
United Nations. (2015). Sustainable Development Goals: Goal 3 – Good Health and Well-being. UN Publications.
World Bank. (2020). Education and Development in South Asia: Challenges and Opportunities. The World Bank Group.
World Bank. (2021). *Education for development: The role of education in reducing poverty*. World Bank.
World Bank. (2023). *Bridging the learning gap in remote regions: Policy strategies for education in India*. World Bank Publications.
World Health Organization (WHO). (2021). Strengthening Healthcare Systems in Remote and Mountainous Regions. WHO Reports.
World Health Organization (WHO). (2022). Integrating Traditional Medicine into Modern Healthcare Systems: A Global Perspective. WHO Reports.
World Health Organization (WHO). (2023a). Global Health Statistics Report.
World Health Organization (WHO). (2023b). Maternal and Child Health Report.
World Health Organization (WHO). (2023c). Primary health care on the road to Universal health coverage: 2023 monitoring report. World Health Organization.
World Health Organization. (2023d). Accelerating Anaemia Reduction: A comprehensive Framework for Action. World Health Organization

Chapter 5

Alkire, S., & Santos, M. E. (2014). Measuring acute poverty in the developing world: Robustness and scope of the Multidimensional Poverty Index. *World Development*, *59*, 251–274.
Anand, I. (2024, July 9). What does the data from the household consumer expenditure survey 2022 23 tell us? *The India Forum*. https://www.theindiaforum.in/public-policy/household-consumption-expenditure-survey-2022-23, viewed on July 10, 2024.
Baruah, S. (2020). In the name of the nation: India and its Northeast.
Bhattacharya, P., & Patel, U. (2020). Poverty, inequality, and tribal welfare in India's Northeast. *Journal of Regional Development*, *45*(2), 65–83.
Chand, R., & Singh, A. (2021). Poverty and livelihoods in India's mountain regions. NITI Discussion Paper.
Chand, R., et al. (2021). Rural Transformation in India: The Role of Public Policy. NITI Aayog.
Chatterjee, S., & Ray, R. (2019). The evolution of consumption inequality in India: 1983–2012. *World Development*, *116*, 252–266.
Chatterjee, U., Murgai, R., & Ravallion, M. (2021). Pathways to reducing inequality in India's rural economy. World Bank Policy Research Working Paper.

Das, P., & Sharma, R. (2021). Empowering rural women through self-help groups: Evidence from the Himalayan states. *Journal of Rural Development*, *40*(3), 345–367.
Deaton, A., & Drèze, J. (2002). Poverty and inequality in India: A re-examination. *Economic and Political Weekly*, *37*(36), 3729–3748.
Dev, S. M. (2020). Social security and welfare in India: A review. IGIDR Working Paper.
Dev, S. M., & Ravi, C. (2019). Human development and state performance in India. Economic and Political Weekly.
Drèze, J., & Khera, R. (2017). Recent social progress in India: Some positive developments. Economic and Political Weekly.
Economic Survey. (2024). Economic survey 2023–24. Ministry of Finance, Government of India.
Engel, E. (1857). Die Productions- und Consumtionsverhältnisse des Königreichs Sachsen.
Ghatak, M., & Kumar, R. (2024, May 29). Determining how many Indians are poor today. *Ideas for India*. https://www.ideasforindia.in/topics/poverty-inequality/determining-how-many-indians-are-poor-today.html, viewed on September 10, 2024.
Government of India. (2024). MGNREGA Annual Report 2023–24. Ministry of Rural Development.
Himanshu. (2019a). Inequality in India: A review of recent trends. Ideas for India.
Himanshu. (2019b). Inequality in India: A review of levels and trends. In *The oxford handbook of the Indian economy*. Oxford University Press.
Himanshu, Lanjouw, P., & Schirmer, P. (2025). Poverty decline in India after 2011–12: Bigger picture evidence. *Economic and Political Weekly*, *60*(15), 36–46.
Jha, R., & Gaiha, R. (2015). Inequality, poverty and well-being in India.
Kapur, R., Mishra, P., & Tiwari, S. (2023). Impact of MGNREGA on rural livelihoods in the Indian Himalayan region. *Economic & Political Weekly*, *58*(14), 22–29.
Khan, F. (2022). Rural livelihoods and women empowerment in Jammu and Kashmir: A case study of UMEED. *Social Change and Development*, *19*(2), 120–137.
Kishore, R., & Jha, A. (2024, February 25). First consumption data released after 2011–2012. *Hindustan Times*. https://www.hindustantimes.com/india-news/first-consumption data-released-after-20112012-101708801139276.html, viewed on September 10, 2024.
Lalnunmawia, F., Zote, H., & Lalmalsawmi, P. (2023). Implementation of PMAY-G in North-East India: Challenges and achievements. *Indian Journal of Social Work*, *84*(1), 71–90.
Mahajan, K. (2022). Urban inequality and policy interventions in India. *Journal of Development Economics*.
Mehrotra, S. (2021). Informality and inequality in India's labour market. IHD Working Paper.
Mehrotra, S., & Kumar, R. R. (2024, February 27). Why the 2023 consumption survey is not comparable with previous rounds. *The Wire*. https://thewire.in/economy/why-the 2023-consumption-survey-is-not-comparable-with-previous-rounds, viewed on September 10, 2024.
Mehrotra, S., & Parida, J. K. (2021). Why inequality persists in India's growth story. IHD Working Paper Series.
Ministry of Housing and Urban Affairs (MoHUA). (2022). National Urban Livelihoods Mission Annual Report.
Nayyar, D., & Sharma, A. (2020). Urbanization and inequality in India. Oxford India Studies.
NITI Aayog. (2021a). National Multidimensional Poverty Index Baseline Report. Government of India.

NITI Aayog. (2021b). SDG India Index & Dashboard 2020–21.
NITI Aayog. (2023). Multidimensional Poverty Index: A Progress Review of Indian States. Government of India.
NITI Aayog. (2024). Multidimensional Poverty in India Since 2005–06. Discussion Paper. Government of India.
OPHI. (2021). Global Multidimensional Poverty Index Report 2021. Oxford Poverty and Human Development Initiative.
Planning Commission. (2014). Report of the Expert Group to Review the Methodology for Measurement of Poverty.
Sen, A. (1997). *On economic inequality*. Oxford University Press.
Sen, A., & Himanshu. (2004). Poverty and inequality in India. *Economic and Political Weekly*.
Singh, B., & Choudhary, N. (2022). Gender and public works: MGNREGA in the Northeast. *Indian Journal of Labour Economics*, *65*(2), 289–305.
UNDP. (2020). Human Development Report 2020: The Next Frontier – Human Development and the Anthropocene. United Nations Development Programme.
UNDP. (2022). Multidimensional Poverty Reduction in India: A Decade of Progress.
UNDP. (2023). South Asia Human Development Report: Changing Consumption and Inequality.
United Nations Development Programme (UNDP) & Oxford Poverty and Human Development Initiative (OPHI). (2021). Global Multidimensional Poverty Index 2021: Unmasking Disparities by Ethnicity, Caste and Gender. UNDP and OPHI, University of Oxford.
Verghese, B. G. (2023). Northeast India: Development, Demography and Policy.
World Bank. (2022). Poverty and Shared Prosperity Report: Correcting Course.

Chapter 6

Andes – Laboratory for Natural Hazards (2018). https://www.fona.de › andes-laboratory-for-natural-ha . . . 05 June
Anees, S. U., & Bhat, M. S. (2016). History of natural disasters in Kashmir Valley, Jammu and Kashmir with special reference to earthquakes. *International Journal of Innovative Research in Science, Engineering and Technology*, *5*(9), 17163–17171.
Awasthi, I. C. (2023, May 4). Uttarakhand's development trajectory: A disaster, business lines. *The Hindu*.
Awasthi, I. C. (2024, July–September). How do disasters impact development? Insights from Indian mountain economies. *IASSI Quarterly, Contributions to Indian Social Science*, *43*(3).
Awasthi, I. C., Mehta, G. S., & Mamgain, R. P. (2014). Uttarakhand disaster: Lessons and way forward. Occasional Paper-6, Giri Institute of Development Studies, Lucknow.
Ballabh, V. S., & Singh, K. (1988). Van panchayats in Uttar Pradesh hills: A critical analysis. *Economic and Political Weekly*, *23*(52).
Byers, E. (1995). Mountain agenda: Environmentally Sustainable and Equitable Development Opportunities, The Mountain Institute, Franklin, West Virginia, USA (Mimeo).
Chandel, V. B., Sharma, S. K., & Wason, R. K. (2010). Seismicity and seismotectonics of Himachal Pradesh and adjoining areas. *Journal of the Geological Society of India*, *75*, 709–720.
Chandel, V. B. S., & Brar, K. K. (2010). Seismicity and vulnerability in Himalayas: The case of Himachal Pradesh, India. *Geomatics, Natural Hazards and Risk, 1*(1), 69–84.
Chopra, R. (2013, August 10). Restoring normalcy in Uttarakhand. *Economic & Political Weekly*, *XLVIIL*(32).

Chopra, R. (2014). *Uttarakhand development and ecological sustainability*. Oxfam India.

Chopra, R. (2023, January 12): Apathy compounds Joshimath's tragedy. *Hindustan Times*.

Dhar, N., & Nandargi, S. (2000). A study of floods in the Brahmaputra basin in India. *International Journal of Climatology*, *20*, 771–781.

Disaster Mitigation and Management Centre (DMMC). (2011). Slope, Instability and Geo-Environmental Issues of the Area around Nainital, Dehradun.

Goyet, C. (2008). *Information gaps in relief, recovery and reconstruction in the aftermath of natural disasters in data against natural disasters* (S. Amin & M. Goldstein). The World Bank.

GRID-Arendal. (2018). Mountain adaptation Outlook series – Outlook on climate change adaptation in the Hindu Kush Himalaya. https://www.grida.no›resources

Gupta, A. K. (2014). *Loss of life in Kashmir: A tale of man-made disaster*. The Water Digest Report.

Gupta, P., Khanna, A., & Majumdar, S. (2012). Disaster management in flash floods in Leh (Ladakh): A case study. *Indian Journal of Community Medicine*, *37*(3), 185–190. https://doi.org/10.4103/0970-0218.99928

Gupta, R., & Joshi, B. (1990). Landslide hazard zoning using the GIS approach – A case study from the Ramganga catchment, Himalayas. *Engineering Geology*, *28*, 119–131.

Hassan, R. (2014). Disasters in Kashmir: Impact and response. *Journal of Humanities and Social Science*, *19*(7), 32–42.

Ives, D. J. (1997). Comparative inequalities – mountain communities and mountain families. In B. Messerli & J. D. Ives (eds.), *Mountains of the world: A global priority*. The Parthenon Publishing Group.

Ives, J. D. (2022). *Sustainable mountain development: Getting the facts right*, 2nd ed. Springer Nature.

Ives, J. D., Messerli, B., & Bishnu, D. U. (1997). *Mountains of the world: A global priority*. Parthenon Publishing Group.

Jodha, N. S., Banskota, M., & Pratap, T. (eds.) (1992). *Sustainable mountain agriculture: Perspectives and issues*, Vol. 1, International Centre for Integrated Mountain Development (ICIMOD), Oxford & IBH.

Kahlon, S., Vishwa, B. S. C., & Brar, K. K. (2014, September). Landslides in Himalayan mountains: A study of Himachal Pradesh, India. *International Journal of IT, Engineering and Applied Sciences Research (IJIEASR)*, *3*(9).

Klein Julia, A., Catherine, T., Anne, N., Kelly, H. A., Adrienne, G. R., Shikui, D., & Margreth, K. (2019). Catalyzing Transformations to Sustainability in the World's Mountains, 2019 American Geophysical Union, Mimeo. https://doi.org/10.1029/2018EF001024

Kumar, N., & Tyagi, P. (2021). Landslides in Jammu & Kashmir union territory: A data inventory from the year 2018 To 2021. *Quest Journals Journal of Research in Environmental and Earth Sciences*, *7*(5), 52–54. ISSN(Online): 2348–2532.

Libiszewski, S., & Bächler, G. (1997). Conflicts in mountain areas – a predicament for sustainable development. In B. Messerli & J. D. Ives (eds.), *Mountains of the world: A global priority* (pp. 103–130). Parthenon Publishing Group.

Li Tianchi, S., Chalise, R., & Upreti, B. N. (eds.) (2001). *Landslide hazard mitigation in the Hindu Kush-Himalayas*. ICIMOD.

Mathew, J., Jha, V. K., & Rawat, G. S. (2007). Weights of evidence modelling for landslide hazard zonation mapping in part of Bhagirathi Valley, Uttarakhand. *Current Science*, *92*, 628–638.

Murthy, S. R. (2000, October). Disaster and mental health: Responses of mental health professionals. *The Indian Journal of Social Work*, *61*(4).

North Eastern Space Applications Centre. (2022). Seasonal Landslide Inventory for NER, North Eastern Regional Node for Disaster Risk Reduction (NERDRR), Government of India, Department of Space, Meghalaya.

Pande, R. K., Pande, A., & Koul, N. K. (2000). Psychological impact of natural disasters: A study of survivors in the Indian context. *Indian Journal of Psychiatry*, *42*(1), 1–7.

Pandey, V. K. (2018). Geological and geotechnical challenges in road widening, national highway-44: Jammu-Udhampur-Banihal-Qazigund, J&K, India. *International Research Journal of Earth Science*, *6*(12), 22–28.

Papola, T. S. (2014a, September 10). *Development of the Indian Himalayan States*, 20th Pandit Govind Ballabh Pant Memorial Lecture delivered at G.B. Pant Institute of Himalayan Environment & Development, Kosi-Katarmal, Almora.

Papola, T. S. (2014b). Uttarakhand disaster–beyond rescue and relief: Some *Lessons for* Reconstruction and Long-Term Development. *Lessons & Learning from Disasters: Uttarakhand State Commentary*, CHEA.

Papola, T. S. (2014c). *Infrastructure development in the North Eastern region: Issues and challenges*. Institute for Studies in Industrial Development.

Papola, T. S. (2014d). *Regional development and disparities in India*. Institute for Studies in Industrial Development, New Delhi.

Papola, T. S. (2014e). *Development in the mountain regions of India: Issues and strategies*. Institute for Studies in Industrial Development, New Delhi.

Parasuraman, S., & Acharya, N. (2000, October). Analysing forms of vulnerability in as disaster. *The Indian Journal of Social Work*, *61*(4).

Patel, S. K., Nanda, A., Singh, G., & Patel, S. (2020). A review of disasters in Jammu and Kashmir, and Ladakh region in India. *International Journal of Population Studies*, *6*(1), 69–81. https://doi.org/10.18063/ijps.v6i1.1180

Planning Commission. (2013, November). Report of the Committee to Study Development in Hill States arising from Management of Forest Lands with Special Focus on Creation of Infrastructure, Livelihood and Human Development, New Delhi.

Price, M. (2004). Introduction: Sustainable mountain development from Rio to Bishkek and beyond. In M. F. Price, L. F. Jansky, & A. A. Iatsenia (eds.), *Key issues for mountain areas*. United Nations, University Press, Tokyo, New York, Paris, United Nations University.

Saha, A. K., Gupta, R. P., & Arora, M. K. (2002). Himalayas GIS based landslide Hazard Zonation in the Bhagirathi (Ganga) Valley, Himalayas. *International Journal of Remote Sensing*, *23*, 357–369.

Sati, V. P. (2023). Geo-hydrological disasters in the Uttarakhand Himalaya: Assessment and mapping, natural hazards. *Natural Hazards*. https://doi.org/10.1007/s11069-023-06287-1

SDMP. (2017). State Disaster Management Plan. India: Department of Disaster Management, Relief, Rehabilitation and Construction, Government of Jammu and Kashmir.

Shafi, M. (1950). Forest in the national economy in India. *The Geographer*, Aligarh (India), *4*, 63–69.

Tolia, R. (2013, June 23). Disastrous management of Uttarakhand – II. *Garhwal Post*, *5*.

UNEP World Conservation Monitoring Centre. (2002). Environmental Change and Sustainable Development in Mountains, Mountain Watch.

Vaidya, R. A., Shrestha, M. S., Nasab, N., Gurung, D. R., Kozo, N., Pradhan, N. S., & Wasson, R. J. (2019). Disaster risk reduction and building resilience in the Hindu Kush Himalaya in the Hindu Kush Himalaya assessment. *Springer Link*. https://link.springer.com›chapter

Valdiya, K. S. (1976). Himalayan transverse faults and their parallelism with subsurface structures of North Indian plains. *Techno-Physics*, 32, 352, 386.
Valdiya, K. S. (1985). Accelerated erosion and landslide-prone zones in the Central Himalayan region. In J. S. Singh (ed.), *Environmental regeneration in Himalaya* (pp. 12–37). Central Himalayan Environment Association and Gyanodaya Prakashan.
World Bank. (2010). *Natural Hazards, unnatural disasters: The economics of effective prevention.* Washington, DC.
World Bank Blogs. (2021, December 15). From the Alps to the Pamirs: Investing in mountain economies to make people and places more resilient. *3*(9). https://blogs.worldbank.org›europeandcentralasia›

Chapter 7

Business Standard (IANS). (2018, October 12). *Sikkim's 100% organic farming wins FAO's Future Policy Gold Award.* Business Standard.
Central Electricity Authority. (2022). *Annual report on hydroelectric generation in India 2021–22.* Ministry of Power, Government of India.
Chauhan, J. S. (2014). Horticulture development in Himachal Pradesh: Lessons for other hill states. *Indian Journal of Agricultural Economics*, *69*(3), 387–400.
CSIR-Institute of Himalayan Bioresource Technology. (2020). *Annual report 2019–20*, Palampur. CSIR-IHBT.
Deccan Herald. (2024, January 25). *12 distinctive products of Arunachal obtain GI tags.* Deccan Herald.
Department of Industries and Commerce Tripura (Government of Tripura). (Year not specified). *Bamboo sector development and promotion in Tripura.* Department of Industries and Commerce.
DIPR Mizoram. (2025). *Chief Minister declares Mizoram the first fully literate state in India.* Dipr Mizoram.
Government of Himachal Pradesh. (2016). *Economic survey of Himachal Pradesh 2015–16.* Department of Economics and Statistics.
Government of Himachal Pradesh. (2023). *Economic survey of Himachal Pradesh 2022–23.* Department of Economics and Statistics.
Government of India. (2024). *Economic survey 2023–24.* Ministry of Finance, Department of Economic Affairs.
The Hans India. (2025). *Tripura's bamboo sector expands with market diversification and cross-border trade with Bangladesh.* The Hans India (News Report).
Himachal Pradesh State Electricity Board. (2021). *Annual administrative report 2020–21.* HPSEB.
HP General Studies. (2019). *Satyanand Stokes – Samuel Evans Stokes . . . .* Himachal Pradesh General Studies.
IBEF. (2020, July 27). *Kashmiri saffron gets GI tag.* IBEF.
ICCA Consortium & TERI. (2018). *Documentation of community-conserved areas of Nagaland.* iccaconsortium.org
IJCRT. (2024). *Sustainable development goals: Comparing Himachal Pradesh . . . .* IJCRT.
India PR Distribution. (2020). Himachal Pradesh Horticulture Development Project (HPHDP): Transforming Horticulture through Scientific Orchard Management and Improved Planting Material. Press Release (IP Press), Government of Himachal Pradesh in collaboration with the World Bank.
Institute for Human Development. (2024). *Human development in the North Eastern region: Issues of environment, livelihoods and sustainability.* New Delhi: Institute for Human Development. (Mimeo).

Jal Jeevan Mission. (2021). *Spring shed management initiatives (Uttarakhand)*. Press Information Bureau.

Krishi Jagran. (2022, December 18). *J&K govt increases cold storage capacity by 700% in 6 years*. Krishi Jagran.

Loktak Development Authority. (2024). *Annual report 2023–24*. Government of Manipur.

Ministry of Education. (2020). *Unified District Information System for Education (UDISE+) 2019–20 report*. Government of India.

Ministry of Environment, Forest and Climate Change. (2020). *Compensatory afforestation and R&R guidelines for hydroelectric projects*. MoEFCC.

Mongabay-India. (2018, May 9). *A Naga village's journey . . . Amur falcon*. Mongabay-India.

National Cooperative Development Corporation. (2020). *Detailed Project Report (DPR) on Integrated Cooperative Development Project (ICDP) in Arunachal Pradesh*. NCDC, Ministry of Agriculture & Farmers Welfare, Government of India.

National Health Mission. (2022). *State programme implementation plan: Himachal Pradesh*. Ministry of Health and Family Welfare.

NITI Aayog. (2021). *SDG India index & dashboard 2020–21: Partnerships in the decade of action*. Government of India.

PeepulTree. (2018). *Satyanand stokes and the apple state*. Peepul Tree World.

Pharma Innovation Journal. (2021). Impact of connectivity and digital technologies on agricultural transformation in Arunachal Pradesh. *The Pharma Innovation Journal*, *10*(6), 1345–1350.

Planning Department, Government of Himachal Pradesh. (2023). *Home stays and dimensions of sustainable tourism in HP*. Planning Department of Himachal Pradesh.

Press Information Bureau. (2023). *Sikkim's organic farming model and promotion of gi-tagged products boost sustainable livelihoods and eco-tourism*. Ministry of Information & Broadcasting, Government of India.

Rajya Sabha, Government of India. (2024, August 5). *Statewise installed hydroelectric capacity (Unstarred Q&A)*. Digital Sansad.

Scroll. (2018, May 14). *The Pangti story: How a Nagaland village turned from hunting ground to safe haven for Amur falcon*. Scroll.in

Sharma, D. (2011, September 13). Samuel Evans Stokes: The man who brought apples to Himachal. *India Today*. https://www.indiatoday.in

Sharma, H. R., & Partap, T. (1993). Apple cultivation in Himachal Pradesh: Impact, problems, and prospects. *Indian Journal of Agricultural Economics*, *48*(3), 345–350.

Sharma, R. (2018). Women's participation in rural tourism: A case study of homestay programmes in Himachal Pradesh. *Journal of Tourism and Hospitality Education*, *8*(1), 24–39.

Times of India. (2025). Mizoram tops literacy charts, becomes 1st fully literate state. *The Times of India*.

Tripathi, P., Joshi, R. K., & Bisht, B. S. (2016). Community institutions and forest management in Uttarakhand: A study of van panchayats. *International Journal of Rural Management*, *12*(1), 1–18.

Tripathi, S., & Bihari, A. (2016). *Van Panchayats of Uttarakhand: A Community-Managed Forest System*. Indian Council of Social Science Research (ICSSR-IMPRESS Project Report).

UNDP. (2024). *Rural women in Ladakh tap solar energy for self-reliance*. Ministry of Food Processing Industries.

United Nations World Tourism Organization. (2019). *Tourism and culture synergies*. UNWTO.

World Bank. (2014, April 10). *Himachal Pradesh horticulture development project.* https://projects.worldbank.org/en/projects-operations/project-detail/P098272
World Bank. (2015, January 28). *Himachal Pradesh: Secrets of success.* The World Bank.
World Intellectual Property Organization (WIPO). (2024a). *Geographical indications and local development: The case of Darjeeling tea and regional value chains.* World Intellectual Property Organization.
World Intellectual Property Organization. (2024b). *Geographical indications and local development: Case studies from India (Sikkim and Kalimpong Floriculture).* WIPO.
WWF-India. (2012). *Community-based natural resource management in the Indian Himalayas: Learning from van panchayats in Uttarakhand.* WWF-India.

Annexures 1

Annexure Chapter 1

Annexure A1.1 Issues of Mountain Economies

European Mountains

Mountain ranges are found across most European countries. In the far north, Iceland and Scandinavia are mountainous, while the southernmost ranges span the Mediterranean islands. To the west, mountains are located in Portugal, Spain, the United Kingdom, and Ireland. The Alps, shared by France, Italy, and Switzerland, are Europe's most renowned mountain range, and other notable ranges in Western Europe include the Pyrenees and the Apennines. These mountains exhibit significant contrasts: western and northern Europe host prosperous economies based on industry and tourism, while southern and eastern Europe have regions of poverty and subsistence living (Mountain Areas in Europe, Final Report, Chapter 1, Introduction). The European Commission's Second Report on Economic and Social Cohesion (2001) states:

> [M]ountainous areas represent geographical barriers. While some mountain regions are economically stable and integrated within the broader EU economy, the majority face challenges; in fact, over 95 per cent of these areas (by land area) qualify for assistance under Objectives 1 or 2 of the Structural Funds.

Appalachian Mountains

The Appalachian Mountains, spanning eastern North America from Quebec to Georgia, once enjoyed dense forest cover prior to the nineteenth century. However, between 1890 and 1910, over 90 per cent of these forests were destroyed by lowland commercial interests. Today, Appalachian forests are generally in good condition, although most of the forestland is privately owned, making timber extraction a tempting option for quick profits. Unfortunately, much of the revenue from this extraction left the mountain communities, with little reinvested in local physical and social infrastructure. Random land use, acid rain, and deforestation led to a loss of cultural landscapes and a decline in biodiversity due to forest fragmentation (Byers, 2000).

African Mountains

African mountains face severe natural resource degradation. In the Ethiopian highlands, soil erosion has reached critical levels, while the water catchments on Zimbabwe's Wedza Mountain are suffering significant soil, water, and vegetation depletion. Drought in the lowlands around Mount Kenya is partly due to the destruction of these crucial water catchments. In Lesotho's highlands, grazing is spreading into sub-pine and alpine grasslands, and agriculture is advancing to elevations of 2,400–2,600 metres, leading to conflicts among mountain stakeholders. In Burundi, land use shifts prioritising human needs have caused biodiversity loss in mountain ecosystems. Some of Africa's densest populations reside in mountainous regions, increasing pressure on these resources. Poverty significantly contributes to unsustainable practices, with many people facing drought and famine, making food security a central concern for the sustainable development of these ecosystems (Gichuki, 2000).

Latin American Mountains

Stretching as the longest mountain range across the continent, the Andes encompass a vast diversity of ecosystems and societies that have adapted to mountain life. Sustainable communities are often located in areas where traditional knowledge is preserved and revitalised. However, the pressures of globalisation and the impact of market forces on less competitive rural communities – particularly in relation to ethnic dynamics – have raised concerns, prompting a reassessment of research priorities amid rapid socio-economic and ecological transformations (Sarmiento, 2000).

South-West Indian Ocean

The South-West Indian Ocean region, encompassing Kenya, Tanzania, Mozambique, South Africa, Madagascar, and their surrounding maritime zones, faces significant risks such as illegal, unregulated, and unreported (IUU) fishing and the impacts of climate change. Establishing a Sustainable Blue Economy (SBE) through robust ocean governance frameworks is urgently needed. However, this endeavour encounters numerous challenges, including the need for stronger institutional coordination for effective SBE implementation, reforming growth-driven policies that overlook sustainability and equity, addressing maritime security issues (such as piracy, trafficking, IUU fishing, and waste dumping), and tackling environmental threats like pollution, overfishing, ecosystem degradation, seabed mining, and climate change

(RESOLVE sarl, 2023). Significant changes may impact mountain livelihoods, downstream resources, and biodiversity conservation. Water scarcity is increasingly evident in lowland areas. For many years, mountain communities have faced marginalisation, yet they have preserved their traditions and cultures, which now represent a valuable source of biological and cultural diversity (Ramamonjisoa, 2000).

The Hindu Kush Himalaya

Alleviating poverty and conserving the environment are key challenges for sustainable development in mountain regions. Tackling these challenges demands a comprehensive approach that integrates economic, political, social, and cultural priorities to ensure the long-term sustainability of mountain ecosystems (Bhadra, 2000). Poverty is widespread in the mountains, often exceeding national averages in HKH countries. The poorest communities, reliant on subsistence farming, face limited market access and basic services. Breaking this poverty cycle requires capacity-building, sustainable agriculture, diversified mountain products, extended market value chains, and natural resource stewardship.

High-value products like non-timber forest goods, medicinal plants, ecotourism, and indigenous honeybee products play a key role in poverty alleviation and community resource management. Livestock products, off-season vegetables, and handicrafts further enhance income opportunities, driving economic transformation in regions like the Sichuan Basin, India, and Nepal.

Mountain products, prized for their purity and nutritional value, need better market linkages, supported by policies promoting their quality and development. ICIMOD is committed to enhancing mountain livelihoods through value chain development and market linkages (ICIMOD, 2015).

Annexure A1.2 Successful Case Studies Across the HKH Regions

The Hindu Kush Himalaya (HKH), often referred to as the "Third Pole," supports the livelihoods of over 240 million people residing in the mountains and 1.65 billion in downstream regions. There is evidence across countries that mountain specificities have been incorporated into development policies and planning, and, as a result, the region has seen rapid transformation from traditional cropping systems to diversified market-oriented products, utilising location-specific diversity in the HKH region (Jodha et al., 1992). The Global Resilience Partnership (GRP) and the International Centre for Integrated Mountain Development (ICIMOD) have recently collaborated to launch the Hindu Kush Himalaya Innovation Challenge for Entrepreneurs (HKH-ICE) 2025. Supported by the UK Foreign, Commonwealth, and Development Office, this initiative aims to foster local innovation and entrepreneurship, promoting scalable solutions to address ecological, market, and value chain challenges. These initiatives focus on (1) resilient innovations for nature: supporting agriculture; (2) water security and resilience; and (3) climate-resilient solutions for sustainable tourism.

India

TRANSFORMATION OF AGRICULTURE TO HORTICULTURE-PRODUCING REGION IN HIMACHAL PRADESH

Himachal Pradesh serves as a distinctive example of successful transformation from traditional agriculture to becoming one of the leading horticulture-producing regions by effectively leveraging its resource-based comparative advantages. Indeed, the government has played a key role by promoting infrastructure (road network, communication, hydroelectric projects, etc.) and by providing institutional support (credit, marketing, price support, processing, and development of ancillary activities). These developments have significant implications for the diversification of the rural economy – from traditional cereal farming to horticultural crops and dairy development – leading to substantial improvements in livelihood opportunities and income levels for the local population.

Nonetheless, this process has also been accompanied by sustained ecological and resource degradation (land and forest, for example) along with inter-regional inequities (Bhati, 1990).

Himachal Pradesh, in north-west India, is known as the "fruit state" or "apple state" due to its significant apple cultivation. Around 31 per cent of its arable land (614,000 ha) is dedicated to horticulture, producing 312,000 tons of fruit annually. Apples are the primary cash crop, covering 42 per cent of horticultural land and making up 90 per cent of fruit production. With 97,438 ha under apple cultivation, about 150,000 growers produce around 510,161 tons yearly. The apple industry contributes approximately $1.7 billion to the state economy, with $150–170 million in direct revenue and $1.5 billion indirectly through job creation (ICIMOD (2012)).

In Himachal Pradesh's Kullu Valley, beekeeping is vital for both honey production and pollination. Beekeepers rent out colonies of indigenous *Apis cerana* and exotic *A. mellifera* bees to apple orchards, boosting apple yields and benefiting both growers and beekeepers. Rental fees range from $13–17 per colony for the apple flowering period. While *A. mellifera* beekeepers manage 100–1500 colonies and practice migratory beekeeping, *A. cerana* keepers operate on a smaller scale with 10–30 stationary colonies. Demand for rented bee colonies for pollination is growing, creating new job opportunities and income for small farmers in the region.

FOREST WATERSHED-BASED CLEAN DEVELOPMENT MECHANISM, HIMACHAL PRADESH

A legal framework that directs carbon credit benefits to the communities actively protecting forests has created strong incentives for watershed and forest conservation. Social and gender equity issues, along with community participation challenges, remain complex but can be partially addressed through fair and transparent sharing of monetary benefits within households. The project's success could further support large-scale afforestation and re-forestation efforts, enhancing benefits for larger downstream communities as well (ICIMOD (2012).

This pioneering mountain project, larger than China's 3,500 hectares CDM project, will aid carbon sequestration and boost income for small farmers. By restoring degraded forestlands in Kangra and Bilaspur districts, it aims to create 343 person-days of employment per hectare while enhancing water storage and other environmental benefits. A recent agreement between the Himachal Pradesh Government and the World Bank, effective until December 2018, guarantees carbon credits to communities, incentivising forest and watershed protection. Ten per cent of carbon revenue goes to the Forest Department, with conditions for tree density, no tree felling, and maintaining forestry use. While social equity and community participation issues remain, this project provides access to green payments.

VAN PANCHAYATS OR COMMUNITY-MANAGED FORESTRY AND THE CONSERVATION AND DEVELOPMENT OF MEDICINAL AND AROMATIC PLANTS AND ORGANIC AGRICULTURE IN UTTARAKHAND – A GREEN SOLUTION FOR MOUNTAIN AGRICULTURE, UTTARAKHAND, INDIA

Van Panchayats (VP: village forest councils) represent the oldest community forestry institution in Uttarakhand, India. Their conservation initiatives provide a range of ecosystem services, including carbon sequestration, which is becoming increasingly vital in addressing climate change. There is potential to incentivise VPs in Uttarakhand through carbon payment schemes, similar to efforts being implemented in Nepal with support from ICIMOD. In India, this approach could be adopted under the Green India Mission, part of the National Action Plan on Climate Change, further contributing to the growth of a green economy (ICIMOD, 2012).

Another notable success story from Uttarakhand is the conservation and development of medicinal and aromatic plants (MAPs). This initiative provides important lessons in sustainable development that can serve as a model for the broader Himalayan region (HKH). MAPs are vital biodiversity resources for socio-economically marginalised Himalayan communities, whose sustainable conservation depends on collaboration among public, private, and civil society sectors. The Uttarakhand experience highlights the MAP sector's positive impact on ecological, economic, and social pillars of sustainability. For continued success, multi-sectoral and interdisciplinary approaches are essential to address cultivation, conservation, processing, marketing, and fair benefit-sharing.

Organic farming reflects the traditional environmental stewardship of local communities, yielding tangible economic benefits. As agriculture is the backbone of mountain economies, sustainable development is closely tied to the growth of the agricultural sector. Organic agriculture, encompassing forestry, range, and pasture development, aligns seamlessly with sustainable mountain development. Global reports show that organic practices support climate change adaptation and enhance resilience for farmers in vulnerable areas. By localising food systems, organic agriculture could potentially reduce global greenhouse gas emissions by nearly 30 per cent and save one-sixth of global energy use.

The formation and empowerment of farmers' associations have played a crucial role in enhancing participation and ensuring equity for small-scale farmers. These associations have also helped address key supply chain issues, including marketing, certification, and the implementation of internal quality management systems to ensure traceability and compliance with organic standards. The Uttarakhand Organic Commodity Board (UOCB) was established in 2003, with support for the initiative sought from the Sri Ratan Tata Trust (SRTT).

CONSERVATION AND DEVELOPMENT OF MEDICINAL AND AROMATIC PLANTS IN UTTARAKHAND, INDIA

Medicinal and aromatic plants (MAPs) are vital to biodiversity and are key to local healthcare, rural livelihoods, and the herbal industry, especially in the Himalayas, where MAP diversity and traditional knowledge are abundant. However, over 90 per cent of MAPs for the herbal industry are sourced from the wild, threatening high-value species. Following Agenda 21 and CBD guidelines, conservation and sustainable use strategies are needed, involving stakeholders at all levels (ICIMOD, 2012).

Uttarakhand, known as India's "herbal state," has about 5,000 vascular plant species, with one-third holding medicinal properties. Since 2000, the state has reformed its MAPs sector to boost local livelihoods through community participation. A Forest and Rural Development Commissioner position was created to connect forestry, biodiversity, and rural development. Key reforms included the State Medicinal Plants Board (SMPB) and Herbal Research and Development Institute (HRDI), fostering sustainable MAPs sector growth with contributions from diverse stakeholders.

The state has also initiated MAP inventory and mapping to integrate Conservation, Development, and Harvest (CDH) plans into forestry management, improving local access to non-timber forest products (NTFPs).

ORGANIC AGRICULTURE IN UTTARAKHAND (INDIA) – A GREEN SOLUTION FOR MOUNTAIN AGRICULTURE

Organic farming in Uttarakhand draws on traditional environmental practices, offering economic benefits and supporting sustainable development. Agriculture is central to the mountain economy, but green revolution methods bypassed these regions due to costly inputs and limited infrastructure. Instead, Uttarakhand has leveraged its agro-biodiversity, forestry resources, and carbon-sequestering practices to promote organic agriculture (ICIMOD (2012).

The state established the Uttarakhand Organic Commodity Board (UOCB) in 2003, with support from the Sri Ratan Tata Trust. Programmes like Himmothan Pariyojna help small farmers with marketing, certification, and quality management. Organic farming here aligns with sustainable development and climate resilience, with potential to reduce global greenhouse gases by 30 per cent and cut energy use significantly.

PIONEERING A CLEAN ENERGY

The Government of Uttarakhand introduced the State Solar Policy 2023 to reduce reliance on fossil fuels, promote renewable energy, and ensure energy security while fostering inclusive development. The policy aims to advance the clean energy transition by integrating solar energy through distributed solar systems, innovative business models, and broader adoption of solar applications across various sectors. By harnessing solar energy, the state seeks to enhance power system stability, boost rural incomes, improve the reliability and quality of electricity supply, and create livelihood opportunities, particularly for youth and women.

IMPROVED NATURAL RESOURCE MANAGEMENT FOR SECURING LIVELIHOODS IN NORTH-EAST INDIA

North-east India, known for its rich biodiversity and high poverty, has historically faced aid dependency. The North Eastern Region Community Resource Management Project for Upland Areas (NERCORMP), funded by IFAD and the Government of India, was launched to sustainably improve the livelihoods of around 87,000 households across Assam, Manipur, and Meghalaya by enhancing resource management and environmental protection. NERCORMP focuses on community capacity-building, economic activities, biodiversity conservation, social services, and infrastructure, now expanding into Arunachal Pradesh and Manipur (ICIMOD (2012).

The project fosters inclusive, community-led development via Natural Resource Management Groups (NaRMGs), enabling local decision-making, gender inclusion, and self-help groups that support savings, micro-credit, and alternative livelihoods like horticulture and handicrafts. Infrastructure improvements include irrigation systems and village roads. By blending traditional practices with new techniques, communities are conserving biodiversity, setting up reserves, and using Participatory 3D Models for planning. NaRMGs also harmonise with traditional institutions and link communities with the private sector to add value to local products and access broader markets.

ICIMOD published a compendium of case studies on the Indian Himalayan region from 2017 to 2019. These studies document the traditional and indigenous knowledge systems of farming communities across the 11 mountain states. They focus on addressing the urgent challenges of sustaining mountain livelihoods and fostering development in the face of climate change (ICIMOD, 2019).

TRANSBOUNDARY ECOTOURISM IN THE EASTERN HIMALAYAS IN SIKKIM (INDIA) AND BHUTAN

Ecotourism in the Eastern Himalayas has become a valuable tool for sustainable mountain development, balancing environmental conservation with cultural preservation and local revenue generation. Both India and Bhutan are promoting ecotourism, leading to increased tourist arrivals, longer stays, and higher spending, benefiting local communities. The region's unique natural beauty and Buddhist heritage attract visitors, who appreciate the safe environment and well-preserved bio-cultural landscape (ICIMOD, 2012).

India and Bhutan have individual tourism policies, yet cross-border cooperation is encouraged to boost tourism and pro-poor enterprises in this region. ICIMOD's Regional Cooperation Framework supports transboundary conservation and harmonises policies to sustainably manage shared landscapes like the Kanchenjunga area.

Nepal

THE EXPERIMENTS OF THE LUMLE AND PAKHRIBAS AGRICULTURAL PROJECTS

Another example is of Nepal, which is not only a land-locked but also a vast area of the country that is still backward and underdeveloped. With increasing pressure of the population and its adverse effect on natural resource use, the country has been facing problems of food deficiency and pervasive poverty. The experiments of the Lumle and Pakhribas agricultural projects were truly pioneering in transforming the western and eastern development regions of the country. The Lumle Project had grown from the strong foundation laid at the Lumle Agricultural Centre (LAC), which integrated institutional, technological, and participatory approaches, with a view to disseminating relevant technologies to farmers. It had built up a strong linkage with research, technology, extension, training, and other inputs and involved farmers at every stage with comprehensive understanding of the field conditions that favoured development of overall farming system. This project had successfully demonstrated that mountain farming could provide sustainable livelihoods to its population (Pound et al., 1992).

Likewise, the Pakhribas Agricultural Centre (PAC) was established in the eastern development region with a view to carrying out multi-disciplinary, farmer-oriented research activities, utilising local resource for sustainable farming, evolving appropriate technologies suiting local conditions, and involving communities so that long-term sustainable farming system could be developed.

The Pakhribas Project has developed suitable technologies for crop production, indigenously bred varieties, fodder and firewood, and overall farming system (Chand et al., 1992). These projects have proved to be not only sustainable in the hill farming context but also highly replicable to other HKH region.

The success of these types of projects largely relied on external funding, autonomous working environment, flexibility, strong linkages, participatory approach, and a zeal to transform, but the lack or absence of these attributes might not have produced the desired results by these pioneering projects. Yet another example is from the northern-most districts of Pakistan, where the Aga Khan Rural Support Programme (AKRSP), with its sustained efforts, had created village-level institutions combining productive physical infrastructure and resource management, which made a significant impact in village economies in terms of increased opportunities of incomes and livelihoods (Husain, 1992). It is one of the finest examples of how subsistence and rather static village economies in the region saw transformation into economies of opportunities and the well-being of the people. Thus, it truly represents a community development project based on strong institutional foundation. But how far such institutional innovations would continue to evolve and spread in village economies in a fast-changing environment largely dictated by the market remains a key question.

The other notable example in the region is Western Sichuan (China), which possessed an enormous diversity of resource base (plant, animal, agro-cottage) that has provided the region the advantage of developing a variety of cottage industries which helped transform the subsistence economy into a commodity-producing and exchanger economy (Zhaoguang et al., 1992). Of course, the locational advantages were also associated with constraints posed by a lack of access to the road network, market, and other support services that had produced considerable bottlenecks in the way to reap the full benefits.

However, the earlier innovative examples are neither many in the regions nor these have been replicated to the extent desired. As a result, the economies in the regions are, by and large, suffer from food deficiency, human poverty and degradation of natural resources thereby posing serious threats to the sustainability of mountain economies. Thus, there are few lessons to be learned within the regions, and numerous lessons to be unlearned from within the regions, which clearly show why certain projects succeeded and why others could not even be designed or evolved.

COMMUNITY FORESTRY AND FOREST GOVERNANCE IN NEPAL

Since the mid-2000s, Nepal's community forestry has shifted to more inclusive, sustainable, and market-oriented practices to address evolving socio-political and environmental challenges. As community forestry expands into carbon markets and PES (payment for ecosystem services) initiatives, local communities play a greater role in global environmental goals, though this can create competition that risks benefiting the most capable more than the marginalised. Community forestry has helped re-green Nepal's mountains, engaging about 40 per cent of the population in managing 25 per cent of the forests (ICIMOD (2012)).

The initiative has moved from subsistence to sustainable practices, supporting local democracy and economic development, particularly through Community Forestry User Groups (CFUGs) which empower rural communities and women. With links to multiple government ministries, CFUGs tackle poverty, environmental fragility, and improve livelihood assets, making community forestry a model for balancing conservation with economic and social progress. Nepal's community forestry allows local ownership and sustainable use of forest resources. Social equity and fair benefit-sharing in forestry are key but challenging, with inclusive policies offering a path forward. Strengthening property rights and leveraging benefits from global services like REDD+ requires external support.

The programme has contributed to social, economic, and environmental goals and supports several MDG targets, proving the effectiveness of community-based resource management in enhancing mountain ecosystems and livelihoods.

NEPAL'S BIOGAS PROGRAMME, THE GREEN ECONOMY, AND SUSTAINABLE MOUNTAIN DEVELOPMENT

Biogas has provided a clean and eco-friendly energy solution to rural households in Nepal since 1977. With support from the Biodiversity Support Programme (BSP), its development has brought together government bodies, donors, the private sector, NGOs, and community organisations. The expansion of biogas usage has been further supported through subsidies and low-interest loans (ICIMOD, 2012).

Biogas systems benefit households by reducing firewood collection time, improving air quality, promoting sanitation with attached toilets, and creating local jobs in plant construction, maintenance, and marketing. Additionally, the leftover slurry serves as an organic fertiliser, enhancing agricultural productivity. The programme aligns with Nepal's sustainable energy goals and poverty reduction efforts by providing accessible energy, supporting rural economies, and cutting emissions.

With over 243,000 biogas plants operational as of 2011 and a high success rate of 93 per cent, Nepal stands out in quality enforcement compared to neighbouring countries. Recently, more focus has shifted towards research and development, addressing both biogas technology and agricultural benefits for rural communities.

Pakistan

AGA KHAN RURAL SUPPORT PROGRAMMES (AKRSP)

Yet another example is from the northern-most districts of Pakistan, where the Aga Khan Rural Support Programme (AKRSP), with its sustained efforts, had created village-level institutions combining productive physical infrastructure and resource management, which made a significant impact in village economies in terms of increased opportunities of incomes and livelihoods (Husain, 1992). It is one of the finest examples of how subsistence and rather static village economies in the region saw transformation into economies of opportunities and the well-being of the people. Thus, it truly represents a community development project based on a strong institutional foundation. But how far such institutional innovations would continue to evolve and spread in village economies in a fast-changing environment largely dictated by the market remains a key question.

MICRO-HYDRO ENERGY DEVELOPMENT IN NORTHERN PAKISTAN

This case study showcases a successful community-driven model for renewable energy and climate change mitigation in the vulnerable mountain regions of Gilgit-Baltistan and Chitral in northern Pakistan. With support from the government, NGOs, and funding agencies, local communities have established nearly 300 micro-hydro projects (MHPs). These initiatives have provided sustainable energy, lowered carbon emissions, and generated certified emission reductions (CERs) under an UN-recognised clean development mechanism (CDM) project (ICIMOD, 2012).

Initiated by the Aga Khan Rural Support Programme in 1990, MHPs now serve as vital energy sources for rural communities, replacing deforestation and diesel use. By 2009, the CDM project bundled 103 new MHPs (totalling up to 15 MW capacity), with communities investing 20 per cent in cash, Pakistan Poverty Alleviation Fund covering 50 per cent as grants, and the remaining 30 per cent funded through carbon income and loans.

The MHP model leverages public funds to raise community equity and is scalable, with larger units operating as utilities, focusing on economic, social, and environmental benefits.

China

DIVERSITY IN RESOURCE BASE IN WESTERN SICHUAN

Another notable example in the region is Western Sichuan (China), which possessed an enormous diversity of resource base (plant, animal, agro-cottage) that has provided the region the advantage of developing a variety of cottage industries, which helped transform the subsistence economy into a commodity-producing and exchanger economy (Zhaoguang, et al., 1992). Of course, locational advantages were also associated with constraints posed by a lack of access to the road network, market, and other support services that had produced considerable bottlenecks in the way to reap the full benefits.

However, the earlier innovative examples are neither many in the regions nor have these been replicated to the extent desired. As a result, the economies in the regions, by and large, suffer from food deficiency, human poverty, and degradation of natural resources, thereby posing serious threats to the sustainability of mountain economies. Thus, there are few lessons to be learned within the regions, and numerous lessons to be unlearned from within the regions, which clearly show why certain projects succeeded and why others could not even be designed or evolved.

INTEGRATED TOURISM AND PARK MANAGEMENT: SHANGRI-LA, CHINA

Tourism development in Shangri-La, Yunnan, China, demonstrates how nature conservation and cultural preservation can go hand in hand. Efforts focus on protecting sensitive habitats, such as those for the golden monkey, and safeguarding local cultural heritage while developing infrastructure. Involving local communities, religious leaders, and stakeholders in planning and tourism management ensures sustainability and supports local livelihoods through revenue-sharing (ICIMOD, 2012).

Education for visitors, tour operators, and local youth is crucial for promoting responsible tourism. Developing local products derived from biodiversity – such as medicinal plants and mushrooms – has the potential to establish distinctive tourism brands. Integrating tourism into park planning enhances conservation and local development, as seen in Shangri-La ecotourism, where environmental impacts are minimised while benefiting local communities. This includes licensing operators and promoting awareness among visitors.

Annexure Chapter 2

Table A2.1 Labour Force Participation Rate (%), 2011–12 (15+ Years, UPSS)

States/UTs	*Rural*			*Urban*			*Total*		
	Male	*Female*	*All*	*Male*	*Female*	*All*	*Male*	*Female*	*All*
Arunachal Pradesh	73.9	41.5	57.9	69.6	21.2	47.5	73.0	37.9	56.0
Himachal Pradesh	76.3	67.2	71.5	77.6	30.1	55.1	76.5	63.3	69.6
Jammu and Kashmir	76.9	36.6	57.5	73.5	19.0	47.5	76.1	32.4	55.1
Manipur	76.8	38.5	58.0	75.1	29.1	51.7	76.3	36.0	56.3
Meghalaya	81.1	62.1	71.7	67.7	30.3	48.4	78.2	54.8	66.5
Mizoram	87.5	59.9	74.2	74.8	38.2	56.0	81.4	48.8	65.1
Nagaland	81.1	47.3	64.0	69.5	29.3	50.3	76.9	41.2	59.2
Sikkim	80.0	68.1	74.1	83.6	37.5	62.6	80.7	62.8	72.0
Tripura	85.3	38.3	62.0	76.8	32.8	54.5	83.9	37.3	60.7
Uttarakhand	71.1	43.8	56.9	73.8	15.0	45.3	71.9	36.5	53.8
All India	81.3	35.8	58.7	76.4	20.5	49.3	79.8	31.2	55.9

Source: National Sample Survey/PLFS.

Table A2.2 Labour Force Participation Rate (%), 2023–24 (15+ Years, UPSS)

States/UTs	*Rural*			*Urban*			*Total*		
	Male	*Female*	*All*	*Male*	*Female*	*All*	*Male*	*Female*	*All*
Arunachal Pradesh	80.0	70.8	75.5	75.1	46.4	60.5	79.2	66.5	73.0
Himachal Pradesh	82.4	70.2	76.0	77.5	45.1	63.2	81.7	67.6	74.4
Jammu and Kashmir	76.0	56.8	66.7	74.6	33.1	54.5	75.7	52.1	64.3
Ladakh	72.5	54.3	63.6	73.1	33.0	55.1	72.5	51.6	62.5
Manipur	71.6	49.6	60.5	68.8	46.6	57.5	70.8	48.7	59.6
Meghalaya	84.8	76.9	80.8	69.5	47.7	57.9	82.3	71.8	76.9
Mizoram	67.4	42.6	55.7	64.5	40.6	52.5	66.1	41.7	54.2
Nagaland	85.4	69.0	77.1	75.3	52.1	64.0	82.4	64.3	73.3
Sikkim	85.7	77.9	81.9	76.2	32.2	57.0	83.4	68.2	76.2
Tripura	81.0	50.7	66.0	69.2	31.4	49.9	78.9	47.1	63.0
Uttarakhand	76.9	52.6	64.5	75.0	24.4	49.5	76.4	45.6	60.7
All India	80.2	47.6	63.7	75.6	28.0	52.0	78.8	41.7	60.1

Source: National Sample Survey/PLFS.

Table A2.3 Work Population Ratio (%), 2011–12 (15+ Years, UPSS)

States/UTs	*Rural*			*Urban*			*Total*		
	Male	*Female*	*All*	*Male*	*Female*	*All*	*Male*	*Female*	*All*
Arunachal Pradesh	72.6	40.9	57.0	67.0	19.3	45.3	71.5	37.0	54.8
Himachal Pradesh	75.5	66.7	70.8	76.1	27.1	52.9	75.6	62.5	68.8
Jammu and Kashmir	75.2	35.5	56.1	70.5	15.4	44.2	74.0	30.7	53.2
Manipur	74.9	37.4	56.5	70.9	25.9	48.0	73.9	34.3	54.3
Meghalaya	80.8	61.9	71.4	66.0	29.2	47.0	77.6	54.4	66.0
Mizoram	86.3	58.3	72.8	71.8	35.6	53.2	79.4	46.7	63.1
Nagaland	69.3	39.6	54.3	56.2	18.7	38.3	64.5	32.6	48.7
Sikkim	79.2	67.4	73.4	81.1	37.4	61.2	79.6	62.2	71.2
Tripura	80.0	30.5	55.4	68.0	14.3	40.7	77.9	27.6	52.9
Uttarakhand	69.2	42.9	55.5	72.5	12.0	43.1	70.1	35.1	52.2
All India	80.0	35.2	57.8	74.1	19.5	47.6	78.1	30.5	54.7

Source: National Sample Survey/PLFS.

Table A2.4 Work Population Ratio (%), 2023–24 (15+ Years, UPSS)

States/UTs	*Rural*			*Urban*			*Total*		
	Male	*Female*	*All*	*Male*	*Female*	*All*	*Male*	*Female*	*All*
Arunachal Pradesh	75.6	67.5	71.7	68.1	38.0	52.8	74.4	62.4	68.5
Himachal Pradesh	79.8	65.3	72.2	73.8	36.9	57.5	78.9	62.3	70.3
Jammu and Kashmir	73.4	52.8	63.4	71.0	24.1	48.3	72.9	47.1	60.4
Ladakh	71.0	50.7	61.1	69.0	21.7	47.7	70.7	47.1	59.3
Manipur	68.2	46.3	57.2	65.0	41.8	53.1	67.2	45.0	56.0
Meghalaya	81.8	71.9	76.7	63.3	37.9	49.8	78.7	65.9	72.1
Mizoram	66.3	42.2	54.9	62.4	39.1	50.7	64.6	40.7	53.0
Nagaland	80.7	65.0	72.7	66.9	46.1	56.8	76.6	59.7	68.1
Sikkim	83.4	76.7	80.1	74.9	30.0	55.3	81.3	66.8	74.4
Tripura	79.7	50.1	65.1	67.4	30.0	48.3	77.5	46.3	62.0
Uttarakhand	73.2	51.2	61.9	72.4	21.2	46.6	73.0	43.7	58.1
All India	78.1	46.5	62.1	72.3	26.0	49.4	76.3	40.3	58.2

Source: National Sample Survey/PLFS.

Table A2.5 Unemployment Rate (%), 2011–12 (15+ Years, UPSS)

States/UTs	*Rural*			*Urban*			*Total*		
	Male	*Female*	*All*	*Male*	*Female*	*All*	*Male*	*Female*	*All*
Arunachal Pradesh	1.7	1.7	1.7	3.7	9.0	4.8	2.1	2.4	2.2
Himachal Pradesh	1.1	0.8	1.0	1.9	9.9	4.0	1.2	1.3	1.2
Jammu and Kashmir	2.2	3.0	2.4	4.1	19.0	7.0	2.7	5.3	3.4
Manipur	2.4	3.0	2.6	5.6	10.8	7.1	3.2	4.7	3.7
Meghalaya	0.4	0.4	0.4	2.5	3.6	2.9	0.8	0.8	0.8
Mizoram	1.3	2.7	1.8	4.0	6.8	5.0	2.5	4.3	3.2
Nagaland	14.6	16.1	15.2	19.1	36.0	23.8	16.1	20.9	17.7
Sikkim	1.0	1.0	1.0	3.0	0.3	2.3	1.4	0.9	1.2
Tripura	6.2	20.3	10.5	11.5	56.5	25.3	7.0	25.9	12.8
Uttarakhand	2.8	2.1	2.5	1.8	20.0	4.7	2.5	4.0	3.0
All India	1.7	1.6	1.7	3.0	5.3	3.4	2.1	2.3	2.1

Source: National Sample Survey/PLFS.

Table A2.6 Unemployment Rate (%), 2023–24 (15+ Years, UPSS)

States/UTs	*Rural*			*Urban*			*Total*		
	Male	*Female*	*All*	*Male*	*Female*	*All*	*Male*	*Female*	*All*
Arunachal Pradesh	5.4	4.6	5.1	9.4	18.1	12.8	6.1	6.2	6.1
Himachal Pradesh	3.2	7.0	5.0	4.8	18.2	9.0	3.4	7.8	5.5
Jammu and Kashmir	3.5	7.1	5.0	4.8	27.2	11.4	3.8	9.7	6.1
Ladakh	2.0	6.6	3.9	5.6	34.4	13.4	2.6	8.8	5.1
Manipur	4.7	6.6	5.5	5.6	10.3	7.5	5.0	7.7	6.1
Meghalaya	3.6	6.6	5.0	8.9	20.6	14.0	4.3	8.2	6.2
Mizoram	1.5	1.0	1.3	3.2	3.9	3.4	2.2	2.4	2.3
Nagaland	5.5	5.8	5.7	11.1	11.6	11.3	7.0	7.1	7.1
Sikkim	2.7	1.6	2.2	1.7	6.9	3.0	2.5	2.1	2.3
Tripura	1.6	1.2	1.4	2.7	4.4	3.2	1.7	1.6	1.7
Uttarakhand	4.8	2.7	3.9	3.5	13.0	5.8	4.5	4.1	4.3
All India	2.7	2.1	2.5	4.4	7.1	5.1	3.2	3.2	3.2

Source: National Sample Survey/PLFS.

Table A2.7 Distribution of GVA by Industrial Classification for Himalayan States and All India at Constant (2011–12) Prices (in %), 2011–12

Item	*Arunachal Pradesh*	*Himachal Pradesh*	*Manipur*	*Meghalaya*	*Mizoram*	*Nagaland*	*Sikkim*	*Tripura*	*Uttarakhand*	*Jammu and Kashmir*	*All India*
Agriculture, forestry, and fishing	42.0	16.8	19.8	14.9	20.1	30.9	8.3	27.2	12.3	17.5	18.5
Mining and quarrying	2.1	0.4	0.0	7.4	0.7	0.5	0.1	6.3	1.7	0.4	3.2
Primary	**44.1**	**17.2**	**19.8**	**22.3**	**20.8**	**31.4**	**8.3**	**33.5**	**14.0**	**17.9**	**21.7**
Manufacturing	1.2	25.9	3.2	24.6	0.9	1.3	39.5	3.9	40.3	10.7	17.4
Electricity, gas, water supply, and other utility services	6.4	8.7	4.3	2.4	6.9	2.4	17.1	2.4	3.7	8.2	2.3
Construction	9.6	9.2	7.9	6.0	12.0	8.7	6.2	7.9	8.2	8.7	9.6
Secondary	**17.2**	**43.8**	**15.4**	**33.0**	**19.8**	**12.4**	**62.8**	**14.1**	**52.1**	**27.6**	**29.3**
Trade, repair, hotels, and restaurants	5.5	6.6	12.3	13.6	10.3	8.7	2.9	12.1	11.0	8.9	10.9
Transport, storage, communication, and services related to broadcasting	2.2	4.3	5.5	5.1	4.3	4.8	2.6	4.5	6.4	6.3	6.5
Financial services	1.9	4.1	1.8	3.0	2.7	4.0	1.5	3.0	2.7	3.0	5.9
Real estate, ownership of dwelling, and professional services	3.5	9.7	10.6	6.1	5.6	10.7	5.4	6.4	5.4	12.7	13.0
Public administration	12.5	5.4	18.2	9.4	18.7	15.1	6.8	12.9	3.7	15.1	6.1
Other services	13.1	8.8	16.4	7.6	17.8	12.9	9.7	13.6	4.6	8.4	6.6
Tertiary	**38.7**	**39.0**	**64.8**	**44.7**	**59.4**	**56.2**	**28.8**	**52.4**	**33.9**	**54.4**	**49.0**
Total	100.0	100.0	100.0	100.0	100.0	100.0	100.0	100.0	100.0	100.0	100.0

Source: MoSPI, National Statistical Office.

Table A2.8 Distribution of GVA by Industrial Classification for Himalayan States and All India at Constant (2011–12) Prices (in %), 2022–23

Item	*Arunachal Pradesh*	*Himachal Pradesh*	*Manipur*	*Meghalaya*	*Mizoram*	*Nagaland*	*Sikkim*	*Tripura*	*Uttarakhand*	*Jammu and Kashmir*	*All India*
Agriculture, forestry, and fishing	23.6	13.5	18.0	16.3	15.3	23.7	6.4	25.6	7.8	15.5	15.3
Mining and quarrying	2.6	0.3	0.1	1.8	0.8	1.5	0.1	13.9	1.1	0.2	2.1
Primary	**26.2**	**13.8**	**18.1**	**18.1**	**16.1**	**25.2**	**6.5**	**39.5**	**8.9**	**15.7**	**17.5**
Manufacturing	1.9	32.0	1.8	11.0	0.6	1.0	37.8	3.7	35.7	7.6	16.9
Electricity, gas, water supply, and other utility services	12.1	6.2	2.2	2.3	19.5	2.4	21.1	3.7	4.3	10.9	2.4
Construction	10.2	7.9	7.0	5.5	9.2	7.1	4.8	6.0	9.2	7.6	8.8
Secondary	**24.2**	**46.1**	**11.0**	**18.8**	**29.3**	**10.5**	**63.7**	**13.4**	**49.2**	**26.2**	**28.1**
Trade, repair, hotels, and restaurants	3.5	7.5	15.0	24.9	18.3	8.7	6.9	11.4	13.8	9.3	12.4
Transport, storage, communication, and services related to broadcasting	2.9	4.9	7.6	7.8	3.1	5.1	2.8	4.0	8.3	6.8	6.3
Financial services	1.5	2.8	3.0	2.8	2.0	6.8	1.5	2.7	3.3	3.8	6.0
Real estate, ownership of dwelling, and professional services	2.1	10.2	6.4	5.1	3.0	6.7	3.4	6.3	5.9	10.5	17.0
Public administration	18.2	5.4	18.7	11.7	15.8	18.4	6.6	12.0	4.3	19.1	5.6
Other services	21.4	9.4	20.1	10.7	12.4	18.6	8.6	10.6	6.2	8.7	7.1
Tertiary	**49.6**	**40.1**	**70.8**	**63.1**	**54.6**	**64.3**	**29.8**	**47.1**	**41.8**	**58.1**	**54.4**
Total	100.0	100.0	100.0	100.0	100.0	100.0	100.0	100.0	100.0	100.0	100.0

Source: MoSPI, National Statistical Office.

Annexure Chapter 3

Table A3.1a Labour Force Participation Rate (15+ Years, UPSS)

States/UTs	*2000*	*2012*	*2024*
Arunachal Pradesh	54.3	56.0	73.0
Himachal Pradesh	72.3	69.6	74.4
Jammu and Kashmir	61.2	55.1	64.3
Manipur	55.4	56.3	59.6
Meghalaya	74.5	66.5	76.9
Mizoram	67.0	65.1	54.2
Nagaland	66.3	59.2	73.3
Sikkim	60.0	72.0	76.2
Tripura	46.3	60.7	63.0
Uttaranchal	61.5	53.8	60.7
All India	61.6	55.9	60.1

Source: EUS and PLFS, NSSO

Table A3.1b Labour Force Participation Rate: Male–Female (15+ Years, UPSS)

States/UTs	*Male*			*Female*		
	2000	*2012*	*2024*	*2000*	*2012*	*2024*
Arunachal Pradesh	62.8	73.0	79.2	44.9	37.9	66.5
Himachal Pradesh	81.4	76.5	81.7	63.8	63.3	67.6
Jammu and Kashmir	81.3	76.1	75.7	39.8	32.4	52.1
Manipur	75.1	76.3	70.8	35.7	36.0	48.7
Meghalaya	85.7	78.2	82.3	63.4	54.8	71.8
Mizoram	81.2	81.4	66.1	52.8	48.8	41.7
Nagaland	73.9	76.9	82.4	57.0	41.2	64.3
Sikkim	80.7	80.7	83.4	36.6	62.8	68.2
Tripura	79.0	83.9	78.9	10.3	37.3	47.1
Uttaranchal	71.9	71.9	76.4	52.7	36.5	45.6
All India	83.6	79.8	78.8	38.9	31.2	41.7

Source: EUS and PLFS, NSSO.

Table A3.1c Labour Force Participation Rate: Rural–Urban (15+ Years, UPSS)

States/UTs	*Rural*			*Urban*		
	2000	*2012*	*2024*	*2000*	*2012*	*2024*
Arunachal Pradesh	55.1	57.9	75.5	45.7	47.5	60.5
Himachal Pradesh	74.7	71.5	76.0	48.9	55.1	63.2
Jammu and Kashmir	65.4	57.5	66.7	43.9	47.5	54.5
Manipur	56.6	58.0	60.5	51.8	51.7	57.5
Meghalaya	80.5	71.7	80.8	47.9	48.4	57.9
Mizoram	75.4	74.2	55.7	55.5	56.0	52.5
Nagaland	72.6	64.0	77.1	51.5	50.3	64.0
Sikkim	60.4	74.1	81.9	56.1	62.6	57.0
Tripura	46.7	62.0	66.0	43.9	54.5	49.9
Uttaranchal	68.6	56.9	64.5	42.5	45.3	49.5
All India	65.6	58.7	63.7	51.0	49.3	52.0

Source: EUS and PLFS, NSSO.

Table A3.2a Worker–Population Ratio (15+ Years, UPSS)

States/UTs	*2000*	*2012*	*2024*
Arunachal Pradesh	53.8	54.8	68.5
Himachal Pradesh	71.1	68.8	70.3
Jammu and Kashmir	60.2	53.2	60.4
Manipur	54.0	54.3	56.0
Meghalaya	73.9	66.0	72.1
Mizoram	65.9	63.1	53.0
Nagaland	63.8	48.7	68.1
Sikkim	58.0	71.2	74.4
Tripura	45.5	52.9	62.0
Uttaranchal	60.2	52.2	58.1
All India	60.2	54.7	58.2

Source: EUS and PLFS, NSSO.

Table A3.2b Worker–Population Ratio: Male–Female (15+ Years, UPSS)

States/UTs	*Male*			*Female*		
	2000	*2012*	*2024*	*2000*	*2012*	*2024*
Arunachal Pradesh	62.2	71.5	74.4	44.67	37.0	62.4
Himachal Pradesh	79.4	75.6	78.9	63.33	62.5	62.3
Jammu and Kashmir	80.0	74.0	72.9	39.21	30.7	47.1
Manipur	73.1	73.9	67.2	34.9	34.3	45.0
Meghalaya	85.0	77.6	78.7	62.82	54.4	65.9
Mizoram	79.6	79.4	64.6	52.24	46.7	40.7
Nagaland	70.6	64.5	76.6	55.47	32.6	59.7
Sikkim	77.9	79.6	81.3	35.56	62.2	66.8
Tripura	77.8	77.9	77.5	9.92	27.6	46.3
Uttaranchal	69.3	70.1	73.0	52.54	35.1	43.7
All India	81.5	78.1	76.3	38.3	30.5	40.3

Source: EUS and PLFS, NSSO.

Table A3.2c Worker–Population Ratio: Rural–Urban (15+ Years, UPSS)

States/UTs	*Rural*			*Urban*		
	2000	*2012*	*2024*	*2000*	*2012*	*2024*
Arunachal Pradesh	54.8	57.0	71.7	44.0	45.3	52.8
Himachal Pradesh	73.7	70.8	72.2	45.6	52.9	57.5
Jammu and Kashmir	64.8	56.1	63.4	41.7	44.2	48.3
Manipur	55.9	56.5	57.2	48.4	48.0	53.1
Meghalaya	80.2	71.4	76.7	45.8	47.0	49.8
Mizoram	74.8	72.8	54.9	53.8	53.2	50.7
Nagaland	71.1	54.3	72.7	46.7	38.3	56.8
Sikkim	58.7	73.4	80.1	51.8	61.2	55.3
Tripura	46.2	55.4	65.1	41.6	40.7	48.3
Uttaranchal	67.4	55.5	61.9	41.2	43.1	46.6
All India	64.6	57.8	62.1	48.6	47.6	49.4

Source: EUS and PLFS, NSSO.

Table A3.3a Unemployment Rate (15+ Years, UPSS)

States/UTs	*2000*	*2012*	*2024*
Arunachal Pradesh	0.5	2.2	6.1
Himachal Pradesh	0.8	1.2	5.5
Jammu and Kashmir	1.4	3.4	6.1
Manipur	2.3	3.7	6.1
Meghalaya	0.9	0.8	6.2
Mizoram	1.0	3.2	2.3
Nagaland	2.7	17.7	7.1
Sikkim	2.8	1.2	2.3
Tripura	4.1	12.8	1.7
Uttaranchal	0.3	3.0	4.3
All India	1.7	2.1	3.2

Source: EUS and PLFS, NSSO.

Table A3.3b Unemployment Rate: Male–Female (15+ Years, UPSS)

States/UTs	*Male*			*Female*		
	2000	*2012*	*2024*	*2000*	*2012*	*2024*
Arunachal Pradesh	1.0	2.1	6.1	0.5	2.4	6.2
Himachal Pradesh	2.5	1.2	3.4	0.8	1.3	7.8
Jammu and Kashmir	1.7	2.7	3.8	1.4	5.3	9.7
Manipur	2.6	3.2	5.0	2.3	4.7	7.7
Meghalaya	0.8	0.8	4.3	0.9	0.8	8.2
Mizoram	2.0	2.5	2.2	1.0	4.3	2.4
Nagaland	4.4	16.1	7.0	2.7	20.9	7.1
Sikkim	3.5	1.4	2.5	2.8	0.9	2.1
Tripura	1.5	7.0	1.7	4.1	25.9	1.6
Uttaranchal	3.6	2.5	4.5	0.3	4.0	4.1
All India	2.5	2.1	3.2	1.7	2.3	3.2

Source: EUS and PLFS, NSSO.

Table A3.3c Unemployment Rate: Rural–Urban (15+ Years, UPSS)

States/UTs	*Rural*			*Urban*		
	2000	*2012*	*2024*	*2000*	*2012*	*2024*
Arunachal Pradesh	0.6	1.7	5.1	3.7	4.8	12.8
Himachal Pradesh	1.4	1.0	5.0	6.7	4.0	9.0
Jammu and Kashmir	1.0	2.4	5.0	5.1	7.0	11.4
Manipur	1.3	2.6	5.5	6.5	7.1	7.5
Meghalaya	0.4	0.4	5.0	4.4	2.9	14.0
Mizoram	0.8	1.8	1.3	3.0	5.0	3.4
Nagaland	2.1	15.2	5.7	9.2	23.8	11.3
Sikkim	2.8	1.0	2.2	7.7	2.3	3.0
Tripura	1.2	10.5	1.4	5.4	25.3	3.2
Uttaranchal	1.8	2.5	3.9	3.0	4.7	5.8
All India	1.5	1.7	2.5	4.8	3.4	5.1

Source: EUS and PLFS, NSSO.

Table A3.3d Youth Employment Rate: 2024 (15+ Years, UPSS)

States/UTs	*Male*			*Female*			*All*		
	YU	*EDYU*	*GRYU*	*YU*	*EDYU*	*GRYU*	*YU*	*EDYU*	*GRYU*
Jammu and Kashmir	11.8	15.3	24.5	26.7	40.1	65.8	17.4	24.2	43.5
Himachal Pradesh	25.8	29.3	24.3	29.9	35.4	36.2	28.1	32.7	31.3
Uttarakhand	8.3	10.4	10.2	12.3	15.0	23.9	9.8	12.2	16.6
Sikkim	8.3	18.4	24.4	6.8	10.5	14.8	7.7	14.7	20.0
Arunachal Pradesh	21.9	33.8	67.9	19.6	34.3	61.7	20.9	34.0	65.0
Nagaland	27.9	45.1	76.3	26.6	47.4	65.7	27.4	46.0	71.3
Manipur	19.9	23.1	38.8	27.5	33.9	49.7	22.9	27.1	43.4
Mizoram	13.4	25.2	42.2	13.0	30.2	40.3	13.3	26.9	41.4
Tripura	6.8	14.1	20.6	6.7	21.4	26.3	6.8	16.2	22.4
Meghalaya	9.9	17.1	29.7	18.7	30.4	34.0	14.0	24.1	32.1
All India	9.8	13.8	23.5	11.0	19.2	33.7	10.2	15.4	27.0

Note: YU, youth unemployment; EDYU, educated youth unemployment; GRYU, graduate youth employment.

Source: PLFS, NSSO.

Table A3.4a Status of Employment: 2024 (15+ Years, UPSS)

States/UTs	*Male*				*Female*				*Total*			
	SE	*RE*	*CW*	*All*	*SE*	*RE*	*CW*	*All*	*SE*	*RE*	*CW*	*All*
Arunachal Pradesh	68.7	24.0	7.3	100	89.5	9.9	0.6	100	77.9	17.7	4.3	100
Himachal Pradesh	50.6	31.1	18.3	100	84.6	12.6	2.8	100	66.1	22.7	11.2	100
Jammu and Kashmir	53.0	29.5	17.5	100	89.5	10.0	0.5	100	66.7	22.1	11.1	100
Manipur	63.4	28.7	7.9	100	86.2	13.2	0.7	100	72.6	22.4	4.9	100
Meghalaya	45.0	17.7	37.4	100	61.2	15.4	23.5	100	52.6	16.6	30.8	100
Mizoram	58.2	32.3	9.4	100	85.7	14.1	0.2	100	68.5	25.5	6.0	100
Nagaland	54.3	36.6	9.1	100	81.8	17.4	0.8	100	66.3	28.2	5.5	100
Sikkim	52.6	35.3	12.1	100	73.1	25.7	1.3	100	61.3	31.2	7.5	100
Tripura	57.4	14.0	28.6	100	68.8	11.3	19.8	100	61.6	13.0	25.3	100
Uttarakhand	51.7	32.0	16.3	100	76.7	17.4	5.8	100	61.3	26.4	12.3	100
Total	53.6	24.9	21.5	100	67.4	15.9	16.7	100	58.4	21.8	19.9	100

Note: SE, self-employed; RE, regularly employed; CW, casual worker.

Source: PLFS, NSSO.

Table A3.4b Status of Employment: Rural–Urban, 2024 (15+ Years, UPSS)

States/UTs	*Rural*				*Urban*			
	SE	*RE*	*CW*	*All*	*SE*	*RE*	*CW*	*All*
Arunachal Pradesh	82.1	13.8	4.2	100	49.9	44.7	5.5	100
Himachal Pradesh	70.1	18.3	11.6	100	30.2	61.5	8.3	100
Jammu and Kashmir	70.1	18.3	11.7	100	49.1	42.6	8.3	100
Manipur	76.1	19.2	4.7	100	63.9	30.7	5.5	100
Meghalaya	55.3	12.3	32.4	100	32.3	48.8	19.0	100
Mizoram	76.6	17.9	5.5	100	58.1	35.2	6.7	100
Nagaland	71.6	23.7	4.7	100	49.7	42.5	7.8	100
Sikkim	65.3	27.6	7.1	100	42.0	48.9	9.1	100
Tripura	63.2	10.1	26.7	100	52.5	30.3	17.2	100
Uttarakhand	65.7	20.8	13.4	100	43.9	48.3	7.8	100
Total	64.7	12.8	22.6	100	40.4	47.5	12.1	100

Note: SE, self-employed; RE, regularly employed; CW, casual worker.

Source: PLFS, NSSO.

Table A3.5a Industry of Employment, 2024 (15+ Years, UPSS)

States/UTs	*Agriculture, etc*	*Mining and Quarrying*	*Manufacturing*	*Electricity, Gas, and Water Supply*	*Construction*	*Trade, Hotel, and Restaurants*	*Transport, Storage, and Communication*	*Finance, Business, Real Estate, etc.*	*Public Admin, Health, Education, etc.*	*Total*
Arunachal Pradesh	62.4	0.1	3.1	1.9	6.3	10.0	2.7	1.0	12.6	100
Himachal Pradesh	53.8	0.0	8.6	1.9	11.5	8.1	4.3	1.4	10.2	100
Jammu and Kashmir	42.8	0.2	9.1	1.7	15.0	11.1	4.9	1.9	13.3	100
Manipur	42.0	0.0	15.3	0.4	7.9	10.4	3.5	3.9	16.6	100
Meghalaya	51.6	2.5	2.1	0.2	15.0	10.1	4.6	2.0	12.1	100
Mizoram	39.1	0.3	4.0	0.2	6.8	19.8	6.6	5.2	18.0	100
Nagaland	45.7	0.0	5.8	0.7	4.6	10.3	6.9	6.4	19.5	100
Sikkim	42.8	0.0	3.4	1.4	8.7	11.7	8.7	1.2	22.2	100
Tripura	44.0	0.0	6.1	0.2	18.4	13.5	4.4	2.0	11.5	100
Uttarakhand	42.0	0.2	13.1	0.5	10.9	15.0	4.8	2.3	11.2	100
Total	46.0	0.2	11.4	0.5	12.0	12.2	5.6	2.9	9.0	100

Note: SE, self-employed; RE, regularly employed; CW, casual worker.

Source: PLFS, NSSO.

Table A3.5b Industry of Employment: Male and Female, 2024 (15+ Years, UPSS)

States/UTs	*Agriculture, etc*	*Mining and Quarrying*	*Manufacturing*	*Electricity, Gas, and Water Supply*	*Construction*	*Trade, Hotel, and Restaurants*	*Transport, Storage, and Communication*	*Finance, Business, Real Estate, etc.*	*Public Admin, Health, Education, etc.*	*Total*	*Agriculture, etc.*	*Mining and Quarrying*	*Manufacturing*	*Electricity, Gas, and Water Supply*	*Construction*	*Trade, Hotel, and Restaurants*	*Transport, Storage, and Communication*	*Finance, Business, Real Estate, etc.*	*Public Admin, Health, Education, etc*	*Total*
	Male										*Female*									
Arunachal Pradesh	51.7	0.2	1.4	2.8	10.8	10.7	4.7	1.6	16.1	100	75.7	0.0	5.3	0.7	0.7	9.1	0.1	0.2	8.1	100
Himachal Pradesh	33.1	0.0	11.4	3.0	19.1	12.9	7.6	2.2	10.6	100	78.4	0.0	5.3	0.6	2.6	2.4	0.5	0.5	9.7	100
Jammu and Kashmir	21.7	0.3	8.7	2.5	23.6	17.1	7.9	2.8	15.5	100	77.8	0.0	9.8	0.4	0.6	1.2	0.0	0.5	9.7	100
Manipur	39.1	0.0	7.0	0.6	13.2	9.0	5.8	5.6	19.6	100	46.2	0.0	27.4	0.0	0.2	12.4	0.1	1.5	12.3	100
Meghalaya	45.2	3.4	2.1	0.4	19.3	9.7	8.5	1.7	9.7	100	58.8	1.4	2.0	0.0	10.1	10.5	0.1	2.3	14.8	100
Mizoram	32.2	0.5	3.2	0.3	10.8	13.4	10.6	5.6	23.4	100	50.6	0.1	5.3	0.0	0.0	30.6	0.0	4.3	9.0	100
Nagaland	34.2	0.0	5.6	1.3	7.6	8.3	12.1	8.5	22.4	100	60.6	0.0	6.1	0.0	0.7	12.9	0.2	3.8	15.6	100
Sikkim	29.2	0.0	4.6	2.3	14.0	11.7	15.2	1.8	21.3	100	61.1	0.0	1.6	0.1	1.5	11.7	0.0	0.3	23.5	100
Tripura	35.3	0.0	5.7	0.2	20.6	17.9	7.0	2.7	10.4	100	58.6	0.0	6.7	0.0	14.5	6.0	0.1	0.9	13.2	100
Uttarakhand	26.0	0.3	16.7	0.9	16.1	19.8	7.2	3.3	9.7	100	67.7	0.0	7.3	0.0	2.5	7.4	0.8	0.6	13.7	100
Total	36.2	0.3	11.4	0.7	16.4	15.5	8.1	3.6	7.7	100	64.3	0.1	11.5	0.2	3.7	6.0	1.1	1.5	11.5	100

Source: PLFS, NSSO.

Table A3.5c Industry of Employment: Rural and Urban, 2024 (15+ Years, UPSS)

States/UTs	*Rural*										*Urban*									
	Agriculture, etc.	*Mining and Quarrying*	*Manufacturing*	*Electricity, Gas, and Water Supply*	*Construction*	*Trade, Hotel, and Restaurants*	*Transport, Storage, and Communication*	*Finance, Business, Real Estate, etc.*	*Public Admin, Health, Education, etc.*	*Total*	*Agriculture, etc.*	*Mining and Quarrying*	*Manufacturing*	*Electricity, Gas, and Water Supply*	*Construction*	*Trade, Hotel, and Restaurants*	*Transport, Storage, and Communication*	*Finance, Business, Real Estate, etc.*	*Public Admin, Health, Education, etc.*	*Total*
Arunachal Pradesh	69.2	0.1	2.9	1.6	5.5	7.9	2.3	0.8	9.6	100	16.2	0.0	4.6	3.5	11.7	23.8	5.4	2.0	32.7	100
Himachal Pradesh	59.3	0.0	6.1	1.8	11.7	7.0	4.4	1.1	8.6	100	5.1	0.2	30.9	2.8	10.6	17.8	3.9	4.0	24.7	100
Jammu and Kashmir	48.9	0.1	8.2	1.5	15.4	8.9	4.3	1.4	11.2	100	10.6	0.6	13.6	2.7	12.6	22.5	8.3	4.6	24.5	100
Manipur	50.6	0.0	14.0	0.2	7.1	7.4	3.1	2.9	14.7	100	19.8	0.0	18.5	0.7	10.1	18.2	4.5	6.7	21.4	100
Meghalaya	57.5	2.6	1.8	0.2	15.8	7.8	3.9	1.3	9.1	100	7.5	1.4	4.0	0.1	8.6	27.2	9.4	7.1	34.7	100
Mizoram	55.0	0.1	2.8	0.1	5.9	14.1	5.6	2.3	14.1	100	18.6	0.6	5.5	0.3	7.9	27.1	8.0	8.8	23.1	100
Nagaland	55.4	0.0	6.3	0.8	3.3	6.4	5.6	3.6	18.7	100	15.3	0.0	4.1	0.4	8.8	22.8	11.2	15.5	21.8	100
Sikkim	51.4	0.0	2.7	1.6	8.4	7.4	7.1	0.5	20.9	100	0.9	0.0	6.6	0.3	10.0	32.5	16.3	4.7	28.5	100
Tripura	49.8	0.0	5.5	0.1	18.9	11.9	3.9	1.1	8.8	100	9.4	0.0	9.4	0.5	14.8	23.0	7.9	7.5	27.5	100
Uttarakhand	51.1	0.3	12.2	0.2	11.3	11.2	4.2	1.1	8.3	100	6.2	0.0	16.6	1.9	9.1	30.0	6.9	6.8	22.6	100
Total	59.8	0.2	8.3	0.4	12.5	8.2	3.7	1.3	5.6	100	6.7	0.3	20.5	1.1	10.6	23.6	11.0	7.4	18.8	100

Source: PLFS, NSSO.

Table A3.6a Reasons of Out-Migration for Male, 2011

States/UTs	*Work/ Employment*	*Business*	*Education*	*Marriage*	*Moved After Birth*	*Moved With Household*	*Others*	*Total*
Arunachal Pradesh	24.0	2.0	20.7	0.7	1.3	28.7	22.7	100
Himachal Pradesh	47.3	0.9	7.7	1.4	4.5	25.5	12.7	100
Jammu and Kashmir	39.4	2.1	8.5	1.1	2.1	28.7	18.1	100
Manipur	35.8	3.4	22.3	0.7	0.7	22.3	14.9	100
Meghalaya	34.1	3.5	9.4	8.2	1.2	27.1	16.5	100
Mizoram	29.5	1.3	19.2	1.3	0.0	24.4	24.4	100
Nagaland	29.0	3.7	12.1	0.9	1.9	33.6	18.7	100
Sikkim	32.9	2.1	20.3	1.4	1.4	19.6	22.4	100
Tripura	37.0	6.8	9.6	1.4	1.4	27.4	16.4	100
Uttaranchal	51.9	1.0	4.0	1.0	2.0	27.3	12.8	100
India	50.6	2.4	3.6	1.2	4.8	23.8	13.7	100

Source: Census of India, 2011.

Table A3.6b Reasons of Out-Migration for Male, 2021

States/UTs	*Work/ Employment*	*Business*	*Education*	*Marriage*	*Moved After Birth*	*Moved With Household*	*Others*	*Total*
Arunachal Pradesh	31.1	5.0	4.7	0.9	1.7	21.4	35.2	100.0
Himachal Pradesh	35.4	1.2	3.7	3.9	7.6	23.0	25.0	100.0
Jammu and Kashmir	12.1	1.7	2.7	5.8	3.8	25.7	48.1	100.0
Manipur	6.8	2.6	2.6	1.9	3.5	30.1	52.4	100.0
Meghalaya	9.6	2.0	2.7	24.7	3.0	15.4	42.7	100.0
Mizoram	23.6	2.4	4.0	2.7	2.6	33.8	30.9	100.0
Nagaland	31.6	6.4	8.2	1.2	0.9	21.3	30.4	100.0
Sikkim	35.5	3.9	3.9	1.6	3.3	20.9	30.9	100.0
Tripura	15.4	2.4	1.5	4.9	1.2	29.3	45.4	100.0
Uttarakhand	37.2	1.0	3.9	1.2	2.6	31.2	22.9	100.0
India	24.0	1.8	2.3	3.7	13.7	20.3	34.2	100.0

Source: PLFS, 2021, NSSO.

Table A3.6c Reasons of Out-Migration for Female, 2011

States/UTs	*Work/ Employment*	*Business*	*Education*	*Marriage*	*Moved after Birth*	*Moved with Household*	*Others*	*Total*
Arunachal Pradesh	3.5	0.6	9.9	35.1	1.2	37.4	12.3	100
Himachal Pradesh	4.3	0.3	3.3	45.7	3.0	35.0	8.3	100
Jammu and Kashmir	4.8	1.0	3.8	27.9	1.9	50.0	10.6	100
Manipur	16.2	1.3	16.2	18.8	0.6	34.4	12.3	100
Meghalaya	6.1	0.9	6.1	44.3	0.9	31.3	10.4	100
Mizoram	10.2	1.1	13.6	18.2	1.1	35.2	20.5	100
Nagaland	6.9	0.8	7.6	32.8	1.5	38.9	11.5	100
Sikkim	6.1	0.5	7.5	49.5	0.9	24.3	11.2	100
Tripura	3.3	1.1	3.3	45.6	1.1	34.4	11.1	100
Uttaranchal	3.6	0.5	1.6	49.3	1.1	36.6	7.3	100
India	6.1	0.5	1.5	43.9	4.1	34.7	9.2	100

Source: Census of India (2011).

Table A3.6d Reasons of Out-Migration for Female, 2021

States/UTs	*Work/ Employment*	*Business*	*Education*	*Marriage*	*Moved after Birth*	*Moved with Household*	*Others*	*Total*
Arunachal Pradesh	7.8	1.1	4.1	31.0	1.3	27.1	27.5	100.0
Himachal Pradesh	3.0	0.1	1.0	76.6	1.9	10.1	7.3	100.0
Jammu and Kashmir	1.1	0.2	0.7	70.2	1.2	10.1	16.4	100.0
Manipur	1.4	0.6	1.2	54.0	1.7	15.3	25.9	100.0
Meghalaya	4.0	0.5	3.4	19.3	3.3	21.6	47.9	100.0
Mizoram	8.8	1.5	3.8	16.8	2.4	38.2	28.4	100.0
Nagaland	8.1	1.6	7.5	24.2	0.8	31.7	26.0	100.0
Sikkim	5.7	0.5	2.6	51.9	2.3	17.1	19.9	100.0
Tripura	2.1	0.2	0.6	60.2	0.5	16.7	19.7	100.0
Uttarakhand	2.3	0.2	1.2	63.4	0.9	22.1	9.8	100.0
India	2.1	0.3	0.7	66.5	4.4	11.7	14.3	100.0

Source: Census of India 2011.

Annexure Chapter 4

Table A4.1 Percentage of Expenditure on Education and Training to Gross State Domestic Product (GSDP)/Gross Domestic Product (GDP)

States/UTs	*% of GSDP/GDP*
Arunachal Pradesh	5.1
Himachal Pradesh	4.2
Jammu and Kashmir	6.2
Manipur	6.1
Meghalaya	5.6
Mizoram	6.2
Nagaland	4.8
Sikkim	4.0
Tripura	4.4
Uttarakhand	3.2
India	3.0

Source: Ministry of Education (Department of Higher Education) Planning, Monitoring, and Statistics Bureau New Delhi (2024).

Table A4.2 Literacy Rates (2001–2024)

States/UTs	*2001*	*2011*	*2023–24**
Arunachal Pradesh	54.3	65.4	84.3
Himachal Pradesh	76.5	82.8	88.9
Jammu and Kashmir	55.5	67.2	82.2
Jharkhand	53.6	66.4	92.1
Manipur	70.5	76.9	94.3
Meghalaya	62.6	74.4	98.2
Mizoram	88.8	91.3	95.8
Nagaland	66.6	79.6	84.7
Sikkim	68.8	81.4	93.7
Tripura	73.2	87.2	84.0
Uttarakhand	71.6	78.8	80.9
All India	64.8	73.0	84.3

Note: * PLFS, NSSO, 2023–24, 7 and above years.

Source: Office of the Registrar General of India, Ministry of Home Affairs.

Table A4.4a Gross Enrolment Ratio (GER) by Level of School Education, 2023–24

States/UTs	*Primary*	*Upper Primary*	*Secondary*	*Higher Secondary*	*Higher Education*
Arunachal Pradesh	114.6	89.3	67.8	45.9	36.5
Himachal Pradesh	106.1	103.8	100.1	81.6	43.1
Jammu and Kashmir	114.2	77.0	65.4	42.8	24.8
Manipur	136.8	91.2	75.9	56.4	35.4
Meghalaya	178.4	115.3	84.7	39.8	25.4
Mizoram	151.8	113.7	98.1	53.3	32.3
Nagaland	93.8	72.0	60.2	40.4	18.8
Sikkim	98.3	78.0	74.2	57.4	38.6
Tripura	120.9	97.6	79.2	56.6	20.7
Uttarakhand	113.3	104.5	93.0	77.5	41.8
India	93.0	89.7	77.4	56.2	28.4

Note: Higher education year is 2021–22.

Source: UDISE+ and AIHES.

Table A4.4b Gross Enrolment Ratio (GER) by Gender and Level of School Education, 2023–24

States/UTs	*Primary*		*Upper Primary*		*Secondary*		*Higher Secondary*		*Higher Education*	
	Boys	*Girls*	*Boys*	*Girls*	*Boys*	*Girls*	*Boys*	*Girls*	*Boys*	*Girls*
Arunachal Pradesh	113.6	115.7	85.7	92.9	65.1	70.5	43.2	48.6	38.4	34.5
Himachal Pradesh	105.3	107.0	102.8	104.9	98.4	102.1	78.8	84.8	37.3	49.7
Jammu and Kashmir	114.0	114.5	75.6	78.5	64.7	66.3	41.6	44.1	22.6	27.2
Manipur	135.2	138.6	89.2	93.4	74.4	77.6	56.3	56.5	35.3	35.5
Meghalaya	176.5	180.4	105.8	125.2	73.0	96.7	32.6	47.3	22.7	28.1
Mizoram	151.2	152.4	111.5	116.0	92.7	103.7	49.4	57.5	31.4	33.2
Nagaland	92.0	95.7	68.5	75.7	55.5	65.2	36.8	44.2	16.5	21.2
Sikkim	100.6	95.9	77.5	78.6	72.5	75.9	51.8	63.0	35.1	42.5
Tripura	118.7	123.2	95.0	100.3	75.9	82.6	53.1	60.5	21.9	19.5
Uttarakhand	110.5	116.6	102.5	106.8	90.8	95.6	73.9	81.5	40.1	43.7
India	91.8	94.3	88.9	90.6	76.8	78.0	54.4	58.2	28.3	28.5

Note: Higher education year is 2021–22.

Table A4.5 Net Enrolment Ratio (NER) by Gender and Level of School Education, 2023–24

States/UTs	*Foundational*			*Preparatory*			*Middle*			*Secondary*		
Location	*Boys*	*Girls*	*All*	*Boys*	*Girls*	*All*	*Boys*	*Girls*	*All*	*Boys*	*Girls*	*All*
Arunachal Pradesh	58.2	59.9	59	64.7	67.2	65.9	51.8	57	54.4	39.6	43.7	41.6
Himachal Pradesh	63.8	63.8	63.8	67.6	66.6	67.2	63.6	62.8	63.2	59.8	61.8	60.8
Jammu and Kashmir	83.3	82.2	82.8	70.9	71.5	71.2	51.5	53.5	52.4	38.2	39.5	38.8
Manipur	72.7	73.6	73.1	87.8	91.4	89.5	59	61.6	60.3	49.8	50.7	50.2
Meghalaya	96.1	100.1	98	89.6	100.4	94.9	63.1	77.5	70.1	37.7	52.8	45.2
Mizoram	79	83.2	81.1	89.3	94.6	91.9	81.8	88.5	85.1	57	65.6	61.2
Nagaland	66.2	68.6	67.4	61.5	65.7	63.5	48	54	50.9	36.3	43.2	39.6
Sikkim	76.4	76	76.2	68.8	67.3	68.1	55	55.4	55.2	47	52.6	49.8
Tripura	47.7	48.7	48.2	97.7	102.7	100.1	81	87.2	84	56.3	62.6	59.3
Uttarakhand	47.7	49.8	48.7	75.4	79	77.1	70.2	72.4	71.2	60.4	64.5	62.3
All India	37.5	38.2	37.8	70.4	72.6	71.4	64.1	64.8	64.4	50	52	50.9

Source: UDISE+.

Table A4.6 Gender Parity Index of GER by Level of Education, 2023–24

States/UTs	*Primary*	*Upper Primary*	*Elementary*	*Secondary*	*Higher Secondary*	*Higher Education*[*]
Arunachal Pradesh	1.02	1.08	1.04	1.08	1.12	0.90
Himachal Pradesh	1.02	1.02	1.02	1.04	1.08	1.33
Jammu and Kashmir	1.00	1.04	1.02	1.02	1.06	1.20
Manipur	1.02	1.05	1.03	1.04	1.00	1.01
Meghalaya	1.02	1.18	1.07	1.32	1.45	1.24
Mizoram	1.01	1.04	1.02	1.12	1.16	1.06
Nagaland	1.04	1.11	1.06	1.17	1.20	1.28
Sikkim	0.95	1.01	0.98	1.05	1.22	1.21
Tripura	1.04	1.06	1.04	1.09	1.14	0.89
Uttarakhand	1.05	1.04	1.05	1.05	1.10	1.09
India	1.03	1.02	1.02	1.02	1.07	1.01

Note: [*]2021–22.

Source: UDISE+ and AIHES.

Table A4.7 Dropout Rate, 2023–24

States/UTs	*Primary*			*Upper Primary*			*Secondary*		
	Boys	*Girls*	*All*	*Boys*	*Girls*	*All*	*Boys*	*Girls*	*All*
Arunachal Pradesh	5.7	5.1	5.4	7.2	6.5	6.8	20.4	18.2	19.3
Himachal Pradesh	0.0	0.0	0.0	0.7	0.4	0.6	5.8	4.0	4.9
Jammu and Kashmir	1.9	1.3	1.6	3.2	3.3	3.2	14.1	12.6	13.4
Ladakh	4.9	3.6	4.3	7.3	4.3	5.8	23.3	16.7	19.8
Manipur	4.5	4.4	4.5	3.9	3.0	3.5	15.6	15.0	15.3
Meghalaya	8.3	6.8	7.5	13.9	11.1	12.4	23.2	21.1	22.0
Mizoram	3.7	3.3	3.5	6.7	4.9	5.9	15.2	14.4	14.8
Nagaland	4.8	4.2	4.5	6.4	5.2	5.8	12.2	11.1	11.6
Sikkim	3.3	1.7	2.6	5.9	4.0	4.9	21.0	17.2	19.0
Tripura	0.8	0.3	0.5	4.5	3.6	4.1	10.7	10.1	10.4
Uttarakhand	0.3	0.0	0.1	2.6	1.9	2.3	8.6	5.3	7.0
India	2.1	1.7	1.9	5.2	5.3	5.2	15.5	12.6	14.1

Source: UDISE+.

Table A4.8a Reasons for Not Enrolled or Not Attending (Male), 2023–24

States/UTs		*1*	*2*	*3*	*4*	*5*	*6*	*7*	*9*	*10*	*11*	*12*	*19*	*All*
Arunachal Pradesh	15.8	13.2	14.7	4.2	1.6	0	0.3	0	0	0	0	0	65.9	100
Himachal Pradesh	5.2	7.8	4.7	15.6	0.7	0	0	0	0	0	0	1.1	70	100
Jammu and Kashmir	10.4	7.9	9.3	0.7	1.1	1.3	0	0	0	0	0	1.9	77.8	100
Manipur	4.2	6.5	4.1	2.3	0.4	0	1.6	0	0	0	0	6.5	78.5	100
Meghalaya	10.2	4.9	14.9	0.6	3	0.5	0	0	0	0	0	0	76.1	100
Mizoram	8.3	3	3.4	0	0	0	0	0	0	0	0	0.4	93.3	100
Nagaland	9.1	6.6	19.7	4.4	0	0	0	0	0.8	0	0	0	68.5	100
Sikkim	1.2	33.3	7.1	12.4	0	0	0	0	0	0	0	0	47.3	100
Tripura	2.8	6.9	5.5	0	0.2	0	0	0	0	0	0	1.2	86.2	100
Uttarakhand	9.5	11.7	2.3	1	3.2	0	5.2	0	0	0	0	2.4	74.2	100
all-India	11	19.3	14.9	1.5	4.5	0.5	0.5	0.1	0	0	0.1	2	56.5	100

Source: Education Survey, NSSO.

Table A4.8b Reasons for Not Enrolled (Female), 2023–24

States/UTs	*1*	*2*	*3*	*4*	*5*	*6*	*7*	*8*	*9*	*10*	*11*	*12*	*17*	*18*	*19*	*20*	*All*
Arunachal Pradesh	20.2	12.6	12.1	7.7	0.5	0.1	0.0	0.0	0.0	0.0	0.0	0.7	0.0	0.0	66.3	0.0	100
Himachal Pradesh	5.8	9.7	9.0	3.2	0.0	14.8	0.0	0.0	0.0	0.0	0.6	5.9	0.0	0.0	56.8	0.0	100
Jammu and Kashmir	15.5	6.0	15.3	3.1	0.4	1.6	0.1	0.0	0.0	0.0	0.0	7.4	0.0	0.7	64.6	0.8	100
Manipur	8.2	7.6	10.3	4.7	1.0	0.0	2.4	0.0	0.0	0.0	0.0	6.9	2.0	0.0	64.8	0.3	100
Meghalaya	10.9	0.9	20.5	1.3	1.1	0.0	0.0	0.0	0.0	0.0	0.0	1.7	0.0	0.0	73.9	0.6	100
Mizoram	8.3	1.5	0.9	0.0	0.0	0.0	0.5	0.0	0.0	0.0	0.0	3.1	0.0	0.0	94.0	0.0	100
Nagaland	11.3	9.0	19.9	3.9	0.0	0.0	0.0	0.0	0.0	0.0	0.0	0.0	0.0	0.0	67.2	0.0	100
Sikkim	1.2	42.1	3.7	9.5	0.0	0.0	0.0	0.0	0.0	0.0	0.0	0.0	0.0	0.0	44.7	0.0	100
Tripura	3.4	2.0	9.5	2.4	0.0	0.0	1.6	0.0	0.0	0.0	0.0	4.8	0.0	0.0	79.7	0.0	100
Uttarakhand	7.7	13.3	6.5	2.0	0.0	0.0	2.5	0.0	0.0	0.8	0.0	6.3	0.0	0.0	67.1	1.4	100
all-India	16.6	19.9	13.6	11.7	1.2	1.4	0.5	0.1	0.1	0.1	0.1	4.8	0.0	0.1	46.0	0.5	100

Note: Reason for never enrolling: not interested in education, 01; financial constraints, 02; engaged in domestic activities, 03; engaged in economic activities, 04; school far off, 05; timings of educational institution not suitable, 06; language/medium of instruction used unfamiliar, 07; inadequate number of teachers, 08; quality of teachers not satisfactory, 10; route to educational institution not safe, 11; no tradition in the community, 12; non-availability of female teacher, 17; non-availability of girls' toilet, 18; others, 19; marriage, 20.

Source: Education Survey, NSSO.

Table A4.9 Transition Rate (%), 2023–24

States/UTs	*Primary to Upper Primary*			*Upper Primary to Secondary*			*Secondary to Higher Secondary*		
	Boys	*Girls*	*All*	*Boys*	*Girls*	*All*	*Boys*	*Girls*	*All*
Arunachal Pradesh	86.1	91.1	88.5	78.6	80.5	79.6	58.3	61.4	59.9
Himachal Pradesh	98.8	98.8	98.8	97.3	98.0	97.7	87.5	91.3	89.3
Jammu and Kashmir	92.5	93.2	92.8	89.2	88.7	89.0	69.6	72.2	70.8
Ladakh	92.3	98.3	95.2	92.1	94.1	93.1	48.1	52.7	50.5
Manipur	81.8	84.5	83.1	83.6	86.1	84.8	65.8	66.7	66.2
Meghalaya	71.5	76.7	74.2	62.1	68.0	65.3	41.2	44.0	42.8
Mizoram	91.9	94.2	93.0	79.8	85.2	82.5	59.9	60.8	60.4
Nagaland	87.3	91.0	89.1	79.0	83.0	81.0	77.3	79.3	78.3
Sikkim	85.7	93.4	89.3	84.0	89.0	86.4	63.1	68.4	65.9
Tripura	91.0	93.2	92.0	86.6	89.4	88.0	85.6	85.8	85.7
Uttarakhand	94.0	95.1	94.5	90.8	92.3	91.5	83.5	89.0	86.1
India	88.4	89.2	88.8	83.7	82.9	83.3	69.1	73.9	71.5

Source: UDISE+.

Table A4.10 Teacher–Student Ratios, 2023–24

States/UTs	*Primary*	*Upper Primary*	*Secondary*	*Higher Secondary*
Arunachal Pradesh	10	7	9	15
Himachal Pradesh	15	8	6	9
Jammu and Kashmir	13	9	12	21
Ladakh	6	3	6	8
Manipur	13	9	9	13
Meghalaya	19	12	10	16
Mizoram	15	7	9	12
Nagaland	9	7	8	16
Sikkim	6	6	5	8
Tripura	17	15	11	15
Uttarakhand	16	14	10	14
All India	21	18	16	24

Source: and UDISE+ and AIHES.

Table A4.11 Pupil–Teacher Ratio (PTR) in Higher Education

States/UTs	*Regular and Distance*	*Regular*
Arunachal Pradesh	28	23
Himachal Pradesh	29	24
Jammu and Kashmir	35	24
Ladakh	16	16
Manipur	20	19
Meghalaya	24	22
Mizoram	21	17
Nagaland	20	18
Sikkim	22	17
Tripura	40	36
Uttarakhand	27	22
All India	26	23

Source: AIHES.

Table A4.12 Type of School by Management (%), 2023–24

States/UTs	*Government*	*Private*	*Total*
Arunachal Pradesh	83.6	16.4	100.0
Himachal Pradesh	85.4	14.6	100.0
Jammu and Kashmir	77.3	22.7	100.0
Manipur	75.7	24.3	100.0
Meghalaya	81.8	18.2	100.0
Mizoram	71.5	28.5	100.0
Nagaland	71.6	28.4	100.0
Sikkim	70.2	29.8	100.0
Tripura	86.9	13.1	100.0
Uttarakhand	74.6	25.4	100.0
India	74.6	25.4	100.0

Note: Government includes government colleges, while *private* includes both private aided and unaided private.

Source: UDISE+.

Table A4.13 Type of Colleges (Higher Education) by Management (%), 2021–22

States/UTs	*Private*	*Government*	*Total*
Arunachal Pradesh	44.2	55.8	100.0
Himachal Pradesh	52.9	47.1	100.0
Jammu and Kashmir	43.9	56.1	100.0
Ladakh	0.0	100.0	100.0
Manipur	43.7	56.3	100.0
Meghalaya	58.0	42.0	100.0
Mizoram	22.5	77.5	100.0
Nagaland	69.1	30.9	100.0
Sikkim	20.0	80.0	100.0
Tripura	20.4	79.6	100.0
Uttarakhand	59.7	40.3	100.0
All India	78.5	21.5	100.0

Source: AIHES.

Table A4.14 Type of Universities

States/UTs	*Government*	*Private*	*Total*
Arunachal Pradesh	10	0	10
Himachal Pradesh	13	17	30
Jammu and Kashmir	16	0	16
Manipur	8	2	10
Meghalaya	3	8	11
Mizoram	2	1	3
Nagaland	2	4	6
Sikkim	3	6	9
Tripura	4	1	5
Uttarakhand	18	20	38
All India	696	472	1168

Source: AIHES.

Table A4.15 Vocational Training Received, 2023–24

States/UTs	*Male*	*Female*	*Total*
Arunachal Pradesh	53.0	42.2	47.8
Himachal Pradesh	59.4	69.0	64.3
Jammu and Kashmir	31.8	25.1	28.6
Manipur	65.5	47.5	56.5
Meghalaya	73.3	53.7	63.5
Mizoram	43.8	31.2	37.8
Nagaland	21.9	11.5	17.0
Sikkim	31.5	7.6	20.2
Tripura	37.5	20.1	29.0
Uttarakhand	24.4	18.3	21.4
All India	44.6	24.1	34.4

Source: PLFS, 2023–24.

Table A4.16 Formal Vocational Training Received, 2023–24

States/UTs	*Male*	*Female*	*Total*
Arunachal Pradesh	23.8	12.1	18.8
Himachal Pradesh	19.2	24.7	22.2
Jammu and Kashmir	9.4	14.2	11.4
Manipur	10.7	5.9	8.7
Meghalaya	9.4	13.8	11.3
Mizoram	19.4	10.1	15.8
Nagaland	45.7	57.8	49.6
Sikkim	11.7	28.3	14.6
Tripura	13.7	16.2	14.5
Uttarakhand	22.8	34.3	27.7
All India	9.5	16.3	11.8

Source: PLFS, 2023–24.

Table A4.17 Performance in Education: Quality of Education

States/UTs	*% Children (Aged 6–14) Enrolled in Govt Schools*	*% Children (Aged 15–16) Not Enrolled in School*	*Std III: % Children Who Can Read Std II-Level Text (Learning Levels)*	*Std III: % Children Who Can Do at Least Subtraction (Learning Levels)*	*Std V: % Children Who Can Read Std II-Level Text (Learning Levels)*	*Std V: % Children Who Can Do Division (Learning Levels)*	*Std VIII: % Children Who Can Read Std II-Level Text (Learning Levels)*	*Std VIII: % Children Who Can Do Division (Learning Levels)*
Arunachal Pradesh	56.3	10.0	19.4	39.8	41.0	30.8	76.0	47.7
Himachal Pradesh	58.6	3.0	50.6	57.9	71.3	50.5	88.3	54.4
Jammu and Kashmir	57.2	3.8	16.6	36.4	37.7	25.1	58.5	35.8
Meghalaya	38.4	13.9	19.5	22.8	42.7	16.0	75.4	19.2
Mizoram	59.3	15.4	29.6	57.2	67.5	44.7	90.7	60.9
Nagaland	45.6	12.6	20.3	37.9	49.2	20.6	79.6	40.2
Sikkim	69.0	3.3	30.4	40.3	53.5	18.9	76.5	27.6
Tripura	73.8	3.4	20.9	33.2	40.7	22.0	68.8	39.4
Uttarakhand	62.8	4.3	39.4	36.0	63.9	39.8	82.2	52.5
All India	66.8	7.9	27.0	33.7	48.7	30.7	71.1	45.7

Source: ASER, 2024.

Table A4.18 Key Infrastructure or Facilities in Schools, 2023–24

States/UTs	*Functional Electricity*	*Functional Drinking Water*	*Toilet Facility*	*Functional Girls' Toilet*	*Librarian*	*Internet*	*Computer Available*
Arunachal Pradesh	58.0	71.3	95.6	70.1	6.2	30.5	42.6
Himachal Pradesh	99.2	100.0	99.9	99.2	8.7	48.7	47.5
Jammu and Kashmir	86.0	96.8	97.1	82.5	9.8	45.3	41.4
Ladakh	74.0	90.4	98.3	86.7	8.8	45.7	53.0
Manipur	60.7	99.4	91.8	74.4	8.6	32.3	33.5
Meghalaya	26.8	49.3	88.8	69.7	1.8	24.5	18.8
Mizoram	82.1	89.8	94.5	80.9	0.7	24.9	46.6
Nagaland	73.2	66.5	92.9	78.2	6.1	56.3	84.3
Sikkim	97.0	98.9	99.8	91.4	9.3	46.8	91.9
Tripura	76.1	86.9	97.1	74.2	3.4	35.3	49.3
Uttarakhand	90.2	92.8	98.6	86.9	12.4	68.5	86.6
All India	89.7	95.9	98.6	92.9	11.5	53.9	57.2

Table A4.19 Expenditure on Health (% of GSDP)

States/UTs	*GHE as % of GSDP*
Arunachal Pradesh	3.4
Himachal Pradesh	1.7
Manipur	2.2
Meghalaya	2.7
Mizoram	3.4
Nagaland	2.3
Sikkim	1.4
Tripura	1.7
Uttarakhand	1.1
Jammu and Kashmir	1.2
All India	1.9

Source: Respective state government, Department of Health.

Table A4.20 Out-of-Pocket Expenditure (% of Total Health Expenditure)

States/UTs	*2019–20*	*2020–21*	*2021–22*
Assam (representing north-eastern states)	34.9	33.2	27.6
Jammu and Kashmir	46.6	31.8	25.9
Uttarakhand	35.8	33.4	26.9
Himachal Pradesh	46.0	45.0	39.6
All India	47.1	44.4	39.4

Source: PIB, GoI.

Table A4.21 Children Under 5 Years Who Are Stunted (Height-for-Age) (%) Across States and UTs of India

States/UTs	*NFHS-3 (2005–06)*	*NFHS-4 (2015–16)*	*NFHS-5 (2019–21)**
Arunachal Pradesh	43.3	29.4	28.0
Himachal Pradesh	38.6	26.3	30.8
Jammu and Kashmir	35.0	27.4	26.9
Manipur	35.6	28.9	23.4
Meghalaya	55.1	43.8	46.5
Mizoram	38.8	28.1	28.9
Nagaland	38.8	28.6	32.7
Sikkim	38.3	29.6	22.3
Uttarakhand	44.4	33.5	27.0
Tripura	35.7	24.3	32.3
All India		38.4	35.5

Source: NFHS.

Table A4.22 Children Under 5 Years Who Are Wasted (Weight-for-Height) (%) Across States and UTs of India

States/UTs	*NFHS-3 (2005–06)*	*NFHS-4 (2015–16)*	*NFHS-5 (2019–21)**
Arunachal Pradesh	15.3	17.3	13.1
Himachal Pradesh	19.3	13.7	17.4
Jammu and Kashmir	14.8	12.2	19.0
Manipur	9.0	6.8	9.9
Meghalaya	30.7	15.3	12.1
Mizoram	9.0	6.1	9.8
Nagaland	13.3	11.3	19.1
Sikkim	9.7	14.2	13.7
Tripura	24.6	16.8	18.2
Uttarakhand	18.8	19.5	13.2
All India	-	21	19.3

Source: NFHS.

Table A4.23 Children Under 5 Years Who Are Underweight (Weight-for-Age) (%) Across States and UTs of India

States/UTs	*NFHS-3 (2005–06)*	*NFHS-4 (2015–16)*	*NFHS-5 (2019–21)**
Arunachal Pradesh	32.5	19.4	15.4
Himachal Pradesh	36.5	21.2	25.5
Jammu and Kashmir	25.6	16.6	21.0
Manipur	22.1	13.8	13.3
Meghalaya	48.8	28.9	26.6
Mizoram	19.9	12.0	12.7
Nagaland	25.2	16.7	26.9
Sikkim	19.7	14.2	13.1
Tripura	39.6	24.1	25.6
Uttarakhand	38.0	26.6	21.0
All India		35.8	32.1

Source: NFHS.

Table A4.24 Infant Mortality Rates (per 1,000 Live Births) Across States and UTs of India

States/UTs	*NFHS-3 (2005–06)*	*NFHS-4 (2015–16)*	*NFHS-5 (2019–21)**
Arunachal Pradesh	60.7	22.9	12.9
Himachal Pradesh	36.1	34.3	25.6
Jammu and Kashmir	44.7	32.4	16.3
Manipur	29.7	21.7	25.0
Meghalaya	44.6	29.9	32.3
Mizoram	34.1	40.1	21.3
Nagaland	38.3	29.5	23.4
Sikkim	33.7	29.5	11.2
Tripura	51.5	26.7	37.6
Uttarakhand	41.9	39.7	39.1
All India	-	40.7	35.2

Source: NFHS.

Table A4.25 Under-Five Mortality Rates (per 1,000 Live Births) Across States and UTs of India

States/UTs	*NFHS-3 (2005–06)*	*NFHS-4 (2015–16)*	*NFHS-5 (2019–21)**
Arunachal Pradesh	87.7	32.9	18.8
Himachal Pradesh	41.5	37.6	28.9
Jammu and Kashmir	51.2	37.6	18.5
Manipur	41.9	25.9	30.0
Meghalaya	70.5	39.6	40.0
Mizoram	52.9	46.0	24.0
Nagaland	64.7	37.5	33.0
Sikkim	40.1	32.2	11.2
Tripura	59.2	32.7	43.3
Uttarakhand	-	46.5	45.6
All India	-	49.7	41.9

Source: NFHS.

Table A4.26 State-Wise Children Aged 6–59 Months Who Are Anaemic (%)

States/UTs	*NFHS 3 (2005–06)*	*NFHS 4 (2015–16)*	*NFHS 5 (2019–21)*
Arunachal Pradesh	56.9	54.2	56.6
Himachal Pradesh	54.4	53.7	55.4
Jammu and Kashmir	58.5	53.8	72.7
Manipur	41.1	23.9	42.8
Meghalaya	63.8	48.0	45.1
Mizoram	43.8	19.3	46.4
Nagaland	-	26.4	42.7
Sikkim	58.1	55.1	56.4
Tripura	62.9	48.3	64.3
Uttarakhand	60.7	59.8	58.8
All India	-	58.6	67.1

Source: NFHS.

Table A4.27 Total Fertility Rate (Children per Women) Across States and UTs of India

States/UTs	*NFHS-3 (2005–06)*	*NFHS-4 (2015–16)*	*NFHS-5 (2019–21)**
Arunachal Pradesh	3.0	2.1	1.8
Himachal Pradesh	1.9	1.9	1.7
Jammu and Kashmir	2.4	2.0	1.4
Manipur	2.8	2.6	2.2
Meghalaya	3.8	3.0	2.9
Mizoram	2.9	2.3	1.9
Nagaland	3.7	2.7	1.7
Sikkim	2.0	1.2	1.1
Tripura	2.2	1.7	1.7
Uttarakhand	-	2.1	1.9
All India	1.9	1.6	1.8

Source: NFHS.

Table A4.28 Percentage of Births Attended by Skilled Health Personnel

States/UTs	*Institutional Births (%)*		*Home Births Conducted by Skilled Health Personnel (%)*	
	NFHS-4 (2015–16)	*NFHS-5 (2019–21)*	*NFHS-4 (2015–16)*	*NFHS-5 (2019–21)*
Arunachal Pradesh	52.2	79.2	2.1	4.0
Himachal Pradesh	76.4	88.2	3.4	1.7
Jammu and Kashmir	#	92.4	2.2	3.0
Manipur	69.1	79.9	8.0	5.8
Meghalaya	51.4	58.1	2.6	6.6
Mizoram	79.7	85.8	3.9	3.5
Nagaland	32.8	45.7	8.8	10.4
Sikkim	94.7	94.7	2.4	2.6
Tripura	79.9	89.2	1.2	1.2
Uttarakhand	68.6	83.2	4.6	3.4
India	78.9	88.6	4.3	3.2

Source: NFHS.

Table A4.29 Prevalence of Anaemia Among Women Aged 15–49 Years

States/UTs	*NFHS-4 (2015–16)*	*NFHS-5 (2019–21)*
Arunachal Pradesh	43.2	40.3
Himachal Pradesh	53.5	53.0
Jammu and Kashmir	48.9	55.9
Manipur	26.4	29.4
Meghalaya	56.2	53.8
Mizoram	24.8	34.8
Nagaland	27.9	28.9
Sikkim	34.9	42.1
Tripura	54.5	67.2
Uttarakhand	45.2	42.6
All India	53.0	57.0

Source: NFHS.

Table A4.30 State-Wise Life Expectancy

States/UTs	*2012–16*			*2016–20*		
	Male	*Female*	*Total*	*Male*	*Female*	*Total*
	59	*60*	*61*	*71*	*72*	*73*
Assam (representing north-eastern states)	64.4	66.8	65.5	67.3	68.6	67.9
Himachal Pradesh	69.4	68.5	72.3	70.3	77.5	73.5
Jammu and Kashmir	71.6	68.5	73.5	72.6	76.3	74.3
Uttarakhand	68.5	68.5	71.5	67.5	73.9	70.6
All India	67.4	68.5	68.7	68.6	71.4	70.0

Source: Registrar General of India, Census.

Table A4.31 Maternal Mortality Rate per 100,000 Live Births (Around 2018–20)

States/UTs	*SRS 2018–20*
Arunachal Pradesh	284
Himachal Pradesh	55
Jammu and Kashmir	97
Manipur	282
Meghalaya	266
Mizoram	19
Nagaland	143
Sikkim	228
Tripura	21
Uttarakhand	103
All India	97

Source: Registrar General of India, Census.

Table A4.32 Percentage of Births Attended by Skilled Health Personnel

States/UTs	*Institutional Births (%)*		*Home Births Conducted by Skilled Health Personnel (%)*	
	NFHS-4 (2015–16)	*NFHS-5 (2019–21)*	*NFHS-4 (2015–16)*	*NFHS-5 (2019–21)*
Arunachal Pradesh	52.2	79.2	2.1	4.0
Himachal Pradesh	76.4	88.2	3.4	1.7
Jammu and Kashmir	#	92.4	2.2	3.0
Manipur	69.1	79.9	8.0	5.8
Meghalaya	51.4	58.1	2.6	6.6
Mizoram	79.7	85.8	3.9	3.5
Nagaland	32.8	45.7	8.8	10.4
Sikkim	94.7	94.7	2.4	2.6
Tripura	79.9	89.2	1.2	1.2
Uttarakhand	68.6	83.2	4.6	3.4
India	78.9	88.6	4.3	3.2

Source: NFHS.

Table A4.33 Total Fertility Rate (Children per Women) Across States and UTs of India

States/UTs	*NFHS-3 (2005–06)*	*NFHS-4 (2015–16)*	*NFHS-5 (2019–21)**
Arunachal Pradesh	3.0	2.1	1.8
Himachal Pradesh	1.9	1.9	1.7
Jammu and Kashmir	2.4	2.0	1.4
Manipur	2.8	2.6	2.2
Meghalaya	3.8	3.0	2.9
Mizoram	2.9	2.3	1.9
Nagaland	3.7	2.7	1.7
Sikkim	2.0	1.2	1.1
Tripura	2.2	1.7	1.7
Uttarakhand		2.1	1.9

Source: NFHS.

Table A4.34 Health Infrastructure (per 100,000 Population), 2022–23

States/UTs	*Doctors/Specialists*	*Hospital*	*Beds*
Arunachal Pradesh	9	12	174
Himachal Pradesh	14	11	224
Jammu and Kashmir	4	13	74
Manipur	7	0	78
Meghalaya	5	5	138
Mizoram	4	8	163
Nagaland	6	8	86
Sikkim	5	5	267
Tripura	6	4	131
Uttarakhand	4	6	74
All India	2	3	62

Source: Health Profile, 2024, GoI.

Annexure Chapter 5

Table A5.1 Average MPCE by 12 Fractile Classes for Himalayan States and All-India (Rural), 2023–24

	F1	F2	F3	F4	F5	F6	F7	F8	F9	F10	F11	F12	All	Fractile Ratios (Inequality)			
	0–5	5–10	10–20	20–30	30–40	40–50	50–60	60–70	70–80	80–90	90–95	95–100		F12/F1	F6/F1	F12/F6	(F10 + F11 + F12)/(F1 + F2 + F3)
Arunachal Pradesh	2,316	2,944	3,669	4,209	4,671	5,170	5,702	6,344	7,144	8,380	10,188	13,873	5,995	6.0	2.2	2.7	3.6
Himachal Pradesh	2,631	3,096	3,530	4,005	4,528	5,064	5,552	6,120	6,831	7,951	9,746	13,841	5,825	5.3	1.9	2.7	3.4
Jammu and Kashmir	2,175	2,621	2,955	3,346	3,719	4,089	4,526	5,024	5,664	6,698	8,052	10,567	4,774	4.9	1.9	2.6	3.3
Manipur	2,159	2,676	3,077	3,452	3,815	4,125	4,477	4,868	5,350	6,026	6,796	8,607	4,531	4.0	1.9	2.1	2.7
Meghalaya	1,792	2,148	2,527	2,936	3,273	3,531	3,790	4,081	4,506	5,116	5,924	7,668	3,852	4.3	2.0	2.2	2.9
Mizoram	2,569	3,165	3,705	4,217	4,714	5,132	5,683	6,331	7,128	8,277	9,806	13,338	5,963	5.2	2.0	2.6	3.3
Nagaland	2,232	2,704	3,317	3,835	4,247	4,665	5,069	5,525	6,070	6,826	7,913	11,136	5,155	5.0	2.1	2.4	3.1
Sikkim	3,194	4,078	5,194	6,310	7,306	8,151	9,057	10,121	11,543	13,384	15,936	22,158	9,377	6.9	2.6	2.7	4.1
Tripura	3,121	3,754	4,260	4,792	5,196	5,613	6,018	6,524	7,136	8,100	9,464	13,585	6,259	4.4	1.8	2.4	2.8
Uttarakhand	2,239	2,750	3,134	3,558	3,967	4,354	4,743	5,215	5,847	6,729	8,203	11,785	5,003	5.3	1.9	2.7	3.3
All-India	**1,677**	2,126	2,473	2,833	3,162	3,498	3,866	4,304	4,885	5,763	6,929	10,137	4,122	6.0	2.1	2.9	3.6

Note: F, fractile classes.

Source: Survey on Household Consumption Expenditure, 2023–24, MoSPI, National Statistical Office, GoI.

Table A5.2 Average MPCE by 12 Fractile Classes for Himalayan States and All-India (Urban), 2023–24

	F1	*F2*	*F3*	*F4*	*F5*	*F6*	*F7*	*F8*	*F9*	*F10*	*F11*	*F12*	*All*	*Fractile Ratios (Inequality)*			
	0–5	*5–10*	*10–20*	*20–30*	*30–40*	*40–50*	*50–60*	*60–70*	*70–80*	*80–90*	*90–95*	*95–100*		*F12/ F1*	*F6/ F1*	*F12/ F6*	*(F10 + F11 + F12)/(F1 + F2 + F3)*
Arunachal Pradesh	3,443	4,676	5,577	6,526	7,421	8,459	9,458	10,472	11,979	14,127	16,956	23,593	9,832	6.9	2.5	2.8	4.0
Himachal Pradesh	3,559	4,352	5,062	5,815	6,658	7,619	8,588	9,616	10,942	13,296	16,632	24,684	9,223	6.9	2.1	3.2	4.2
Jammu and Kashmir	2,720	3,122	3,645	4,210	4,722	5,303	5,884	6,613	7,683	8,945	10,646	16,064	6,327	5.9	1.9	3.0	3.8
Manipur	2,709	3,449	3,972	4,451	4,905	5,361	5,822	6,321	6,946	7,925	9,196	12,153	5,945	4.5	2.0	2.3	2.9
Meghalaya	3,305	3,915	4,680	5,398	5,976	6,563	7,401	8,248	9,103	10,994	13,016	19,812	7,839	6.0	2.0	3.0	3.7
Mizoram	4,254	5,088	5,713	6,424	7,097	7,671	8,314	9,057	9,976	11,496	13,499	19,832	8,709	4.7	1.8	2.6	3.0
Nagaland	3,851	4,661	5,485	6,124	6,626	7,111	7,799	8,525	9,455	10,635	12,046	16,379	8,022	4.3	1.8	2.3	2.8
Sikkim	5,386	6,660	7,925	9,099	10,109	11,329	12,715	14,338	16,460	20,297	25,492	36,468	13,927	6.8	2.1	3.2	4.1
Tripura	4,064	4,774	5,340	5,853	6,362	6,903	7,575	8,348	9,244	10,676	12,535	18,704	8,034	4.6	1.7	2.7	3.0
Uttarakhand	2,726	3,476	4,083	4,780	5,326	6,036	6,951	7,816	9,114	11,078	13,662	19,497	7,486	7.2	2.2	3.2	4.3

Note: F, fractile classes.

Source: Survey on Household Consumption Expenditure, 2023–24, MoSPI, National Statistical Office, GoI.

Table A5.3 Average MPCE by 12 Fractile Classes for Himalayan States and All-India (Rural), 2011–12

	F1	*F2*	*F3*	*F4*	*F5*	*F6*	*F7*	*F8*	*F9*	*F10*	*F11*	*F12*	*All*	*Fractile Ratios (Inequality)*			
	0–5	*5–10*	*10–20*	*20–30*	*30–40*	*40–50*	*50–60*	*60–70*	*70–80*	*80–90*	*90–95*	*95–100*		*F12/ F1*	*F6/ F1*	*F12/ F6*	*(F10 + F11 + F12)/(F1 + F2 + F3)*
Arunachal Pradesh	571	665	790	943	1081	1236	1440	1758	2205	2930	3944	5700	1782	10.0	2.2	4.6	6.2
Himachal Pradesh	776	991	1128	1290	1437	1606	1799	2023	2290	2782	3597	6582	2034	8.5	2.1	4.1	4.5
Jammu and Kashmir	699	915	1080	1220	1347	1478	1617	1801	2019	2381	2868	4488	1743	6.4	2.1	3.0	3.6
Manipur	742	827	959	1108	1192	1288	1396	1544	1730	2047	2469	3469	1502	4.7	1.7	2.7	3.2
Meghalaya	721	911	1004	1097	1227	1313	1398	1531	1707	1924	2284	3175	1475	4.4	1.8	2.4	2.8
Mizoram	659	846	979	1121	1242	1380	1550	1728	1958	2359	2870	3874	1644	5.9	2.1	2.8	3.7
Nagaland	1123	1261	1404	1568	1673	1770	1900	2106	2340	2681	3181	4726	2059	4.2	1.6	2.7	2.8
Sikkim	879	980	1071	1171	1244	1317	1420	1558	1763	2091	2471	3667	1565	4.2	1.5	2.8	2.8
Tripura	607	735	845	956	1052	1145	1243	1378	1556	1835	2256	3076	1334	5.1	1.9	2.7	3.3
Uttarakhand	776	929	1044	1175	1286	1370	1522	1735	1989	2380	2990	4823	1726	6.2	1.8	3.5	3.7
All-India	521	666	783	905	1018	1136	1266	1427	1645	2007	2556	4481	1430	8.6	2.2	3.9	4.6

Note: F, fractile classes.

Source: Survey on Household Consumption Expenditure, 2011–12, MoSPI, National Statistical Office, GoI.

Table A5.4 Average MPCE by 12 Fractile Classes for Himalayan States and All-India (Urban), 2011–12

	F1	*F2*	*F3*	*F4*	*F5*	*F6*	*F7*	*F8*	*F9*	*F10*	*F11*	*F12*	*All*	*Fractile Ratios (Inequality)*			
	0–5	*5–10*	*10–20*	*20–30*	*30–40*	*40–50*	*50–60*	*60–70*	*70–80*	*80–90*	*90–95*	*95–100*		*F12/ F1*	*F6/ F1*	*F12/ F6*	*(F10 + F11 + F12)/(F1 + F2 + F3)*
Arunachal Pradesh	641	784	1007	1318	1624	1926	2267	2742	3352	4305	5945	8578	2654	13.4	3.0	4.5	7.7
Himachal Pradesh	992	1299	1685	2056	2322	2599	2893	3373	3928	4955	5916	9166	3259	9.2	2.6	3.5	5.0
Jammu and Kashmir	836	1039	1219	1488	1736	1936	2197	2573	2977	3688	4680	7522	2485	9.0	2.3	3.9	5.1
Manipur	710	793	924	1132	1224	1313	1404	1486	1633	2042	2498	3353	1483	4.7	1.8	2.6	3.3
Meghalaya	951	1093	1449	1824	2002	2186	2344	2478	2808	3389	3982	5710	2436	6.0	2.3	2.6	3.7
Mizoram	1029	1193	1424	1784	2034	2292	2518	2729	3164	3712	4359	5435	2568	5.3	2.2	2.4	3.7
Nagaland	1009	1125	1262	1434	1723	2020	2308	2586	2897	3271	3857	4705	2284	4.7	2.0	2.3	3.5
Sikkim	1118	1414	1700	1911	2076	2277	2414	2641	3036	3679	4309	5756	2608	5.1	2.0	2.5	3.2
Tripura	762	969	1087	1247	1425	1597	1929	2299	2687	3227	3996	6148	2144	8.1	2.1	3.8	4.7
Uttarakhand	721	938	1129	1326	1593	1848	2086	2382	2802	3494	4631	7132	2339	9.9	2.6	3.9	5.5

Note: F, fractile classes.

Source: Survey on Household Consumption Expenditure, 2011–12, MoSPI, National Statistical Office, GoI.

Annexure 2
Concepts and Definitions

2.1 Economy and Employment Concepts and Definitions

Activity status. It is the activity situation in which a person is found during the reference period. According to this, a person could be in one or a combination of the three broad activity statuses during the reference period, viz., (1) working or being engaged in economic activity (work), (2) not being engaged in economic activity (work) but either making tangible efforts to seek work or being available for work if work is available, and (3) not being engaged in economic activity (work) and also not available for work.

Usual principal activity status (UPS). The usual activity status relates to the activity status of a person during the reference period of 365 days preceding the date of survey. The activity status on which a person spent relatively long time (major time criterion) during the 365 days preceding the date of survey was considered the usual principal activity status of the person.

Subsidiary economic activity status (SS). Subsidiary status workers are those who are engaged in an economic activity for a smaller duration in the reference period of the last 30 days preceding the date of the survey.

Usual principal and subsidiary status (UPSS). All those engaged in principal activity (UPS) and subsidiary activity are included in UPSS employment.

Labour force participation rate (LFPR). LFPR is defined as the share of the population that is actively engaged in the labour market, either working or seeking work.

Worker–population ratio (WPR). WPR is the share of the population who are employed or engaged in work.

Unemployment rate (UR). Unemployment rate is the share of the labour force that does not have employment and is seeking and/or available for work.

Employment status. Employment status is classified into three categories, viz., self-employment, regular employment, and casual employment.

- *Regular employment.* All those wage/salary workers who are on relatively longer tenure of works and who are usually paid wages/salary on a weekly or monthly basis.

- *Casual employment.* All those who do not have any tenure and are mostly employed on daily wage basis are casual workers.
- *Self-employment.* All those who are 'own account workers', working employers, unpaid family workers, and home-based workers are included under self-employment.

Unorganised/informal sector. Unorganised or informal sector includes those organisations which are categorised as follows: proprietary, male and female; partnership, with members from the same household; and Partnership, with members from different households and with fewer than ten workers. Additionally, it includes the household sector, that is, people employed in private households as maids, servants, security guards, cooks, etc. Even enterprises whose number of workers is not known or cannot be ascertained, and that do not give their workers any social security benefits, are included in the unorganised sector.

Organised formal sector. Government/local body, public sector enterprises, public/private limited companies, autonomous bodies, co-operative societies, and trust/other non-profit institutions are all considered to be part of the organised/formal sector. Enterprises are categorised as follows: Proprietary: male and female; Partnership: with members from the same household; and Partnership: with members from different households and with more than ten workers. Enterprises whose number of workers is unknown or cannot be ascertained, and that give their workers social security benefits, are also included in the organised formal sector.

Informal workers (or informal employment). All self-employed own-account workers, self-employed unpaid workers, and workers in the household sector are informal workers. Regular salaried workers and casual workers who have no form of social security benefit are also informal workers. Self-employed workers who are employers and in the informal sector are informal workers.

Formal workers (or formal employment). Formal workers include self-employed workers who are employers in the formal sector, and regular salaried and casual workers who receive social security.

Gross value added (GVA). Gross value added represents the total value of all goods and services produced within an industry, sector, manufacturing unit, area, or region in an economy.

Gini coefficient. It is a statistical indicator used to measure income or wealth inequality within a defined population, typically a country. Ranging from 0 to 1, a value of 0 represents perfect equality – where everyone has the same income or wealth – while a value closer to 1 indicates greater inequality, with wealth concentrated in the hands of a few.

Source: India Employment Report, ILO and IHD, 2024;
Periodic Labour Force Survey (PLFS), 2023–24;
National Statistical Office

2.2 Education Concepts and Definitions

Gross enrolment rate (GER). Total enrolment in a particular level of school education, regardless of age, expressed as a percentage of the population of the official age group which corresponds to the given level of school education in a given school year. Example: GER primary = Enrolment in classes 1 to 5 ÷ projected population in age group 6–10 years.

Net enrolment rate (NER). Total number of pupils enrolled in a particular level of school education who are of the corresponding official age group expressed as a percentage of the population of the official age group which corresponds to the given level of school education in a given school year. Example: NER primary = children of age 6–10 years enrolled in classes 1 to 5 ÷ projected population in age group 6–10 years.

Dropout rate. Proportion of pupil from a cohort enrolled in a given level at a given school year who are no longer enrolled at any grade in the following school year.

Transition rate. Proportion of pupil moving from one stage or level to another in the schooling system. For example, the transition rate is the proportion of students moving from primary to upper primary, upper primary to secondary, or secondary to higher secondary.

Gender parity index (GPI) of GER. Ratio of GER of girls to GER of boys. It measures the progress towards gender parity in education participation and/or learning opportunities available for girls in relation to those available to boys. It also represents the level of girls' empowerment in the society.

Pupil–teacher ratio (PTR). Pupil–teacher ratio (PTR) is the average number of pupils (at a specific level of education) per teacher (teaching at that level of education) in a given school year.

Source: Report on Unified District Information System for Education Plus (UDISE+), Government of India (GoI), Ministry of Education, 2023–24

2.3 Income Inequality, Demography, and Health Concepts and Definitions

Monthly per capita consumption expenditure (MPCE). MPCE represents a household's consumer expenditure over a 30-day period divided by the household size. This measure serves as an indicator of the household's standard of living.

Fractile classes. For any fraction f ($0 < f < 1$), the corresponding fractile of the distribution of MPCE is the level of MPCE, Y_f, such that the proportion of the population whose household MPCE lies below Y_f is f. A fractile class of MPCE is a segment of the population lying within two fractiles, f_1 and f_2. In the analysis in this book, 12 fractile classes are represented as "0–5 per cent," "5–10 per cent," "10–20 per cent," . . ., "95–100 per cent." Each of the fractile classes contains 5 per cent of the estimated population ranked by MPCE in ascending order.

Survey on Household Consumption Expenditure, 2023–24, MoSPI, National Statistical Office, GoI

Sex ratio. It is defined as the number of females per 1,000 males in the population.

Total fertility rate. It is derived from the cumulative values of age-specific fertility rates at the end of the childbearing years. It represents the average number of children a woman is expected to have throughout her reproductive lifespan assuming that the prevailing age-specific fertility rates remain constant and there is no mortality.

Infant mortality rate. It refers to the measurement of mortality in the first year of life and is computed as the number of deaths under one year of age divided by 1,000 live births in a given year.

Life expectancy. It is a measure that is often used to gauge the overall health of a community. Life expectancy at birth measures health status across all age groups. Shifts in life expectancy are used to describe trends in mortality.

Maternal mortality rate. It refers to the number of women who die as a result of complications of pregnancy or childbearing in a given year per 100,000 live births in that year. It is a crucial health indicator, as most maternal deaths result from known causes that are largely preventable and treatable with proper healthcare interventions.

Women and Men in India, 2024: Selected Indicators, Social Statistics Division, MoSPI, GoI

Index

D

E

M

N

For Product Safety Concerns and Information please contact our EU representative GPSR@taylorandfrancis.com
Taylor & Francis Verlag GmbH, Kaufingerstraße 24, 80331 München, Germany

www.ingramcontent.com/pod-product-compliance
Lightning Source LLC
LaVergne TN
LVHW010651300926
849161LV00005B/1095

* 9 7 8 1 0 3 2 9 7 5 8 8 7 *